ADVANCE PRAISE FOR *A FIRE STORY*

"Coping with loss is a deeply personal thing, and anyone who experiences tragedy must find his or her own way. A route to some kind of normalcy. To someplace safe . . . So Fies did what came naturally when the home he shared with his wife, Karen, went up in flames. He started drawing."
   —**San Francisco Chronicle**

"Subtle and heart-wrenching."
   —**Press Democrat**

"As striking as it is detailed . . . Fies's attention to process—knowing the how, why, when, and where of very specific moments—gives the comic a sense of immediacy."
   —**Entertainment Weekly**

"An effective snapshot of a broad disaster."
   —**io9**

"Brian Fies sat down with some Sharpies and some paper to process his pain the way he knows best. He began to draw. The result is *A Fire Story* . . . a webcomic that recounts the heart-wrenching devastation the California wildfires has wrought . . . Fies is a graphic novelist, one of the best in his field. A few years ago, when his mom was battling terminal cancer, he processed his grief by writing the comic *Mom's Cancer*. It won an Eisner Award, one of the comic world's highest achievements. Now he's had to do it all over again."
   —**CNN**

ALSO BY BRIAN FIES

Mom's Cancer

Whatever Happened to the World of Tomorrow?

The Last Mechanical Monster

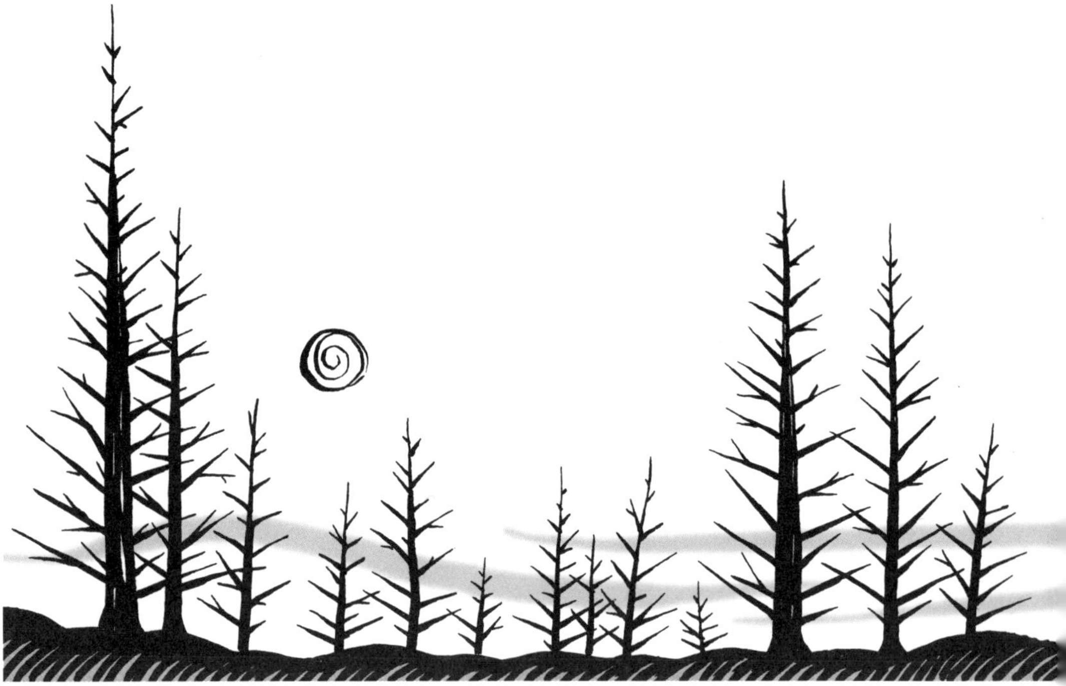

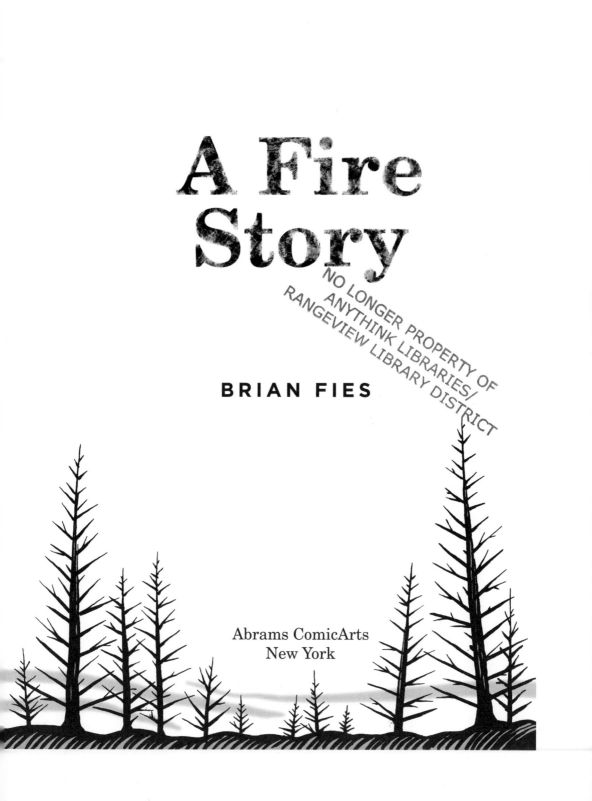

A Fire Story

BRIAN FIES

Abrams ComicArts
New York

Editor: Charles Kochman
Art Director: Pamela Notarantonio
Managing Editor: Amy Vreeland
Production Manager: Alison Gervais

Cataloging-in-Publication Data has been applied for
and may be obtained from the Library of Congress.

ISBN 978-1-4197-3585-1

Published in 2019 by Abrams ComicArts®, an imprint of ABRAMS.

Printed and bound in China
10 9 8 7 6 5 4 3 2 1

Abrams ComicArts books are available at special discounts when
purchased in quantity for premiums and promotions as well as fundraising or
educational use. Special editions can also be created to specification.
For details, contact specialsales@abramsbooks.com or the address below.

ABRAMS The Art of Books
195 Broadway, New York, NY 10007
abramsbooks.com

To the memory of the forty-four

Acknowledgments

Special thanks to Mike, Dottie, Mary, Larry, Jerry, and Sunny for trusting me with their fire stories.

People who read early drafts of this book and gave me valuable feedback, not all of which I heeded, included Stephan Pastis, Richard Pini, Mike Peterson, MK Czerwiec, Don Rubin, and Jeff Kinney. Thank you, my friends. My best critiques came from Karen, Laura, and Robin Fies—eyewitnesses who vetoed surprisingly little.

Thanks to Charlie Kochman, the best kind of editor who makes me better without leaving fingerprints, and art director Pam Notarantonio, who made it easy. Thanks to the many people at Abrams who championed *A Fire Story*. Thanks also to the patient Stu Rees.

Thanks to Kelly Whalen, Farrin Abbott, and Gabe Meline at KQED for their expert storytelling and my astonishing Emmy.

Thanks to everyone who read the original webcomic or watched KQED's video. There'd be no book without you.

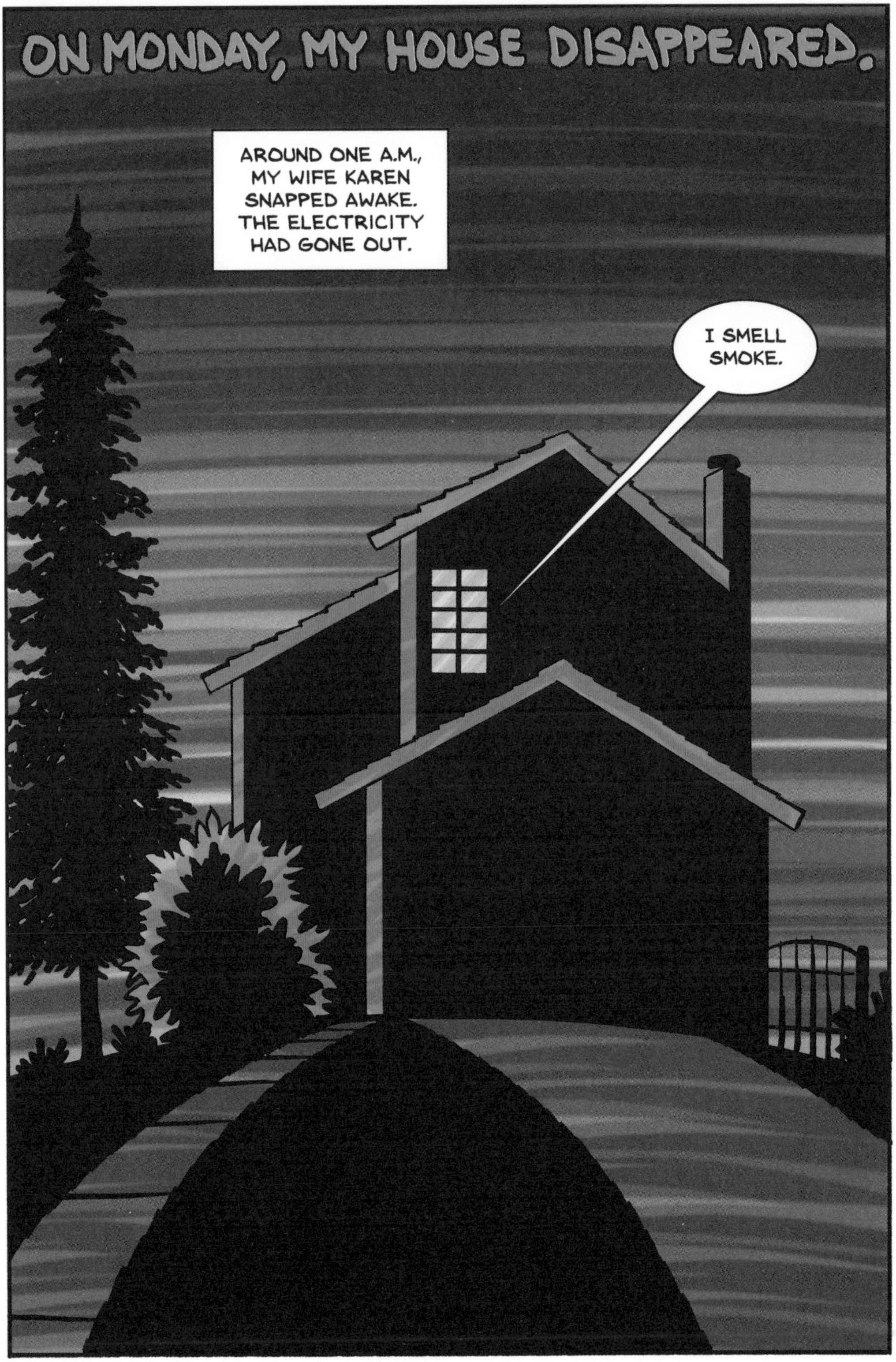
ON MONDAY, MY HOUSE DISAPPEARED.
AROUND ONE A.M., MY WIFE KAREN SNAPPED AWAKE. THE ELECTRICITY HAD GONE OUT.
I SMELL SMOKE.

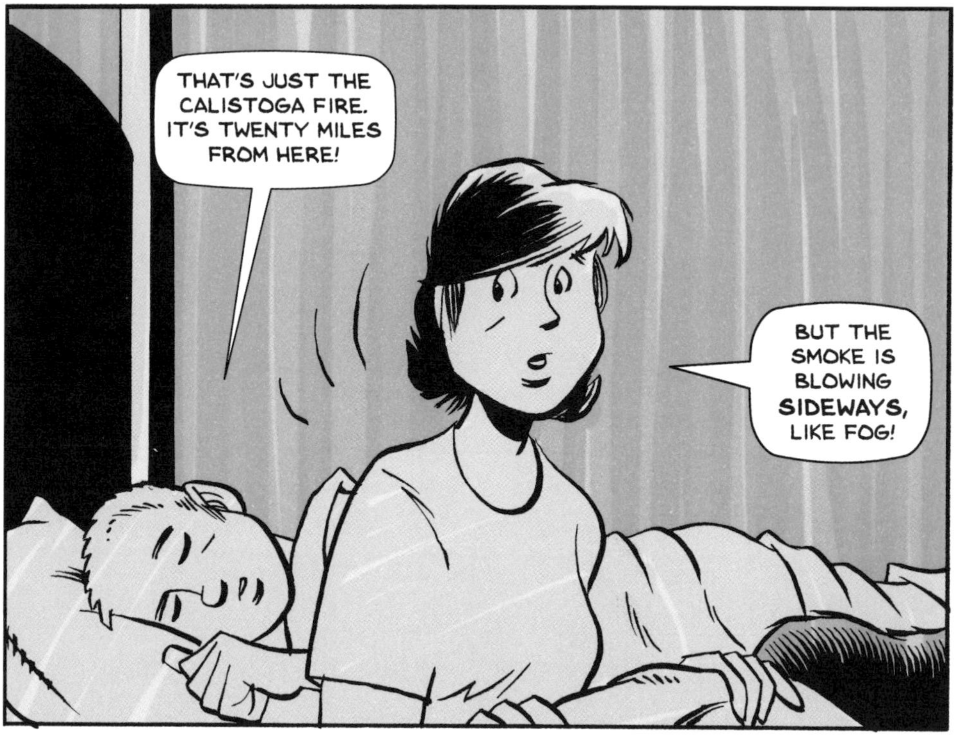
THAT'S JUST THE CALISTOGA FIRE. IT'S TWENTY MILES FROM HERE!
BUT THE SMOKE IS BLOWING SIDEWAYS, LIKE FOG!

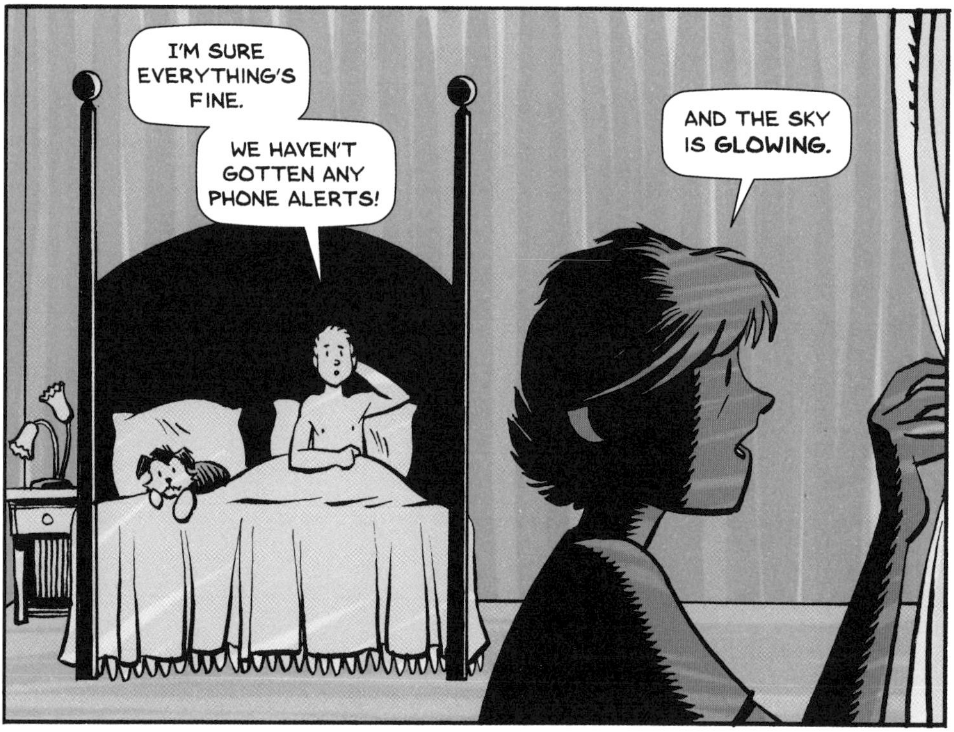
I'M SURE EVERYTHING'S FINE.
WE HAVEN'T GOTTEN ANY PHONE ALERTS!
AND THE SKY IS GLOWING.

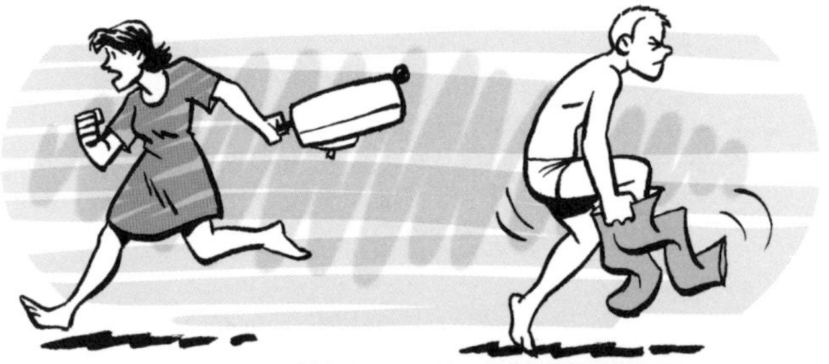

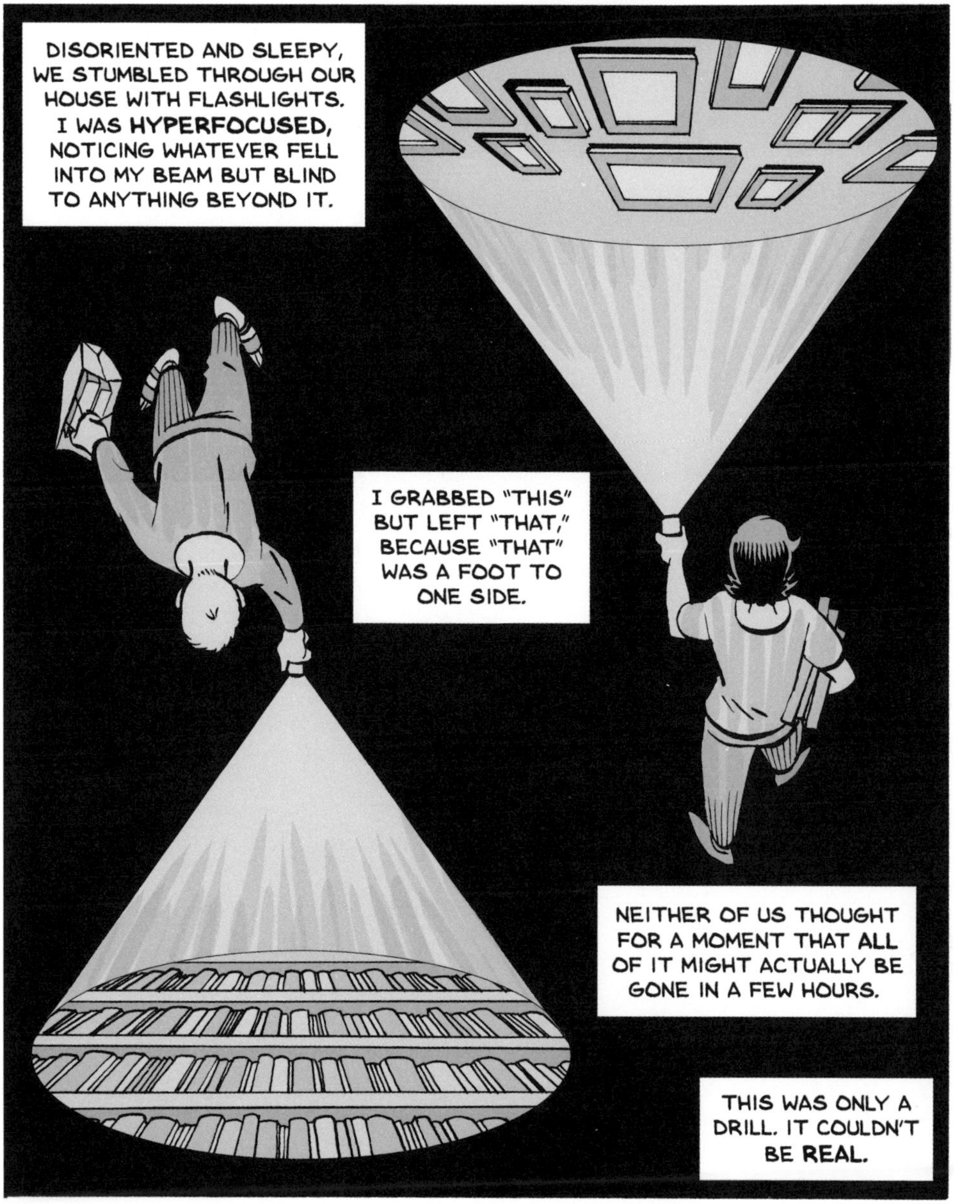
DISORIENTED AND SLEEPY, WE STUMBLED THROUGH OUR HOUSE WITH FLASHLIGHTS. I WAS **HYPERFOCUSED,** NOTICING WHATEVER FELL INTO MY BEAM BUT BLIND TO ANYTHING BEYOND IT.
I GRABBED "THIS" BUT LEFT "THAT," BECAUSE "THAT" WAS A FOOT TO ONE SIDE.
NEITHER OF US THOUGHT FOR A MOMENT THAT **ALL** OF IT MIGHT ACTUALLY BE GONE IN A FEW HOURS.
THIS WAS ONLY A DRILL. IT COULDN'T BE **REAL.**

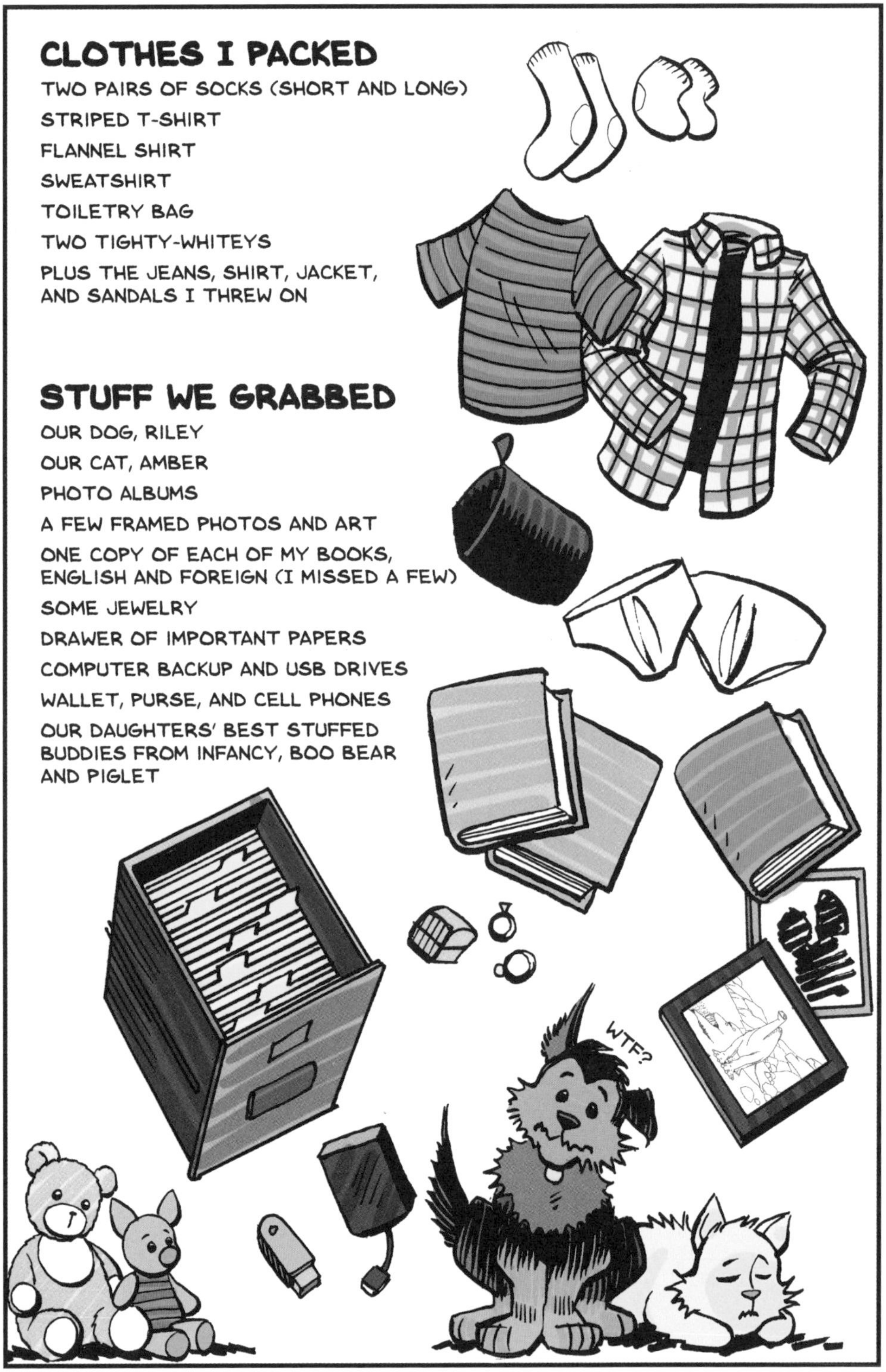
CLOTHES I PACKED
TWO PAIRS OF SOCKS (SHORT AND LONG)
STRIPED T-SHIRT
FLANNEL SHIRT
SWEATSHIRT
TOILETRY BAG
TWO TIGHTY-WHITEYS
PLUS THE JEANS, SHIRT, JACKET, AND SANDALS I THREW ON
STUFF WE GRABBED
OUR DOG, RILEY
OUR CAT, AMBER
PHOTO ALBUMS
A FEW FRAMED PHOTOS AND ART
ONE COPY OF EACH OF MY BOOKS, ENGLISH AND FOREIGN (I MISSED A FEW)
SOME JEWELRY
DRAWER OF IMPORTANT PAPERS
COMPUTER BACKUP AND USB DRIVES
WALLET, PURSE, AND CELL PHONES
OUR DAUGHTERS' BEST STUFFED BUDDIES FROM INFANCY, BOO BEAR AND PIGLET
WTF?

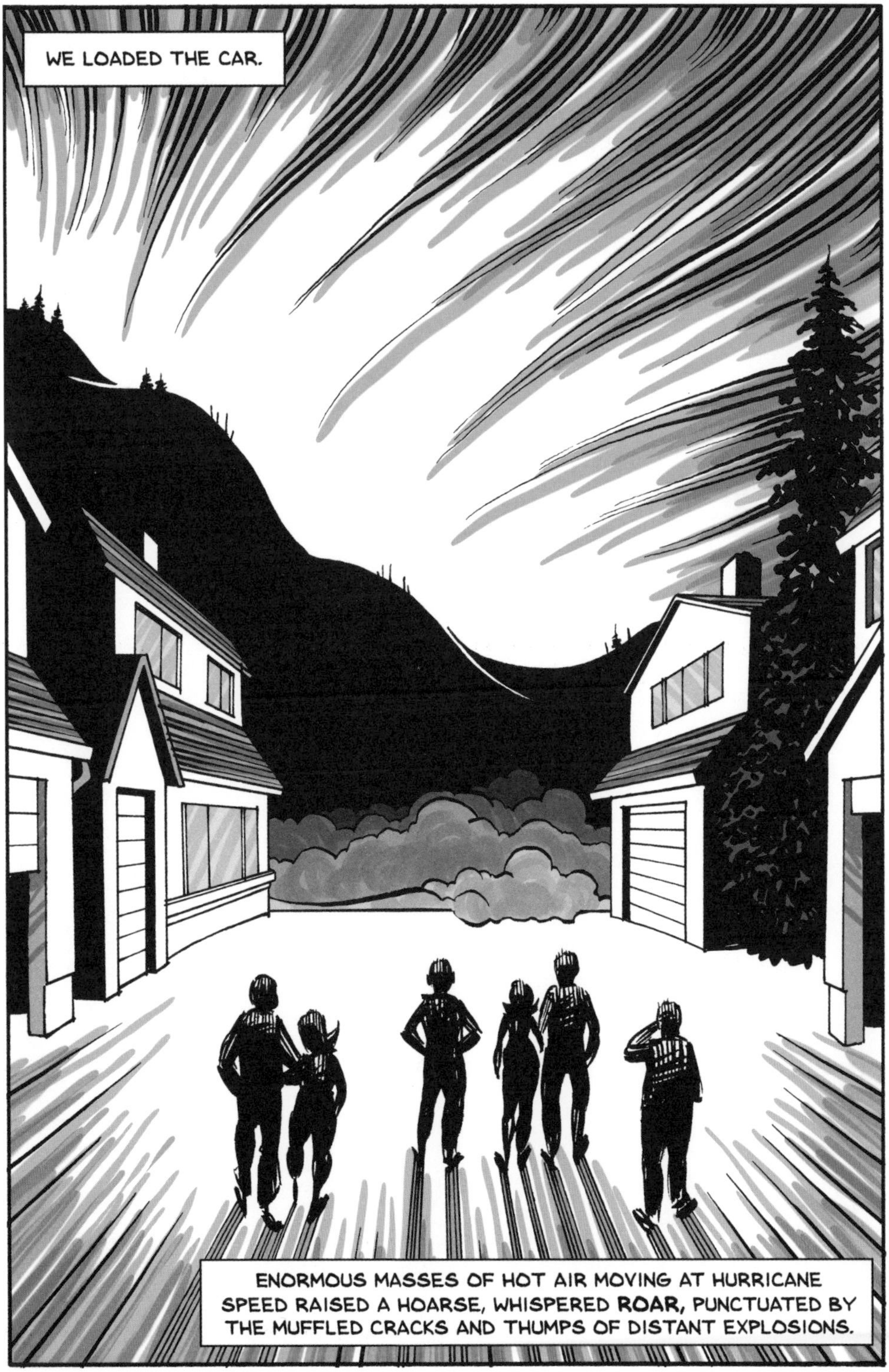
WE LOADED THE CAR.
ENORMOUS MASSES OF HOT AIR MOVING AT HURRICANE SPEED RAISED A HOARSE, WHISPERED ROAR, PUNCTUATED BY THE MUFFLED CRACKS AND THUMPS OF DISTANT EXPLOSIONS.

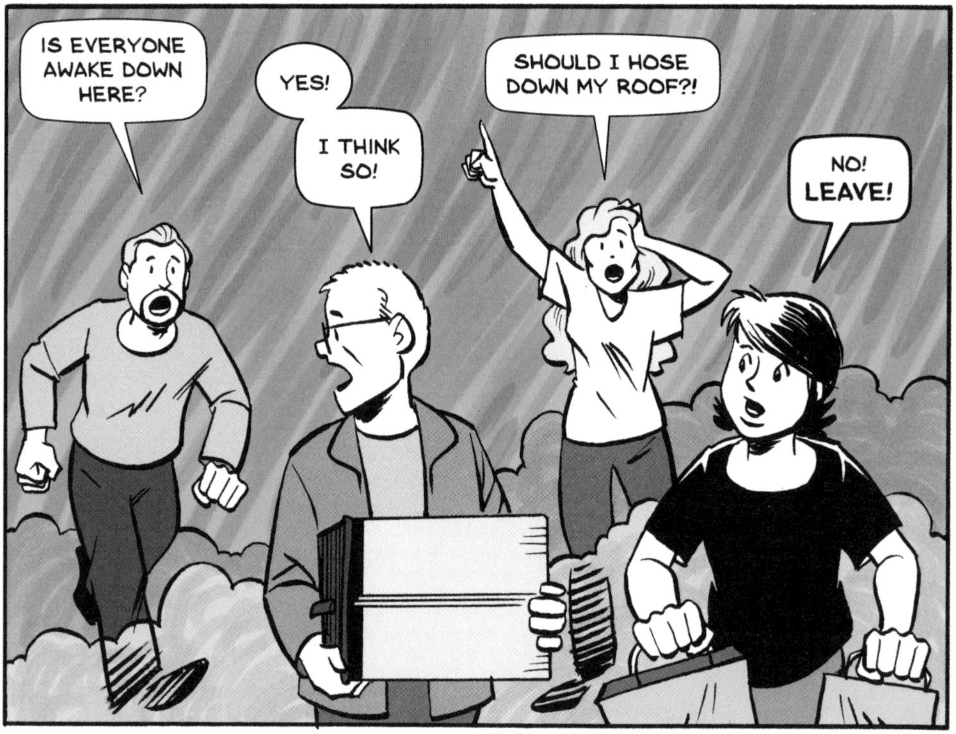
IS EVERYONE AWAKE DOWN HERE?
YES!
I THINK SO!
SHOULD I HOSE DOWN MY ROOF?!
NO! LEAVE!

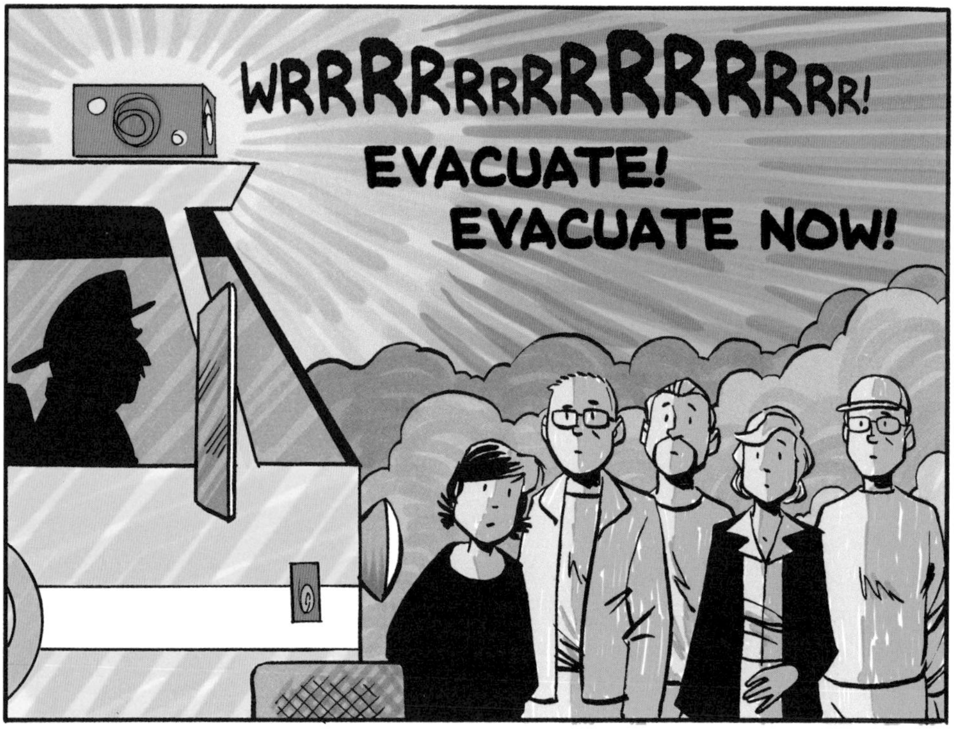
WRRRRRRRRRRRRRR!
EVACUATE!
EVACUATE NOW!

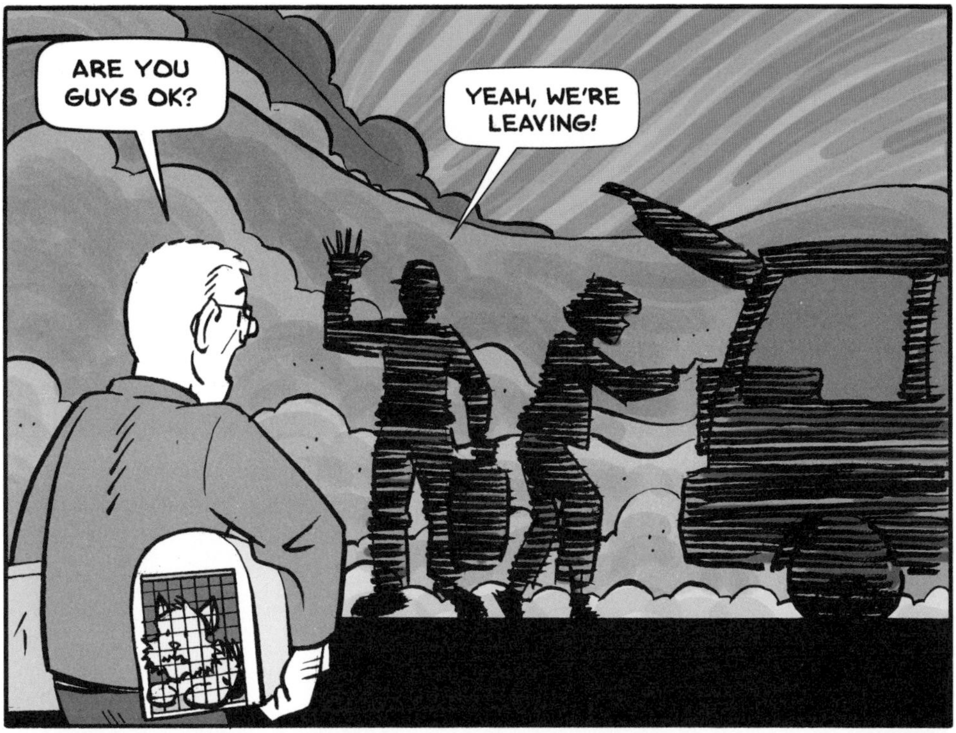
ARE YOU GUYS OK?
YEAH, WE'RE LEAVING!

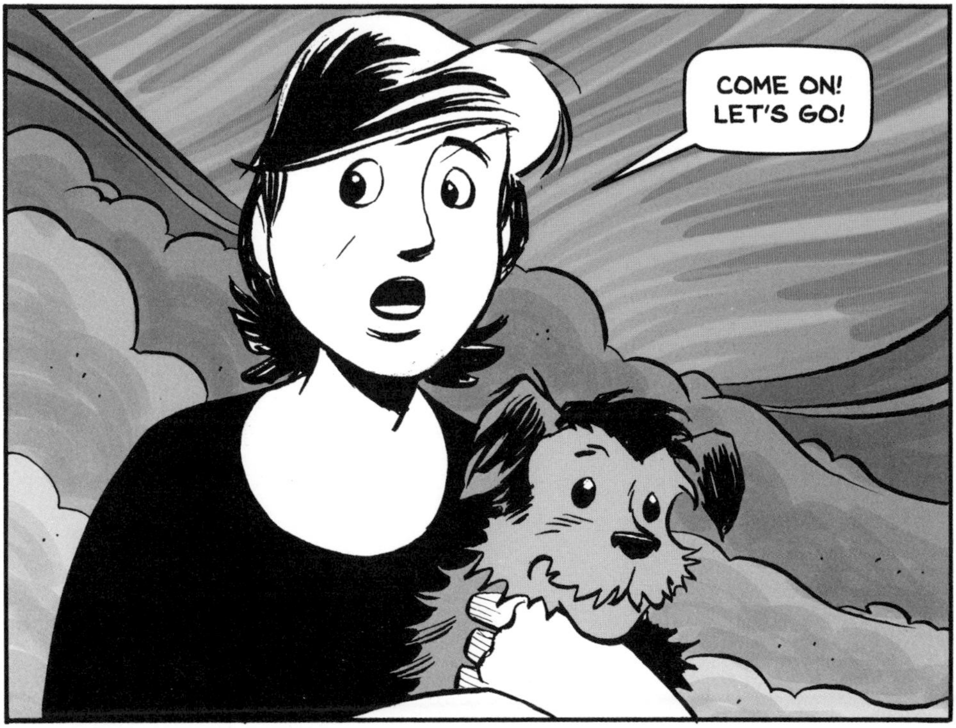
COME ON! LET'S GO!

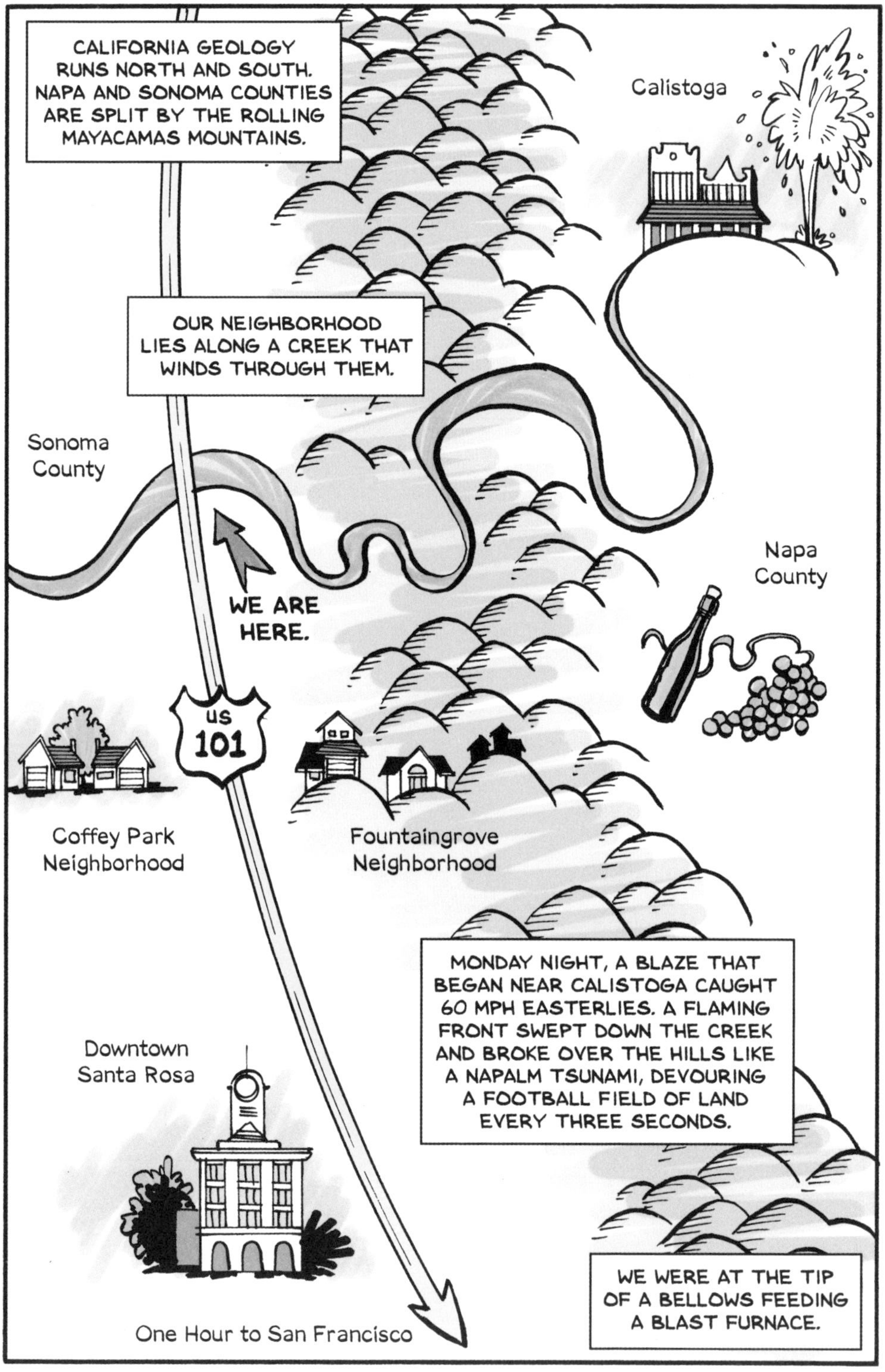
CALIFORNIA GEOLOGY RUNS NORTH AND SOUTH. NAPA AND SONOMA COUNTIES ARE SPLIT BY THE ROLLING MAYACAMAS MOUNTAINS.
Calistoga
OUR NEIGHBORHOOD LIES ALONG A CREEK THAT WINDS THROUGH THEM.
Sonoma County
WE ARE HERE.
Napa County
US 101
Coffey Park Neighborhood
Fountaingrove Neighborhood
MONDAY NIGHT, A BLAZE THAT BEGAN NEAR CALISTOGA CAUGHT 60 MPH EASTERLIES. A FLAMING FRONT SWEPT DOWN THE CREEK AND BROKE OVER THE HILLS LIKE A NAPALM TSUNAMI, DEVOURING A FOOTBALL FIELD OF LAND EVERY THREE SECONDS.
Downtown Santa Rosa
WE WERE AT THE TIP OF A BELLOWS FEEDING A BLAST FURNACE.
One Hour to San Francisco

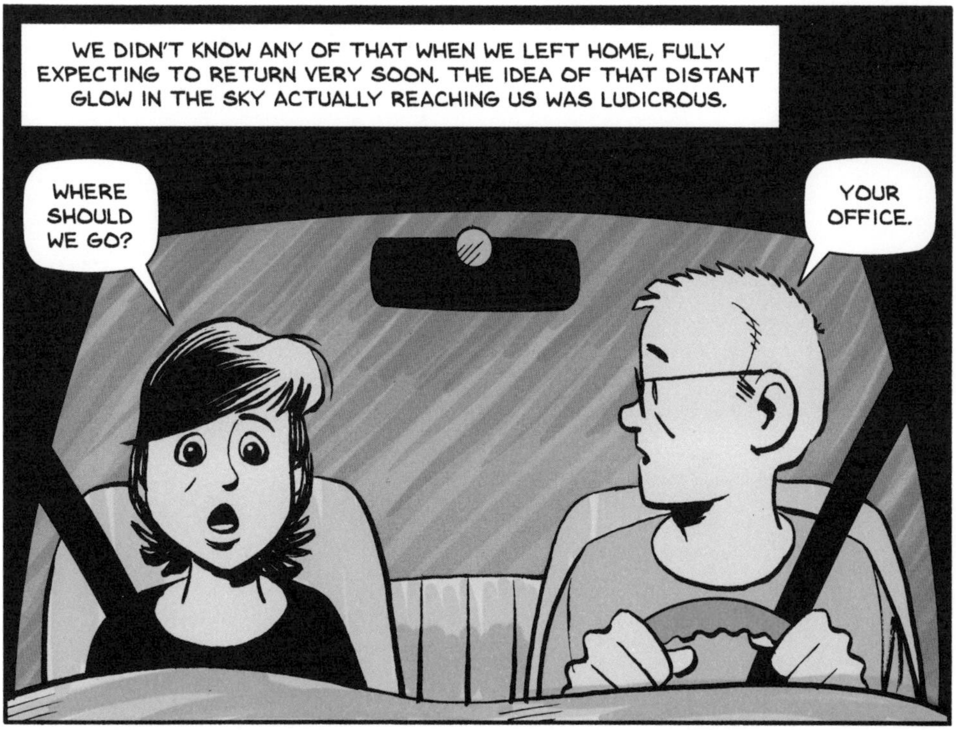
WE DIDN'T KNOW ANY OF THAT WHEN WE LEFT HOME, FULLY EXPECTING TO RETURN VERY SOON. THE IDEA OF THAT DISTANT GLOW IN THE SKY ACTUALLY REACHING US WAS LUDICROUS.
WHERE SHOULD WE GO?
YOUR OFFICE.

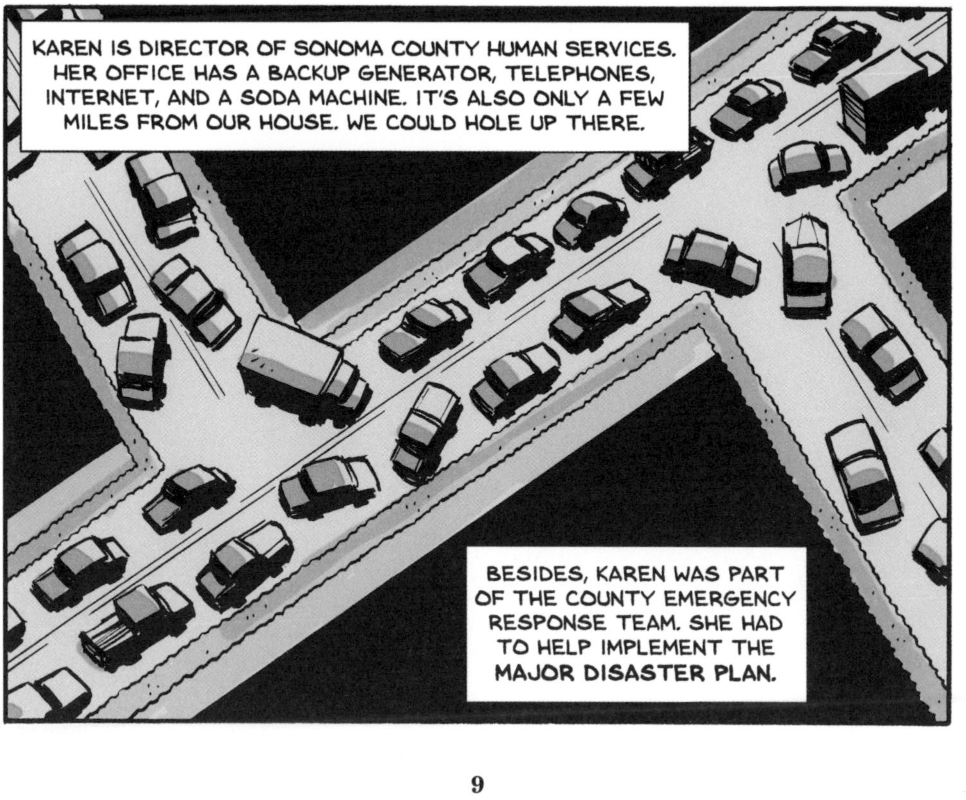
KAREN IS DIRECTOR OF SONOMA COUNTY HUMAN SERVICES. HER OFFICE HAS A BACKUP GENERATOR, TELEPHONES, INTERNET, AND A SODA MACHINE. IT'S ALSO ONLY A FEW MILES FROM OUR HOUSE. WE COULD HOLE UP THERE.
BESIDES, KAREN WAS PART OF THE COUNTY EMERGENCY RESPONSE TEAM. SHE HAD TO HELP IMPLEMENT THE **MAJOR DISASTER PLAN.**

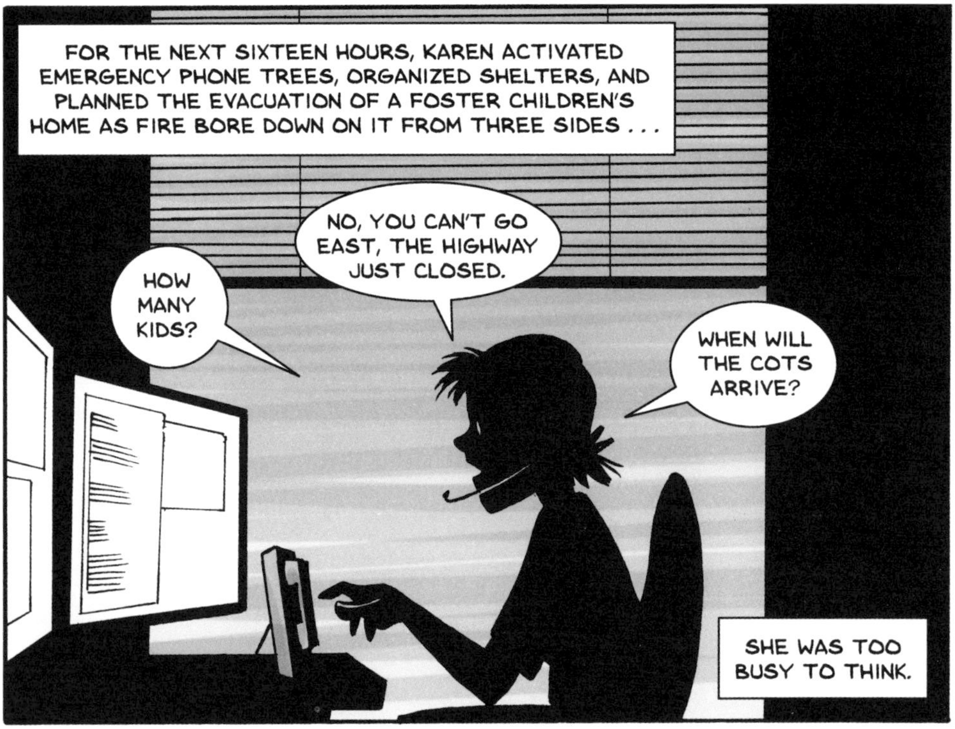
FOR THE NEXT SIXTEEN HOURS, KAREN ACTIVATED EMERGENCY PHONE TREES, ORGANIZED SHELTERS, AND PLANNED THE EVACUATION OF A FOSTER CHILDREN'S HOME AS FIRE BORE DOWN ON IT FROM THREE SIDES . . .
HOW MANY KIDS?
NO, YOU CAN'T GO EAST, THE HIGHWAY JUST CLOSED.
WHEN WILL THE COTS ARRIVE?
SHE WAS TOO BUSY TO THINK.

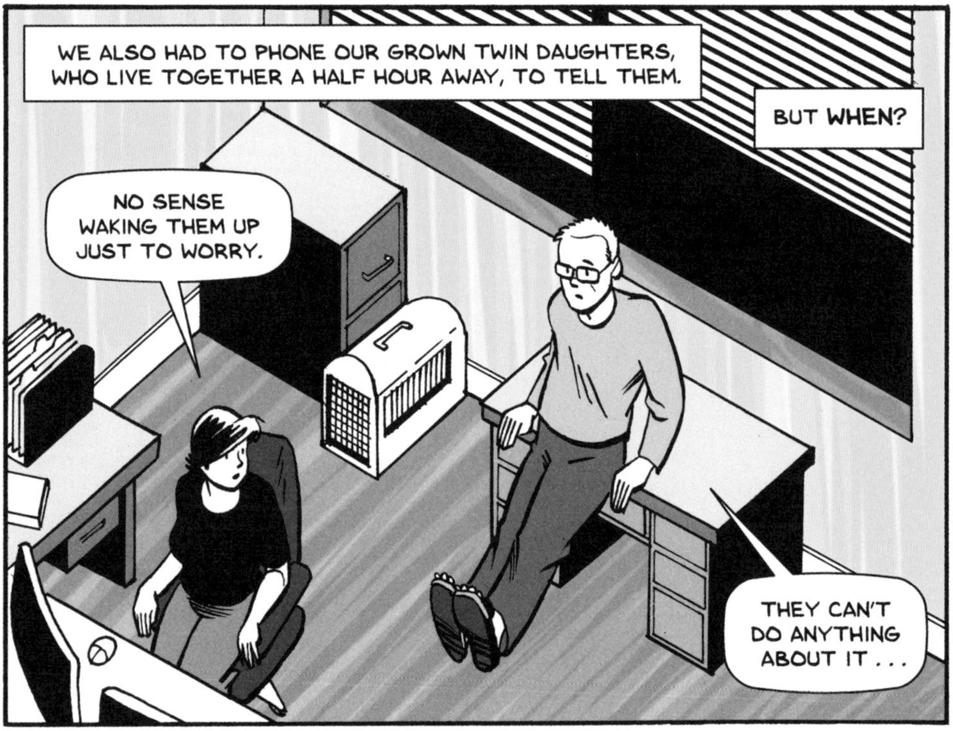
WE ALSO HAD TO PHONE OUR GROWN TWIN DAUGHTERS, WHO LIVE TOGETHER A HALF HOUR AWAY, TO TELL THEM.
BUT WHEN?
NO SENSE WAKING THEM UP JUST TO WORRY.
THEY CAN'T DO ANYTHING ABOUT IT . . .

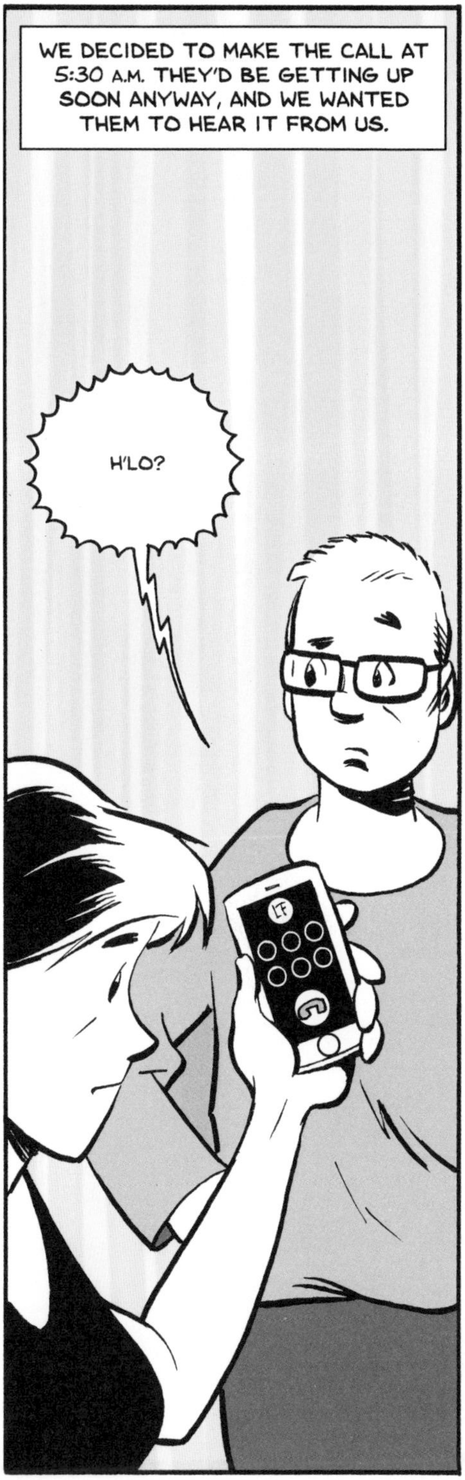
WE DECIDED TO MAKE THE CALL AT 5:30 A.M. THEY'D BE GETTING UP SOON ANYWAY, AND WE WANTED THEM TO HEAR IT FROM US.
H'LO?

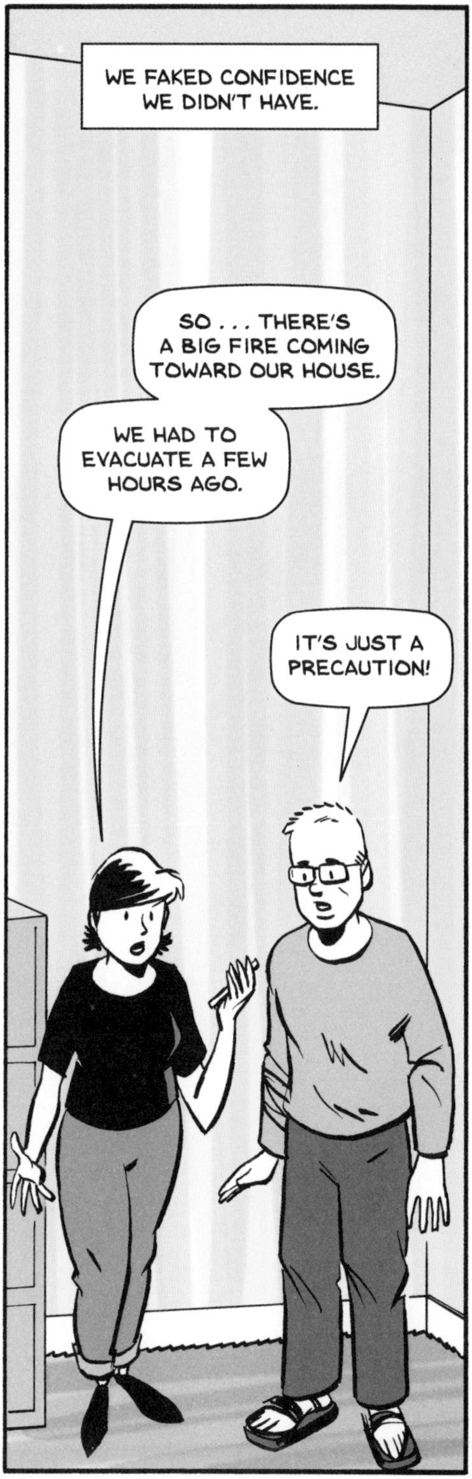
WE FAKED CONFIDENCE WE DIDN'T HAVE.
SO . . . THERE'S A BIG FIRE COMING TOWARD OUR HOUSE.
WE HAD TO EVACUATE A FEW HOURS AGO.
IT'S JUST A PRECAUTION!

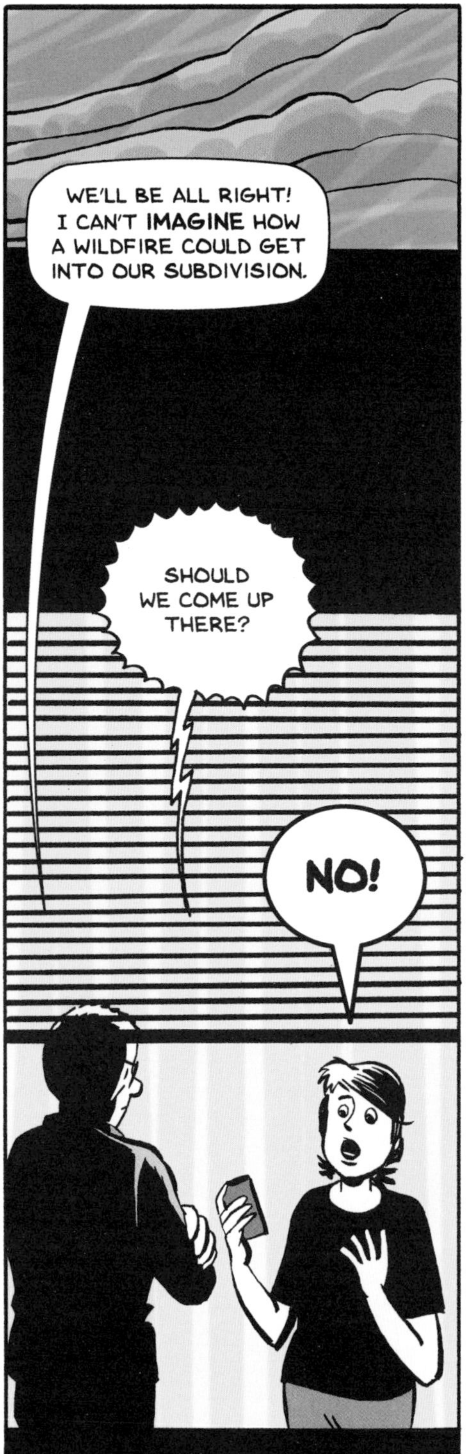
WE'LL BE ALL RIGHT! I CAN'T IMAGINE HOW A WILDFIRE COULD GET INTO OUR SUBDIVISION.
SHOULD WE COME UP THERE?
NO!

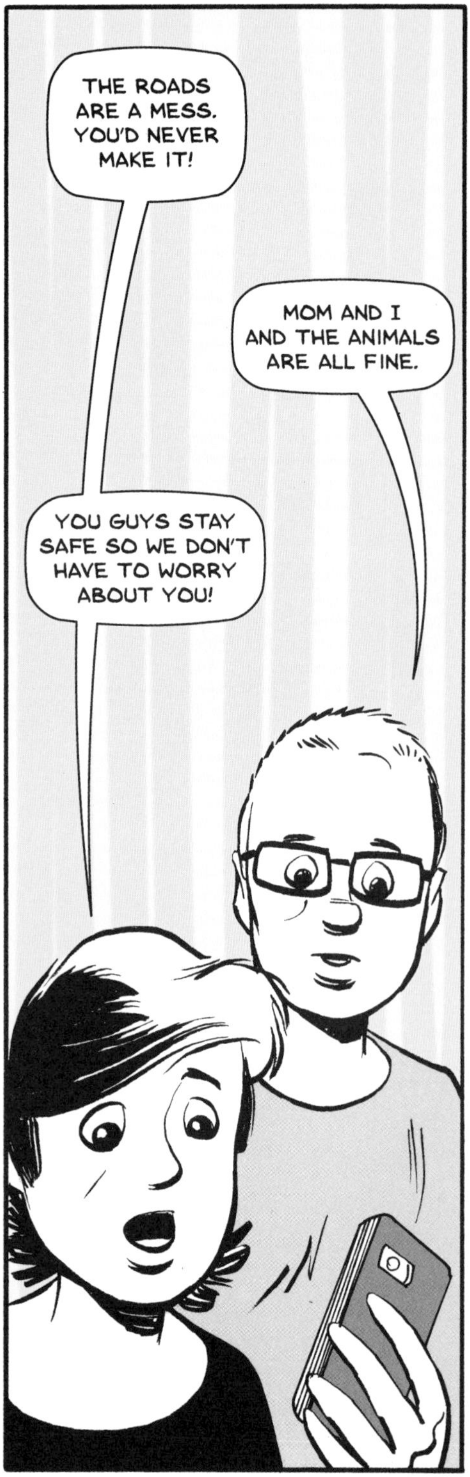
THE ROADS ARE A MESS. YOU'D NEVER MAKE IT!
MOM AND I AND THE ANIMALS ARE ALL FINE.
YOU GUYS STAY SAFE SO WE DON'T HAVE TO WORRY ABOUT YOU!

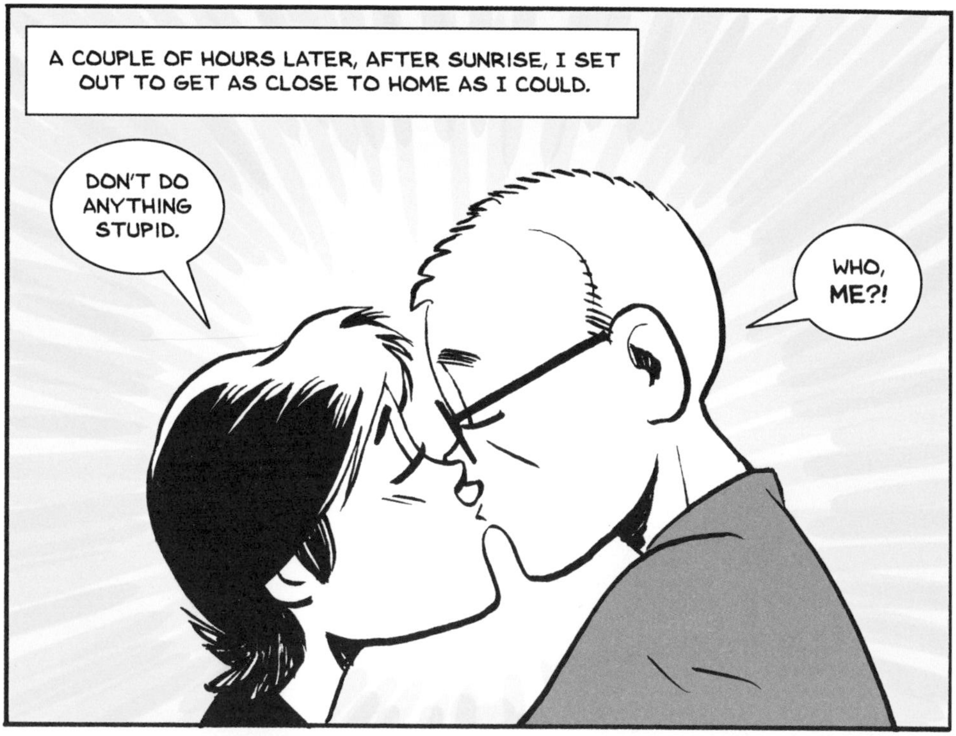
A COUPLE OF HOURS LATER, AFTER SUNRISE, I SET OUT TO GET AS CLOSE TO HOME AS I COULD.
DON'T DO ANYTHING STUPID.
WHO, ME?!

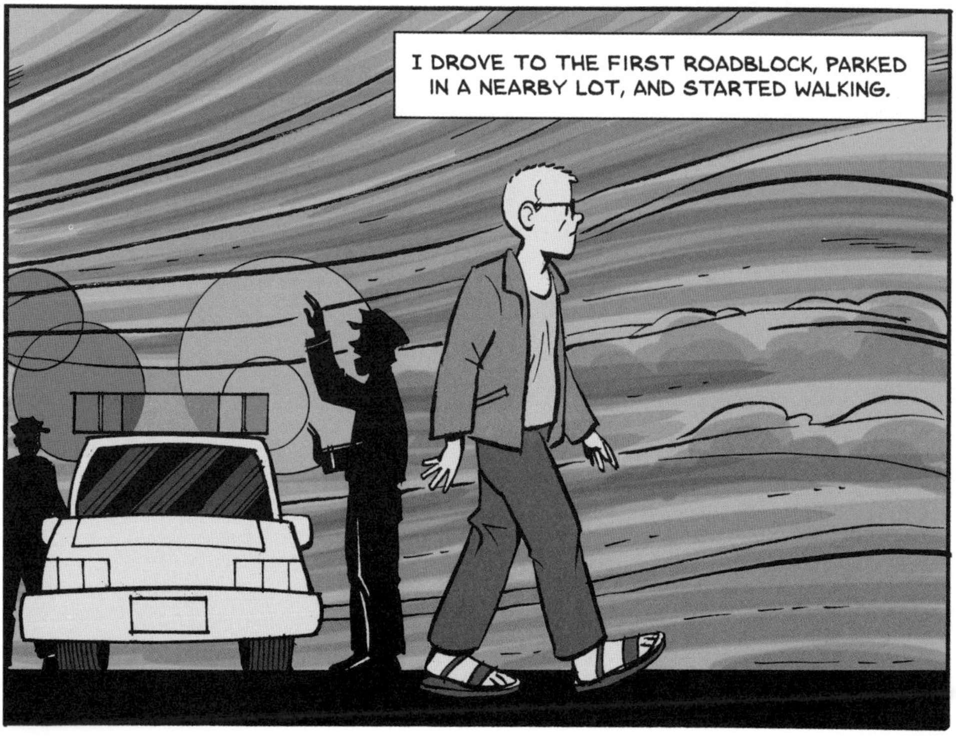
I DROVE TO THE FIRST ROADBLOCK, PARKED IN A NEARBY LOT, AND STARTED WALKING.

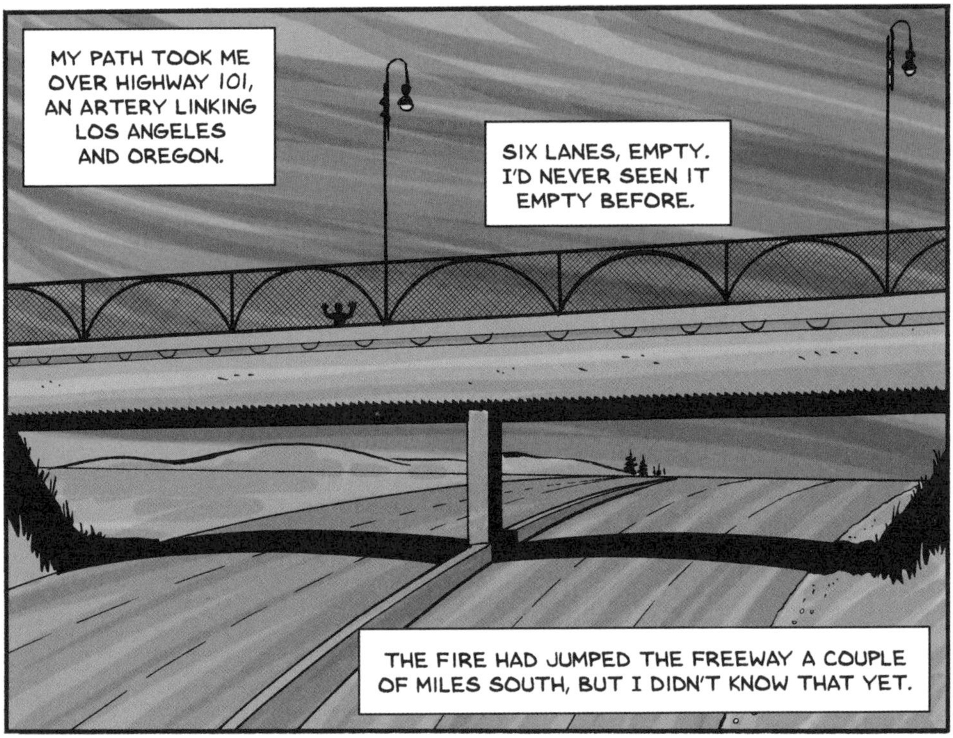
MY PATH TOOK ME OVER HIGHWAY 101, AN ARTERY LINKING LOS ANGELES AND OREGON.
SIX LANES, EMPTY. I'D NEVER SEEN IT EMPTY BEFORE.
THE FIRE HAD JUMPED THE FREEWAY A COUPLE OF MILES SOUTH, BUT I DIDN'T KNOW THAT YET.

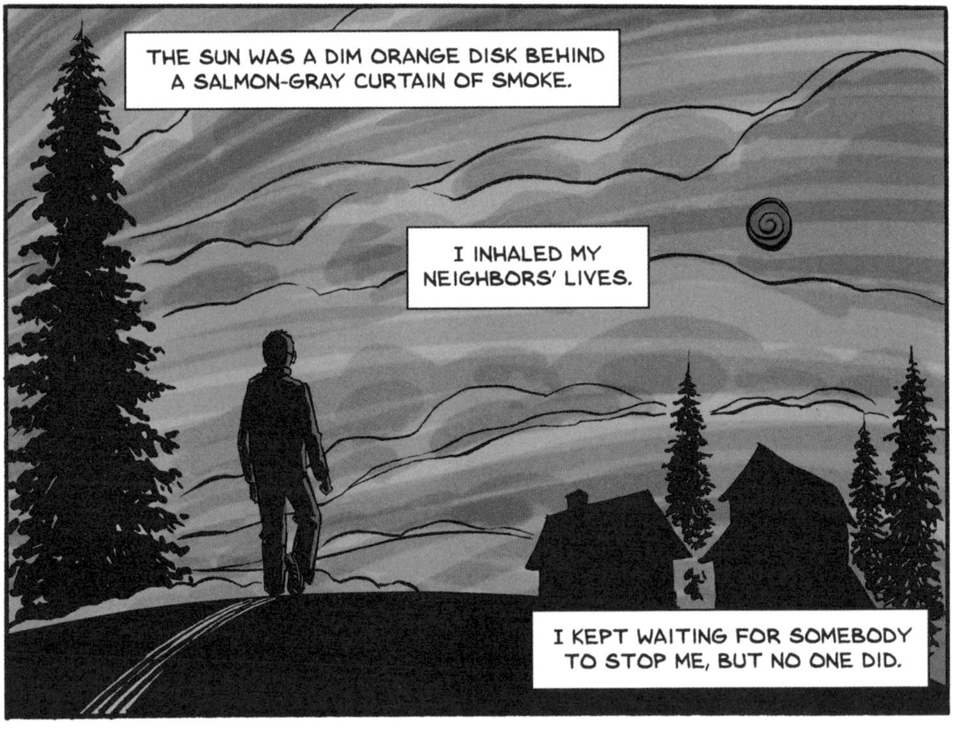
THE SUN WAS A DIM ORANGE DISK BEHIND A SALMON-GRAY CURTAIN OF SMOKE.
I INHALED MY NEIGHBORS' LIVES.
I KEPT WAITING FOR SOMEBODY TO STOP ME, BUT NO ONE DID.

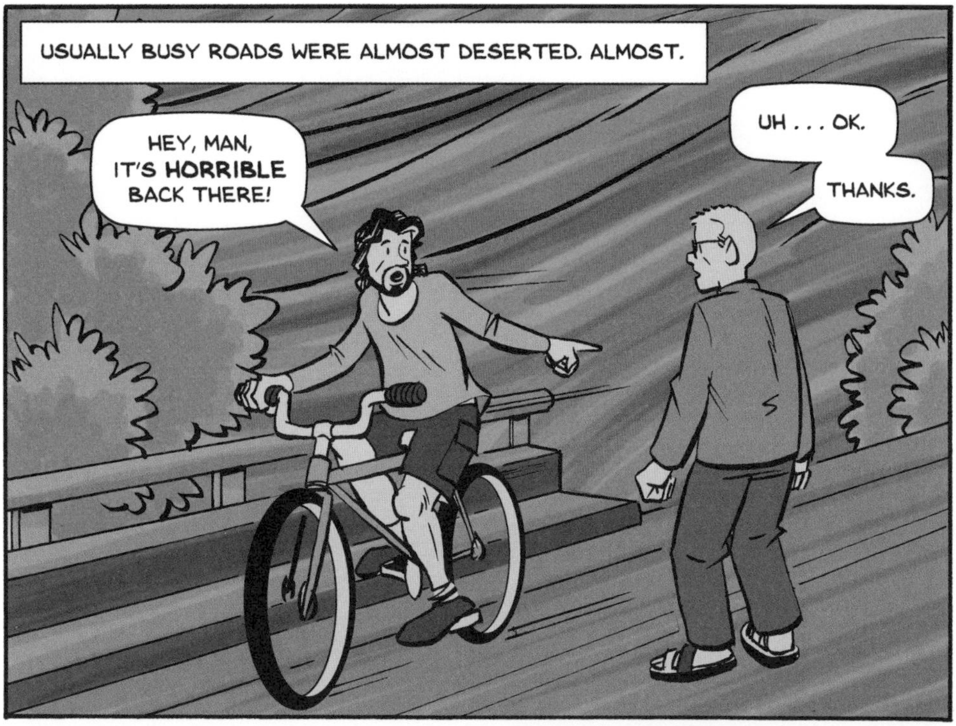
USUALLY BUSY ROADS WERE ALMOST DESERTED. ALMOST.
HEY, MAN, IT'S **HORRIBLE** BACK THERE!
UH . . . OK.
THANKS.

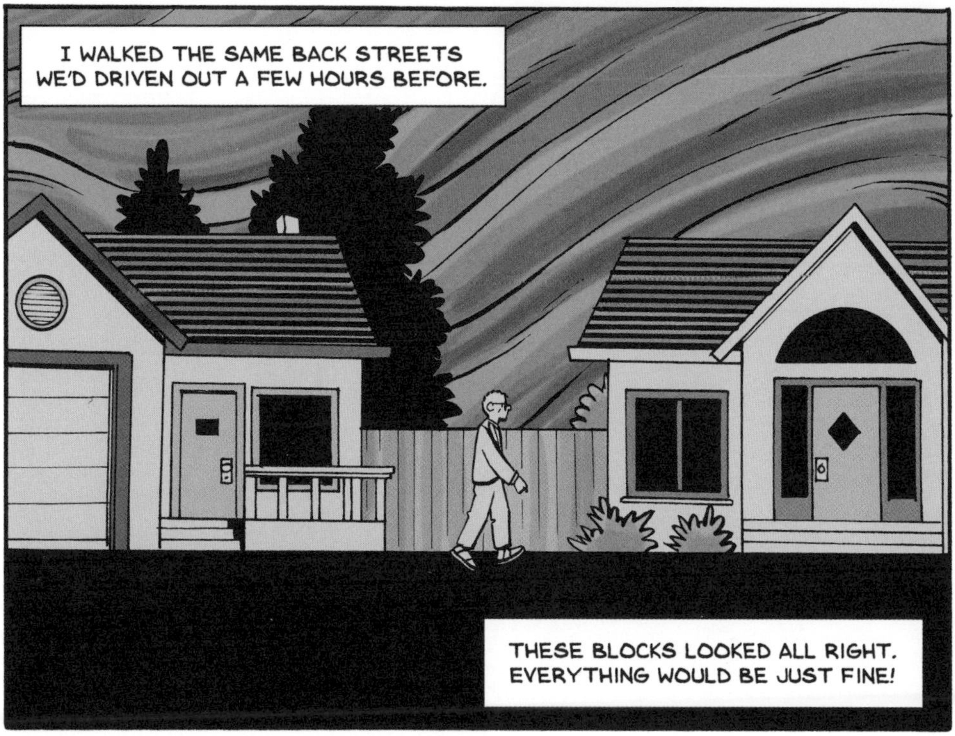
I WALKED THE SAME BACK STREETS WE'D DRIVEN OUT A FEW HOURS BEFORE.
THESE BLOCKS LOOKED ALL RIGHT. EVERYTHING WOULD BE JUST FINE!

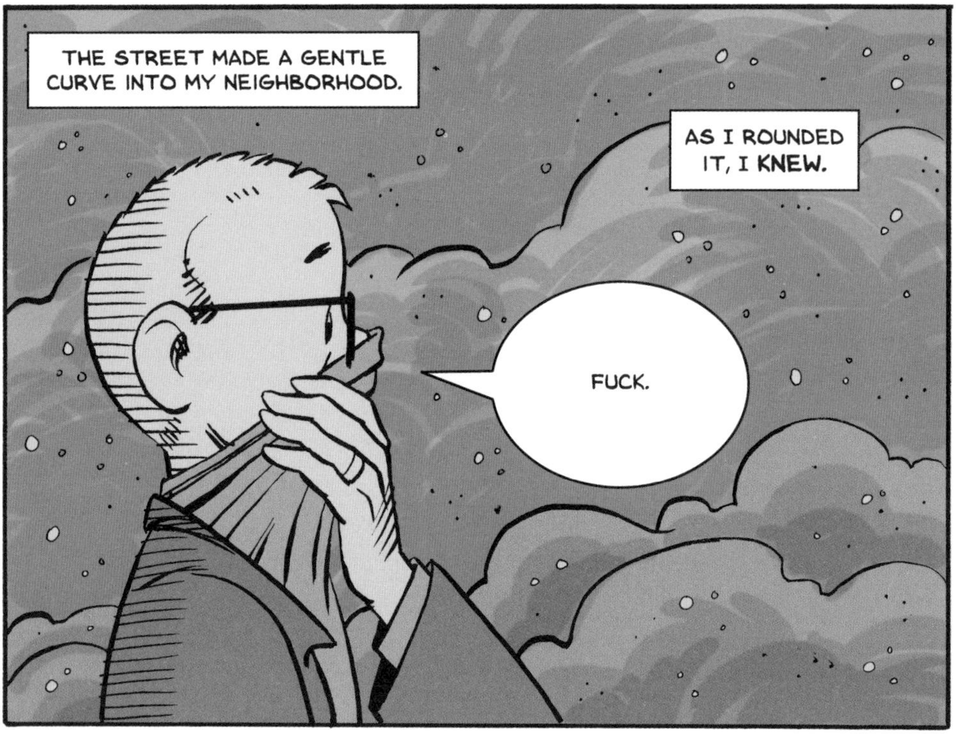
THE STREET MADE A GENTLE CURVE INTO MY NEIGHBORHOOD.
AS I ROUNDED IT, I KNEW.
FUCK.

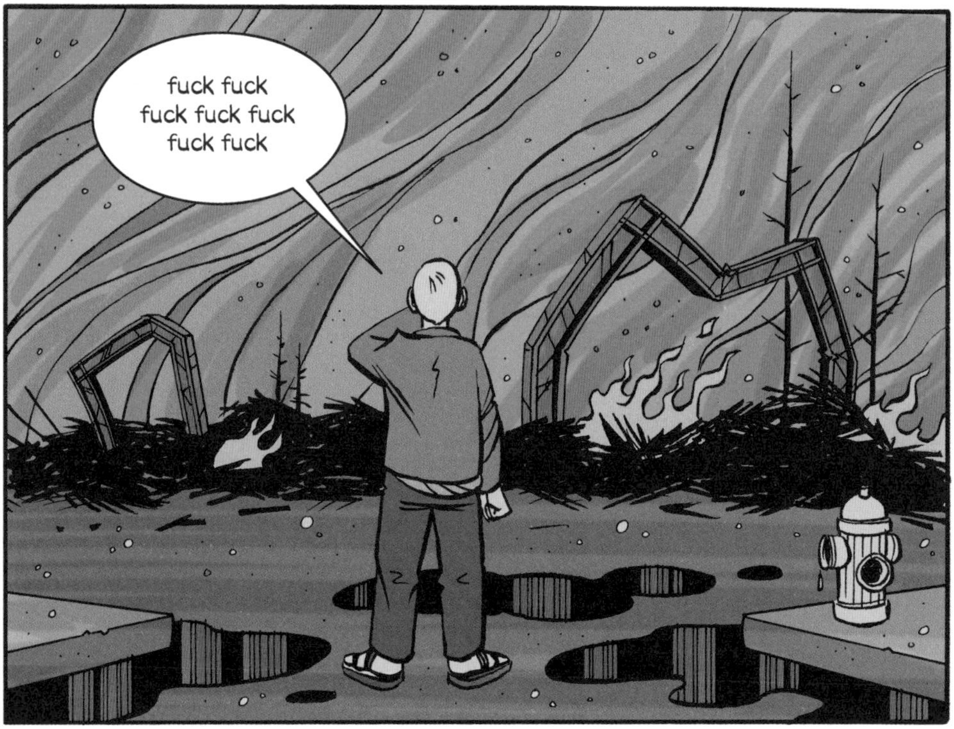
fuck fuck
fuck fuck fuck
fuck fuck

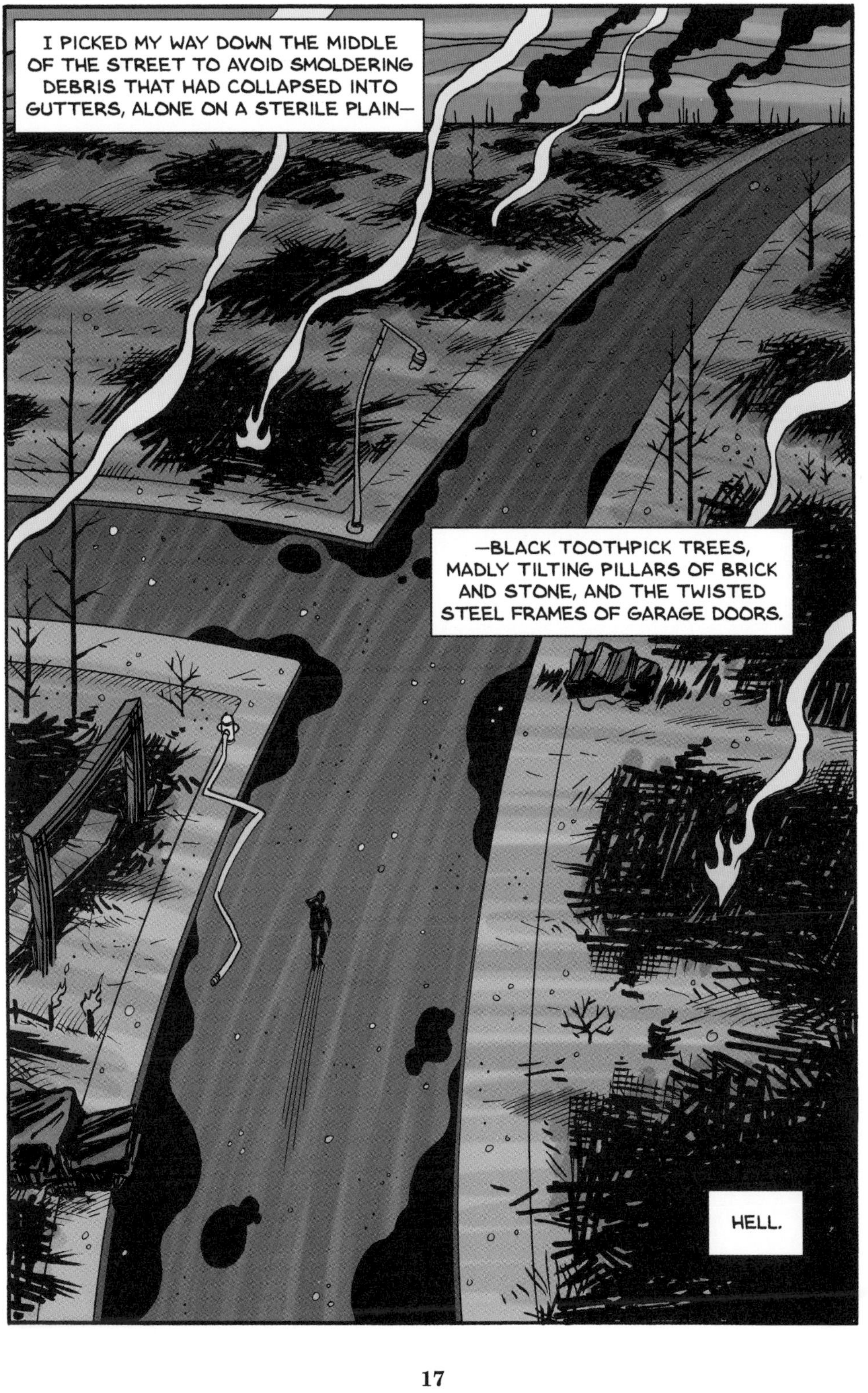
I PICKED MY WAY DOWN THE MIDDLE OF THE STREET TO AVOID SMOLDERING DEBRIS THAT HAD COLLAPSED INTO GUTTERS, ALONE ON A STERILE PLAIN—
—BLACK TOOTHPICK TREES, MADLY TILTING PILLARS OF BRICK AND STONE, AND THE TWISTED STEEL FRAMES OF GARAGE DOORS.
HELL.

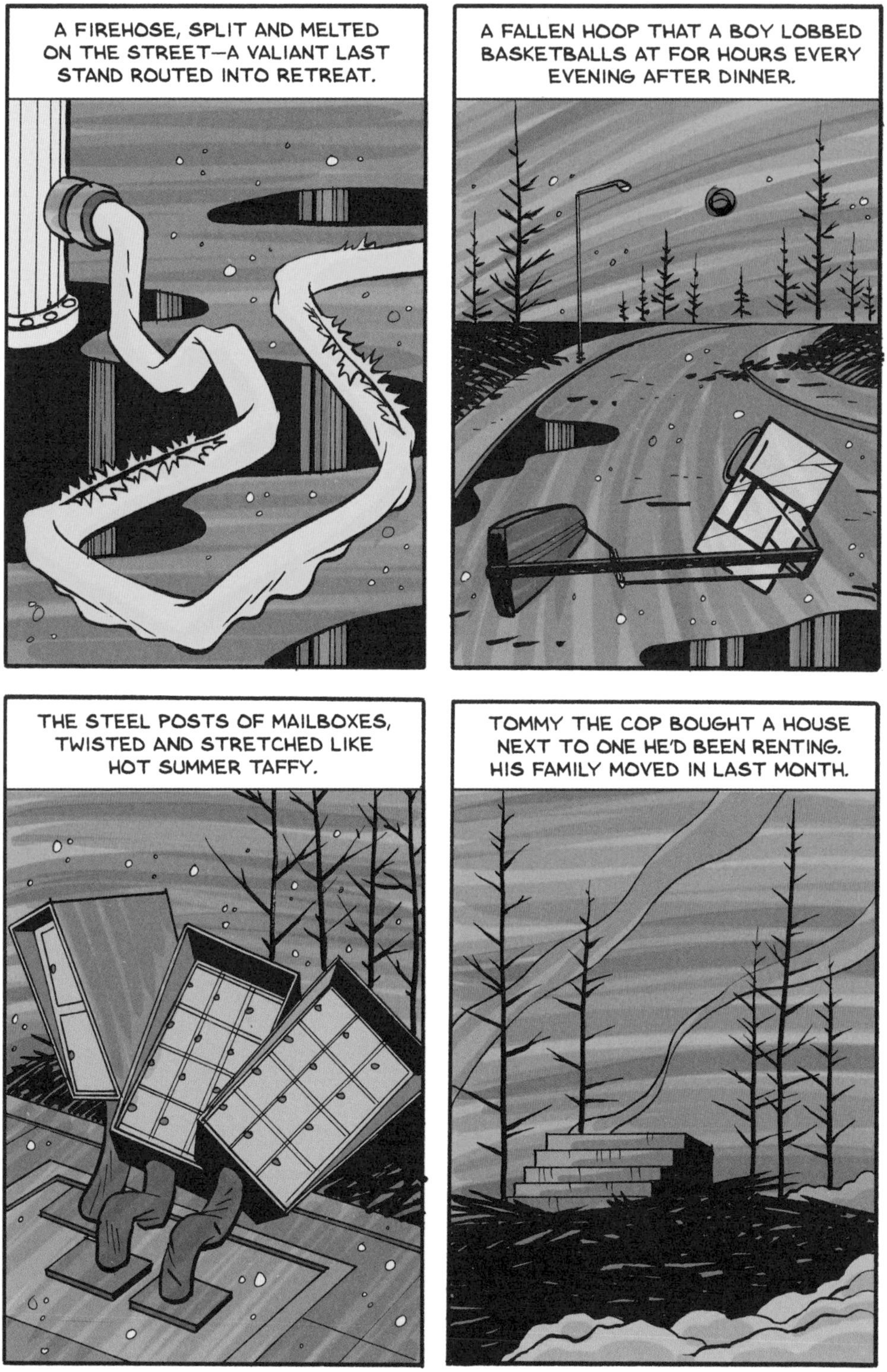
A FIREHOSE, SPLIT AND MELTED ON THE STREET—A VALIANT LAST STAND ROUTED INTO RETREAT.
A FALLEN HOOP THAT A BOY LOBBED BASKETBALLS AT FOR HOURS EVERY EVENING AFTER DINNER.
THE STEEL POSTS OF MAILBOXES, TWISTED AND STRETCHED LIKE HOT SUMMER TAFFY.
TOMMY THE COP BOUGHT A HOUSE NEXT TO ONE HE'D BEEN RENTING. HIS FAMILY MOVED IN LAST MONTH.

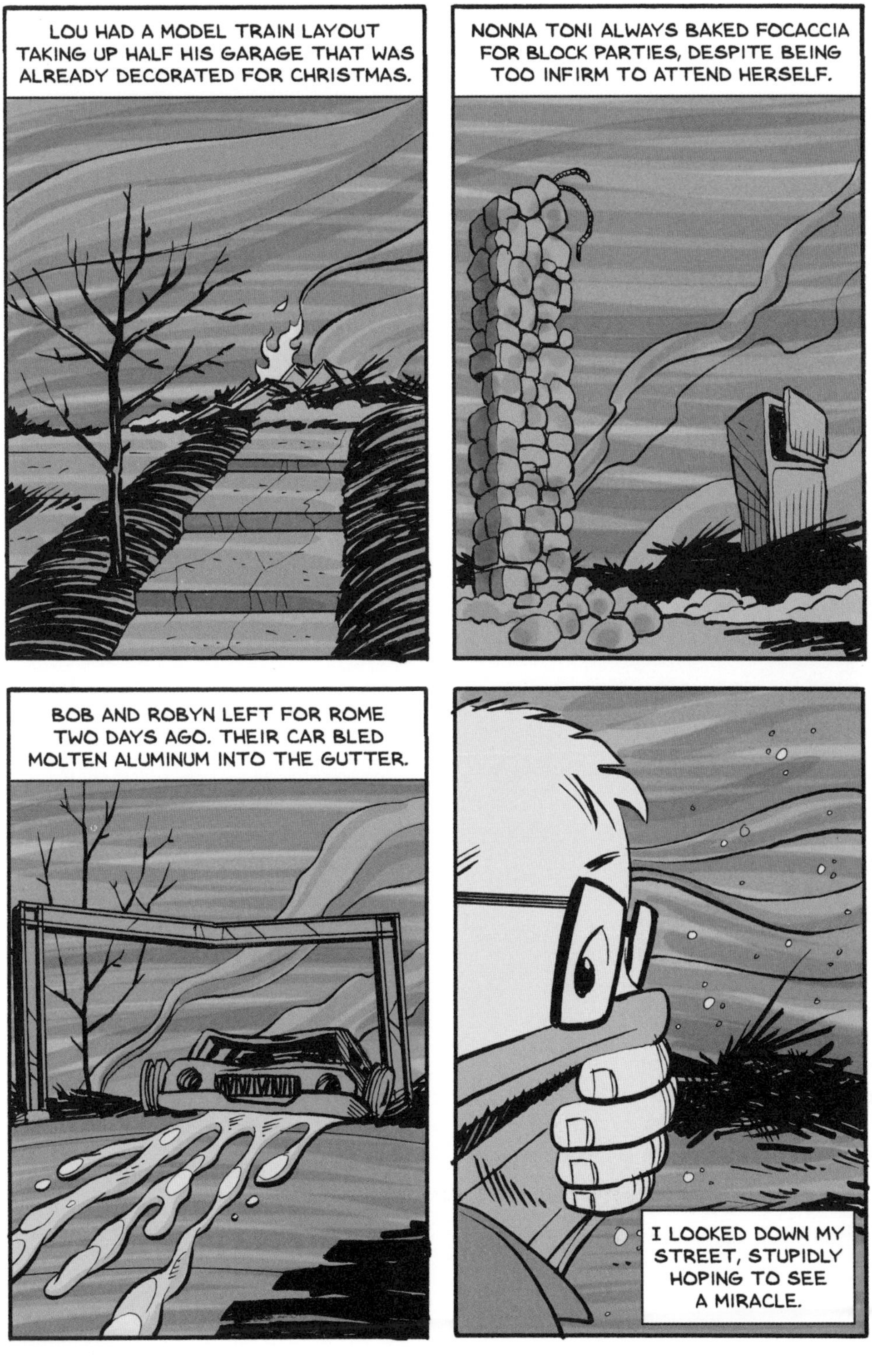
LOU HAD A MODEL TRAIN LAYOUT TAKING UP HALF HIS GARAGE THAT WAS ALREADY DECORATED FOR CHRISTMAS.
NONNA TONI ALWAYS BAKED FOCACCIA FOR BLOCK PARTIES, DESPITE BEING TOO INFIRM TO ATTEND HERSELF.
BOB AND ROBYN LEFT FOR ROME TWO DAYS AGO. THEIR CAR BLED MOLTEN ALUMINUM INTO THE GUTTER.
I LOOKED DOWN MY STREET, STUPIDLY HOPING TO SEE A MIRACLE.

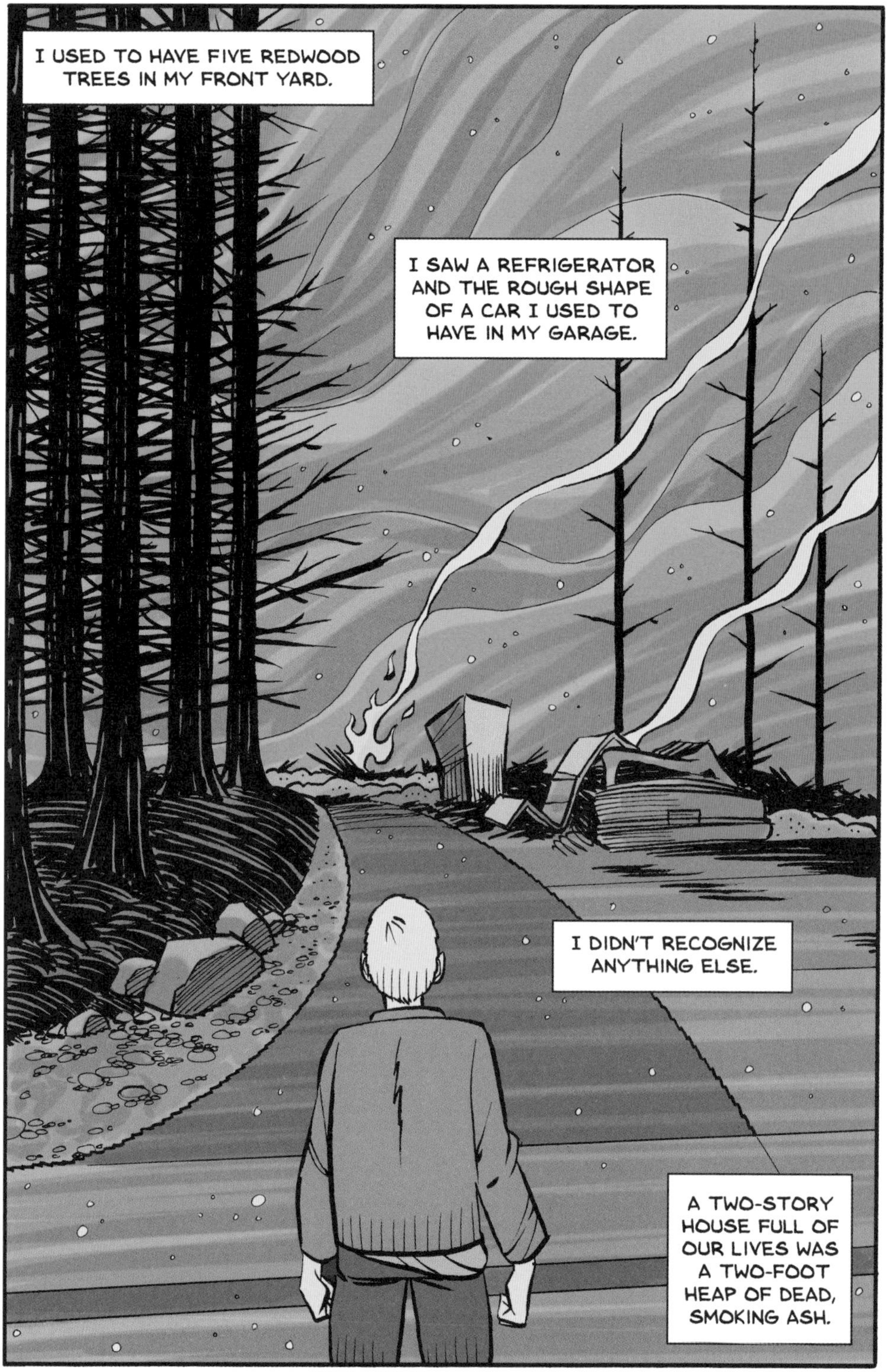
I USED TO HAVE FIVE REDWOOD TREES IN MY FRONT YARD.
I SAW A REFRIGERATOR AND THE ROUGH SHAPE OF A CAR I USED TO HAVE IN MY GARAGE.
I DIDN'T RECOGNIZE ANYTHING ELSE.
A TWO-STORY HOUSE FULL OF OUR LIVES WAS A TWO-FOOT HEAP OF DEAD, SMOKING ASH.

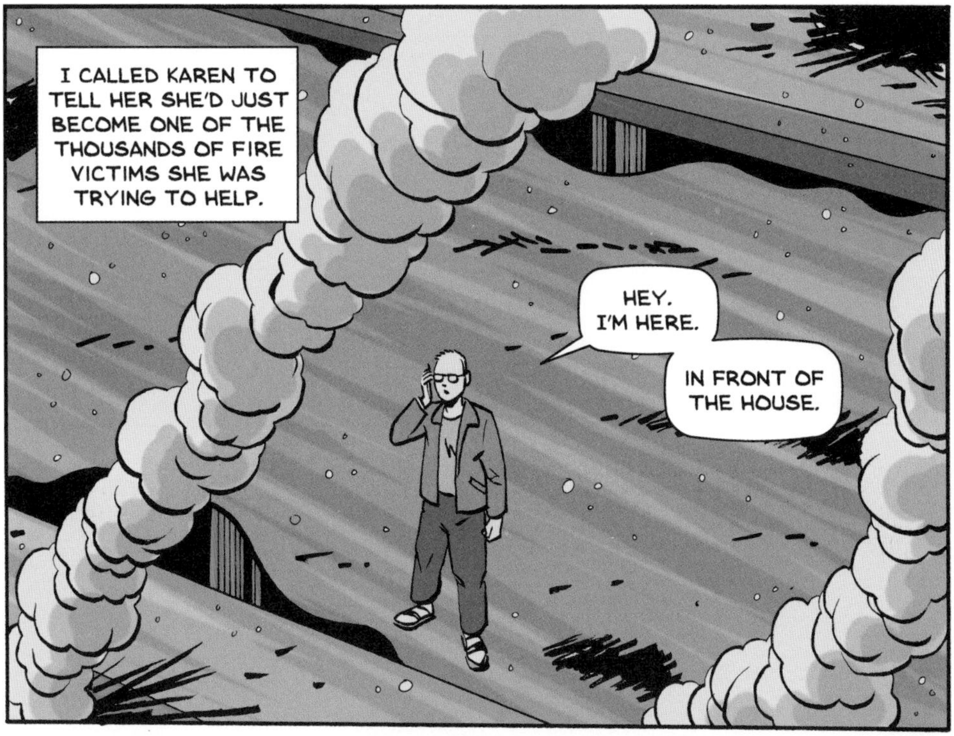
I CALLED KAREN TO TELL HER SHE'D JUST BECOME ONE OF THE THOUSANDS OF FIRE VICTIMS SHE WAS TRYING TO HELP.
HEY. I'M HERE.
IN FRONT OF THE HOUSE.

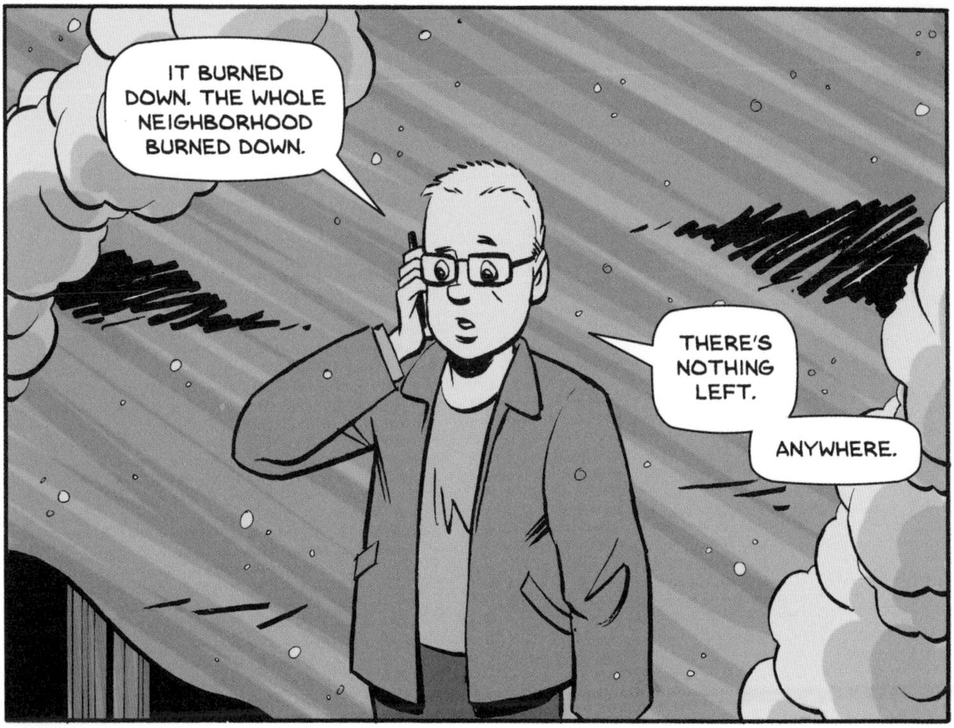
IT BURNED DOWN. THE WHOLE NEIGHBORHOOD BURNED DOWN.
THERE'S NOTHING LEFT.
ANYWHERE.

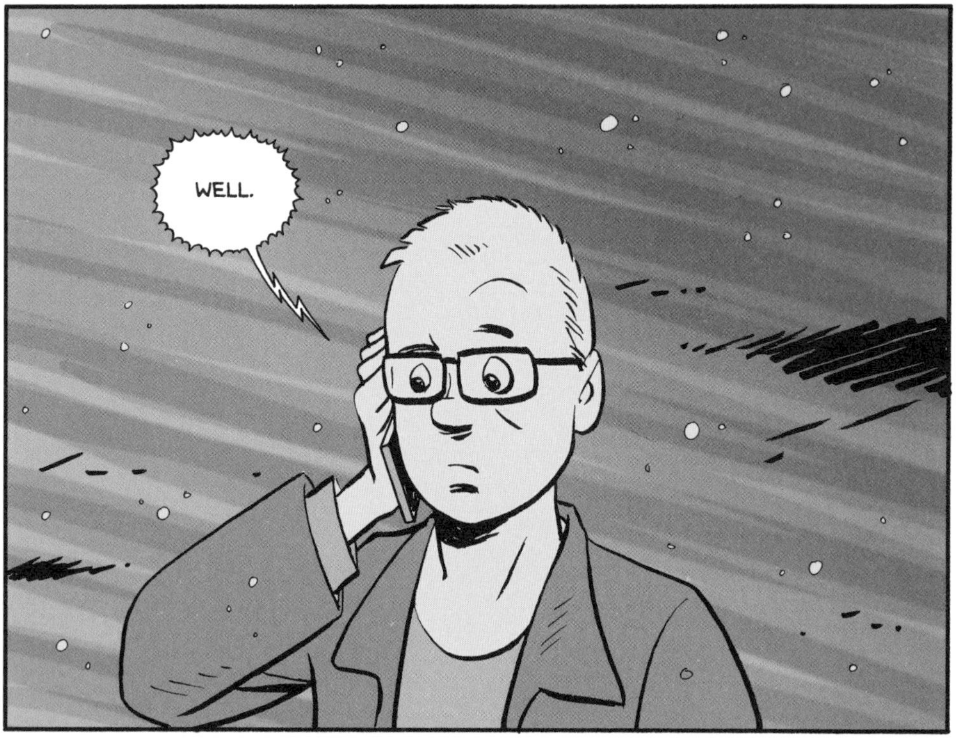
WELL.

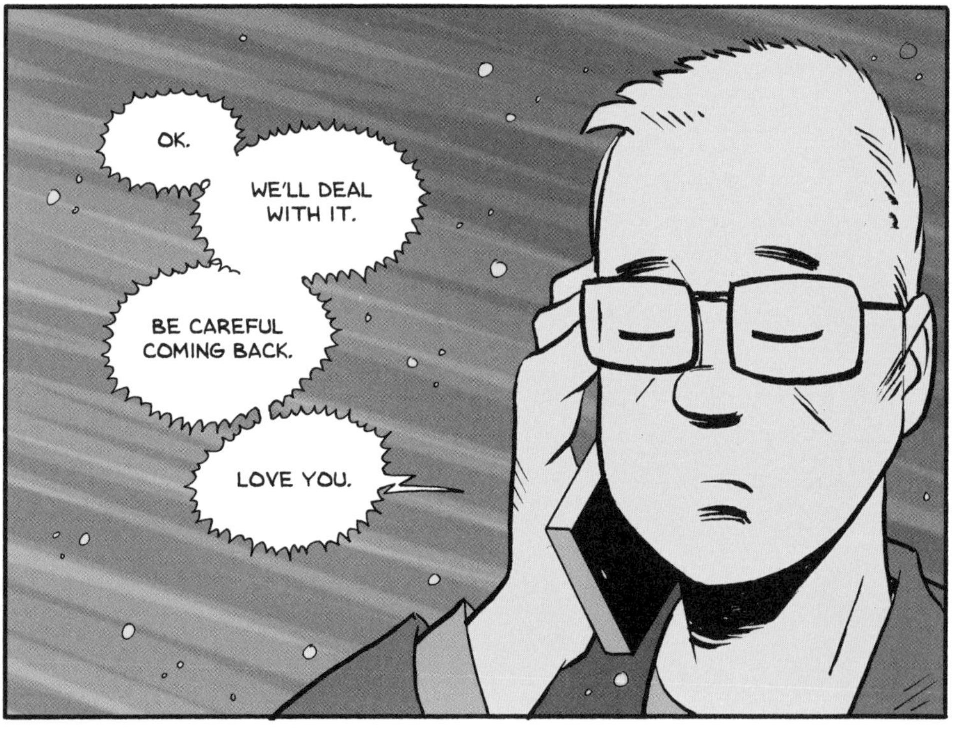
OK.
WE'LL DEAL WITH IT.
BE CAREFUL COMING BACK.
LOVE YOU.

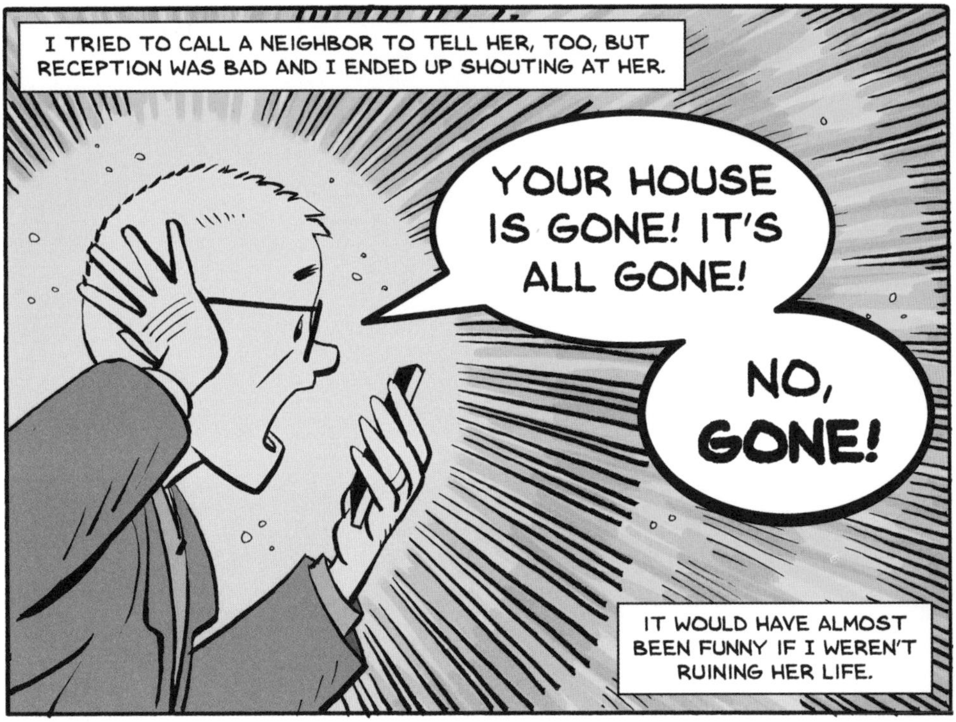
I TRIED TO CALL A NEIGHBOR TO TELL HER, TOO, BUT RECEPTION WAS BAD AND I ENDED UP SHOUTING AT HER.
YOUR HOUSE IS GONE! IT'S ALL GONE!
NO, GONE!
IT WOULD HAVE ALMOST BEEN FUNNY IF I WEREN'T RUINING HER LIFE.

I TOOK A FEW PHOTOS BUT DIDN'T LINGER.

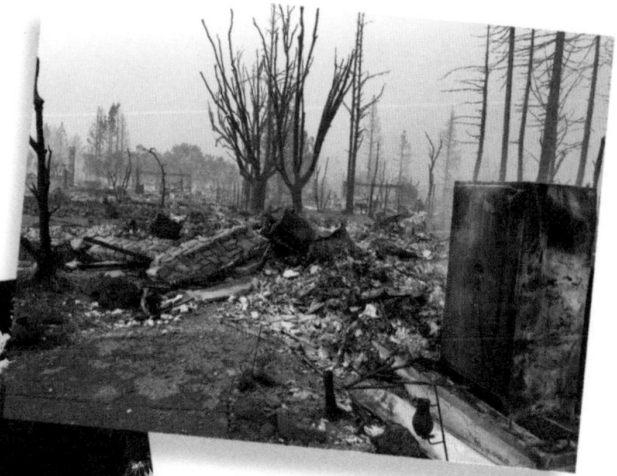

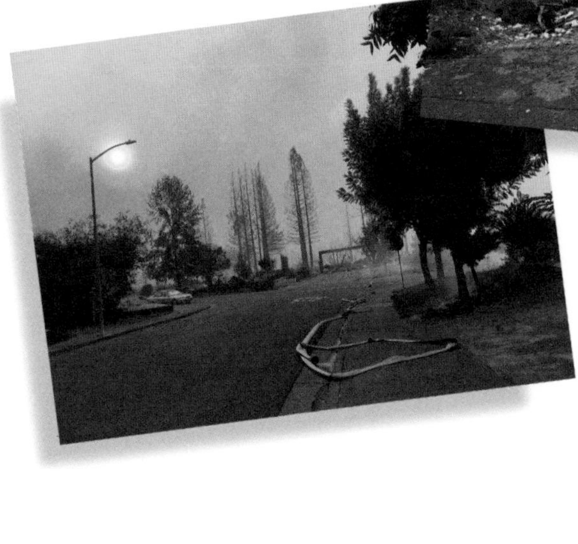

SPOTS WERE STILL BURNING, AND I SUDDENLY FELT EXPOSED AND VULNERABLE.

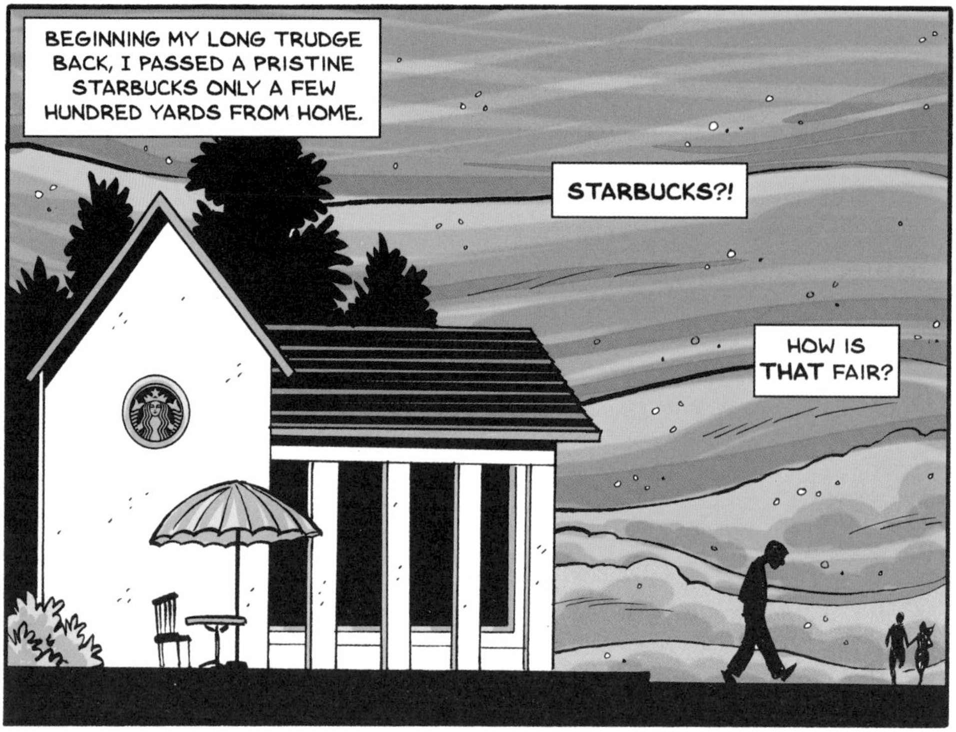
BEGINNING MY LONG TRUDGE BACK, I PASSED A PRISTINE STARBUCKS ONLY A FEW HUNDRED YARDS FROM HOME.
STARBUCKS?!
HOW IS THAT FAIR?

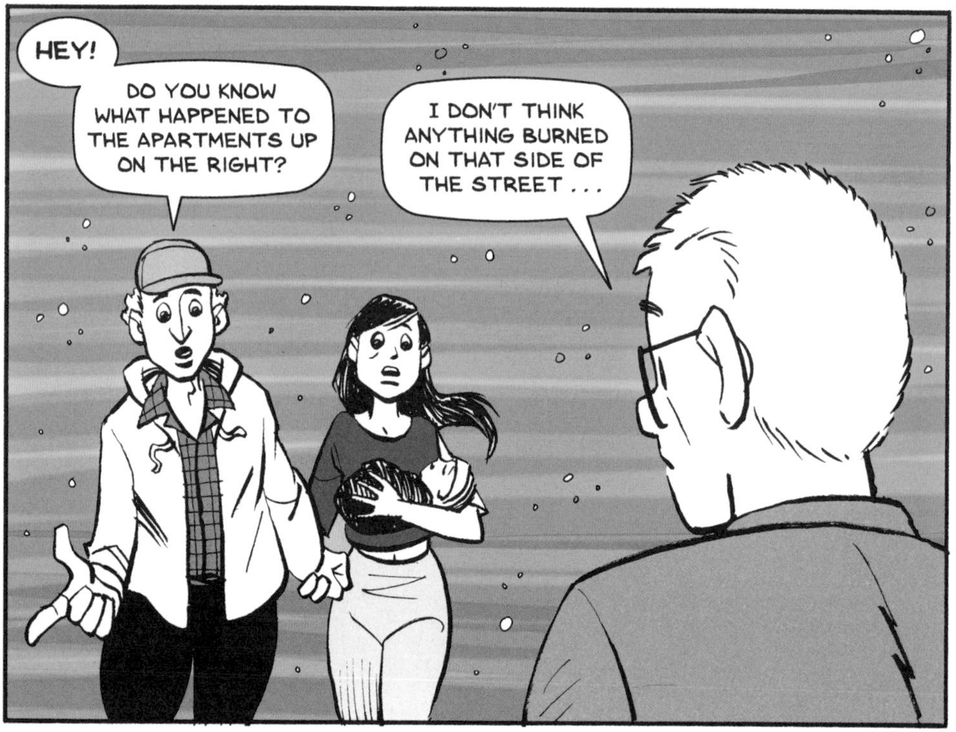
HEY!
DO YOU KNOW WHAT HAPPENED TO THE APARTMENTS UP ON THE RIGHT?
I DON'T THINK ANYTHING BURNED ON THAT SIDE OF THE STREET . . .

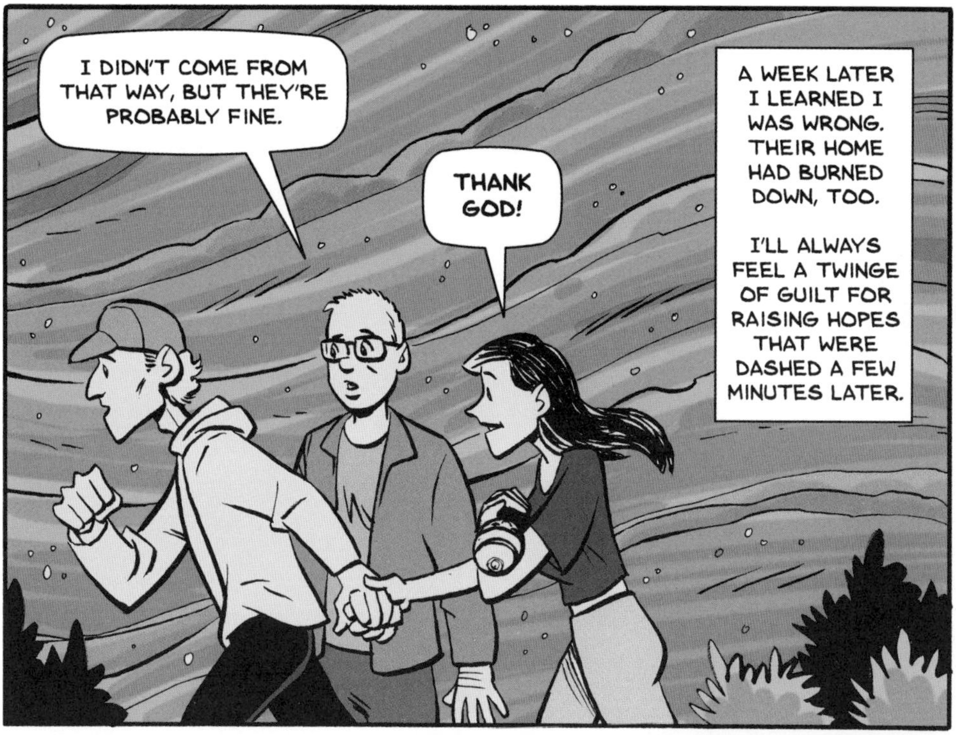
I DIDN'T COME FROM THAT WAY, BUT THEY'RE PROBABLY FINE.
THANK GOD!
A WEEK LATER I LEARNED I WAS WRONG. THEIR HOME HAD BURNED DOWN, TOO.
I'LL ALWAYS FEEL A TWINGE OF GUILT FOR RAISING HOPES THAT WERE DASHED A FEW MINUTES LATER.

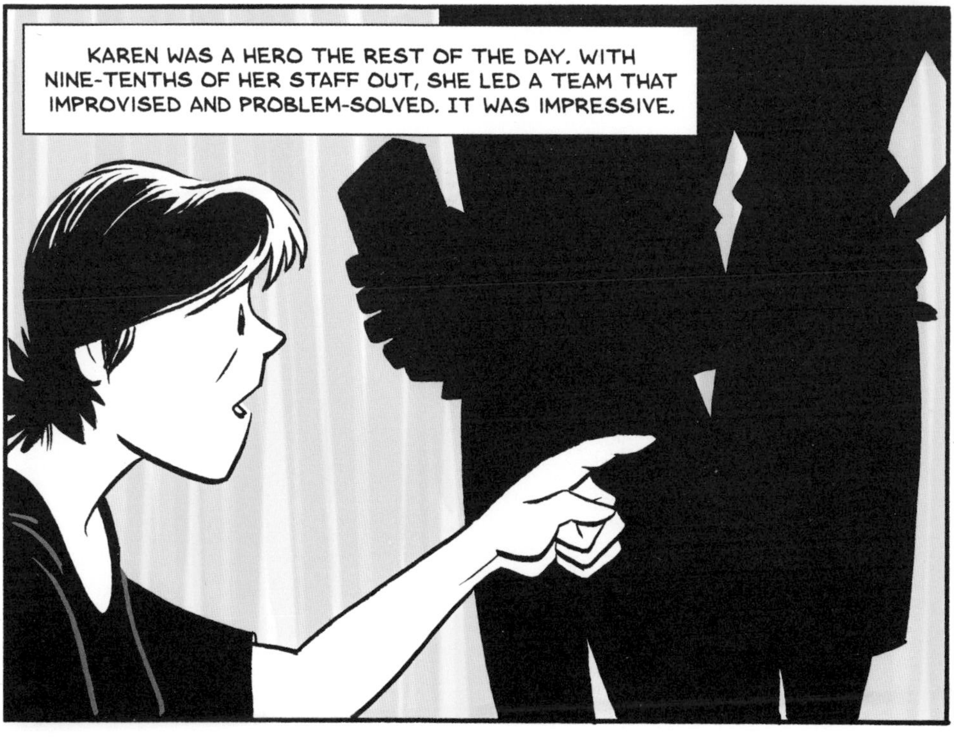
KAREN WAS A HERO THE REST OF THE DAY. WITH NINE-TENTHS OF HER STAFF OUT, SHE LED A TEAM THAT IMPROVISED AND PROBLEM-SOLVED. IT WAS IMPRESSIVE.

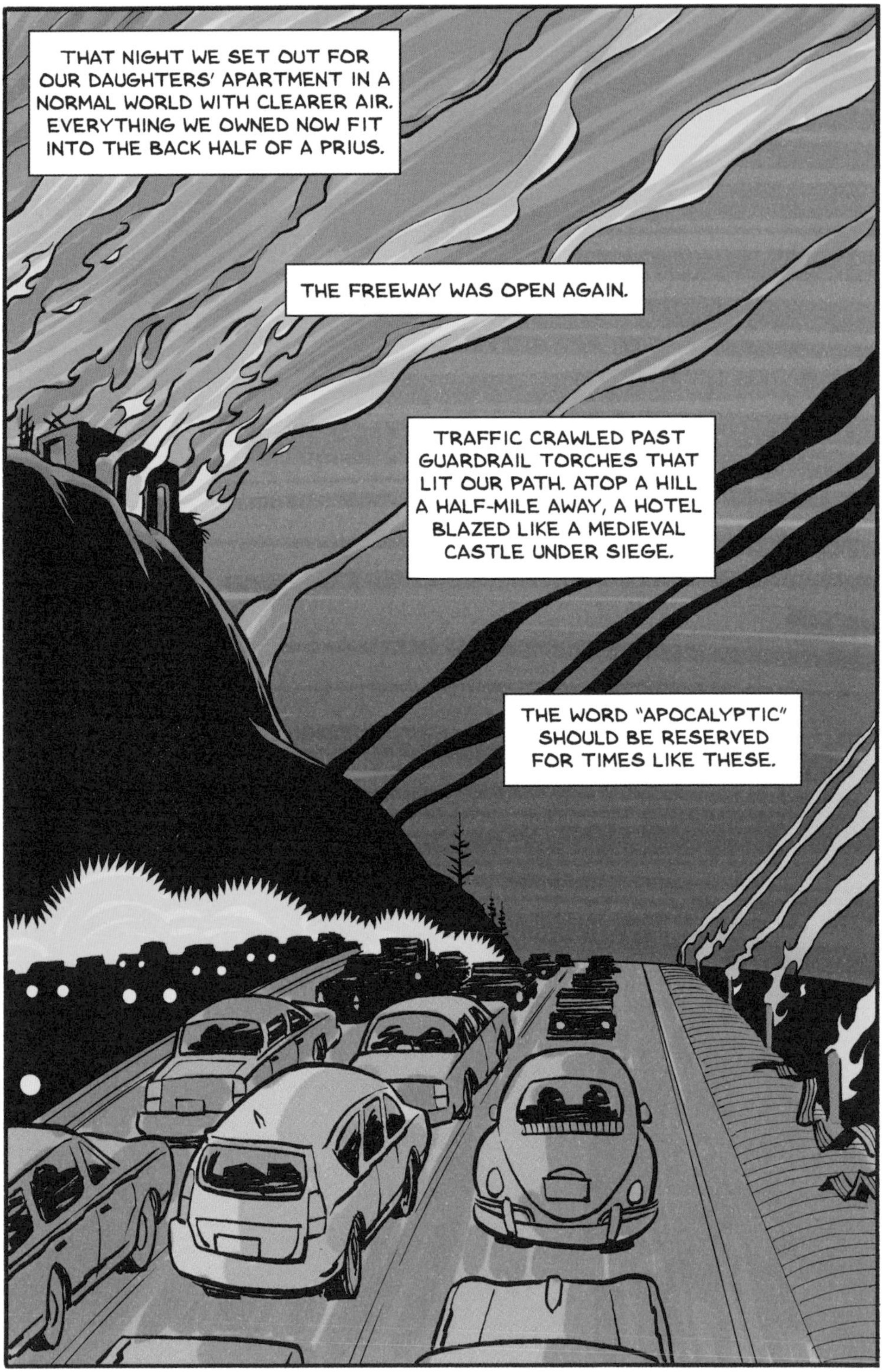
THAT NIGHT WE SET OUT FOR OUR DAUGHTERS' APARTMENT IN A NORMAL WORLD WITH CLEARER AIR. EVERYTHING WE OWNED NOW FIT INTO THE BACK HALF OF A PRIUS.
THE FREEWAY WAS OPEN AGAIN.
TRAFFIC CRAWLED PAST GUARDRAIL TORCHES THAT LIT OUR PATH. ATOP A HILL A HALF-MILE AWAY, A HOTEL BLAZED LIKE A MEDIEVAL CASTLE UNDER SIEGE.
THE WORD "APOCALYPTIC" SHOULD BE RESERVED FOR TIMES LIKE THESE.

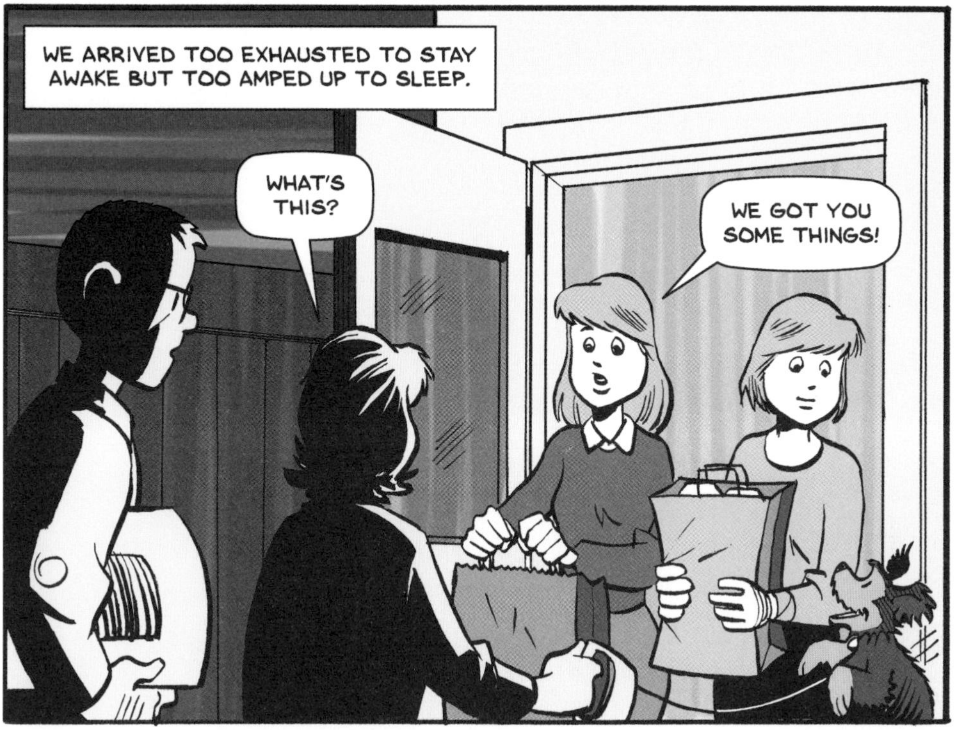
WE ARRIVED TOO EXHAUSTED TO STAY AWAKE BUT TOO AMPED UP TO SLEEP.
WHAT'S THIS?
WE GOT YOU SOME THINGS!

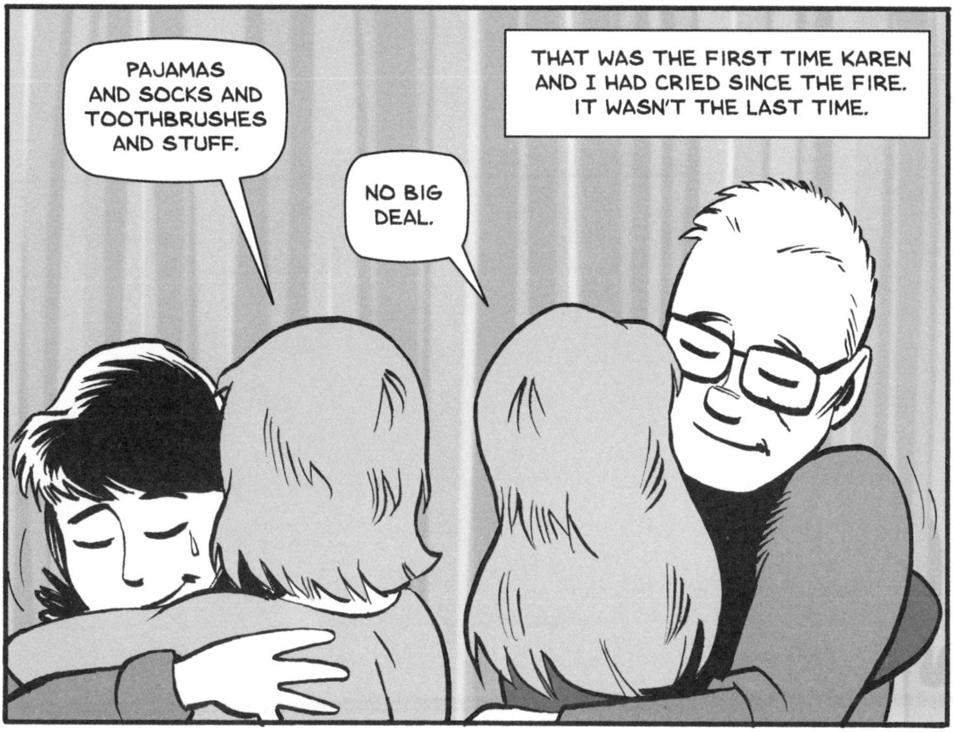
PAJAMAS AND SOCKS AND TOOTHBRUSHES AND STUFF.
NO BIG DEAL.
THAT WAS THE FIRST TIME KAREN AND I HAD CRIED SINCE THE FIRE. IT WASN'T THE LAST TIME.

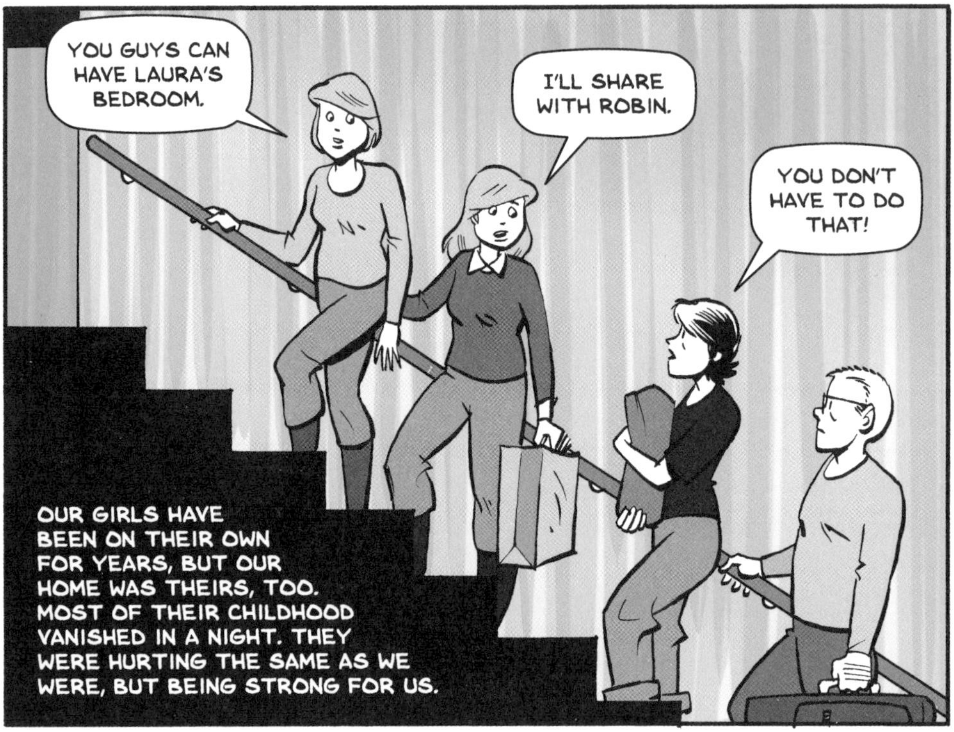
YOU GUYS CAN HAVE LAURA'S BEDROOM.
I'LL SHARE WITH ROBIN.
YOU DON'T HAVE TO DO THAT!
OUR GIRLS HAVE BEEN ON THEIR OWN FOR YEARS, BUT OUR HOME WAS THEIRS, TOO. MOST OF THEIR CHILDHOOD VANISHED IN A NIGHT. THEY WERE HURTING THE SAME AS WE WERE, BUT BEING STRONG FOR US.

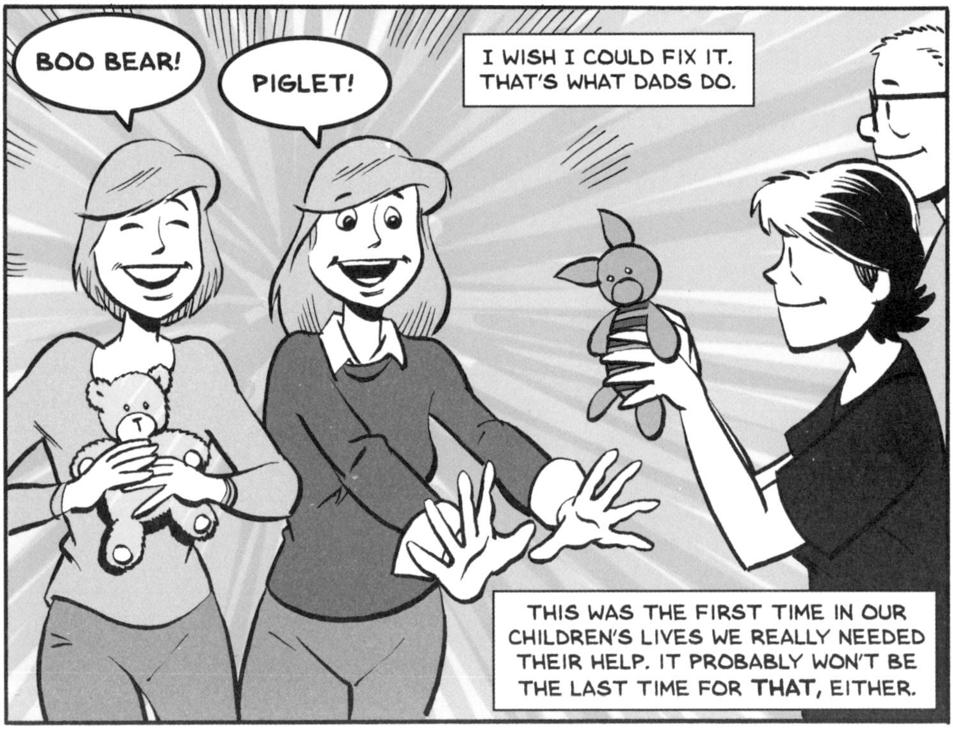
BOO BEAR!
PIGLET!
I WISH I COULD FIX IT. THAT'S WHAT DADS DO.
THIS WAS THE FIRST TIME IN OUR CHILDREN'S LIVES WE REALLY NEEDED THEIR HELP. IT PROBABLY WON'T BE THE LAST TIME FOR THAT, EITHER.

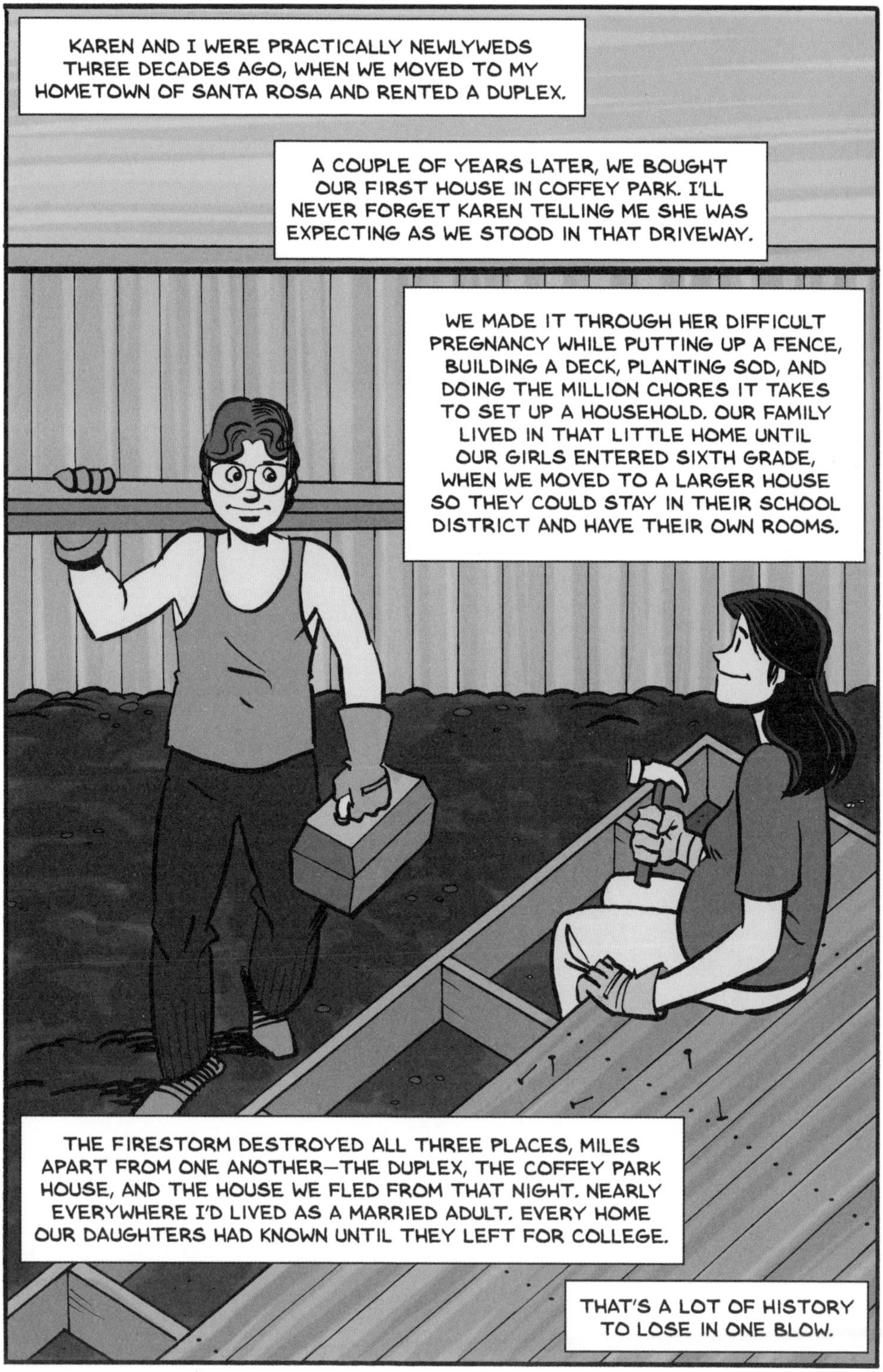
KAREN AND I WERE PRACTICALLY NEWLYWEDS THREE DECADES AGO, WHEN WE MOVED TO MY HOMETOWN OF SANTA ROSA AND RENTED A DUPLEX.
A COUPLE OF YEARS LATER, WE BOUGHT OUR FIRST HOUSE IN COFFEY PARK. I'LL NEVER FORGET KAREN TELLING ME SHE WAS EXPECTING AS WE STOOD IN THAT DRIVEWAY.
WE MADE IT THROUGH HER DIFFICULT PREGNANCY WHILE PUTTING UP A FENCE, BUILDING A DECK, PLANTING SOD, AND DOING THE MILLION CHORES IT TAKES TO SET UP A HOUSEHOLD. OUR FAMILY LIVED IN THAT LITTLE HOME UNTIL OUR GIRLS ENTERED SIXTH GRADE, WHEN WE MOVED TO A LARGER HOUSE SO THEY COULD STAY IN THEIR SCHOOL DISTRICT AND HAVE THEIR OWN ROOMS.
THE FIRESTORM DESTROYED ALL THREE PLACES, MILES APART FROM ONE ANOTHER—THE DUPLEX, THE COFFEY PARK HOUSE, AND THE HOUSE WE FLED FROM THAT NIGHT. NEARLY EVERYWHERE I'D LIVED AS A MARRIED ADULT. EVERY HOME OUR DAUGHTERS HAD KNOWN UNTIL THEY LEFT FOR COLLEGE.
THAT'S A LOT OF HISTORY TO LOSE IN ONE BLOW.

IN QUIET MOMENTS, WE INVENTORIED LOST TREASURES, EACH A SHARP STAB
TO THE HEART. WE DIDN'T SAVE THE **WRONG** STUFF, LIKE THE PEOPLE WHO RISK
THEIR LIVES FOR A JAR OF PICKLES. WE JUST DIDN'T SAVE **ENOUGH** OF IT.

THINGS I WILL NEVER SEE AGAIN

MY GRANDMA'S DEPRESSION-ERA GLASS CANDY JAR

MY GRANDPA'S WORLD WAR II FIELD CAP

OUR ANTIQUE PHONOGRAPH

CHILD-MADE CHRISTMAS ORNAMENTS

A TIME CAPSULE OF NEWSPAPERS AND MAGAZINES
I BOUGHT THE DAY MY GIRLS WERE BORN

AN APOLLO SPACECRAFT MODEL SIGNED
BY ASTRONAUT DICK GORDON, WHO
DIED A MONTH AFTER THE FIRE

A LITTLE BOOK MY FRIEND JIM AND I WROTE
IN EIGHTH GRADE, WHICH HE ENTRUSTED TO
ME WHEN HE DIED TWENTY YEARS AGO

MY GREAT-GRANDMOTHER'S SET OF
THE 1892 ENCYCLOPEDIA BRITANNICA

MY MOM'S DIAMOND EARRINGS WE
PLANNED TO RE-SET AND GIVE TO
OUR GIRLS ON THEIR NEXT BIRTHDAY

A SERIES OF FAMILY PICTURES TAKEN BY
CRAMMING ALL OF US INTO A PHOTO BOOTH
AT THE COUNTY FAIR EVERY SUMMER FOR
TWENTY YEARS

EVERYTHING I EVER DREW OR PAINTED
OR MADE

EVERYTHING ELSE.

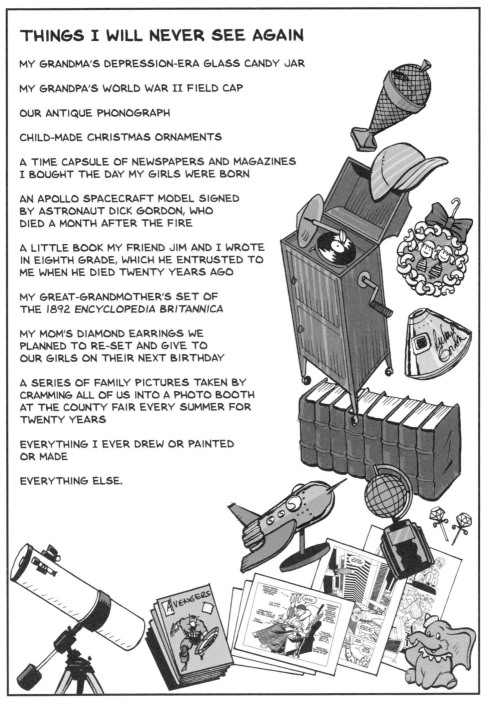

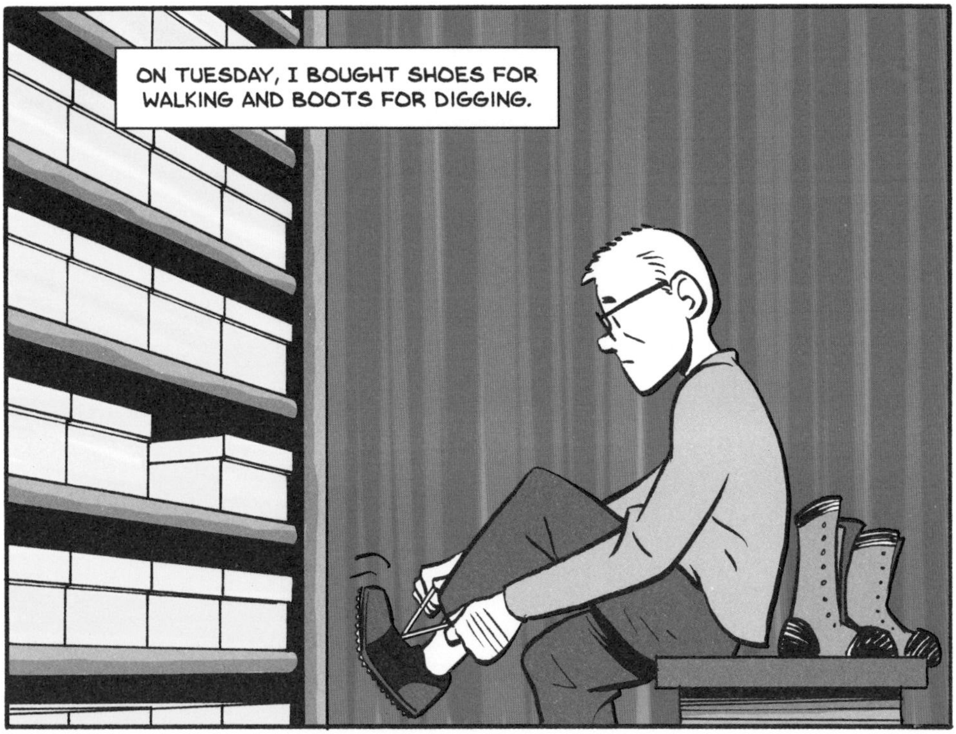
ON TUESDAY, I BOUGHT SHOES FOR WALKING AND BOOTS FOR DIGGING.

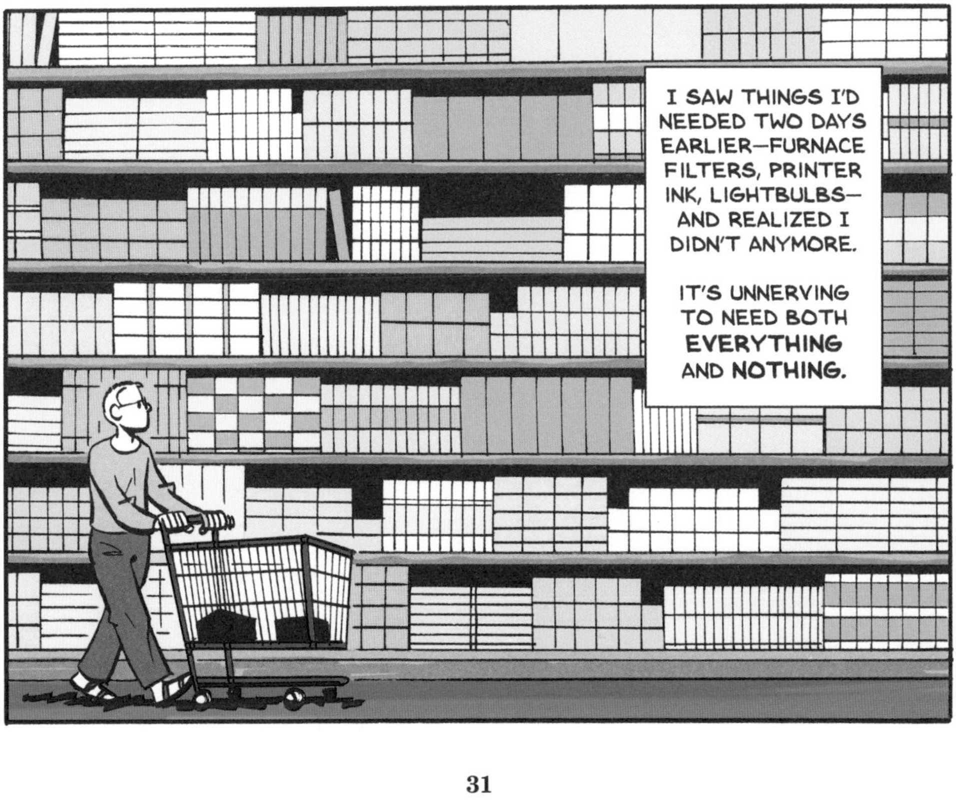
I SAW THINGS I'D NEEDED TWO DAYS EARLIER—FURNACE FILTERS, PRINTER INK, LIGHTBULBS—AND REALIZED I DIDN'T ANYMORE.
IT'S UNNERVING TO NEED BOTH **EVERYTHING** AND **NOTHING.**

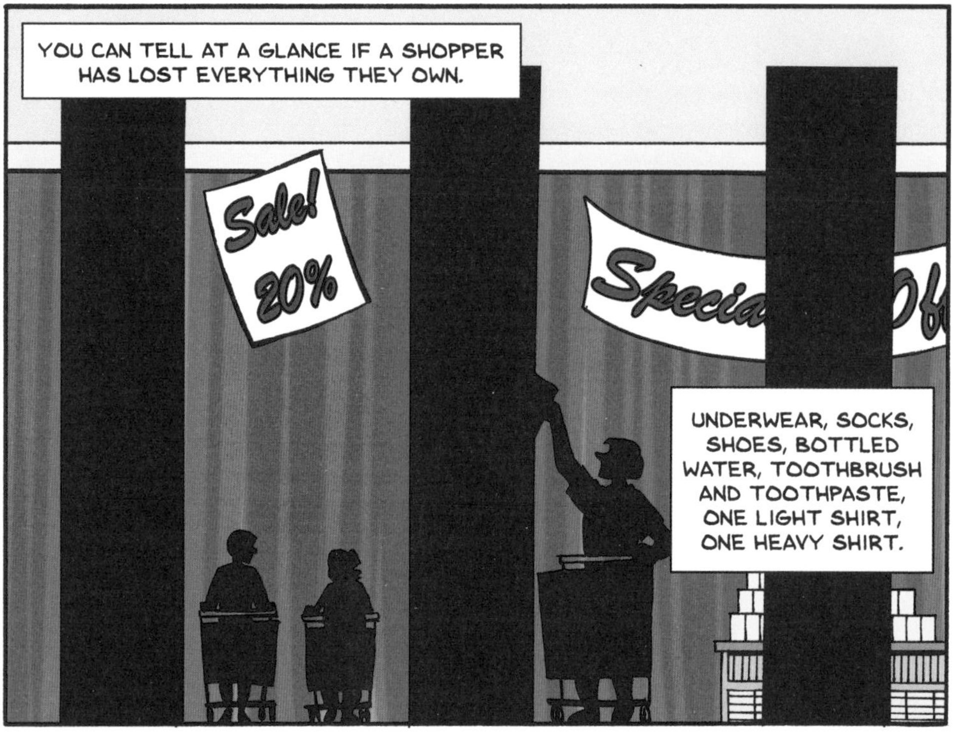
YOU CAN TELL AT A GLANCE IF A SHOPPER HAS LOST EVERYTHING THEY OWN.
Sale! 20%
UNDERWEAR, SOCKS, SHOES, BOTTLED WATER, TOOTHBRUSH AND TOOTHPASTE, ONE LIGHT SHIRT, ONE HEAVY SHIRT.

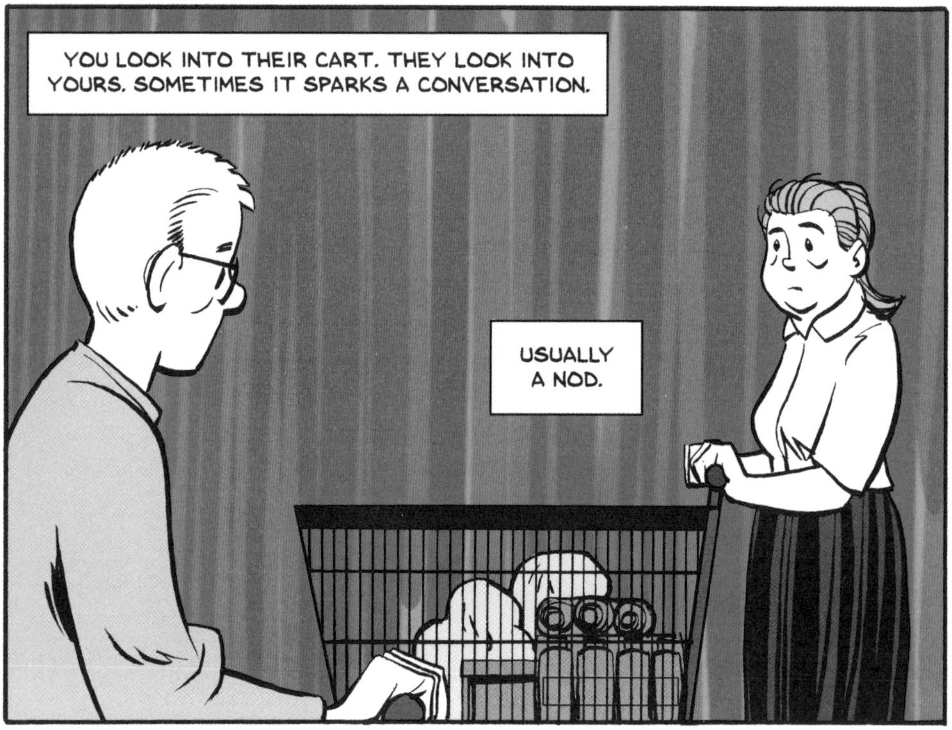
YOU LOOK INTO THEIR CART. THEY LOOK INTO YOURS. SOMETIMES IT SPARKS A CONVERSATION.
USUALLY A NOD.

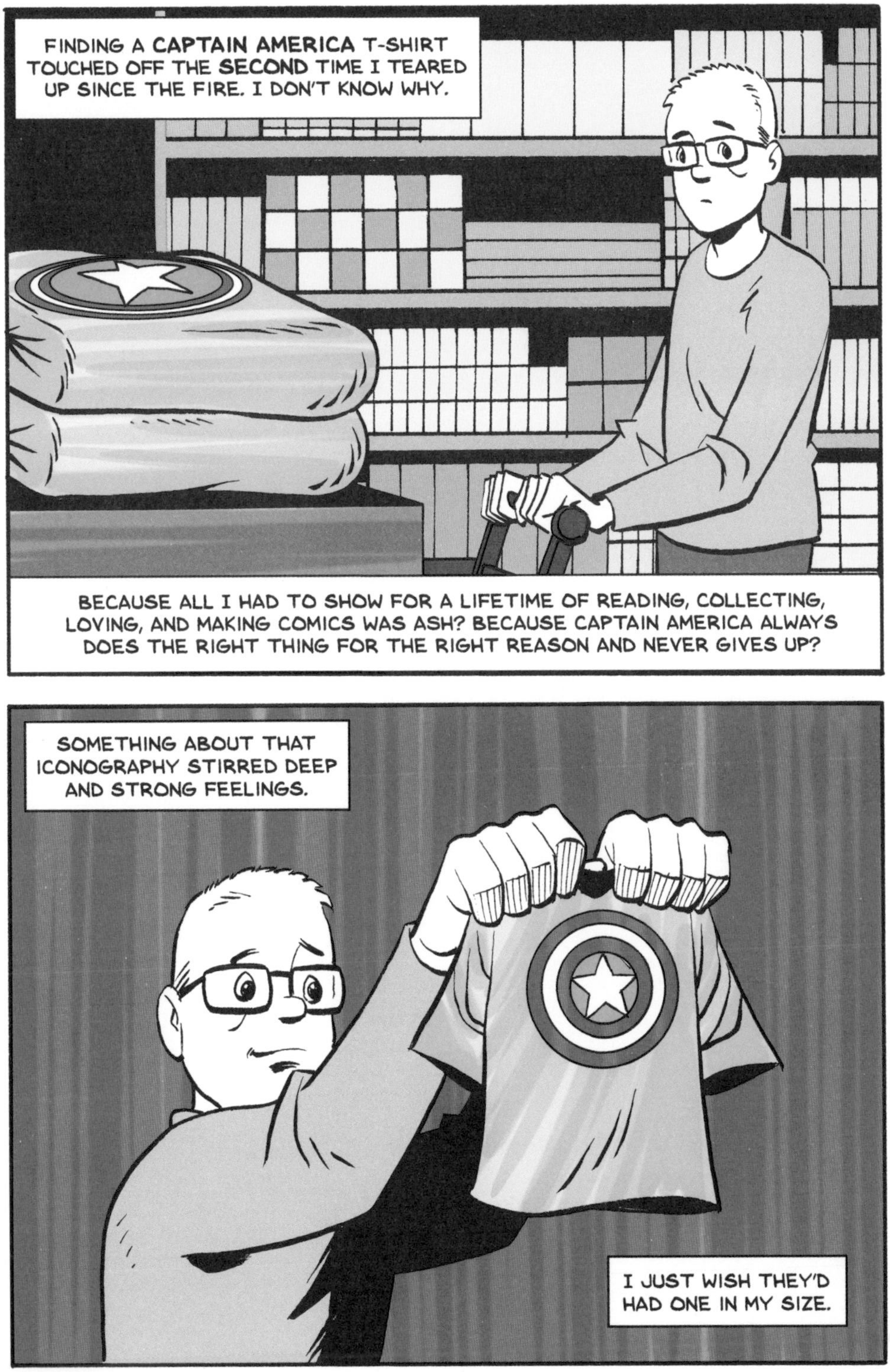
FINDING A CAPTAIN AMERICA T-SHIRT TOUCHED OFF THE SECOND TIME I TEARED UP SINCE THE FIRE. I DON'T KNOW WHY.
BECAUSE ALL I HAD TO SHOW FOR A LIFETIME OF READING, COLLECTING, LOVING, AND MAKING COMICS WAS ASH? BECAUSE CAPTAIN AMERICA ALWAYS DOES THE RIGHT THING FOR THE RIGHT REASON AND NEVER GIVES UP?
SOMETHING ABOUT THAT ICONOGRAPHY STIRRED DEEP AND STRONG FEELINGS.
I JUST WISH THEY'D HAD ONE IN MY SIZE.

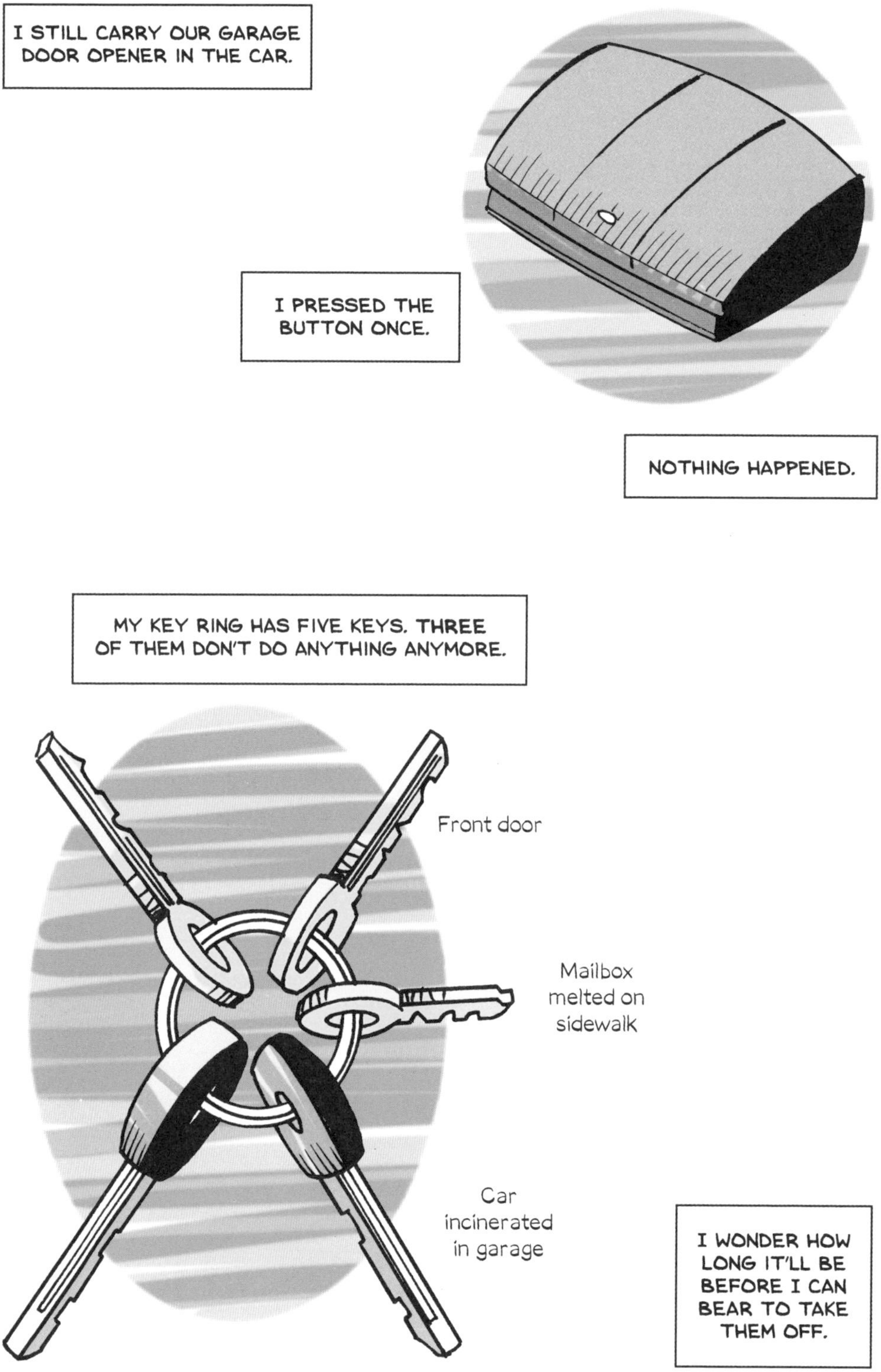
I STILL CARRY OUR GARAGE DOOR OPENER IN THE CAR.
I PRESSED THE BUTTON ONCE.
NOTHING HAPPENED.
MY KEY RING HAS FIVE KEYS. THREE OF THEM DON'T DO ANYTHING ANYMORE.
Front door
Mailbox melted on sidewalk
Car incinerated in garage
I WONDER HOW LONG IT'LL BE BEFORE I CAN BEAR TO TAKE THEM OFF.

MIKE'S FIRE STORY

OTHER PEOPLE HAVE THEIR OWN FIRE STORIES TO TELL. MICHAEL W. HARKINS IS A JOURNALIST, MEDIA CONSULTANT, AND AUTHOR OF THE BOOK MOVE TO FIRE. HIS WIFE, ELIZABETH, IS AN ATTORNEY. THEY LIVED IN A SMALL NEIGHBORHOOD NEAR COFFEY PARK.

I was awake. It was probably 1:30 in the morning, and I've had this habit for decades, before turning off the lights, of channel-surfing to different news stations.

Only one news station had a live remote reporting on the fires. I was watching it, and Elizabeth woke up and came down the hall and said, "What's going on?" I pointed at the TV and said, "This."

As we watched, they said the fire had just jumped 101. We said, "Huh." Then the power went out, and we said, "OK, time to pack." We made a major error in judgment, which I think many people did; we packed thinking we'd be back in a day or so.

Our neighbor Maria is handicapped, so I went outside to check on her. Maria was thinking she might actually try to stay. We just couldn't sort out the situation because we had no idea about the enormity of what was happening. We couldn't see anything. But the sky got oranger and oranger.

I went inside and said, "Elizabeth, you have to go." She said, "You're coming with me." I said, "I can't. I have to make sure Maria's out of here." Elizabeth looked at me and said, "You're going to be right behind me, right?" I said "Yes," and I meant that. So Elizabeth left.

Maria's housemate, Dane, and I got Maria into a van. They got out all right. By then the fire was coming across a field to the first house in our neighborhood. Our neighbor Matt had a power washer and a generator, and was trying to keep the flames back. I took my hose over to his house and hooked it up.

We could feel the superheated air. After a while another neighbor came over and said, "We have to go." Matt got his stuff together and left. I went back to my house and reconnected the hose. Pretty soon it was just me.

I turned on the hose at the front of the house and another at the back, and left them on. Then, for the rest of the night, I ran from front to back, and across the street and down the block, to stomp out little fires as they started.

Embers on roofs were not a problem. They hit the asphalt shingles; they were featherweight and glowing, but their conductivity wasn't such that they could get through the shingles. What happened was, embers would float down and land on vegetation: dry grass and leaves. They'd be blown under trees and bushes, and fires would flare up.

The turning point of the night was when the fire flanked me. My neighbor Tony's son had a car parked in his driveway with a car cover on, and I heard this *fwoomp* to my left, which was the entire car cover going up at once. That surprised me. That's the first time during the night I thought, "You need to be more aware! You *think* you're aware, but you are not in charge."

As the fire spread behind me from places I couldn't see, there would be an explosion followed by a kind of jet stream of glowing golden particles. Like a special effect from a fantasy film.

There was one in particular that I looked up and remember thinking that it was, in the weirdest way, beautiful. Mesmerizing. I couldn't *not* watch it. Like a golden Milky Way. Then I realized that I should actually watch where they landed! I could see them drop down, and knew I had to note where they went. After a while it happened so much I couldn't note them anymore.

When a car explodes, first the windows blow out. Then oil and fluids in the engine go. Tires go next. But the big one is the gas tank. I was fifteen feet away and it went with a *boom!*

So Tony's kid's car goes up. His garage is starting to go, his house is going to go. I knew if the fire came around the front and turned the corner toward my house, it was going to be extremely difficult for me to do any more.

One of the reasons I stayed is I had just seen my dad in July. I went to Ireland; he and his wife, Marian, built a cottage about two miles from where he was born. I went for his ninetieth birthday, and every time I see him I hear stories I'd never heard before . . .

He was once out boating on Lake Michigan. There was a huge storm. Something had come apart on the boat and he had to crawl out and up to repair the thing, or die. The man is so capable. In his life he's been a karate instructor. He's been an engineer. He's been an officer in the Coast Guard Reserve and a ski patrol guy. And he came back into the boat looking like hell, but fine. He said, "I knew if I could get to it, I could fix it." That was in my mind. I thought, "If I can just maintain this, I can make it."

MIKE FOUGHT THE FIRE ALONE WITH A GARDEN HOSE FROM ABOUT 4 TO 7 A.M.

I'm a Buddhist, raised Catholic. I became a Buddhist as a teenager after martial arts introduced me to Zen and Buddhism in grammar school. People say Buddhism is the religion that has no god. The more appropriate modern response is, "If there is a god, it doesn't matter. I still try to live my life right, in harmony with the universe." But that night, when I decided to stay, I did say out loud to the universe, "You've gotta give me this!"

Whatever I was talking to replied, "I'll give you a few hours. We'll see what happens."

Explosions were constant. I haven't been in a war but I was in the Army, with plenty of training exercises. They sounded like different calibers going off, all night long.

The fire's coming around. Superheated air is so hot! Within a minute, it started to blister my skin. Embers came down and burned through my shirt—I still have the shirt, Elizabeth kept it for me. I backed off and knew (a) I didn't have enough water to reach it, and (b) I couldn't get any closer. As I watched, the walls of my house started to bubble. And I thought, "That's it. My house is done." Then I heard a power saw.

Suddenly he's just there: a firefighter from Berkeley Engine 6, next to me with a real hose. He barely glances at me, just walks a little closer than I can get, and says as he's walking by, "Let's see if we can save your house."

He hits it with this beautiful stream of water I would have given my leg for earlier in the evening. He's hitting my house, he's hitting Tony's house. He worked on it for about a minute. We both saw: the windows had blown out of my house. We could see flames inside coming up the hallway. And through the foundation vents, we could look down there and see flames under the house.

He said, "I don't think we can save this." I said, "I know."

The firefighter looked right at me and said, "I'm sorry I couldn't save your house."

I'm thinking, "With all the shit you have to do, you're taking a moment to look at me and convey, 'I know you're losing everything and I'm really sorry.'" It's one of the most humanitarian moments of my life. Then he and his crew saved the rest of my neighborhood.

Mike took this final photo of his home.

MIKE BEGAN HIS CAREER IN MUSIC AS A ROADIE FOR THE BAND JOURNEY IN 1976, BEFORE THEY BECAME FAMOUS.

Journey, in their early days, were kind of an extended jam band, perfect for a young man who plays guitar to become enamored with. As Journey got big, they became pioneers in the large-screen projection video that's now part of every big concert. They formed their own production company called Nocturne to do those shows. I'd been a film and video major before I left art school, so I joined Nocturne and worked with all these bands: Santana, Prince, the Police, Springsteen.

My last gig was road manager for Michael Jackson's *Bad* tour in Japan and Australia in 1987. I dealt with the guest lists, everybody from Cheryl Tiegs to Gregory Peck. One of the most memorable moments of my rock-and-roll career was shooting the breeze with Gregory Peck at a stadium in Tokyo.

I had kept all the lists I'd made of famous people calling, all the visitor passes and tour passes. Documents from the venues. Things that nobody in the world had but me. I lost all my Michael Jackson stuff. All my Journey stuff. All these things I'd made an effort to keep, not just because they were memorabilia but because they meant so much to me. The fire took them all. ∎

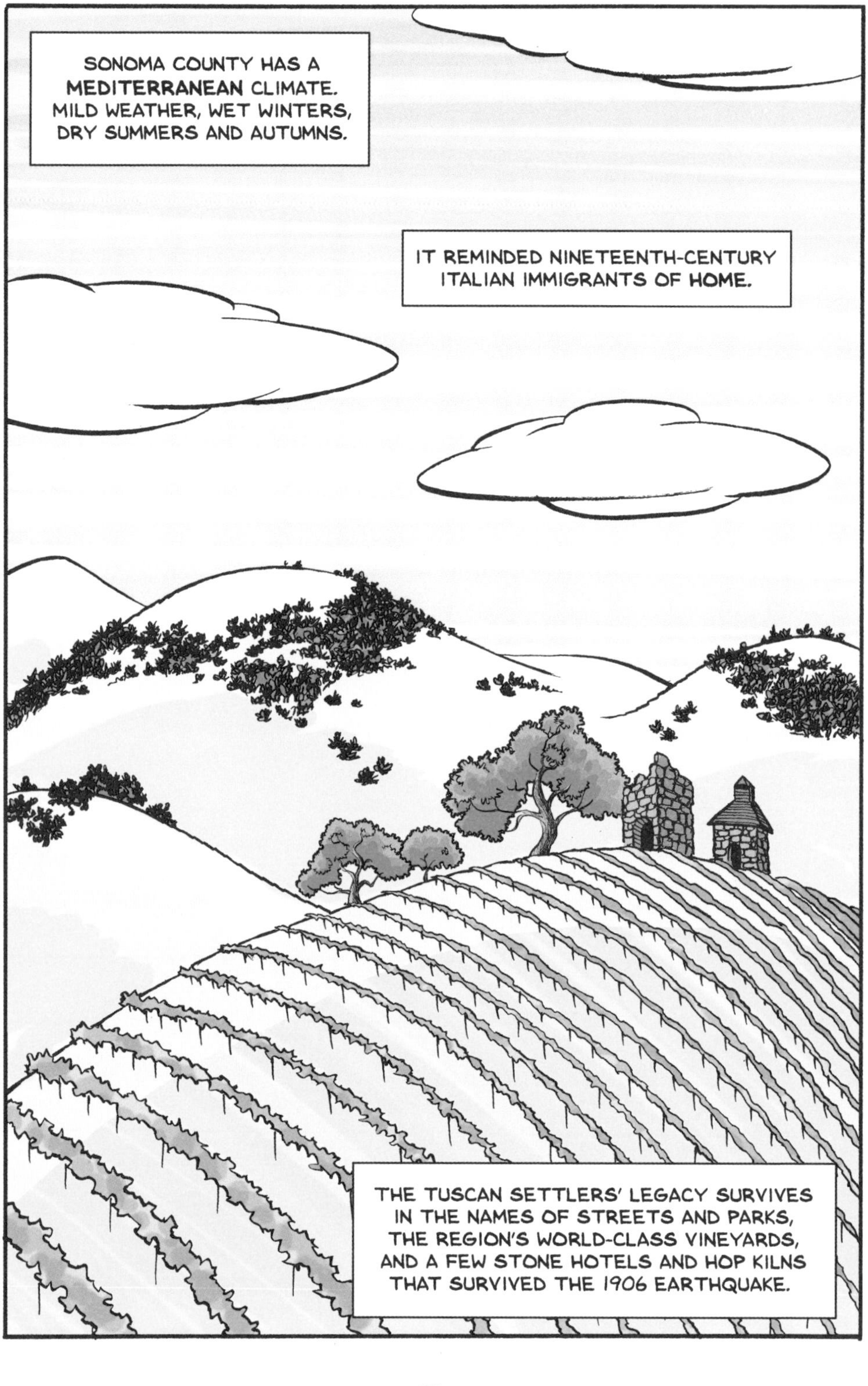
SONOMA COUNTY HAS A **MEDITERRANEAN** CLIMATE. MILD WEATHER, WET WINTERS, DRY SUMMERS AND AUTUMNS.
IT REMINDED NINETEENTH-CENTURY ITALIAN IMMIGRANTS OF **HOME**.
THE TUSCAN SETTLERS' LEGACY SURVIVES IN THE NAMES OF STREETS AND PARKS, THE REGION'S WORLD-CLASS VINEYARDS, AND A FEW STONE HOTELS AND HOP KILNS THAT SURVIVED THE 1906 EARTHQUAKE.

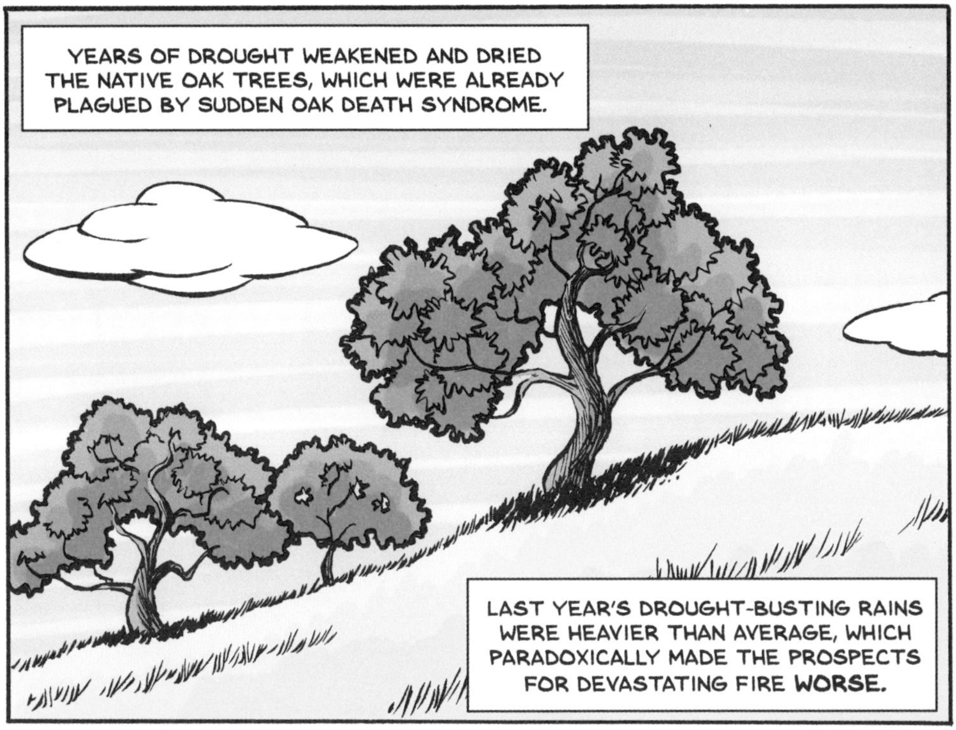
YEARS OF DROUGHT WEAKENED AND DRIED THE NATIVE OAK TREES, WHICH WERE ALREADY PLAGUED BY SUDDEN OAK DEATH SYNDROME.
LAST YEAR'S DROUGHT-BUSTING RAINS WERE HEAVIER THAN AVERAGE, WHICH PARADOXICALLY MADE THE PROSPECTS FOR DEVASTATING FIRE **WORSE.**

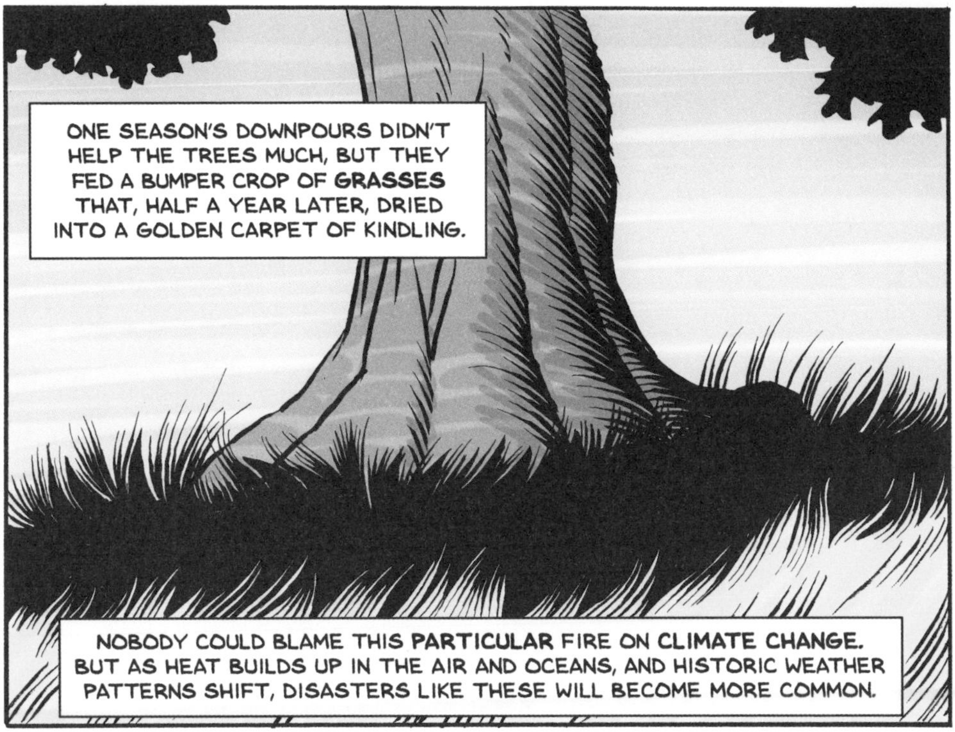
ONE SEASON'S DOWNPOURS DIDN'T HELP THE TREES MUCH, BUT THEY FED A BUMPER CROP OF **GRASSES** THAT, HALF A YEAR LATER, DRIED INTO A GOLDEN CARPET OF KINDLING.
NOBODY COULD BLAME THIS **PARTICULAR** FIRE ON **CLIMATE CHANGE.** BUT AS HEAT BUILDS UP IN THE AIR AND OCEANS, AND HISTORIC WEATHER PATTERNS SHIFT, DISASTERS LIKE THESE WILL BECOME MORE COMMON.

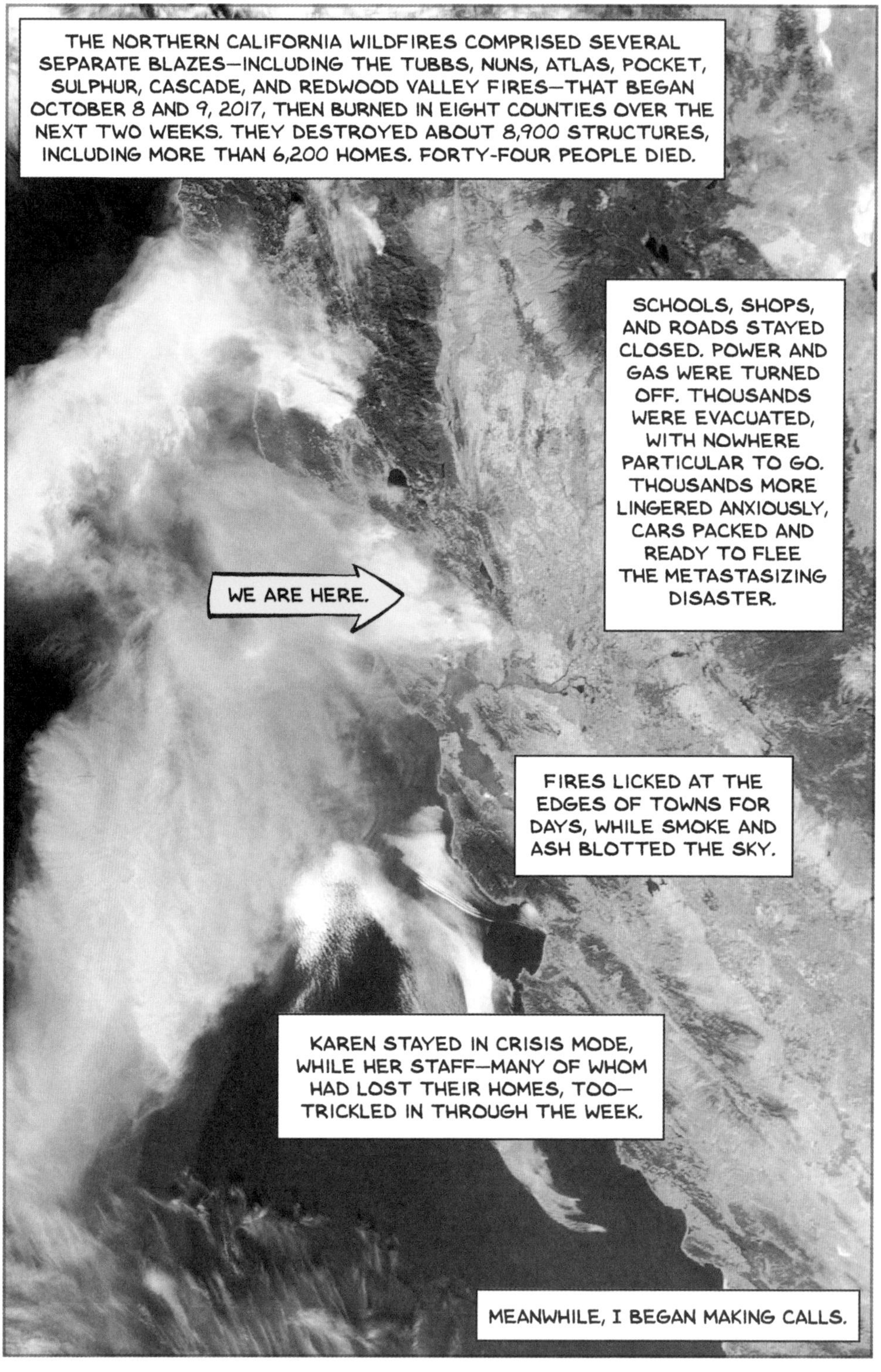
THE NORTHERN CALIFORNIA WILDFIRES COMPRISED SEVERAL SEPARATE BLAZES—INCLUDING THE TUBBS, NUNS, ATLAS, POCKET, SULPHUR, CASCADE, AND REDWOOD VALLEY FIRES—THAT BEGAN OCTOBER 8 AND 9, 2017, THEN BURNED IN EIGHT COUNTIES OVER THE NEXT TWO WEEKS. THEY DESTROYED ABOUT 8,900 STRUCTURES, INCLUDING MORE THAN 6,200 HOMES. FORTY-FOUR PEOPLE DIED.
SCHOOLS, SHOPS, AND ROADS STAYED CLOSED. POWER AND GAS WERE TURNED OFF. THOUSANDS WERE EVACUATED, WITH NOWHERE PARTICULAR TO GO. THOUSANDS MORE LINGERED ANXIOUSLY, CARS PACKED AND READY TO FLEE THE METASTASIZING DISASTER.
WE ARE HERE.
FIRES LICKED AT THE EDGES OF TOWNS FOR DAYS, WHILE SMOKE AND ASH BLOTTED THE SKY.
KAREN STAYED IN CRISIS MODE, WHILE HER STAFF—MANY OF WHOM HAD LOST THEIR HOMES, TOO—TRICKLED IN THROUGH THE WEEK.
MEANWHILE, I BEGAN MAKING CALLS.

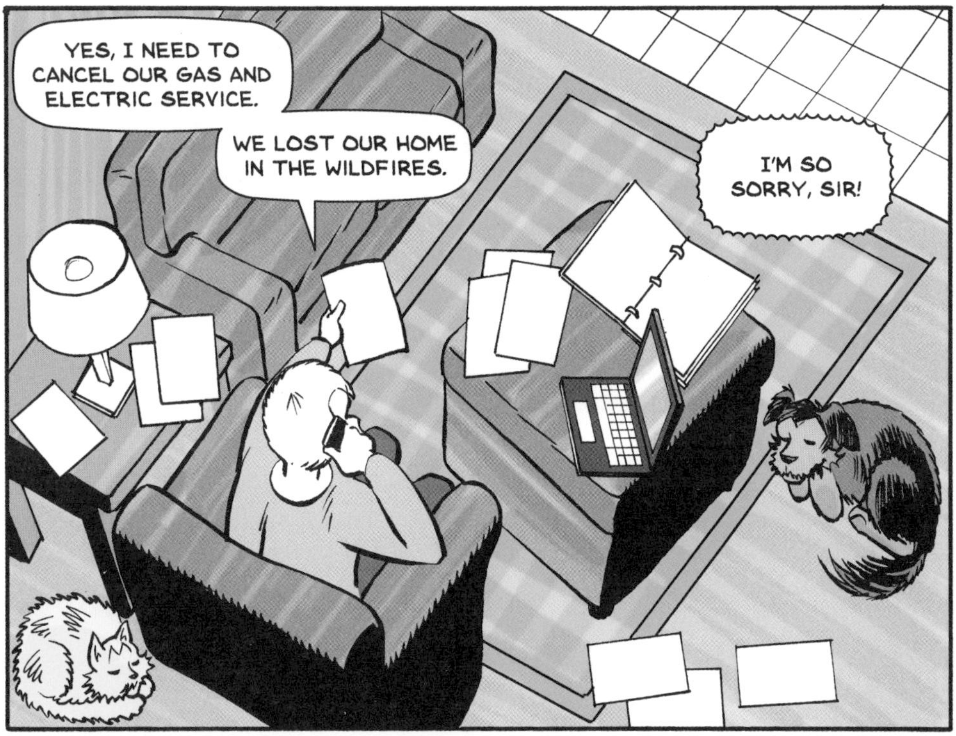
YES, I NEED TO CANCEL OUR GAS AND ELECTRIC SERVICE.
WE LOST OUR HOME IN THE WILDFIRES.
I'M SO SORRY, SIR!

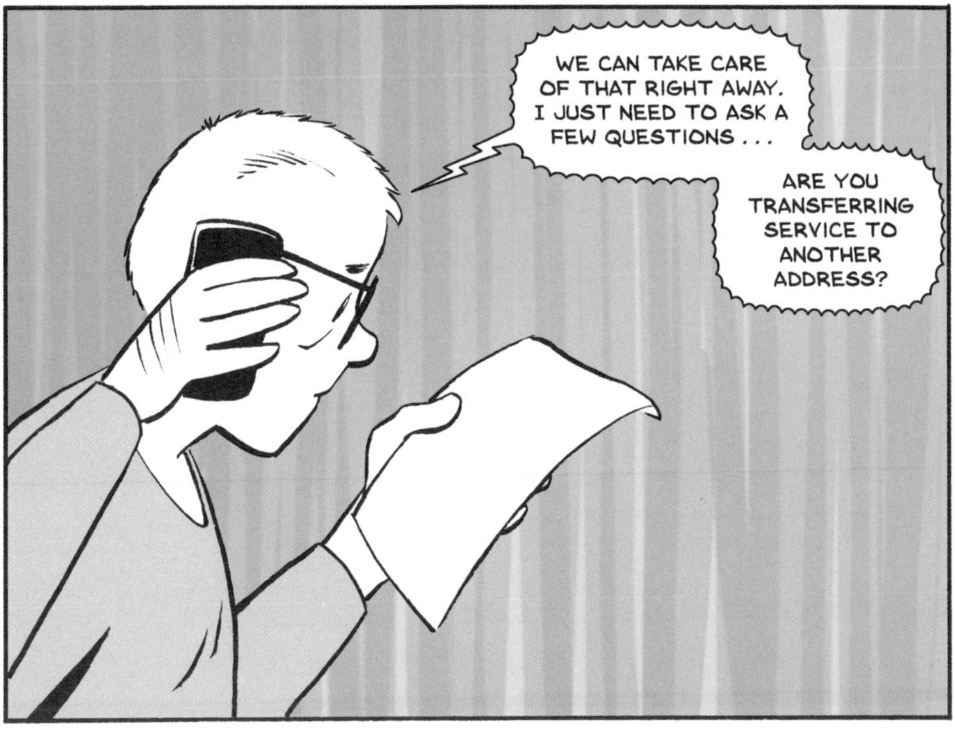
WE CAN TAKE CARE OF THAT RIGHT AWAY. I JUST NEED TO ASK A FEW QUESTIONS . . .
ARE YOU TRANSFERRING SERVICE TO ANOTHER ADDRESS?

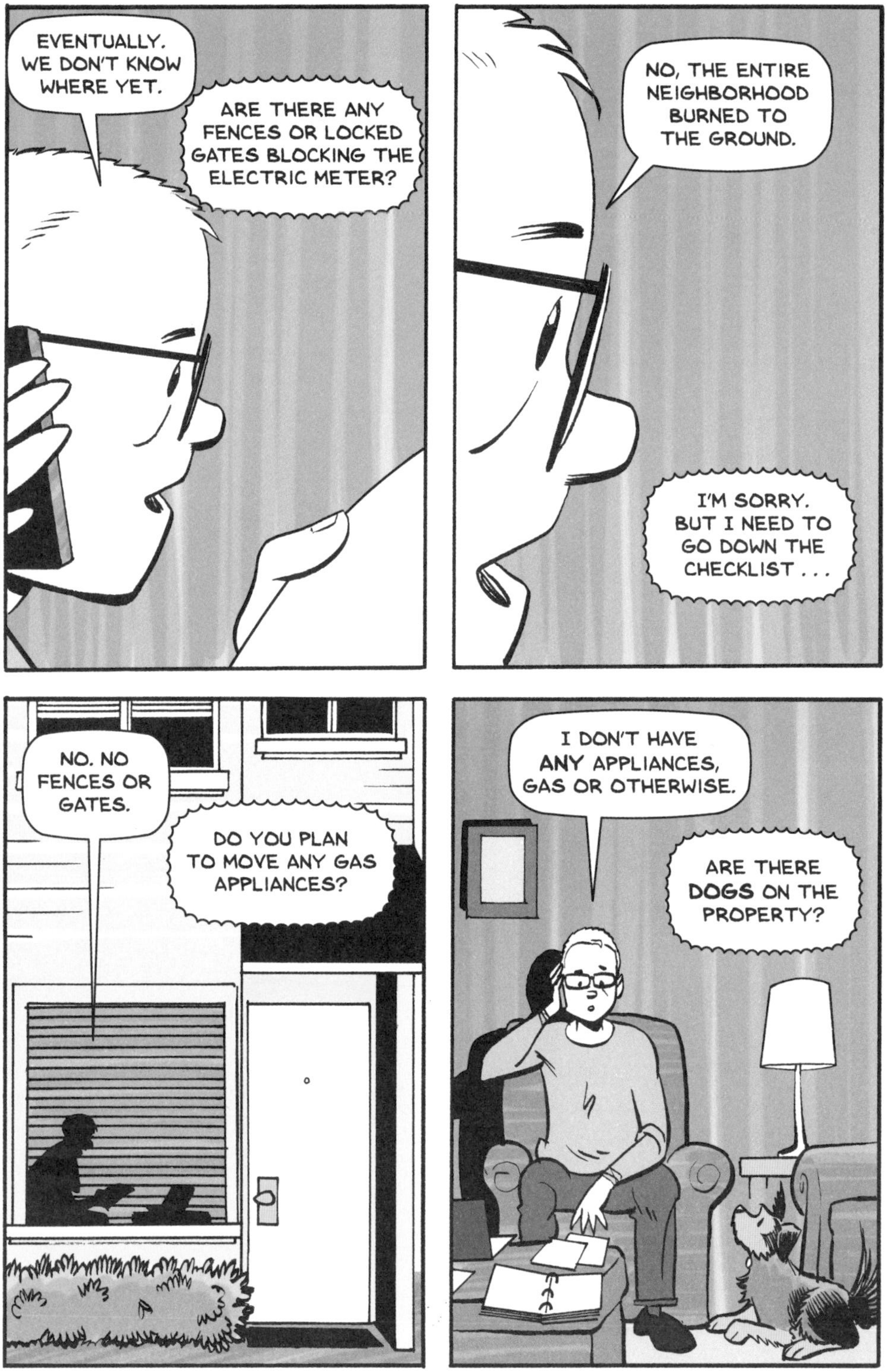
EVENTUALLY. WE DON'T KNOW WHERE YET.
ARE THERE ANY FENCES OR LOCKED GATES BLOCKING THE ELECTRIC METER?
NO, THE ENTIRE NEIGHBORHOOD BURNED TO THE GROUND.
I'M SORRY. BUT I NEED TO GO DOWN THE CHECKLIST . . .
NO. NO FENCES OR GATES.
DO YOU PLAN TO MOVE ANY GAS APPLIANCES?
I DON'T HAVE ANY APPLIANCES, GAS OR OTHERWISE.
ARE THERE DOGS ON THE PROPERTY?

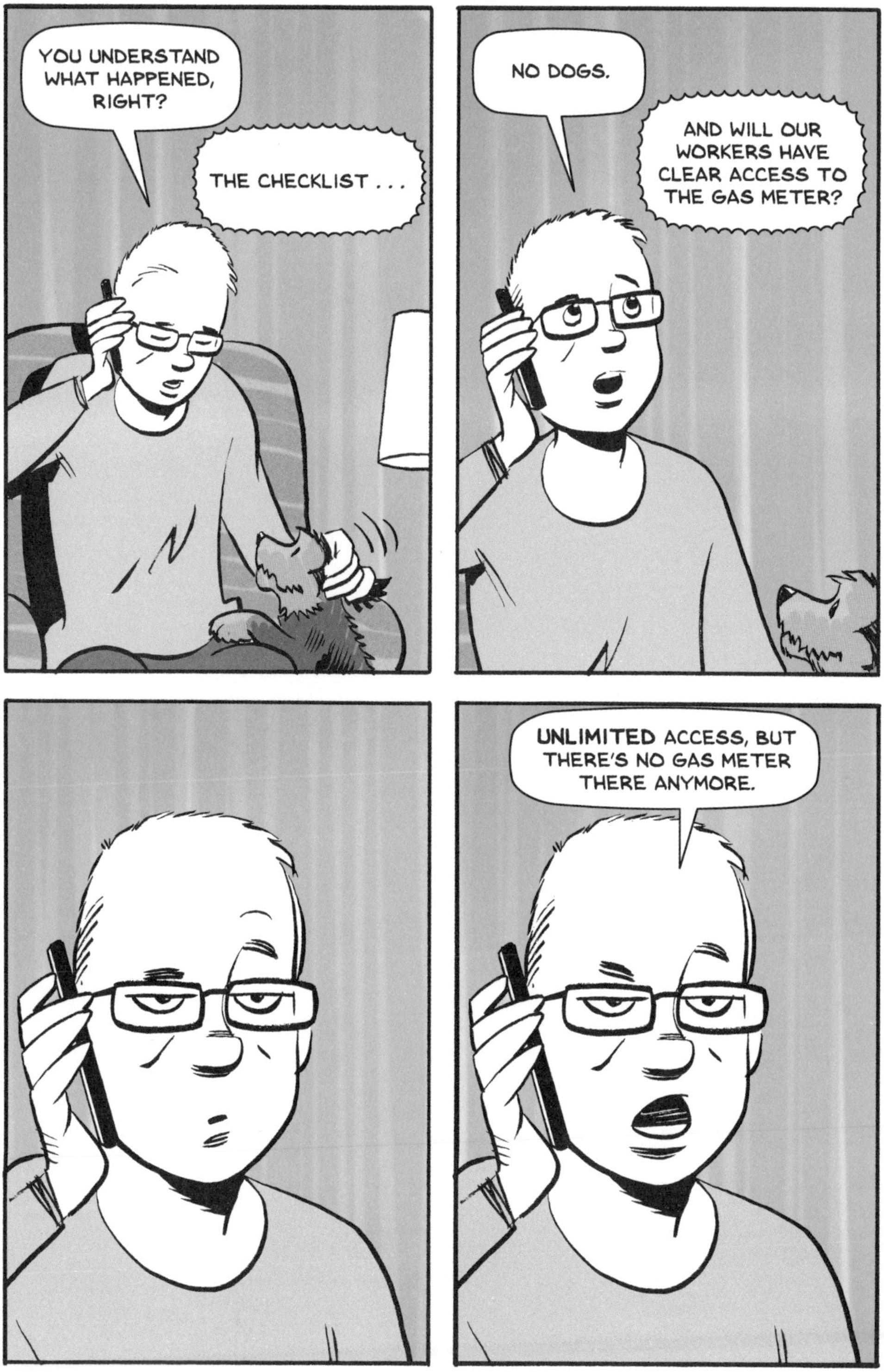
YOU UNDERSTAND WHAT HAPPENED, RIGHT?
THE CHECKLIST . . .
NO DOGS.
AND WILL OUR WORKERS HAVE CLEAR ACCESS TO THE GAS METER?
UNLIMITED ACCESS, BUT THERE'S NO GAS METER THERE ANYMORE.

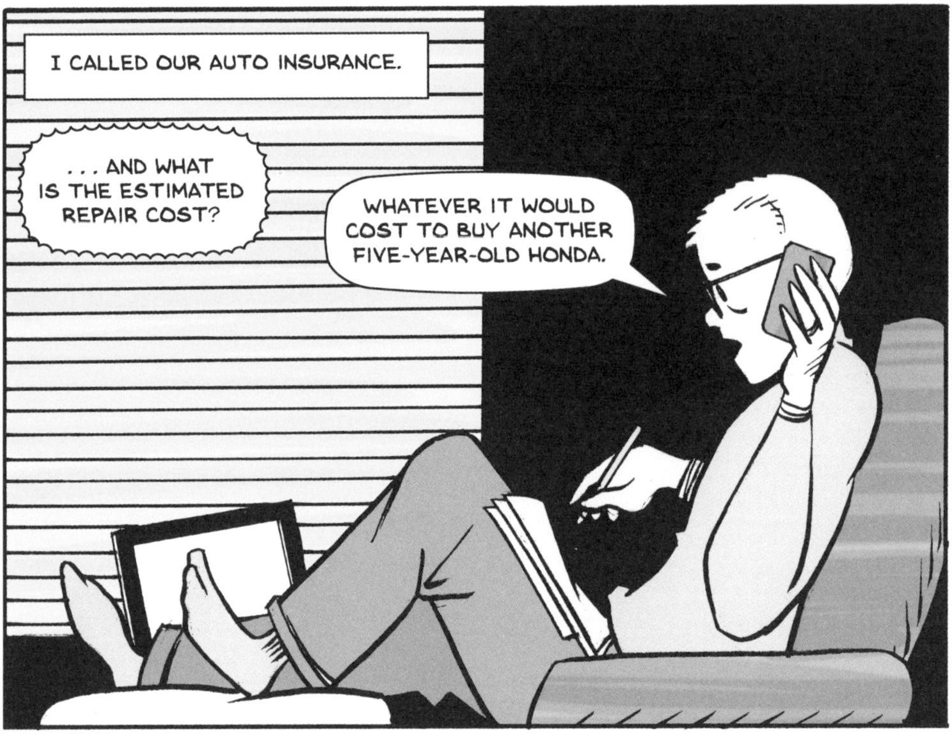
I CALLED OUR AUTO INSURANCE.
. . . AND WHAT IS THE ESTIMATED REPAIR COST?
WHATEVER IT WOULD COST TO BUY ANOTHER FIVE-YEAR-OLD HONDA.

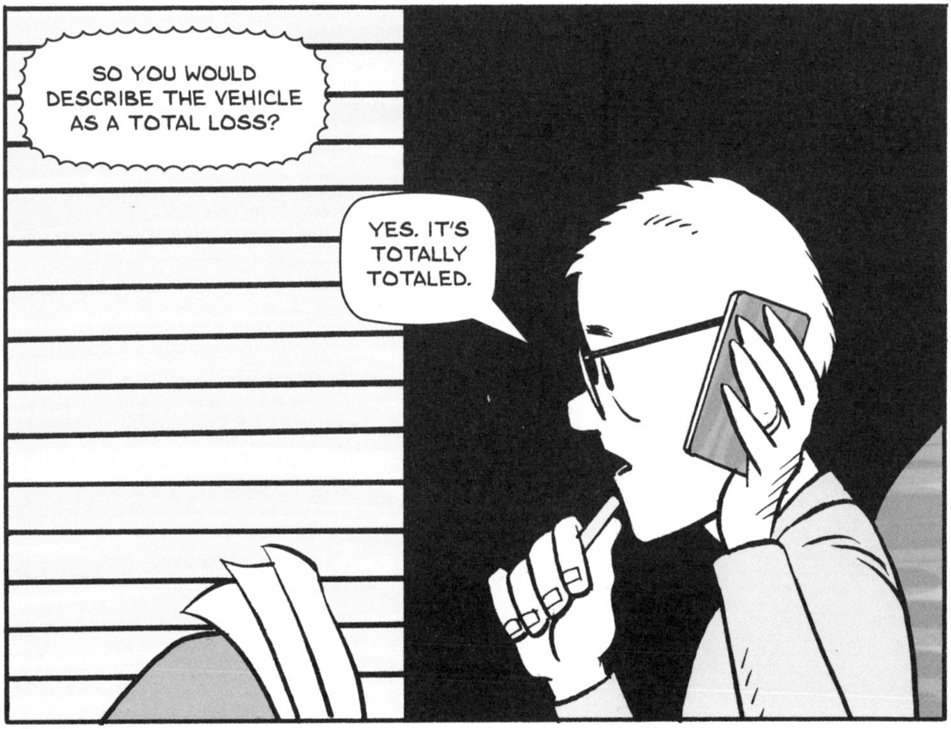
SO YOU WOULD DESCRIBE THE VEHICLE AS A TOTAL LOSS?
YES. IT'S TOTALLY TOTALED.

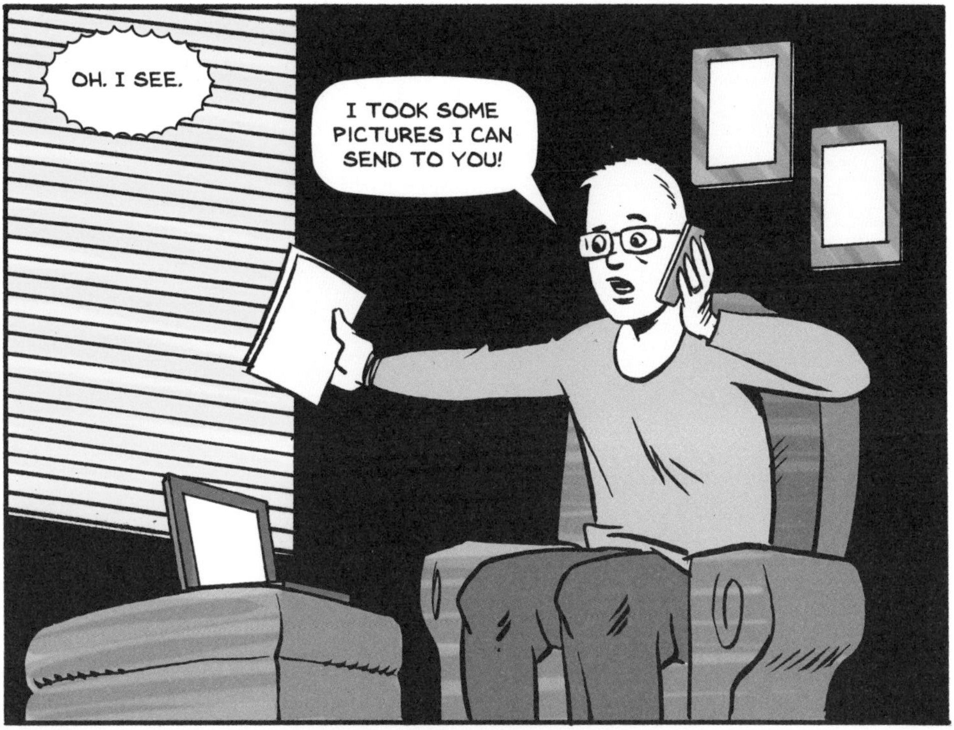
OH. I SEE.
I TOOK SOME PICTURES I CAN SEND TO YOU!

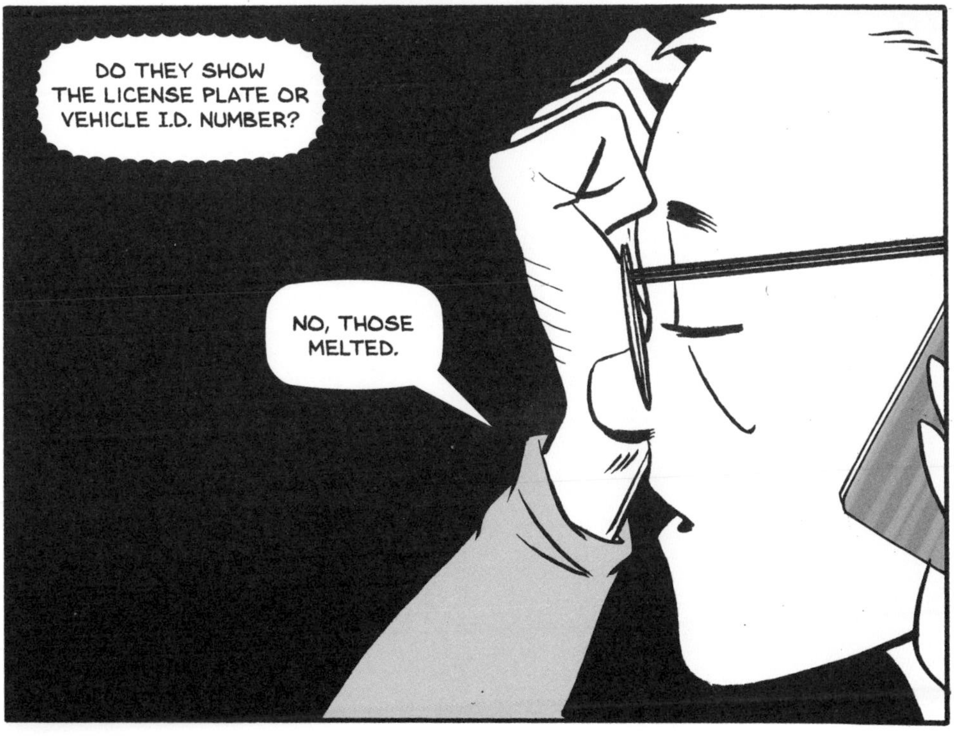
DO THEY SHOW THE LICENSE PLATE OR VEHICLE I.D. NUMBER?
NO, THOSE MELTED.

A DAY IN THE NEW LIFE

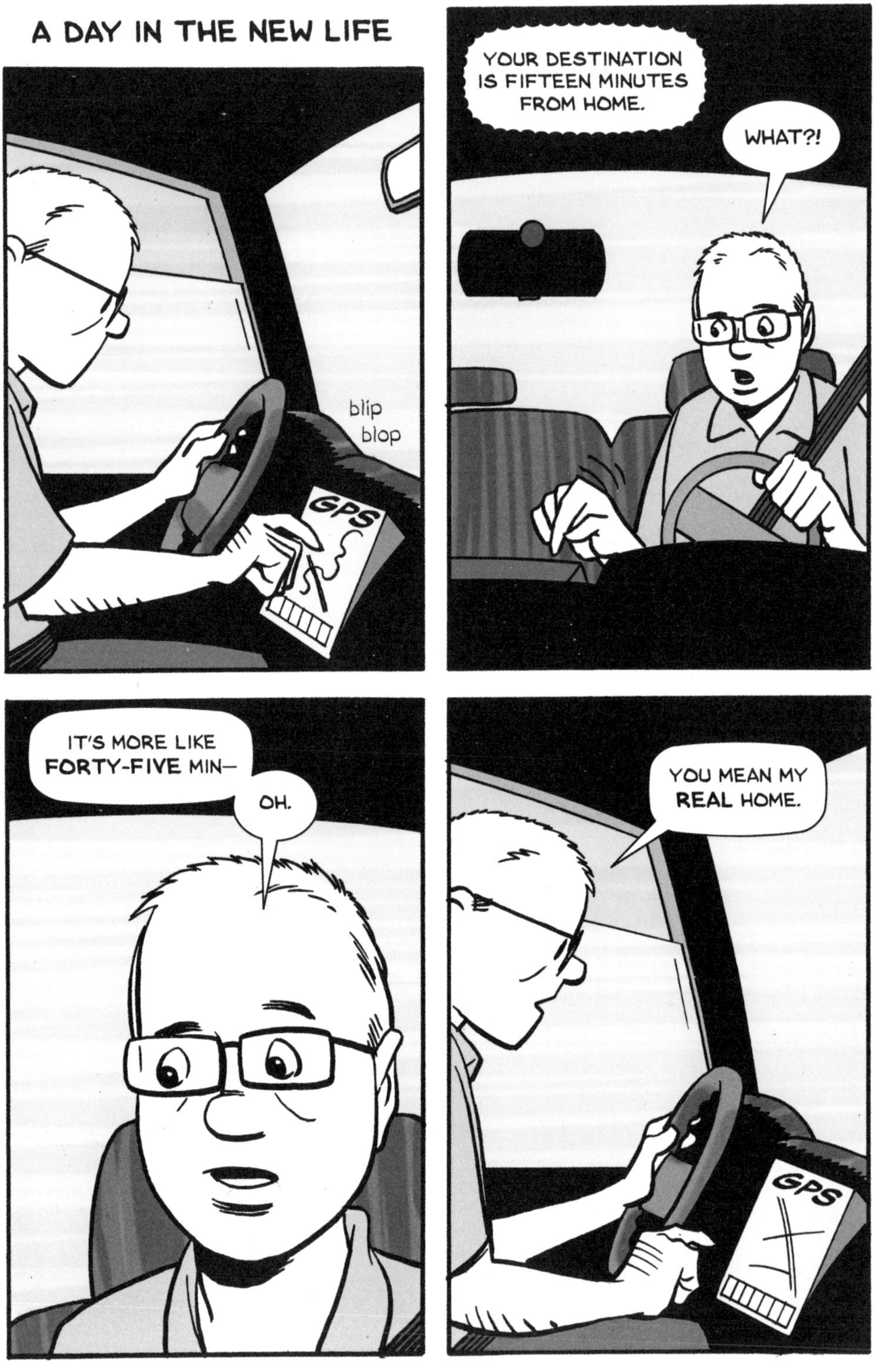
blip
blop
GPS
YOUR DESTINATION IS FIFTEEN MINUTES FROM HOME.
WHAT?!
IT'S MORE LIKE **FORTY-FIVE** MIN—
OH.
YOU MEAN MY **REAL** HOME.
GPS

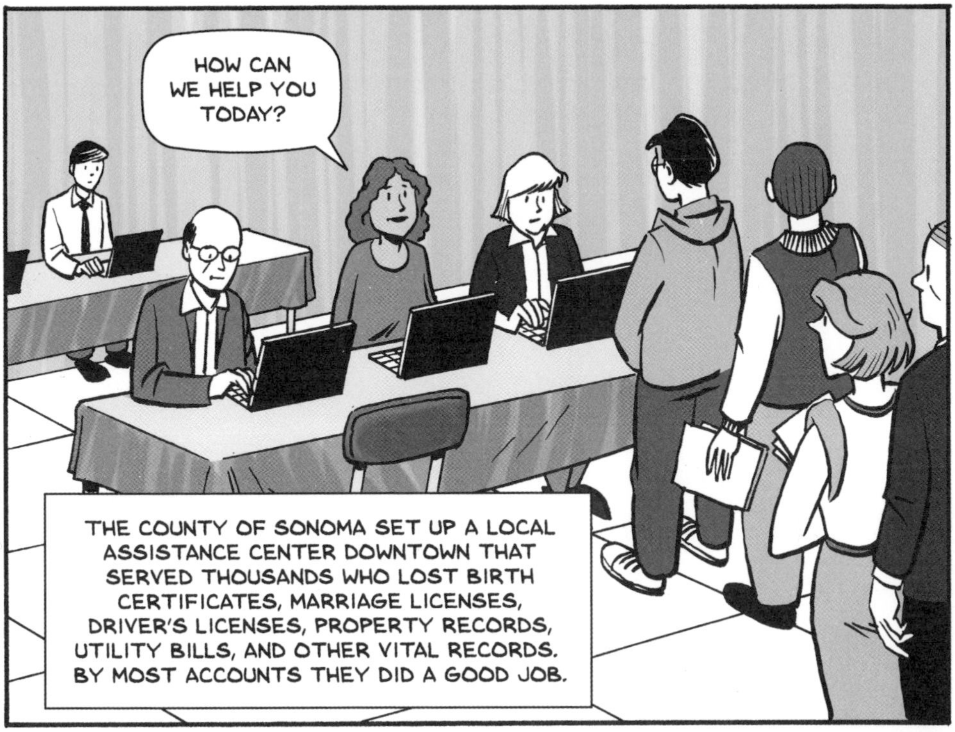
HOW CAN WE HELP YOU TODAY?
THE COUNTY OF SONOMA SET UP A LOCAL ASSISTANCE CENTER DOWNTOWN THAT SERVED THOUSANDS WHO LOST BIRTH CERTIFICATES, MARRIAGE LICENSES, DRIVER'S LICENSES, PROPERTY RECORDS, UTILITY BILLS, AND OTHER VITAL RECORDS. BY MOST ACCOUNTS THEY DID A GOOD JOB.

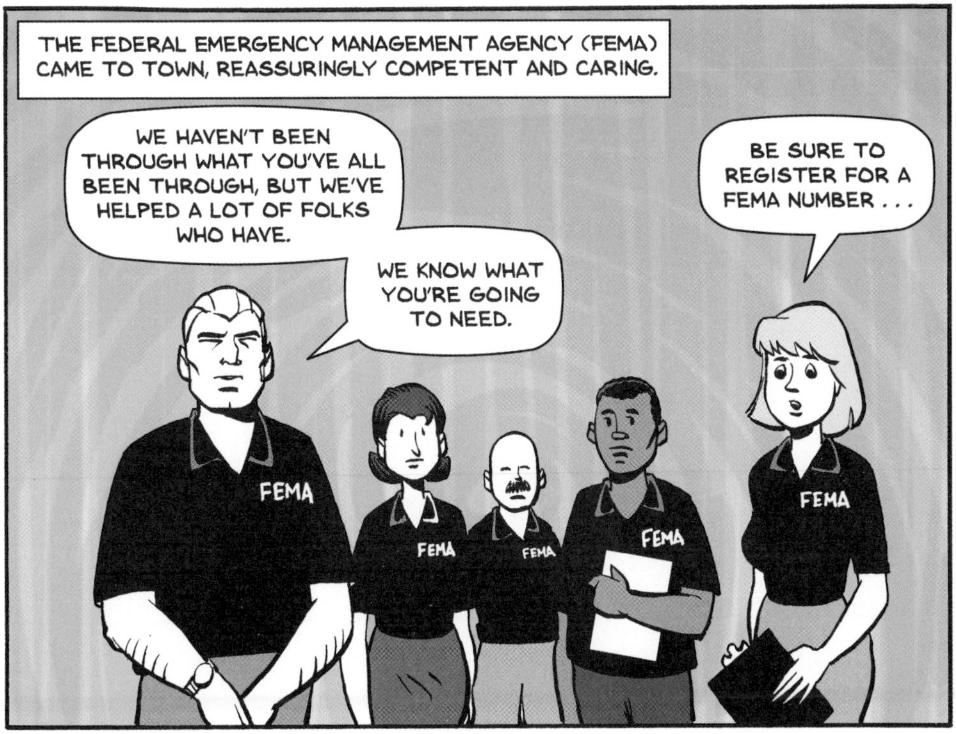
THE FEDERAL EMERGENCY MANAGEMENT AGENCY (FEMA) CAME TO TOWN, REASSURINGLY COMPETENT AND CARING.
WE HAVEN'T BEEN THROUGH WHAT YOU'VE ALL BEEN THROUGH, BUT WE'VE HELPED A LOT OF FOLKS WHO HAVE.
WE KNOW WHAT YOU'RE GOING TO NEED.
BE SURE TO REGISTER FOR A FEMA NUMBER . . .
FEMA
FEMA
FEMA
FEMA
FEMA

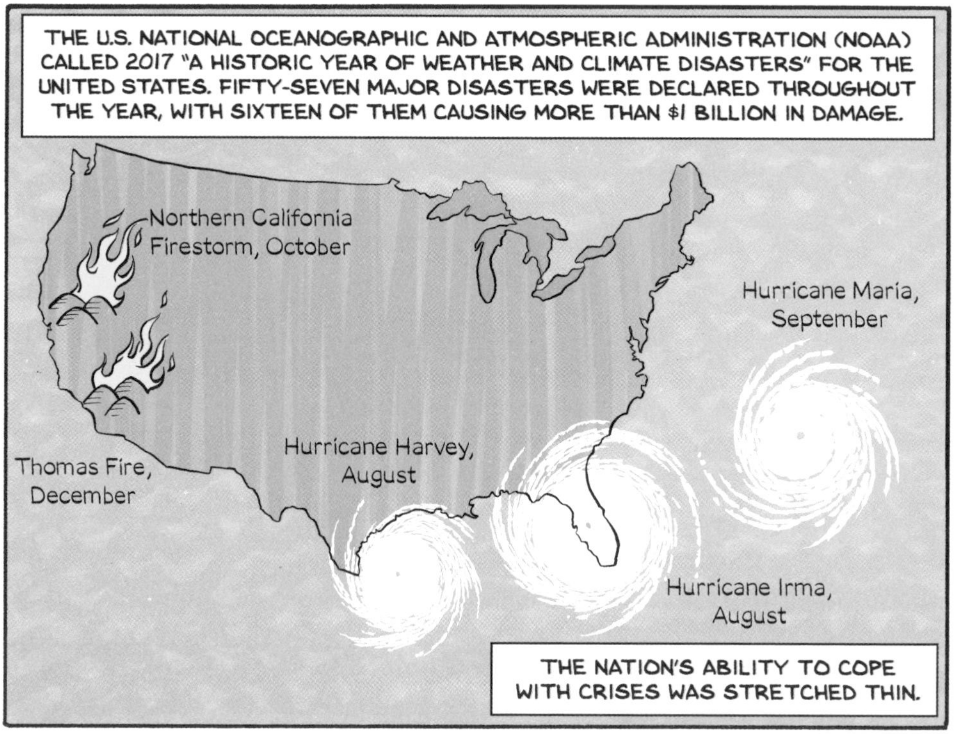
THE U.S. NATIONAL OCEANOGRAPHIC AND ATMOSPHERIC ADMINISTRATION (NOAA) CALLED 2017 "A HISTORIC YEAR OF WEATHER AND CLIMATE DISASTERS" FOR THE UNITED STATES. FIFTY-SEVEN MAJOR DISASTERS WERE DECLARED THROUGHOUT THE YEAR, WITH SIXTEEN OF THEM CAUSING MORE THAN $1 BILLION IN DAMAGE.
Northern California Firestorm, October
Thomas Fire, December
Hurricane Harvey, August
Hurricane Irma, August
Hurricane Maria, September
THE NATION'S ABILITY TO COPE WITH CRISES WAS STRETCHED THIN.

FEMA'S CRITICAL CONCERN WAS **HOUSING**: RENTALS, TRAILERS, HOTEL VOUCHERS. BECAUSE OUR DAUGHTERS TOOK US IN, FEMA DIDN'T NEED TO DO ANYTHING FOR US. BUT OTHER GROUPS FUNNELED CHARITABLE GIVING INTO CASH THAT WE COULD USE.

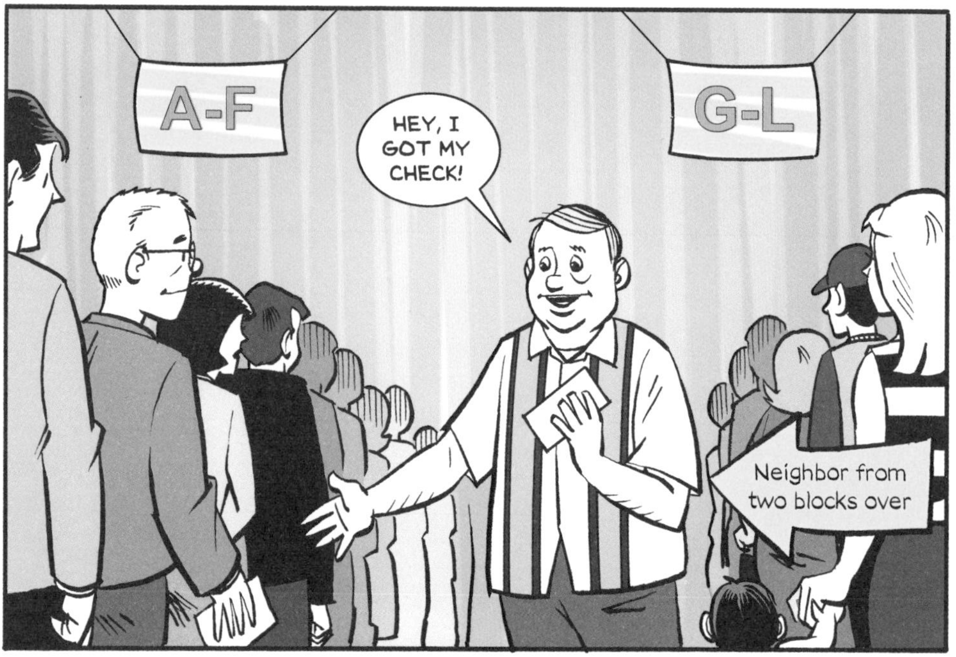
A-F
G-L
HEY, I GOT MY CHECK!
Neighbor from two blocks over

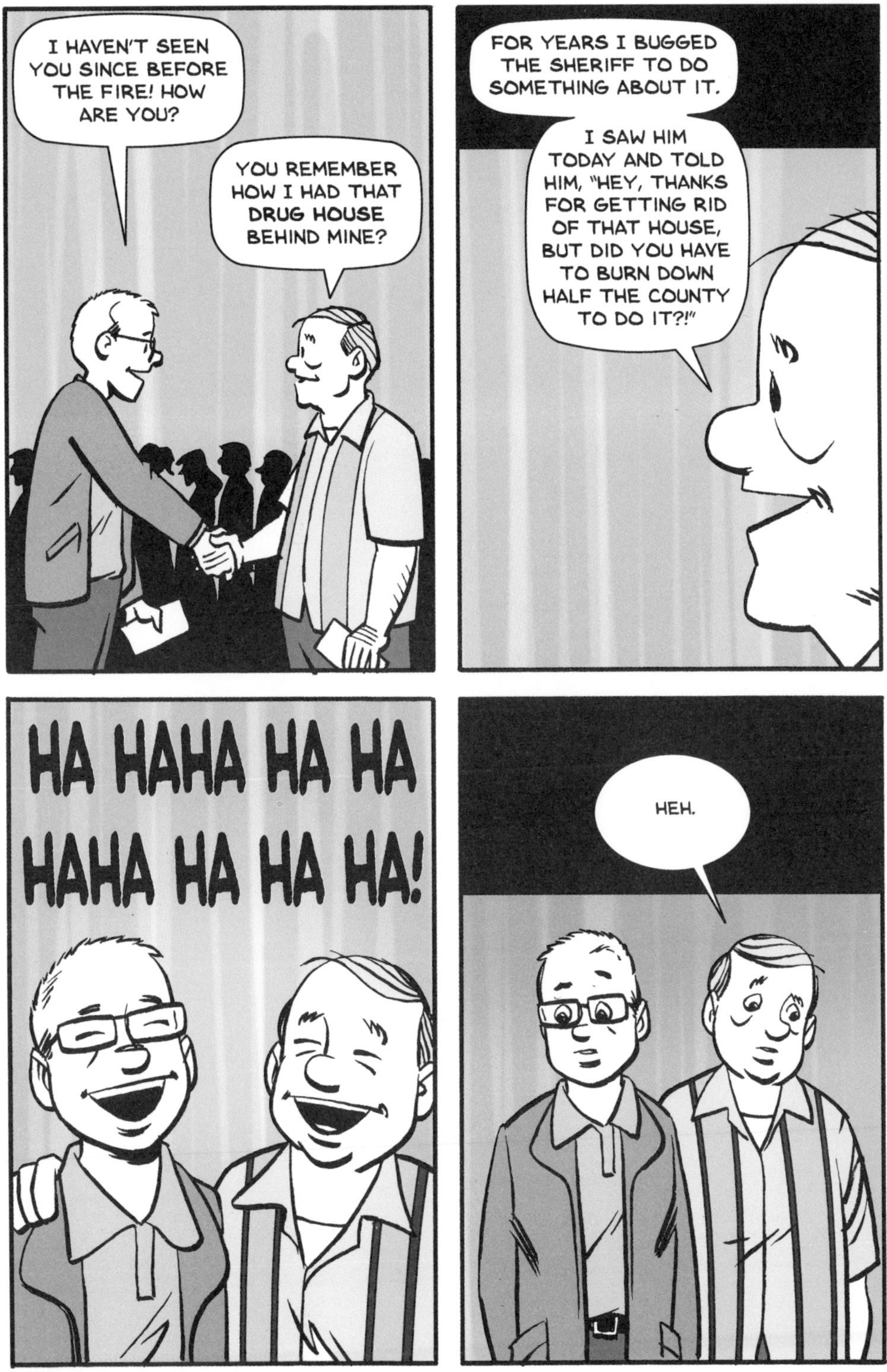

I HAVEN'T SEEN YOU SINCE BEFORE THE FIRE! HOW ARE YOU?
YOU REMEMBER HOW I HAD THAT DRUG HOUSE BEHIND MINE?
FOR YEARS I BUGGED THE SHERIFF TO DO SOMETHING ABOUT IT.
I SAW HIM TODAY AND TOLD HIM, "HEY, THANKS FOR GETTING RID OF THAT HOUSE, BUT DID YOU HAVE TO BURN DOWN HALF THE COUNTY TO DO IT?!"
HA HAHA HA HA HAHA HA HA HA!
HEH.

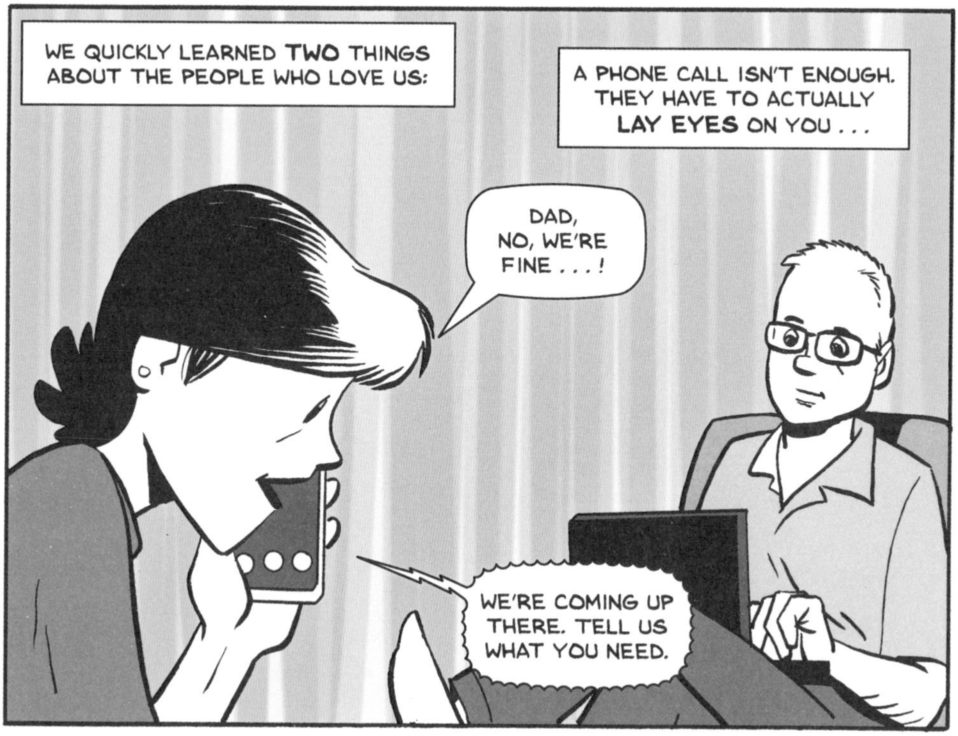
WE QUICKLY LEARNED **TWO** THINGS ABOUT THE PEOPLE WHO LOVE US:
A PHONE CALL ISN'T ENOUGH. THEY HAVE TO ACTUALLY **LAY EYES** ON YOU . . .
DAD, NO, WE'RE FINE . . . !
WE'RE COMING UP THERE. TELL US WHAT YOU NEED.

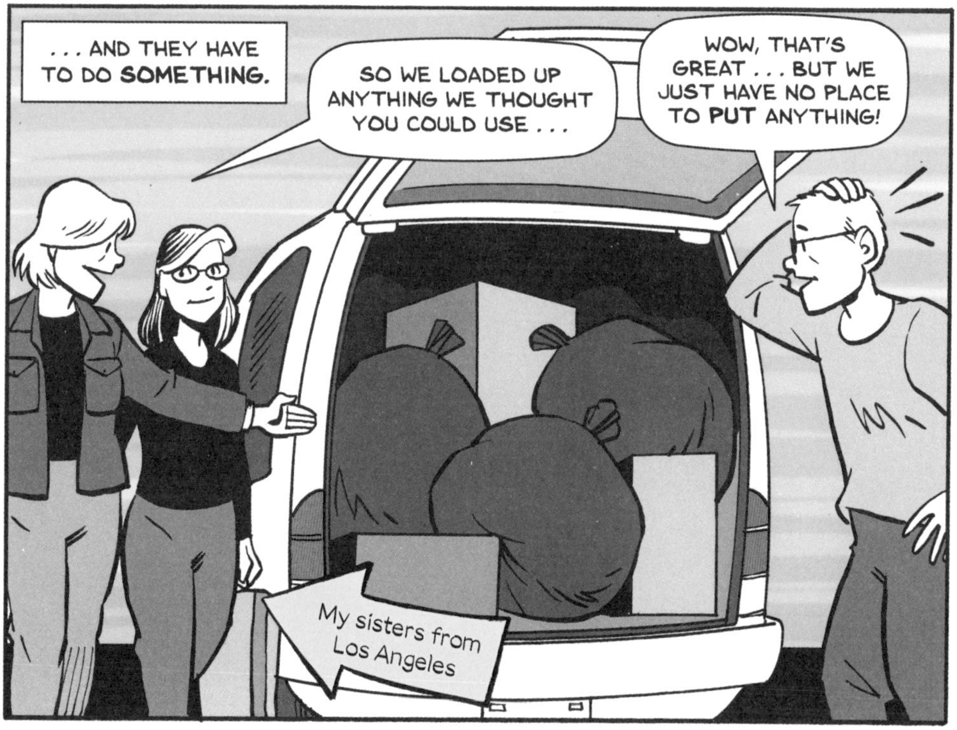
. . . AND THEY HAVE TO DO **SOMETHING.**
SO WE LOADED UP ANYTHING WE THOUGHT YOU COULD USE . . .
WOW, THAT'S GREAT . . . BUT WE JUST HAVE NO PLACE TO **PUT** ANYTHING!
My sisters from Los Angeles

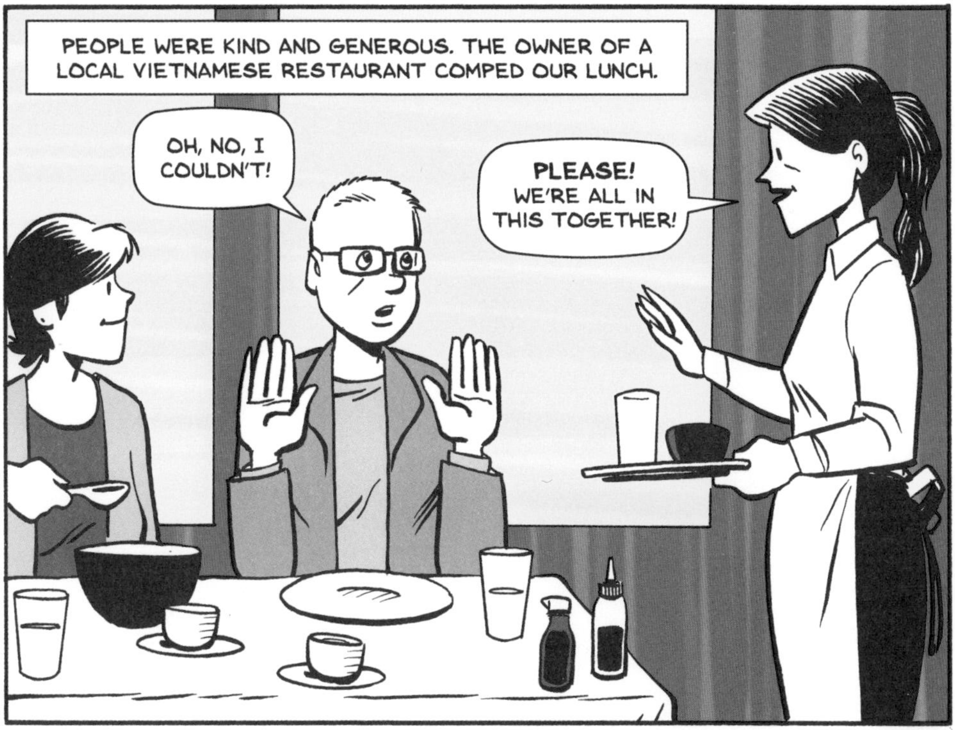
PEOPLE WERE KIND AND GENEROUS. THE OWNER OF A LOCAL VIETNAMESE RESTAURANT COMPED OUR LUNCH.
OH, NO, I COULDN'T!
PLEASE! WE'RE ALL IN THIS TOGETHER!

A VETERINARY OFFICE GAVE US A CASE OF PRESCRIPTION DOG FOOD.

A SYNDICATED CARTOONIST I'VE NEVER MET MAILED ME PENS AND PENCILS. OTHER CARTOONISTS SENT ART, BOOKS, EVEN MONEY.

A LOCAL GOVERNMENT-BACKED ARTS GROUP, CREATIVE SONOMA, GAVE ME CASH TOWARD NEW ART EQUIPMENT AND MATERIALS.

A STATIONER SENT US HOME WITH TWO BAGS OF FREE OFFICE SUPPLIES.

BOY SCOUT TROOPS AND OTHERS BUILT SIFTING SCREENS BY THE HUNDREDS.

SCHOOLKIDS IN OCEANSIDE, NEW YORK, HAND-PAINTED WOODEN STARS THAT HUNG IN OUR BURNED TREES LIKE ORNAMENTS.

FOOD AND CLOTHES BANKS POPPED UP IN VACANT STOREFRONTS.

MANY STORES OFFERED DISCOUNTS TO FIRE VICTIMS, NO PROOF REQUIRED.

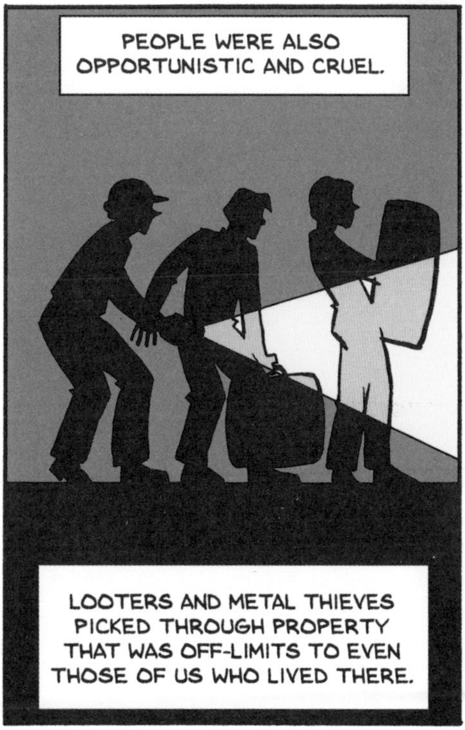
PEOPLE WERE ALSO OPPORTUNISTIC AND CRUEL.
LOOTERS AND METAL THIEVES PICKED THROUGH PROPERTY THAT WAS OFF-LIMITS TO EVEN THOSE OF US WHO LIVED THERE.

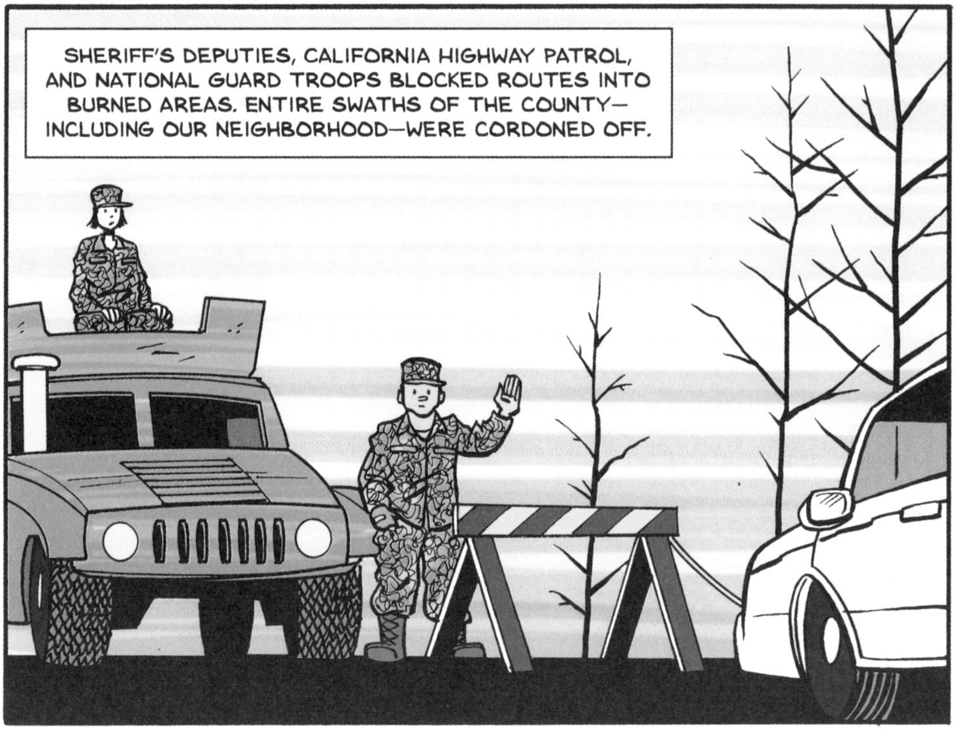
SHERIFF'S DEPUTIES, CALIFORNIA HIGHWAY PATROL, AND NATIONAL GUARD TROOPS BLOCKED ROUTES INTO BURNED AREAS. ENTIRE SWATHS OF THE COUNTY—INCLUDING OUR NEIGHBORHOOD—WERE CORDONED OFF.

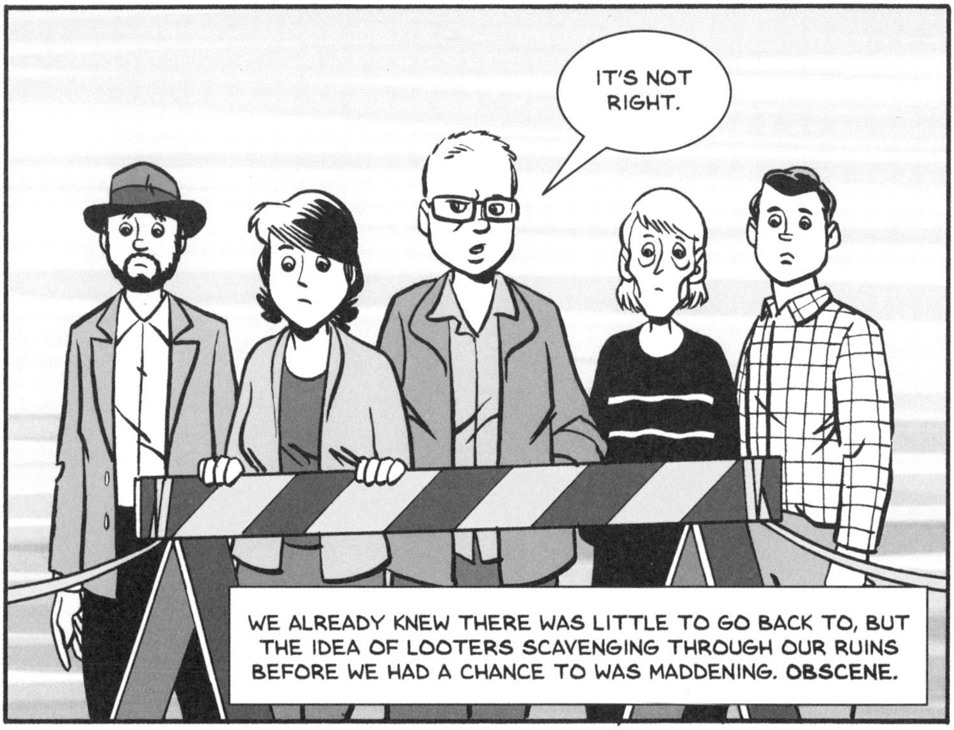
IT'S NOT RIGHT.
WE ALREADY KNEW THERE WAS LITTLE TO GO BACK TO, BUT THE IDEA OF LOOTERS SCAVENGING THROUGH OUR RUINS BEFORE WE HAD A CHANCE TO WAS MADDENING. **OBSCENE.**

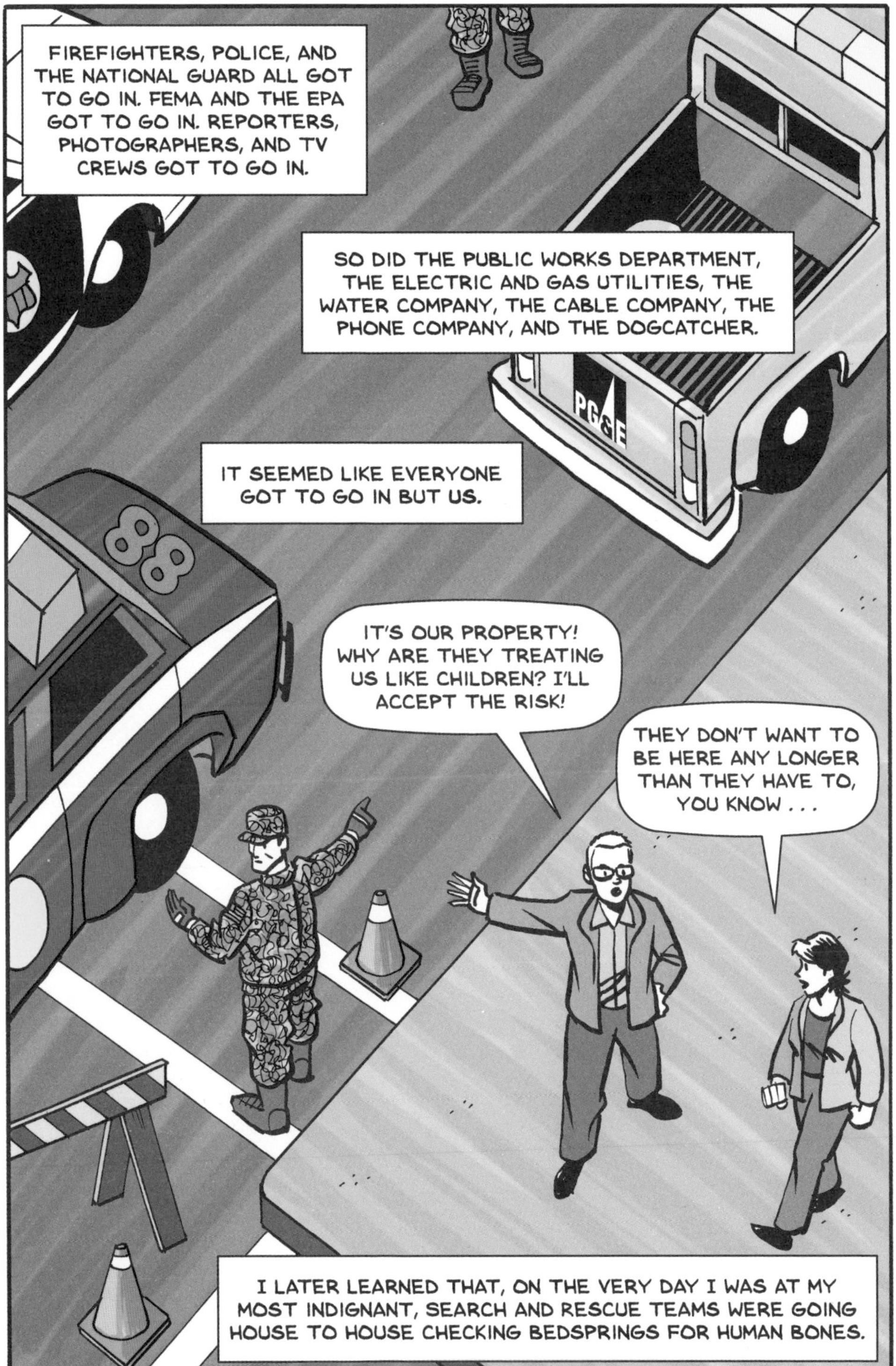
FIREFIGHTERS, POLICE, AND THE NATIONAL GUARD ALL GOT TO GO IN. FEMA AND THE EPA GOT TO GO IN. REPORTERS, PHOTOGRAPHERS, AND TV CREWS GOT TO GO IN.
SO DID THE PUBLIC WORKS DEPARTMENT, THE ELECTRIC AND GAS UTILITIES, THE WATER COMPANY, THE CABLE COMPANY, THE PHONE COMPANY, AND THE DOGCATCHER.
PG&E
IT SEEMED LIKE EVERYONE GOT TO GO IN BUT US.
88
IT'S OUR PROPERTY! WHY ARE THEY TREATING US LIKE CHILDREN? I'LL ACCEPT THE RISK!
THEY DON'T WANT TO BE HERE ANY LONGER THAN THEY HAVE TO, YOU KNOW . . .
I LATER LEARNED THAT, ON THE VERY DAY I WAS AT MY MOST INDIGNANT, SEARCH AND RESCUE TEAMS WERE GOING HOUSE TO HOUSE CHECKING BEDSPRINGS FOR HUMAN BONES.

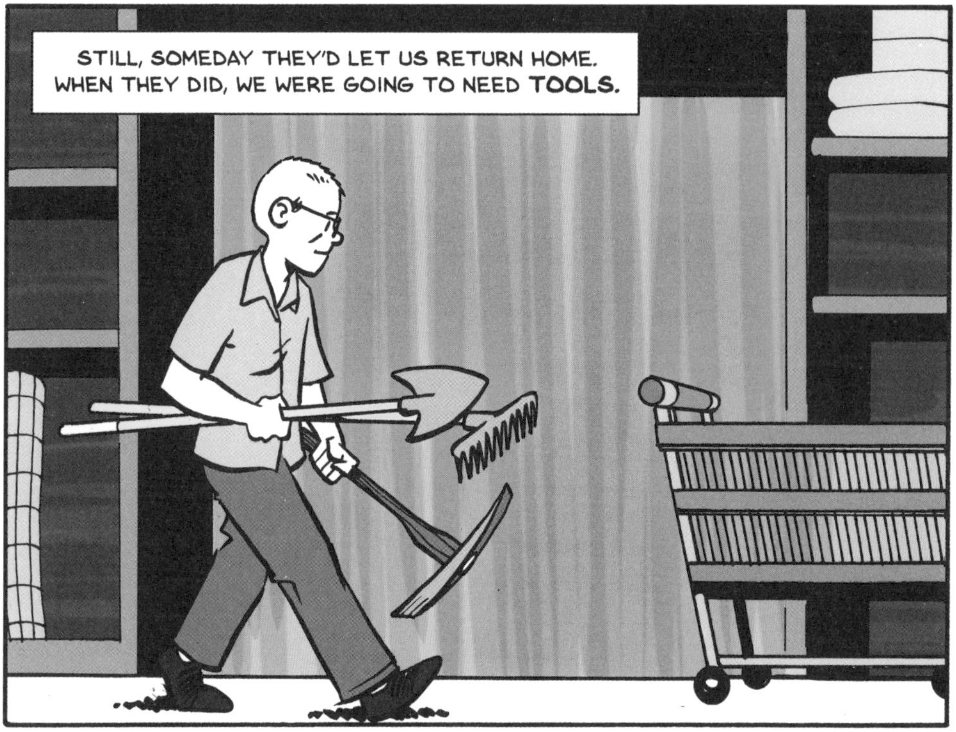
STILL, SOMEDAY THEY'D LET US RETURN HOME. WHEN THEY DID, WE WERE GOING TO NEED **TOOLS.**

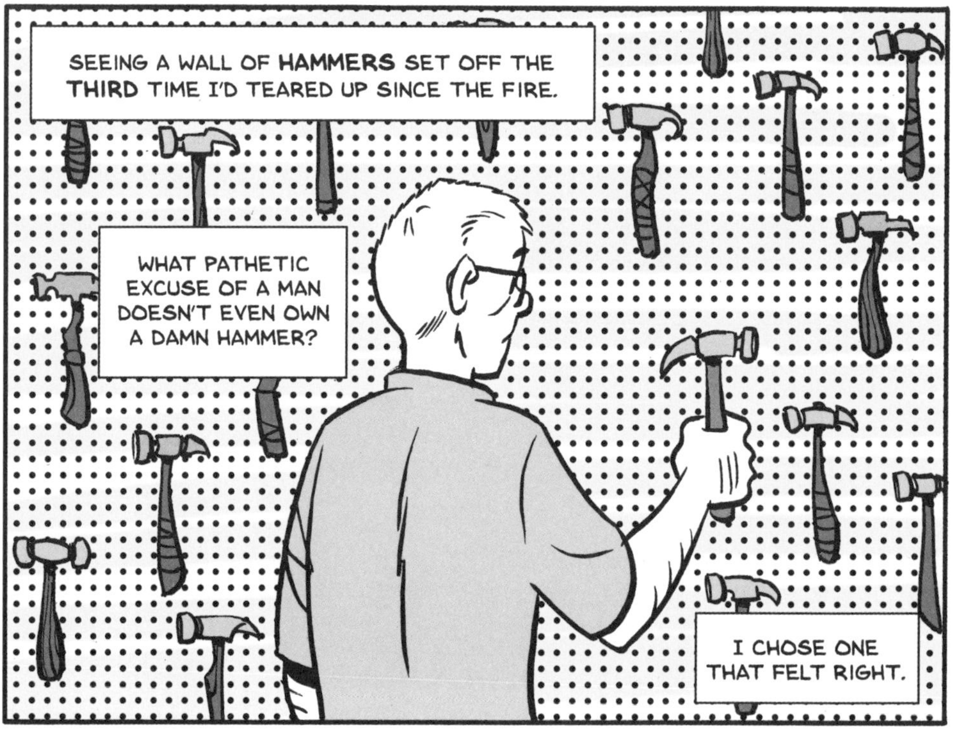
SEEING A WALL OF **HAMMERS** SET OFF THE **THIRD** TIME I'D TEARED UP SINCE THE FIRE.
WHAT PATHETIC EXCUSE OF A MAN DOESN'T EVEN OWN A DAMN HAMMER?
I CHOSE ONE THAT FELT RIGHT.

DOTTIE'S FIRE STORY

DOROTHY HUGHES LIVED IN JOURNEY'S END, A MOBILE HOME PARK OCCUPIED BY
LOW-INCOME SENIORS. IT WAS NEXT TO HIGHWAY 101, JUST WEST OF THE FOUNTAINGROVE
NEIGHBORHOOD. ONLY FORTY-FOUR OF ITS 160 HOMES SURVIVED. DOTTIE WAS EIGHTY-ONE
AT THE TIME OF THE FIRE.

My niece called me. She said, "Auntie, if
you're on any kind of medication, grab your
medications and come up to my house." She
didn't say "fire," she just said, "Get up to my
house." I could tell by the tone of her voice
to listen to her.

I grabbed some insurance papers and things
like that, and got in my car. As I was driving
out, the wind was blowing the fire across
the street from Fountaingrove.

I knew it was going to hit Journey's End.
My street had newer mobile homes, but it
hit the older ones first. I know how mobile
courts go. If one starts, they all go.

I got to my niece's house, but they were in
jeopardy, too. We drove to one evacuation
center, bumper to bumper, but people came
out into the street and said, "Turn around,
they're full." So we went to the Veterans'
Memorial Building.

I saw a man from Journey's End named
John. He was with his little dog, and he was
barefoot. So I took off my socks and went
over and said, "Put these on to keep your
feet warm and I'll go get you a bottle of
water." About that time, they told him he
had to leave because of his dog, which was
all he had in the world. I couldn't find him
after that.

We stayed there all night long. Finally my son wanted to go see if my place was still
standing. Well, they wouldn't even let us go down the street. And I didn't really want
to see, to tell you the truth. I was scared.

My son said, "Let's sneak in through the Kaiser hospital next door," because my
house backs right up against it. So we went around and through Kaiser. And my house
was still standing! When the firemen were fighting to save the hospital they hosed
down my whole street. That's why those forty-four homes survived.

I just thanked God for blessing us. But it's a Catch-22, since Journey's End is too
unsafe to live in, but insurance won't pay for the houses because they're still standing.

The Journey's End owners locked us out. I was picketing. "Let us go home!" "We're too old to start over!" I was in the newspapers. That's not like me, I don't do those things! But it's like we've fallen through the cracks. You hear about Fountaingrove and Coffey Park, but Journey's End is the truly forgotten one.

Some people have given up and moved to Sacramento because they couldn't afford to stay here. That hurts us more, because it means fewer people are here fighting to get back what's ours.

At the beginning, they said it was feasible to open up the forty-four houses and let us return. But now they're saying no, it's too hard to get new utilities in there for us. But they're going to have to put in utilities for whatever replaces us, so that doesn't add up to me.

I hate to give up hope, but it doesn't look good at all. I try very hard not to think about it because I get so upset about never, ever being able to live there again.

DOTTIE'S HUSBAND, ALBERT, DIED IN FEBRUARY 2017.

Every night I wake up worrying about something. I think the hardest part is not having my husband with me. I just miss him. I feel like he'd have some ideas of what to do or where to go. I'm doing the best I can. Every day I'm going someplace, trying to figure out what to do or where to get help. I'm thankful for any help I get, but if I had him it would be so much easier.

But I don't know if he could have lived through what I've been through. Sometimes women are stronger when it comes to that, you know.

We were together fifty-nine years. He wanted so much to make it to sixty.

I love my mobile, but it's too old to be moved. It's a really nice double-wide. I had a nice patio, a nice yard. I was very comfortable. We lived there twenty-nine years and I thought it was where my life would come to an end.

I have a key to the gate now. I guess I think I'm still going to be able to move back sometime, because I fill up jugs and take them over there to water my flowers.

DOTTIE LIVED IN A FEMA-SUBSIDIZED MOTEL ROOM, ACROSS THE FREEWAY FROM HER FORMER HOME, FOR EIGHT MONTHS.

I managed with a little refrigerator and a toaster oven. I washed dishes, sometimes in the little sink and some-times in the bathtub. I tried to go to the grocery store to get my mind off things. It was just horrible living that way.

I get supplements because I know I'm not eating like I should be. We eat out a lot, but I'm Italian, so I love to cook. I say I have pasta withdrawal. That's the one thing I can't do without.

IN JUNE 2018, DOTTIE MOVED INTO A SMALL APARTMENT PROVIDED BY THE NON-PROFIT BURBANK HOUSING.

From what I hear I'm very lucky to get a place, because most of the Journey's End people keep getting refusal letters. I wasn't happy about going there, but I know I'm blessed to have a place because so many don't. It's just so far from what I used to have.

I just hope that God blesses me with a little more time on this Earth to be happy and not sad every day, and not wake up in the middle of the night wondering what's going to happen tomorrow. It's been hell since the fire. ∎

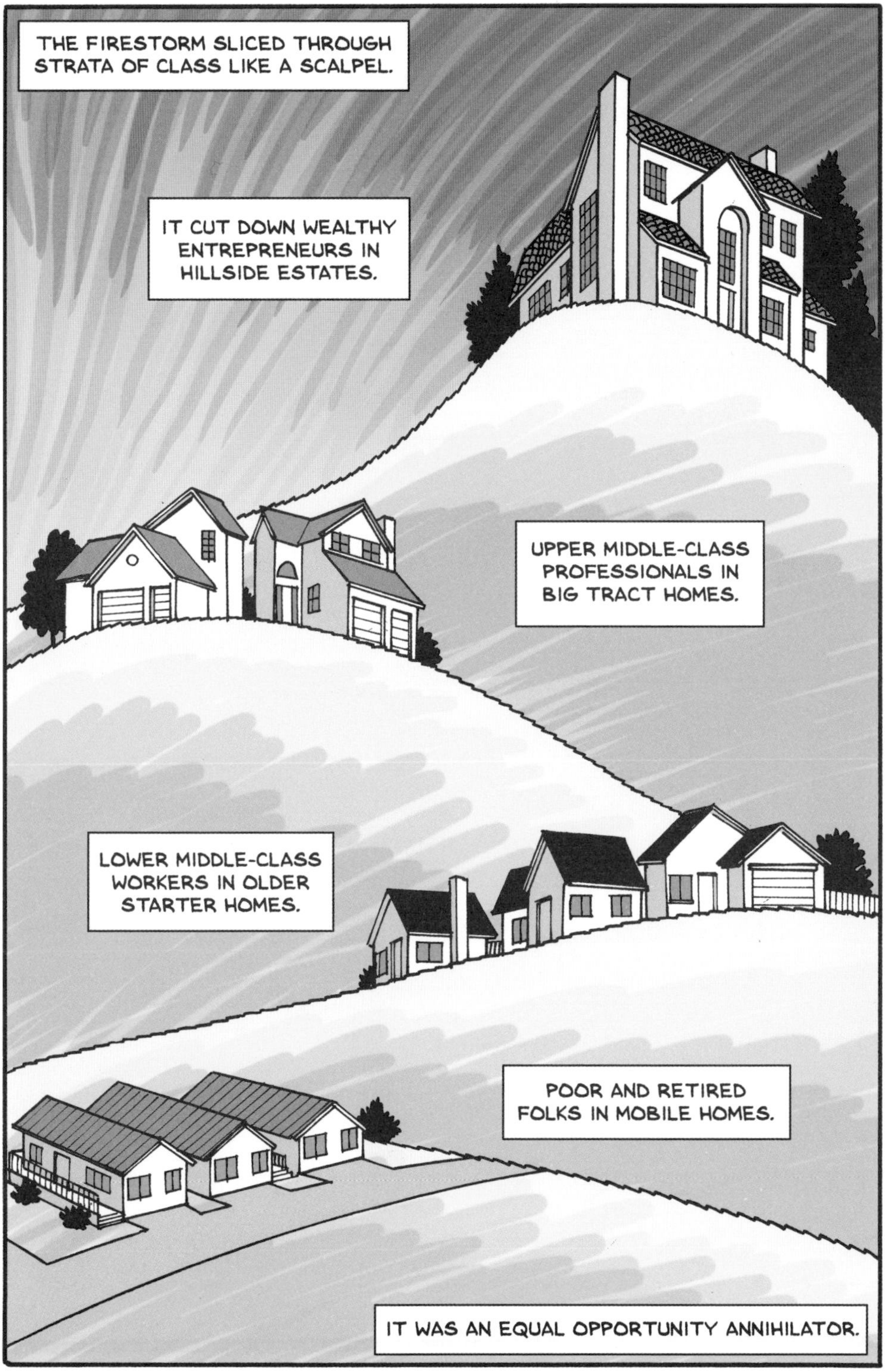
THE FIRESTORM SLICED THROUGH STRATA OF CLASS LIKE A SCALPEL.
IT CUT DOWN WEALTHY ENTREPRENEURS IN HILLSIDE ESTATES.
UPPER MIDDLE-CLASS PROFESSIONALS IN BIG TRACT HOMES.
LOWER MIDDLE-CLASS WORKERS IN OLDER STARTER HOMES.
POOR AND RETIRED FOLKS IN MOBILE HOMES.
IT WAS AN EQUAL OPPORTUNITY ANNIHILATOR.

IMAGINE THE IMPACT THAT TEN THOUSAND PEOPLE INSTANTLY HOMELESS, AND THOUSANDS MORE INSTANTLY JOBLESS, HAVE ON A LOCAL ECONOMY.

THE RICH WERE FINE. THEIR INSURERS SNAPPED UP EVERY AVAILABLE VACANCY AND BID UP RENTS THAT FORCED THE LESS WELL-OFF TO PAY INFLATED RATES FOR SHACKS FORTY MILES AWAY.

HOMEOWNERS ALREADY PLANNING TO SELL MADE QUICK DEALS AT PEAK PRICES.

RENTERS WERE EVICTED BY LANDLORDS WHO'D LOST THEIR OWN HOMES AND DESPERATELY NEEDED A ROOF OF THEIR OWN.

LAWS WERE QUICKLY PASSED FORBIDDING RENT HIKES MORE THAN 10 PERCENT OVER PRE-FIRE PRICES, BUT LOOPHOLES AND SHARKS ABOUNDED.

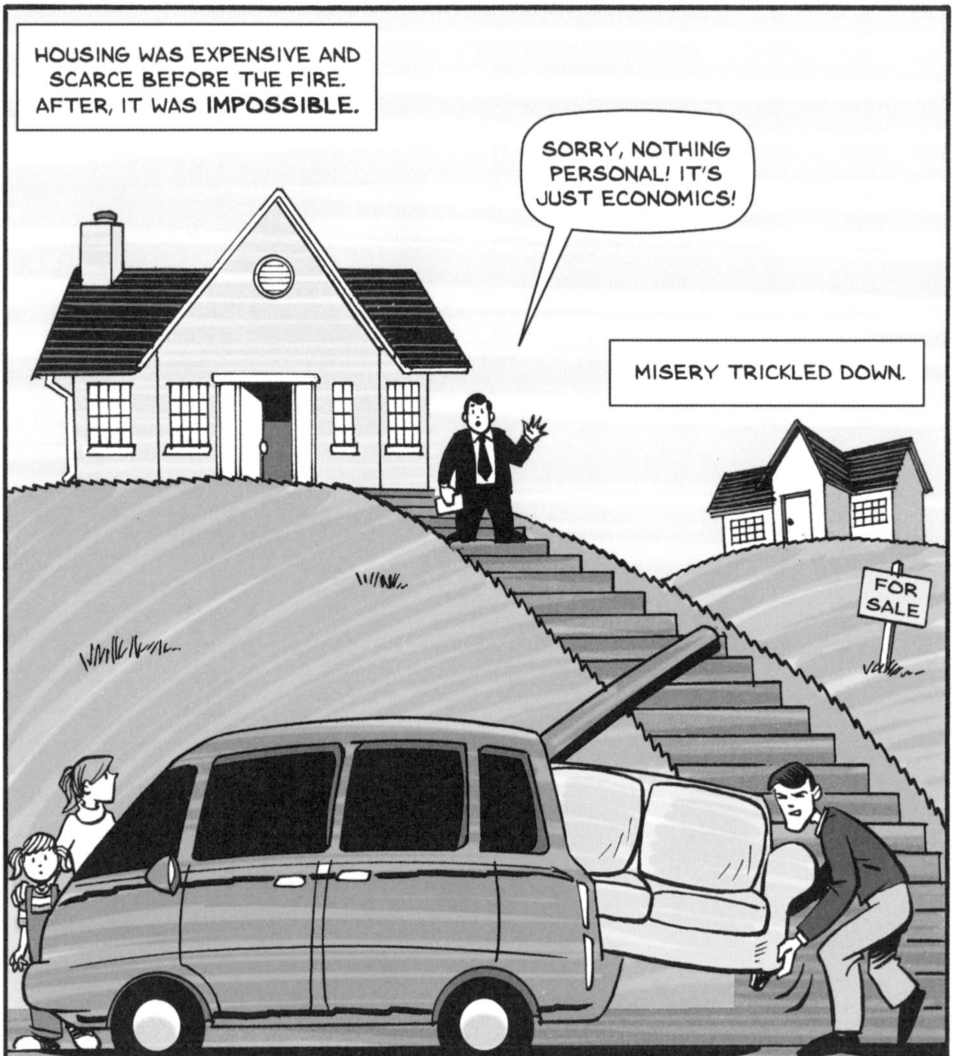
HOUSING WAS EXPENSIVE AND SCARCE BEFORE THE FIRE. AFTER, IT WAS **IMPOSSIBLE.**
SORRY, NOTHING PERSONAL! IT'S JUST ECONOMICS!
MISERY TRICKLED DOWN.
FOR SALE

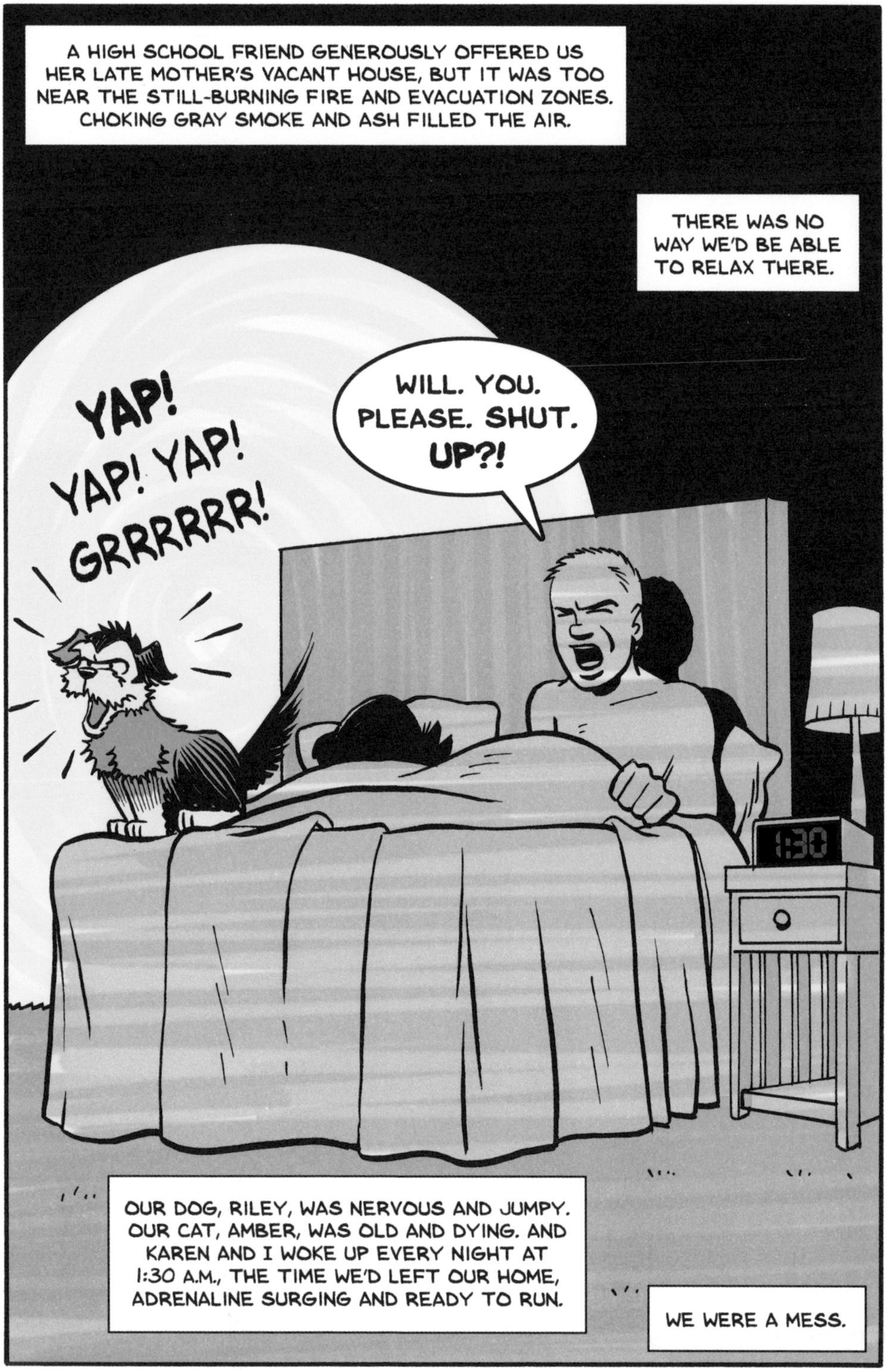
A HIGH SCHOOL FRIEND GENEROUSLY OFFERED US HER LATE MOTHER'S VACANT HOUSE, BUT IT WAS TOO NEAR THE STILL-BURNING FIRE AND EVACUATION ZONES. CHOKING GRAY SMOKE AND ASH FILLED THE AIR.
THERE WAS NO WAY WE'D BE ABLE TO RELAX THERE.
YAP! YAP! YAP! GRRRRRR!
WILL. YOU. PLEASE. SHUT. UP?!
1:30
OUR DOG, RILEY, WAS NERVOUS AND JUMPY. OUR CAT, AMBER, WAS OLD AND DYING. AND KAREN AND I WOKE UP EVERY NIGHT AT 1:30 A.M., THE TIME WE'D LEFT OUR HOME, ADRENALINE SURGING AND READY TO RUN.
WE WERE A MESS.

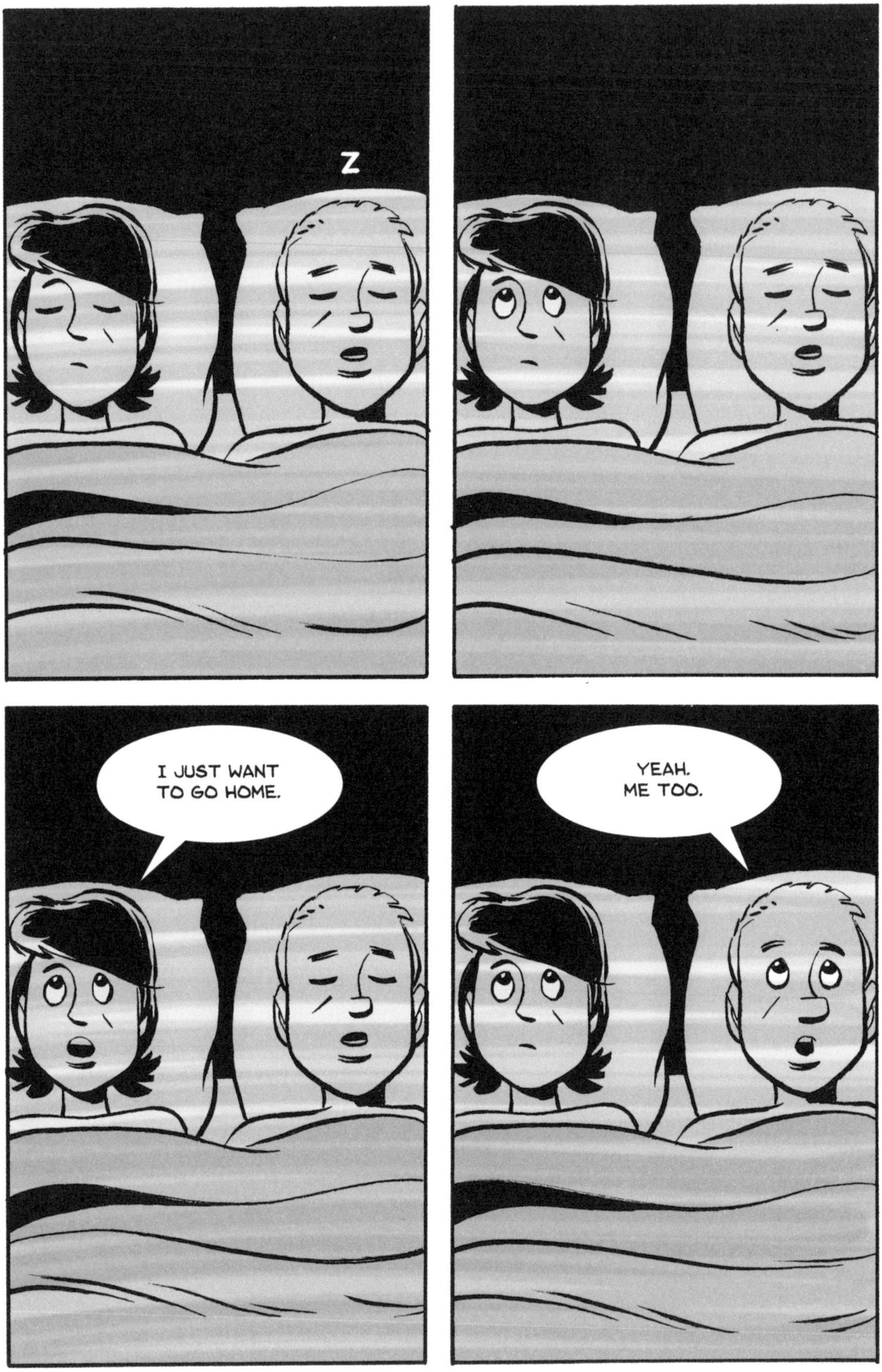
Z
I JUST WANT TO GO HOME.
YEAH. ME TOO.

A DAY IN THE NEW LIFE

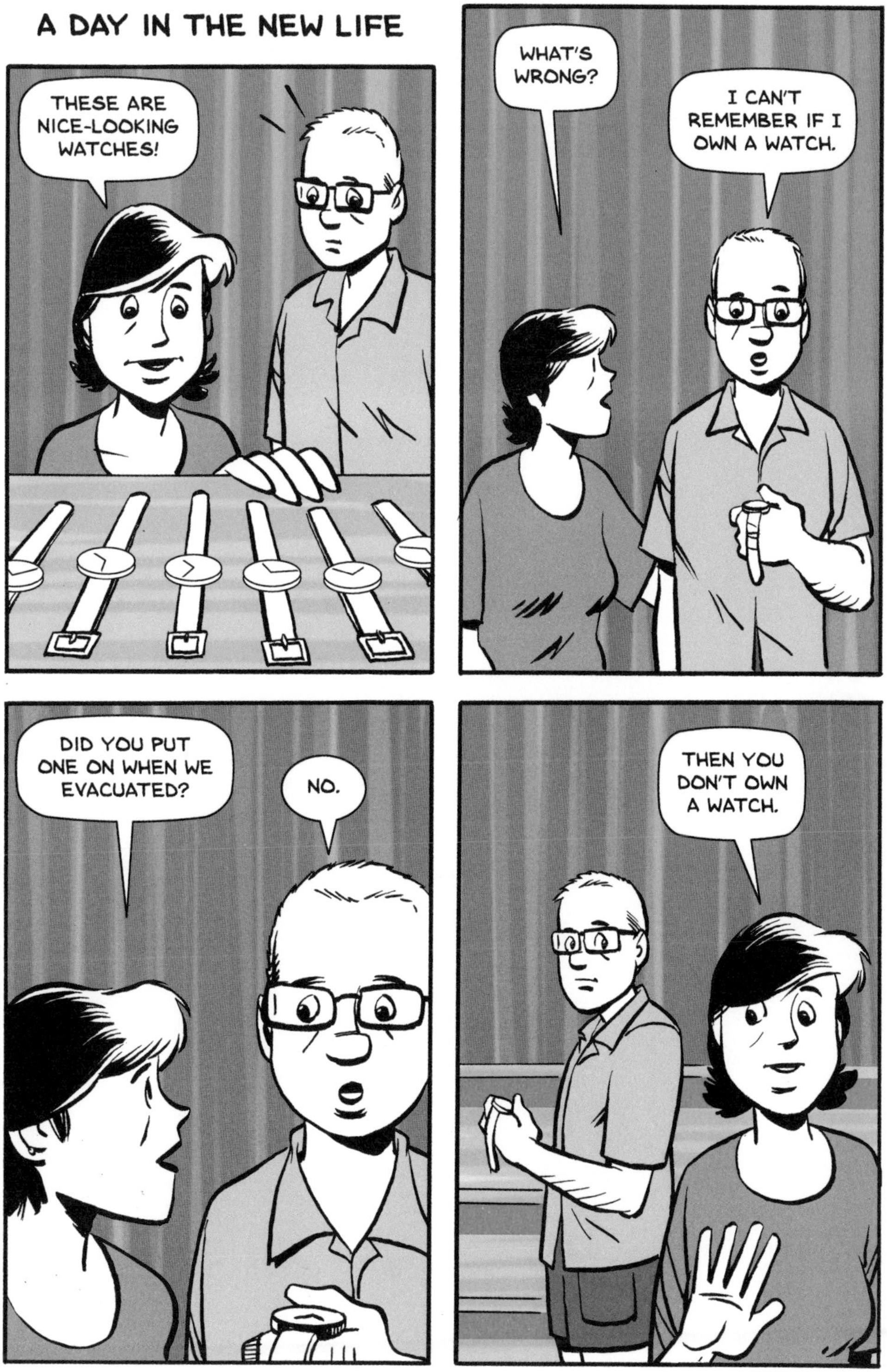
THESE ARE NICE-LOOKING WATCHES!
WHAT'S WRONG?
I CAN'T REMEMBER IF I OWN A WATCH.
DID YOU PUT ONE ON WHEN WE EVACUATED?
NO.
THEN YOU DON'T OWN A WATCH.

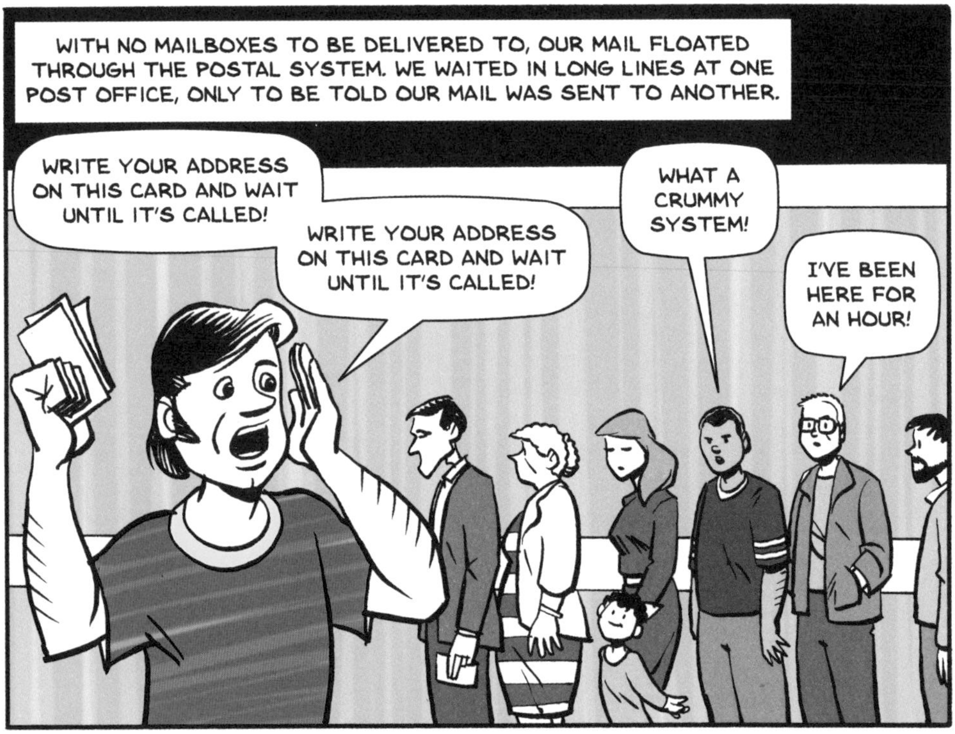
WITH NO MAILBOXES TO BE DELIVERED TO, OUR MAIL FLOATED THROUGH THE POSTAL SYSTEM. WE WAITED IN LONG LINES AT ONE POST OFFICE, ONLY TO BE TOLD OUR MAIL WAS SENT TO ANOTHER.
WRITE YOUR ADDRESS ON THIS CARD AND WAIT UNTIL IT'S CALLED!
WRITE YOUR ADDRESS ON THIS CARD AND WAIT UNTIL IT'S CALLED!
WHAT A CRUMMY SYSTEM!
I'VE BEEN HERE FOR AN HOUR!

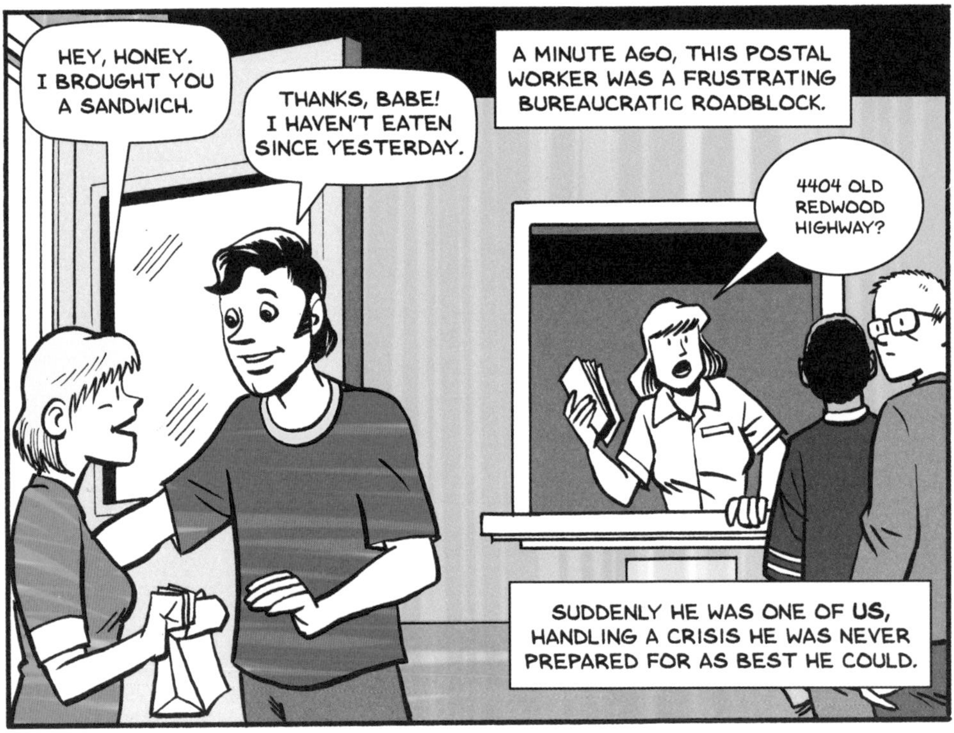
HEY, HONEY. I BROUGHT YOU A SANDWICH.
THANKS, BABE! I HAVEN'T EATEN SINCE YESTERDAY.
A MINUTE AGO, THIS POSTAL WORKER WAS A FRUSTRATING BUREAUCRATIC ROADBLOCK.
4404 OLD REDWOOD HIGHWAY?
SUDDENLY HE WAS ONE OF **US**, HANDLING A CRISIS HE WAS NEVER PREPARED FOR AS BEST HE COULD.

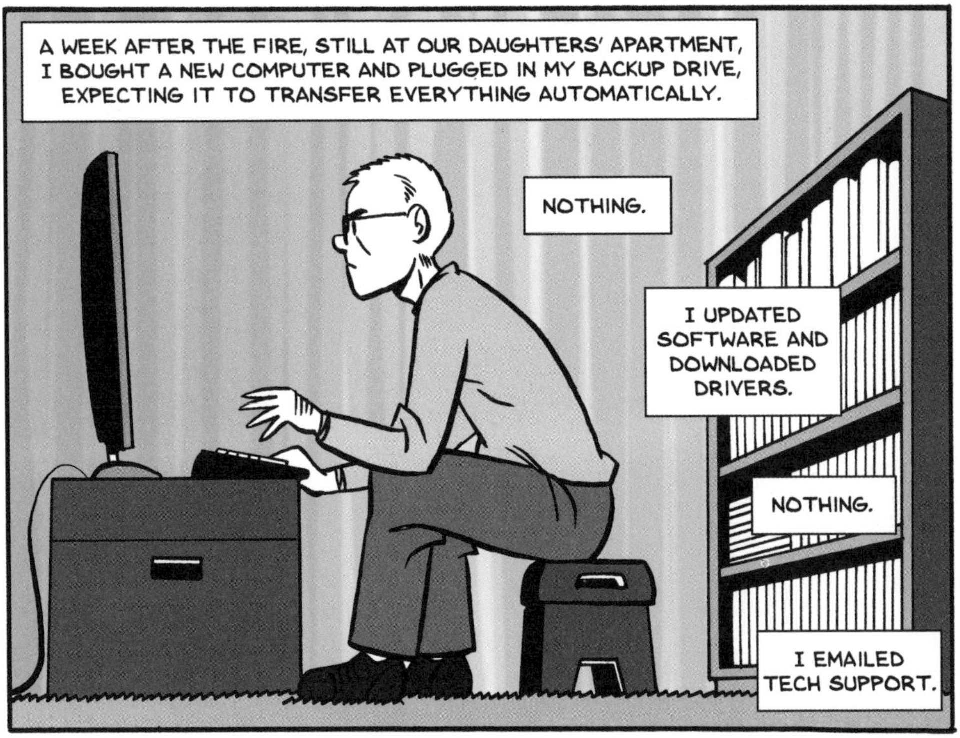
A WEEK AFTER THE FIRE, STILL AT OUR DAUGHTERS' APARTMENT, I BOUGHT A NEW COMPUTER AND PLUGGED IN MY BACKUP DRIVE, EXPECTING IT TO TRANSFER EVERYTHING AUTOMATICALLY.
NOTHING.
I UPDATED SOFTWARE AND DOWNLOADED DRIVERS.
NOTHING.
I EMAILED TECH SUPPORT.

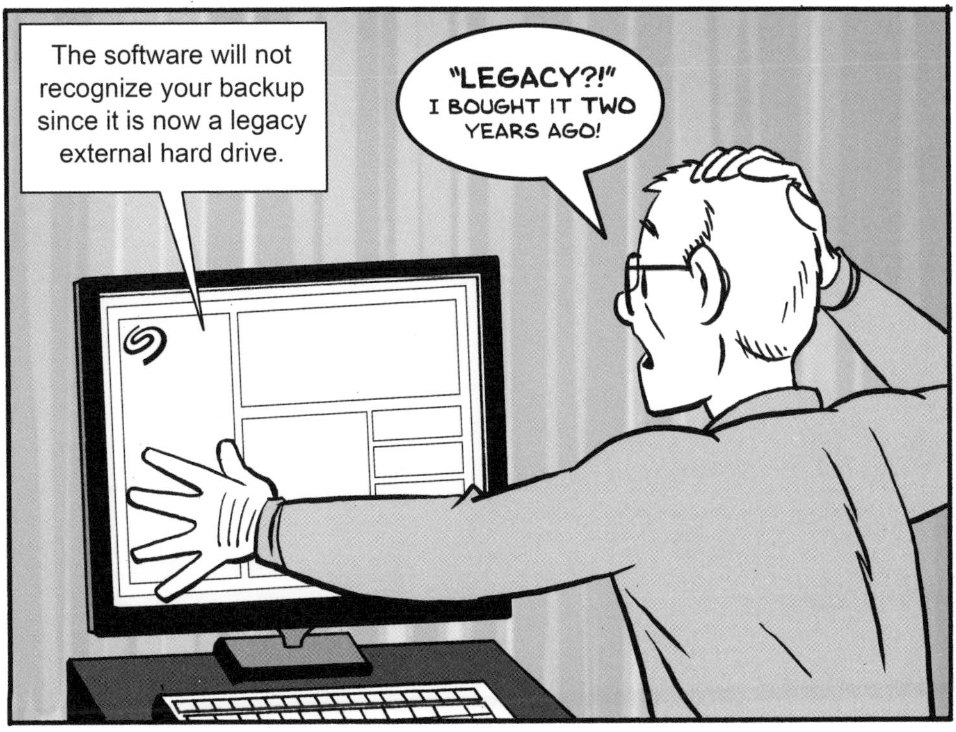
The software will not recognize your backup since it is now a legacy external hard drive.
"LEGACY?!" I BOUGHT IT TWO YEARS AGO!

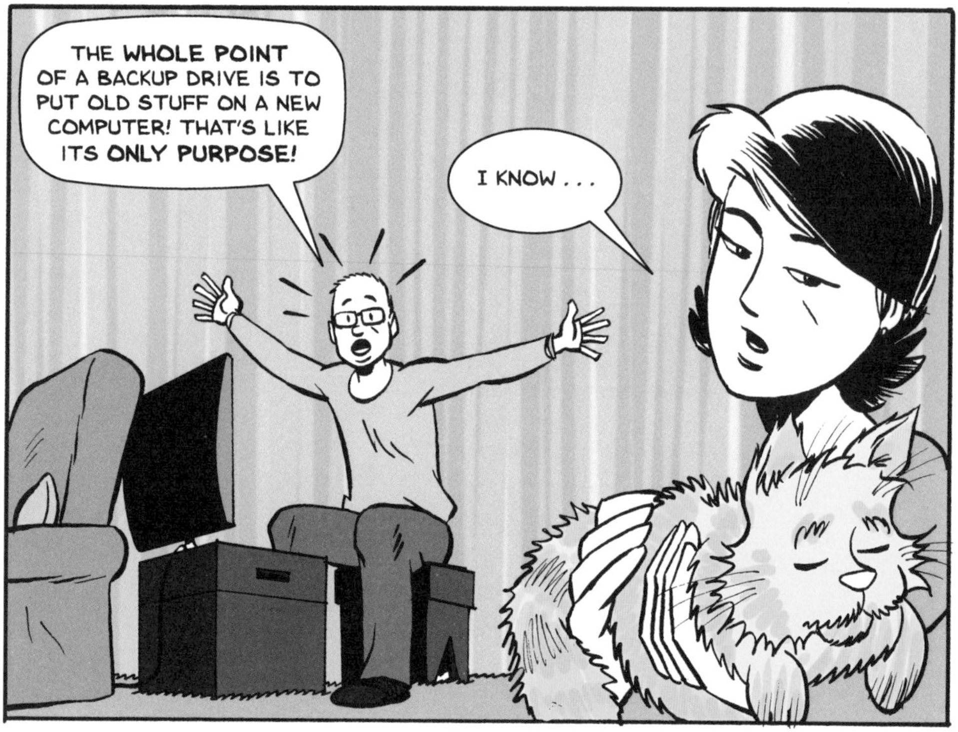
THE **WHOLE POINT** OF A BACKUP DRIVE IS TO PUT OLD STUFF ON A NEW COMPUTER! THAT'S LIKE ITS **ONLY PURPOSE!**
I KNOW . . .

I SPENT THE NEXT THREE DAYS COPYING AND PASTING **THOUSANDS** OF INDIVIDUAL FILES FROM THE BACKUP TO MY NEW HARD DRIVE. BUT AT LEAST I STILL HAD THEM.

THE ELECTRONS CLINGING TO THAT FRAGILE MAGNETIC DISC WERE NEARLY ALL THAT REMAINED OF THE PHOTOS I'D TAKEN, THE ARTICLES I'D WRITTEN, THE BOOKS I'D DONE, THE BOOKS I PLANNED TO DO, AND EVERYTHING ELSE I'D EVER CREATED.

I NEVER TRUSTED CLOUD STORAGE. BUT IF I HADN'T GRABBED THAT BACKUP THE NIGHT OF THE FIRE, I'D HAVE LOST IT ALL.

I'M A CONVERT TO THE CLOUD.

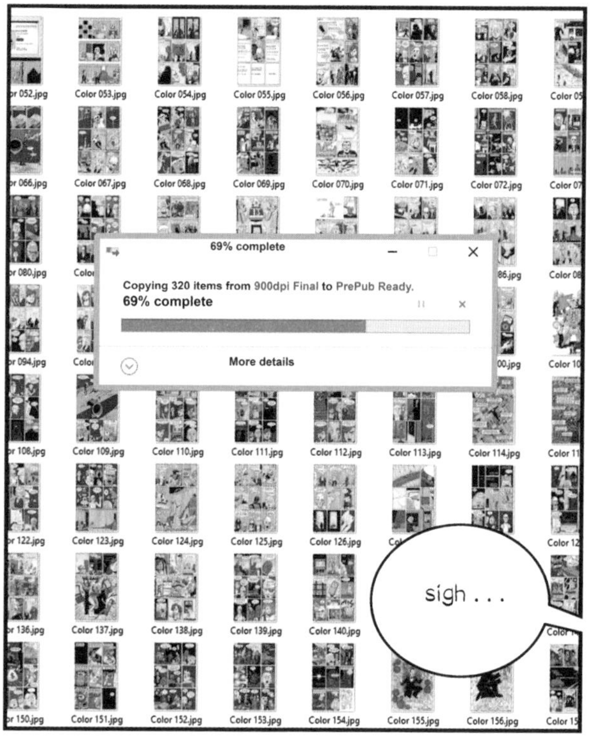
69% complete
Copying 320 items from 900dpi Final to PrePub Ready.
69% complete
More details
sigh . . .

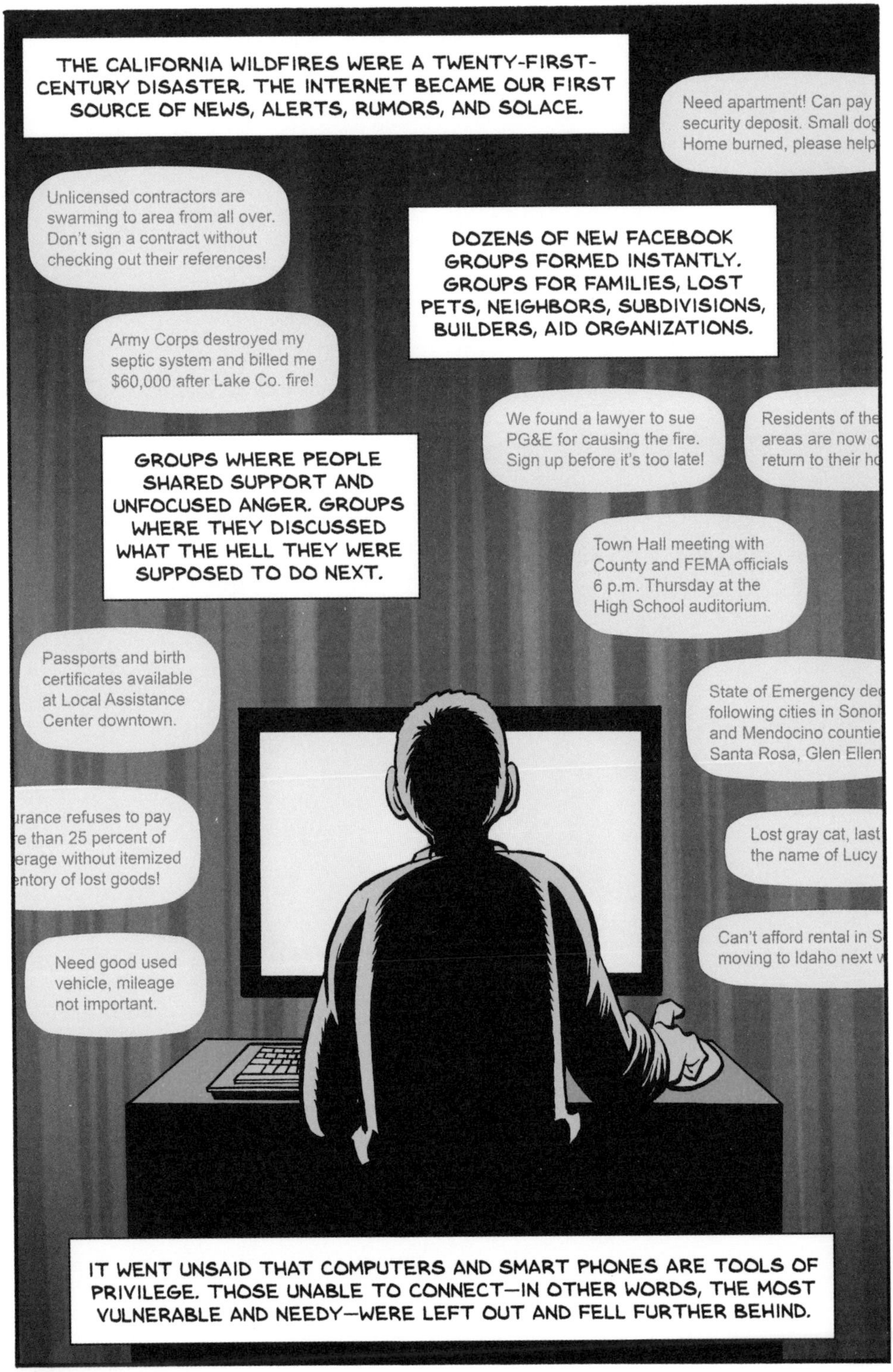
THE CALIFORNIA WILDFIRES WERE A TWENTY-FIRST-CENTURY DISASTER. THE INTERNET BECAME OUR FIRST SOURCE OF NEWS, ALERTS, RUMORS, AND SOLACE.
Need apartment! Can pay security deposit. Small dog Home burned, please help
Unlicensed contractors are swarming to area from all over. Don't sign a contract without checking out their references!
DOZENS OF NEW FACEBOOK GROUPS FORMED INSTANTLY. GROUPS FOR FAMILIES, LOST PETS, NEIGHBORS, SUBDIVISIONS, BUILDERS, AID ORGANIZATIONS.
Army Corps destroyed my septic system and billed me $60,000 after Lake Co. fire!
We found a lawyer to sue PG&E for causing the fire. Sign up before it's too late!
Residents of the areas are now c return to their h
GROUPS WHERE PEOPLE SHARED SUPPORT AND UNFOCUSED ANGER. GROUPS WHERE THEY DISCUSSED WHAT THE HELL THEY WERE SUPPOSED TO DO NEXT.
Town Hall meeting with County and FEMA officials 6 p.m. Thursday at the High School auditorium.
Passports and birth certificates available at Local Assistance Center downtown.
State of Emergency de following cities in Sonor and Mendocino countie Santa Rosa, Glen Ellen
urance refuses to pay e than 25 percent of erage without itemized entory of lost goods!
Lost gray cat, last the name of Lucy
Can't afford rental in S moving to Idaho next
Need good used vehicle, mileage not important.
IT WENT UNSAID THAT COMPUTERS AND SMART PHONES ARE TOOLS OF PRIVILEGE. THOSE UNABLE TO CONNECT—IN OTHER WORDS, THE MOST VULNERABLE AND NEEDY—WERE LEFT OUT AND FELL FURTHER BEHIND.

SONOMA COUNTY HAD **FOUR** WAYS TO WARN AND INFORM PEOPLE IN A DISASTER:

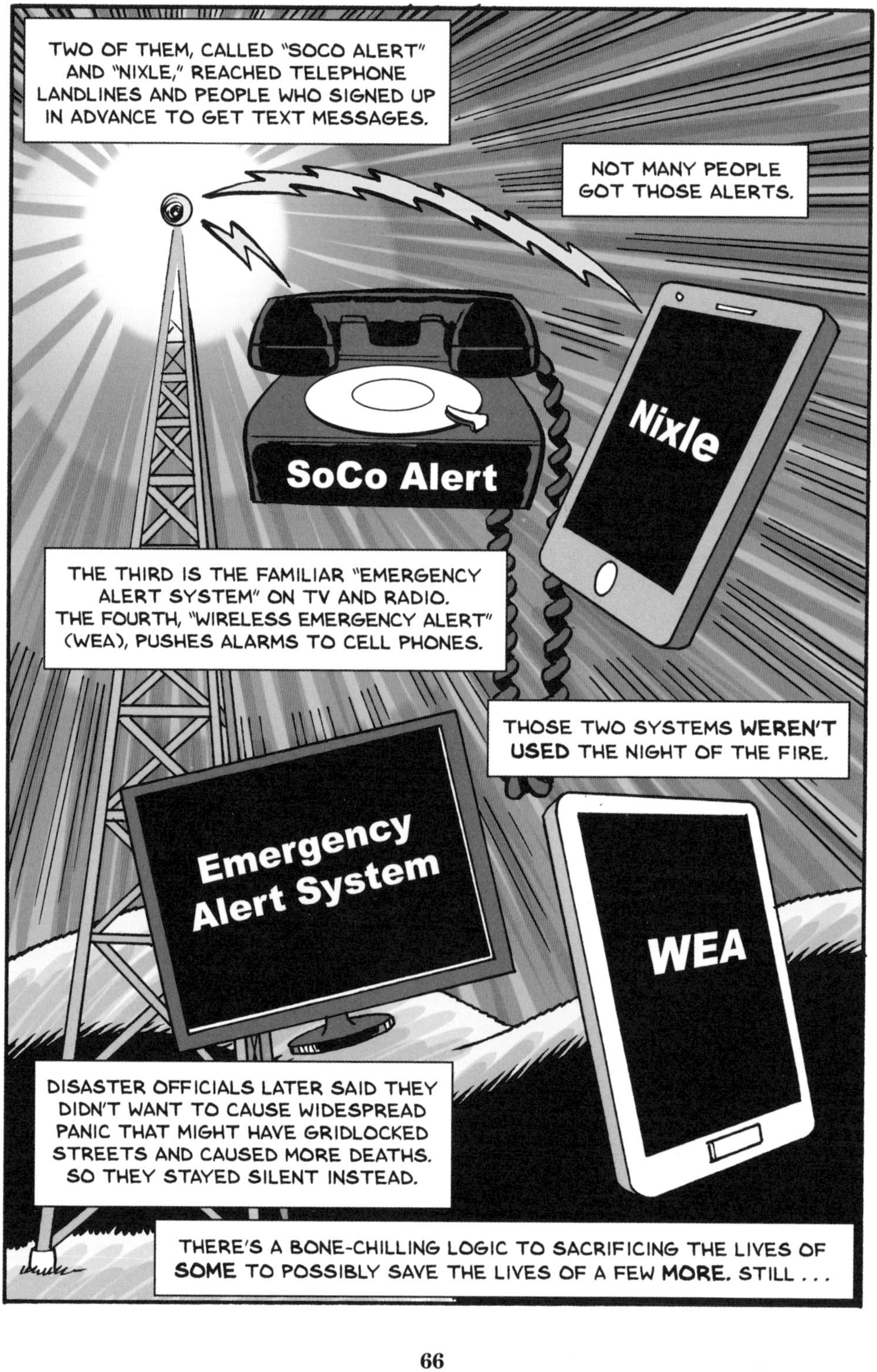

TWO OF THEM, CALLED "SOCO ALERT" AND "NIXLE," REACHED TELEPHONE LANDLINES AND PEOPLE WHO SIGNED UP IN ADVANCE TO GET TEXT MESSAGES.
NOT MANY PEOPLE GOT THOSE ALERTS.
SoCo Alert
Nixle
THE THIRD IS THE FAMILIAR "EMERGENCY ALERT SYSTEM" ON TV AND RADIO. THE FOURTH, "WIRELESS EMERGENCY ALERT" (WEA), PUSHES ALARMS TO CELL PHONES.
THOSE TWO SYSTEMS **WEREN'T USED** THE NIGHT OF THE FIRE.
Emergency Alert System
WEA
DISASTER OFFICIALS LATER SAID THEY DIDN'T WANT TO CAUSE WIDESPREAD PANIC THAT MIGHT HAVE GRIDLOCKED STREETS AND CAUSED MORE DEATHS. SO THEY STAYED SILENT INSTEAD.
THERE'S A BONE-CHILLING LOGIC TO SACRIFICING THE LIVES OF **SOME** TO POSSIBLY SAVE THE LIVES OF A FEW **MORE**. STILL . . .

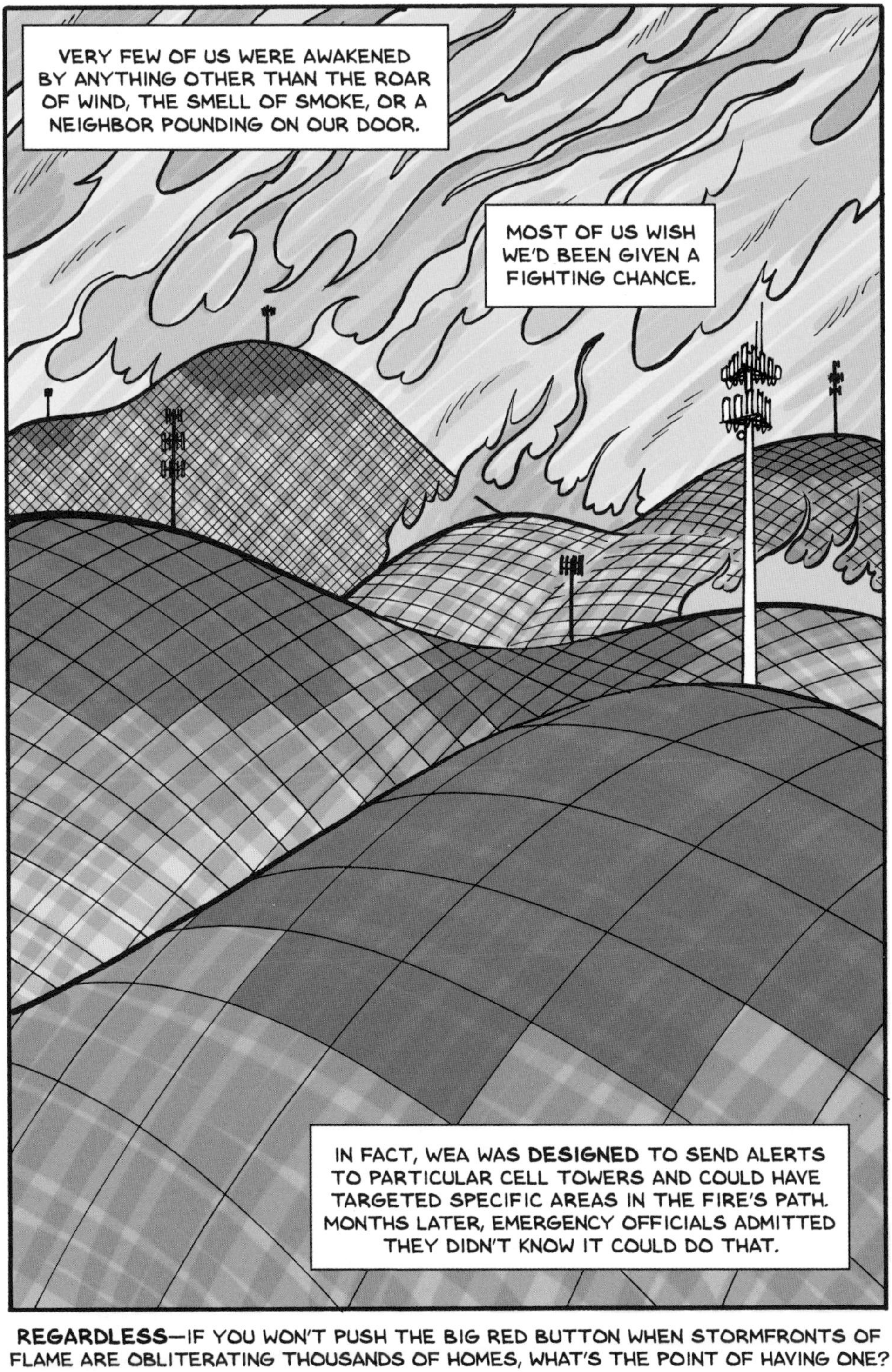
VERY FEW OF US WERE AWAKENED BY ANYTHING OTHER THAN THE ROAR OF WIND, THE SMELL OF SMOKE, OR A NEIGHBOR POUNDING ON OUR DOOR.
MOST OF US WISH WE'D BEEN GIVEN A FIGHTING CHANCE.
IN FACT, WEA WAS **DESIGNED** TO SEND ALERTS TO PARTICULAR CELL TOWERS AND COULD HAVE TARGETED SPECIFIC AREAS IN THE FIRE'S PATH. MONTHS LATER, EMERGENCY OFFICIALS ADMITTED THEY DIDN'T KNOW IT COULD DO THAT.

REGARDLESS—IF YOU WON'T PUSH THE BIG RED BUTTON WHEN STORMFRONTS OF FLAME ARE OBLITERATING THOUSANDS OF HOMES, WHAT'S THE POINT OF HAVING ONE?

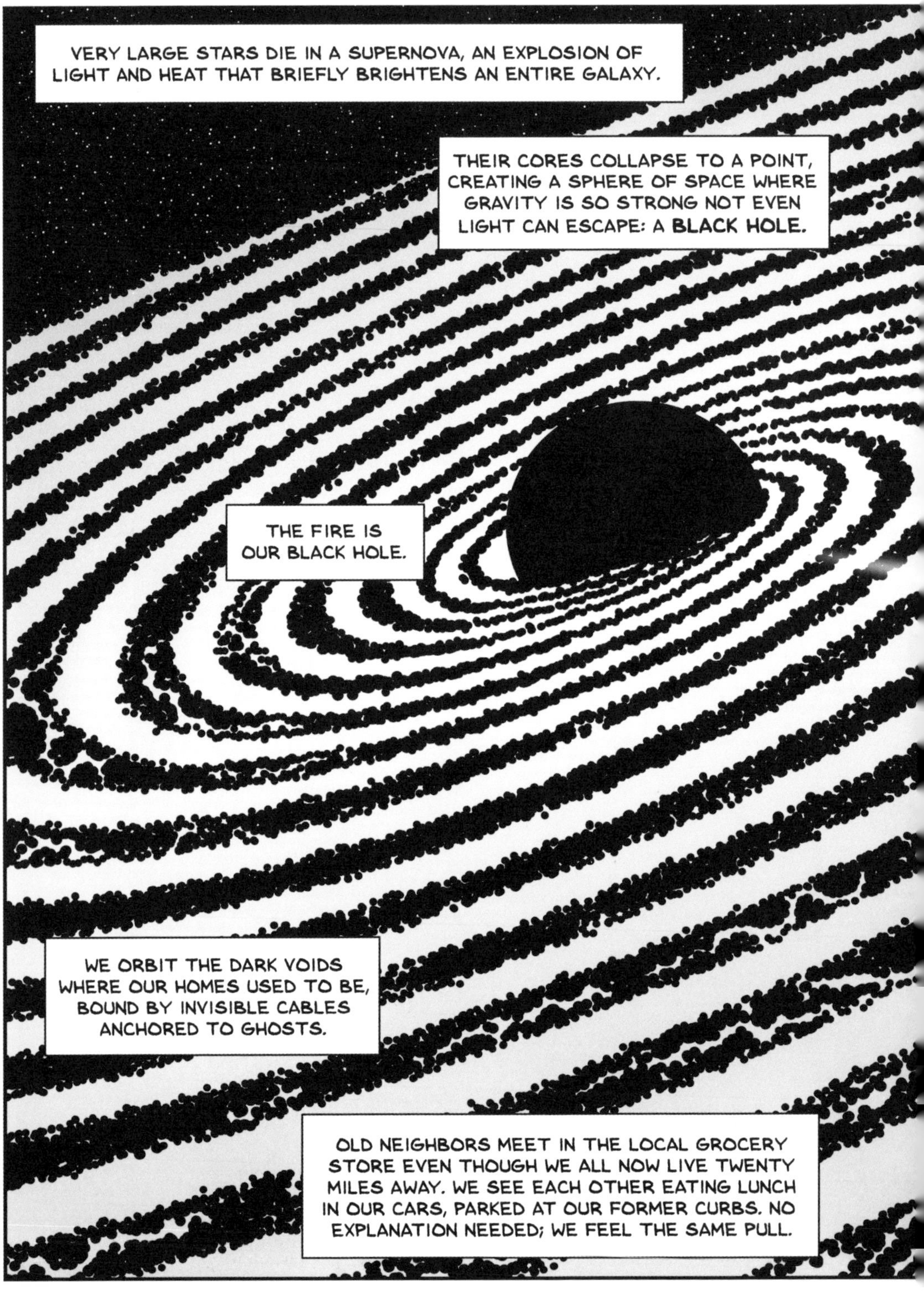
VERY LARGE STARS DIE IN A SUPERNOVA, AN EXPLOSION OF LIGHT AND HEAT THAT BRIEFLY BRIGHTENS AN ENTIRE GALAXY.
THEIR CORES COLLAPSE TO A POINT, CREATING A SPHERE OF SPACE WHERE GRAVITY IS SO STRONG NOT EVEN LIGHT CAN ESCAPE: A **BLACK HOLE.**
THE FIRE IS OUR BLACK HOLE.
WE ORBIT THE DARK VOIDS WHERE OUR HOMES USED TO BE, BOUND BY INVISIBLE CABLES ANCHORED TO GHOSTS.
OLD NEIGHBORS MEET IN THE LOCAL GROCERY STORE EVEN THOUGH WE ALL NOW LIVE TWENTY MILES AWAY. WE SEE EACH OTHER EATING LUNCH IN OUR CARS, PARKED AT OUR FORMER CURBS. NO EXPLANATION NEEDED; WE FEEL THE SAME PULL.

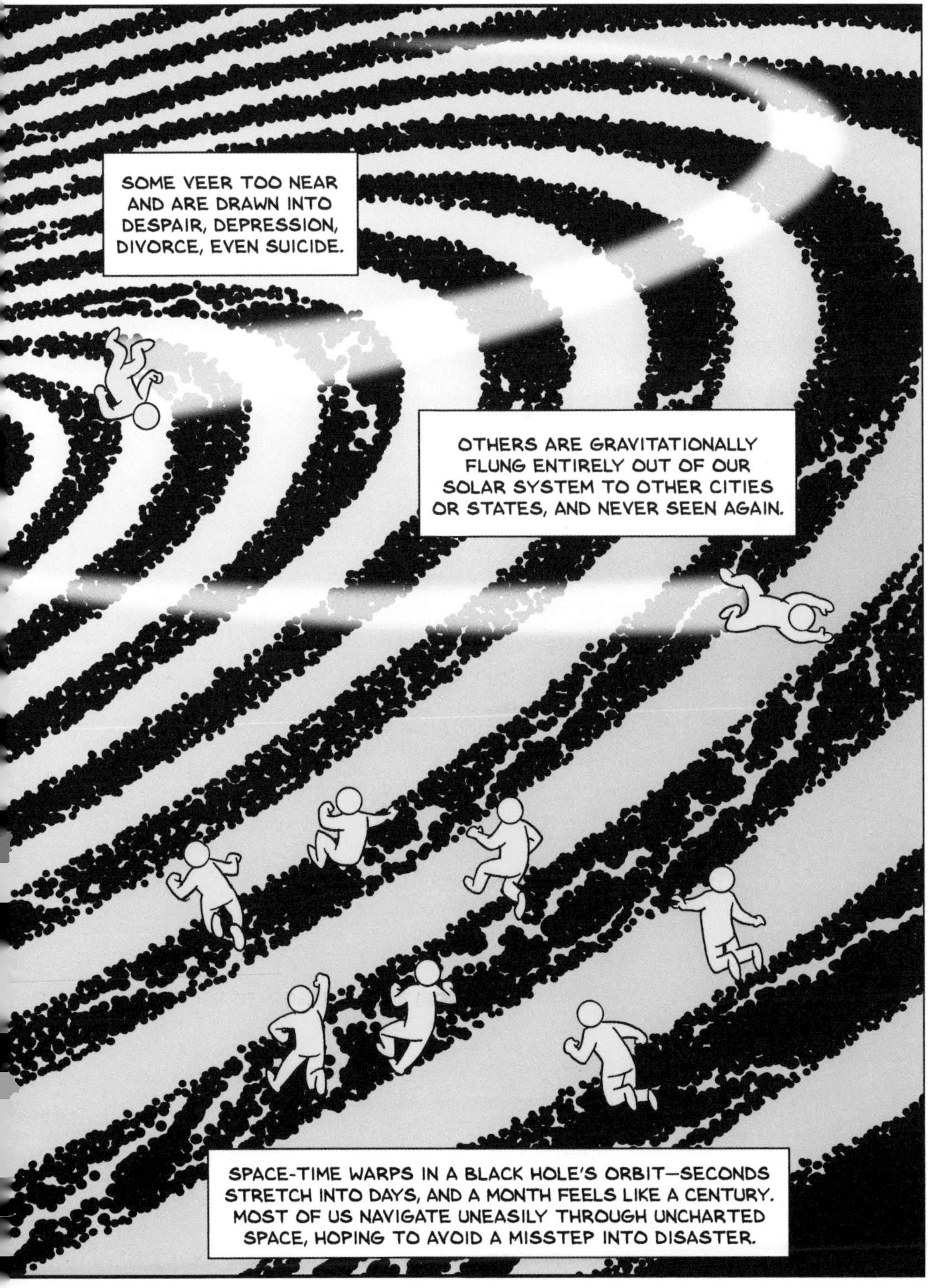
SOME VEER TOO NEAR AND ARE DRAWN INTO DESPAIR, DEPRESSION, DIVORCE, EVEN SUICIDE.
OTHERS ARE GRAVITATIONALLY FLUNG ENTIRELY OUT OF OUR SOLAR SYSTEM TO OTHER CITIES OR STATES, AND NEVER SEEN AGAIN.
SPACE-TIME WARPS IN A BLACK HOLE'S ORBIT—SECONDS STRETCH INTO DAYS, AND A MONTH FEELS LIKE A CENTURY. MOST OF US NAVIGATE UNEASILY THROUGH UNCHARTED SPACE, HOPING TO AVOID A MISSTEP INTO DISASTER.

MARY & LARRY'S FIRE STORY

LARRY TERBUSH IS RETIRED FROM A THIRTY-FIVE-YEAR CAREER WITH THE FBI. HIS WIFE, MARY, BEGAN HER CAREER AS FBI CLERICAL STAFF, WHERE SHE MET LARRY, AND RECENTLY RETIRED FROM HER JOB AS A HEALTH CLUB TRAINER. ONE OF THEIR DAUGHTERS, ERIN, IS MARRIED TO A FIREFIGHTER, HAS TWO SONS, AND LIVES A FEW MILES NORTH OF THEM. THE TERBUSHES HAD THEIR HOME FOR THIRTY YEARS.

Larry: I'd gotten up and smelled smoke. I looked out the bedroom window toward the north and saw a little bit of glow in that direction. So I called Erin. Then I looked out our bathroom window to the east, where the fire came down the creek, and it was definitely glowing. I could see the bright bright red. I woke up Mary, and we started getting our things together.

Mary: We figured we'd be back. What I find so interesting is the things you grab. I grabbed some of my mother's jewelry that was irreplaceable emotionally. But I didn't bring any clothes. Larry got a folder of important papers and the computer.

Larry: I went into the garage, got a suitcase, and threw in our binders of photos—

Mary: I grabbed those. You grabbed water.

Larry (laughing): I grabbed a flat of bottled water that was on the shelf. I had no idea what the situation was going to be. The water was right there, we had space in the car, so I threw it in.

Mary: I had tunnel vision. I never thought of anything else except let's get the stuff and just go. I don't remember being nervous or scared. I just thought: Action!

Larry: We weren't doing a lot of talking, just methodically getting things together. We're very much alike, Mary and I, and I was very pleased with how we went through the whole thing that night.

Mary: We got to Erin's and just sat. Our grandsons Jake and Trent were wide awake. Erin had completely outfitted a bedroom for us. She got the bed ready and filled the drawers with pajamas and clothes and toiletries. Nobody went to sleep, we all just sat up and waited. I started getting a lot of phone calls about 7 A.M. from my brothers calling to check on me. Lots of phone calls from cousins. A friend in Australia.

MARY IS THE NEIGHBOR I YELLED AT OVER A BAD CELL PHONE CONNECTION.

Mary: When you said, "It's all gone," I was numb. How can you picture your house being gone? But when you said, "The whole neighborhood is gone," that hurt my heart. I felt that in my chest.

LARRY AND MARY'S OTHER TWO CHILDREN, ALLISON AND MICHAEL, ARE BOTH MARRIED AND LIVE IN DUBLIN, IRELAND.

Mary: We were in constant contact with the kids in Ireland, back and forth phone calls. It was hard for them. They wanted to be here so badly, and they couldn't. As long as we talked to them every single day and kept them in the loop . . .

The fire was big news in Ireland, and the kids have many friends who approached them and asked, "Were your parents affected?" People there who knew us said, "We're so sorry to hear about your folks." I felt better knowing they were taken care of by friends.

It's still hard. They definitely realize they are so far away from what happened that they don't know exactly what it feels like. They see the photos, but it's so different to actually stand there in front of your destroyed home.

LARRY JOINED THE FBI IN 1962 AND BECAME A SPECIAL AGENT IN 1970.

Larry: The squad I worked on did domestic and international terrorism, which in the seventies in San Francisco included a lot of bombings. Our squad worked all those crime scenes.

We had a saying after a bombing: "Everything is still here, it just changed shape." Of course, a fire *consumes* so much stuff. Most bombs don't burn, they just blow things apart.

Mary: You were not daunted when you looked at our pile of a house. I looked at it and said, "There's nothing here," but you looked right at it and focused.

Larry: Everything was still there. It just changed shape.

Mary: I don't wake up in the middle of the night anymore because I talk to a guy. Not a psychologist, a life coach. I went to him because I was worried I was handling it *too* well. I actually had two very well-meaning people come up to me and say, "I think that you're not grieving properly." I said, "OK, what do you want me to do?" I thought maybe I was missing something. I *was* waking up and having a hard time getting back to sleep, replaying that night like a movie.

After chatting with him, he said we could redirect my thinking. We really got into what makes me happy, what I'm grateful for. The hardest part was for me to feel worthy. More accepting of people's help. To me, there was always somebody who had it harder. But why wouldn't I feel worthy? I just lost my house!

Larry: I wish I'd found my dad's wedding ring, and his town marshal badge. Other than that . . . I still haven't gotten around to having my credentials and service medals replaced. They will be, but for some reason it really isn't a priority.

MARY'S MOTHER, MARGARET, LIVED WITH THE TERBUSHES BEFORE HER DEATH IN 2016.

Mary: I miss the feeling of physically being in my mom's sitting room. That's gone. That room was a hub. It's not so much my things I'll miss, it's that I will no longer have that room. The week before the fire, Larry and I had our morning coffee in there and said, "This is the house we're going to live in the rest of our lives." ■

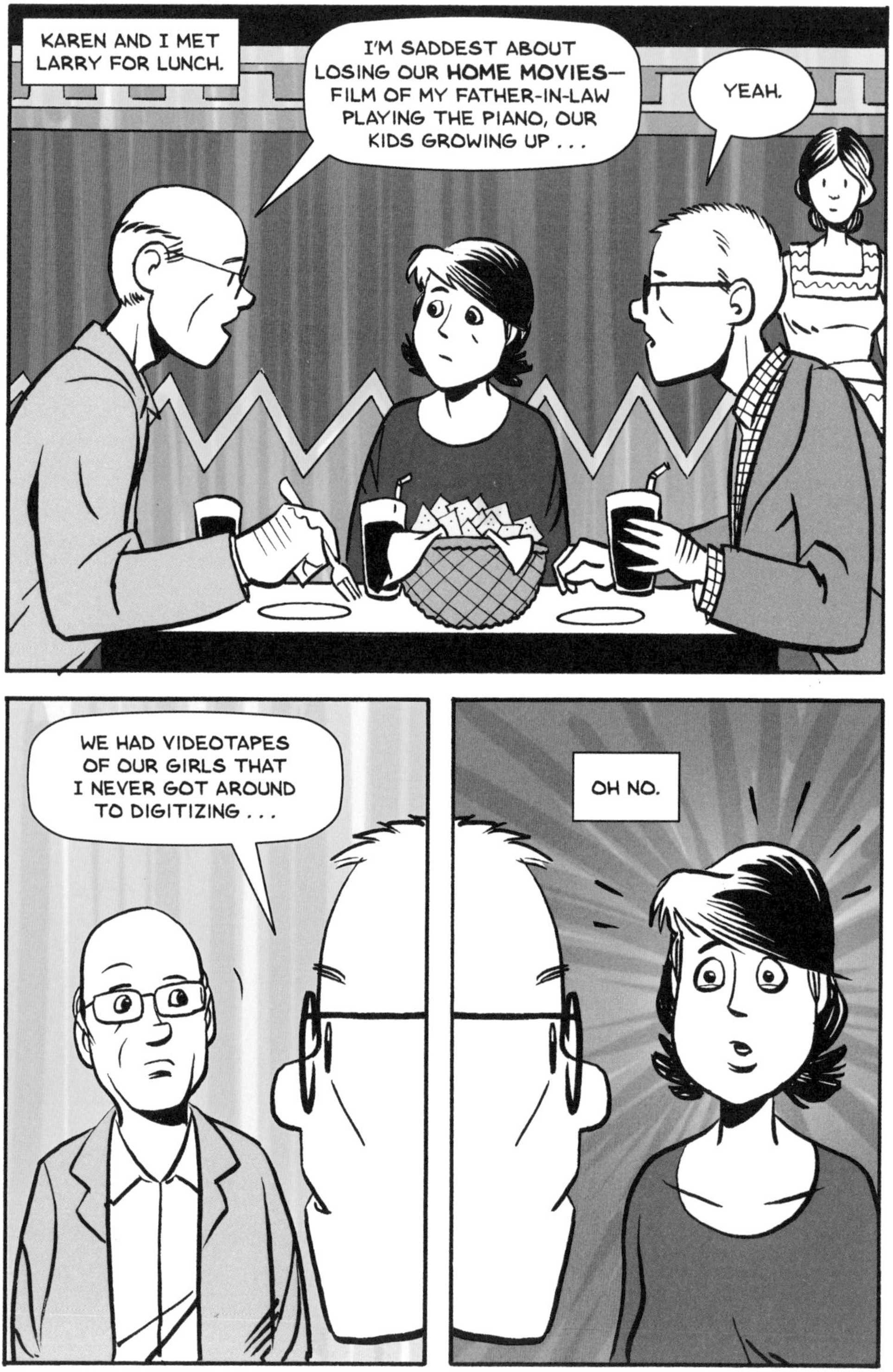
KAREN AND I MET LARRY FOR LUNCH.
I'M SADDEST ABOUT LOSING OUR **HOME MOVIES**— FILM OF MY FATHER-IN-LAW PLAYING THE PIANO, OUR KIDS GROWING UP . . .
YEAH.
WE HAD VIDEOTAPES OF OUR GIRLS THAT I NEVER GOT AROUND TO DIGITIZING . . .
OH NO.

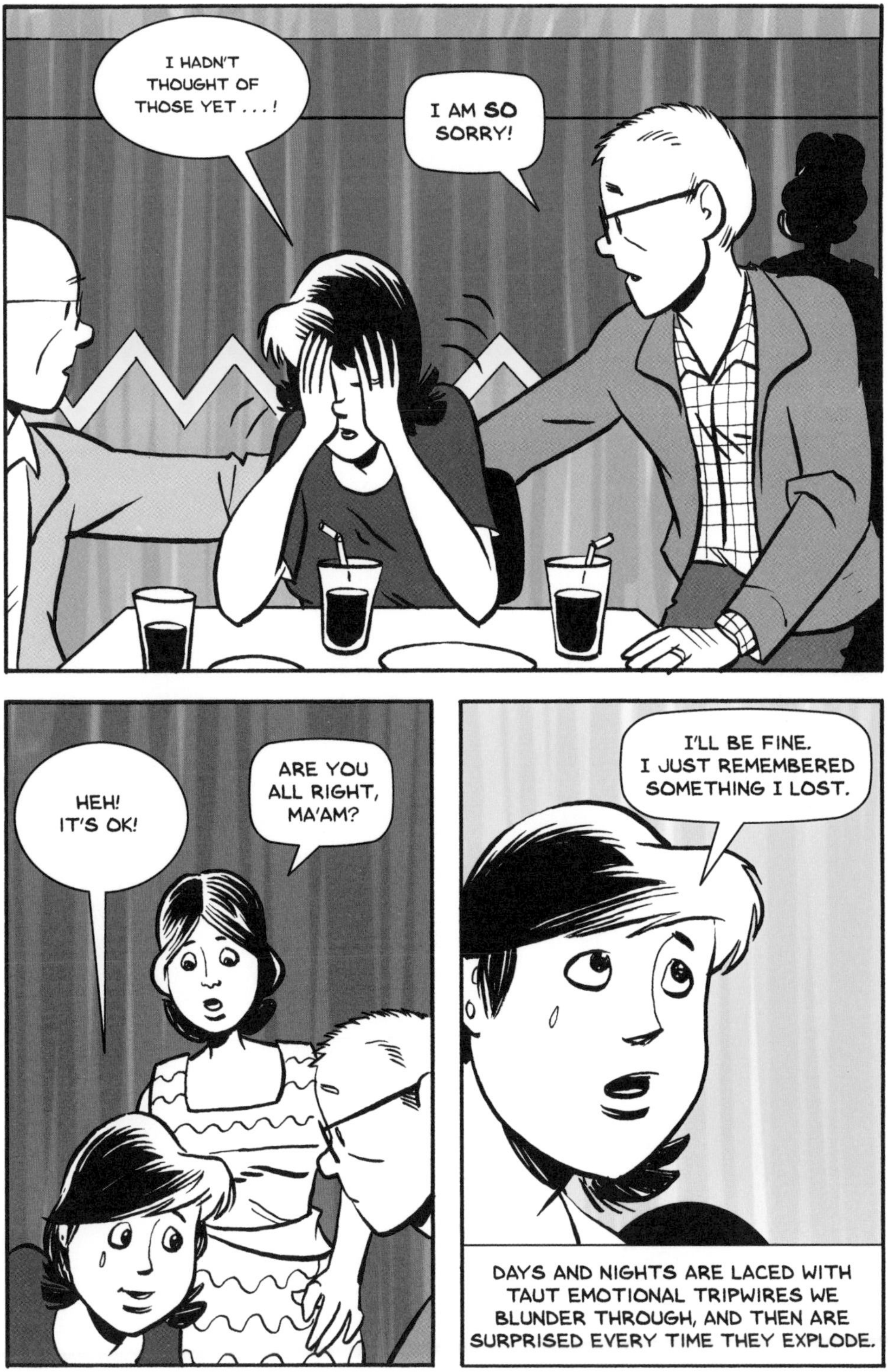
I HADN'T THOUGHT OF THOSE YET . . . !
I AM **SO** SORRY!
HEH! IT'S OK!
ARE YOU ALL RIGHT, MA'AM?
I'LL BE FINE. I JUST REMEMBERED SOMETHING I LOST.
DAYS AND NIGHTS ARE LACED WITH TAUT EMOTIONAL TRIPWIRES WE BLUNDER THROUGH, AND THEN ARE SURPRISED EVERY TIME THEY EXPLODE.

A DAY IN THE NEW LIFE

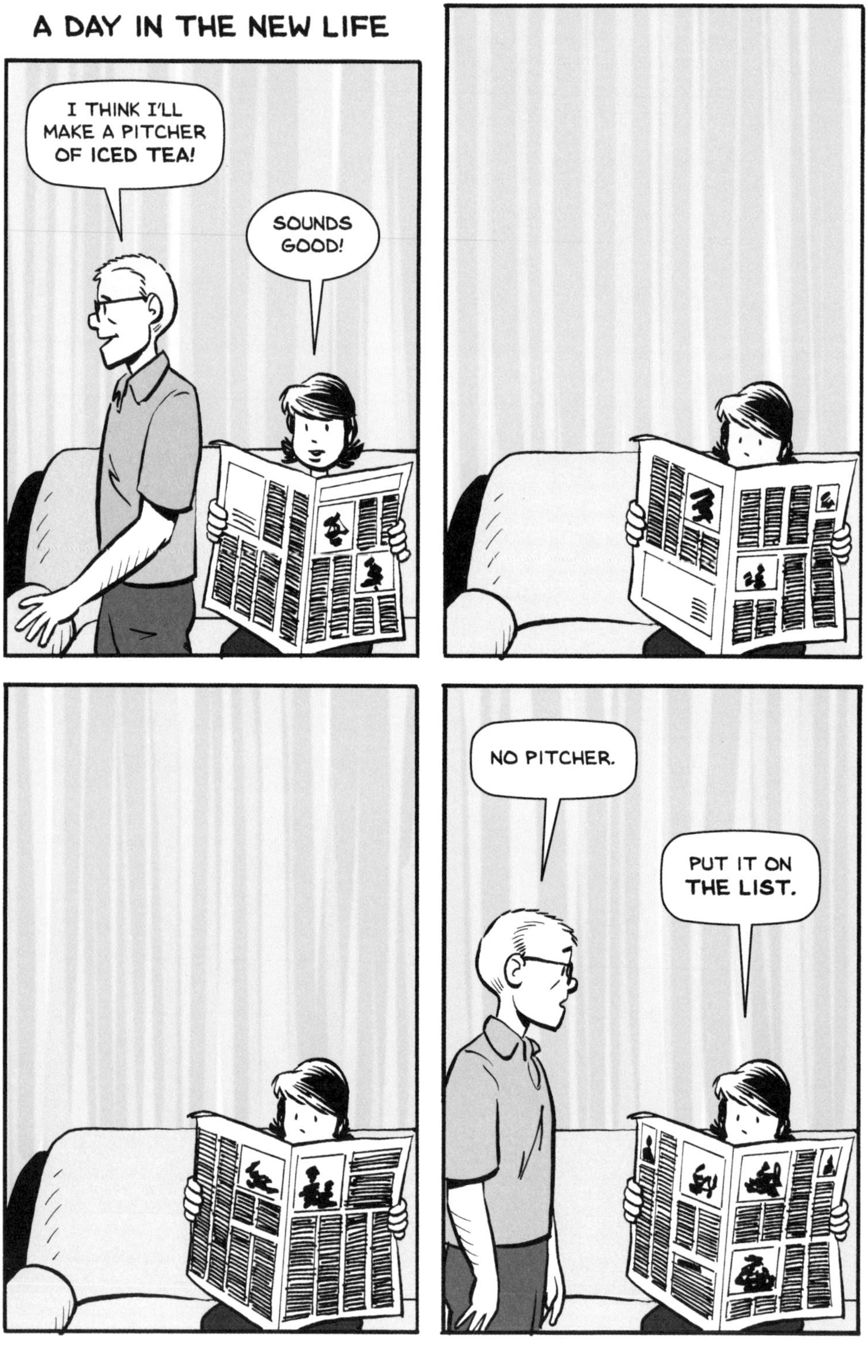
I THINK I'LL MAKE A PITCHER OF ICED TEA!
SOUNDS GOOD!
NO PITCHER.
PUT IT ON THE LIST.

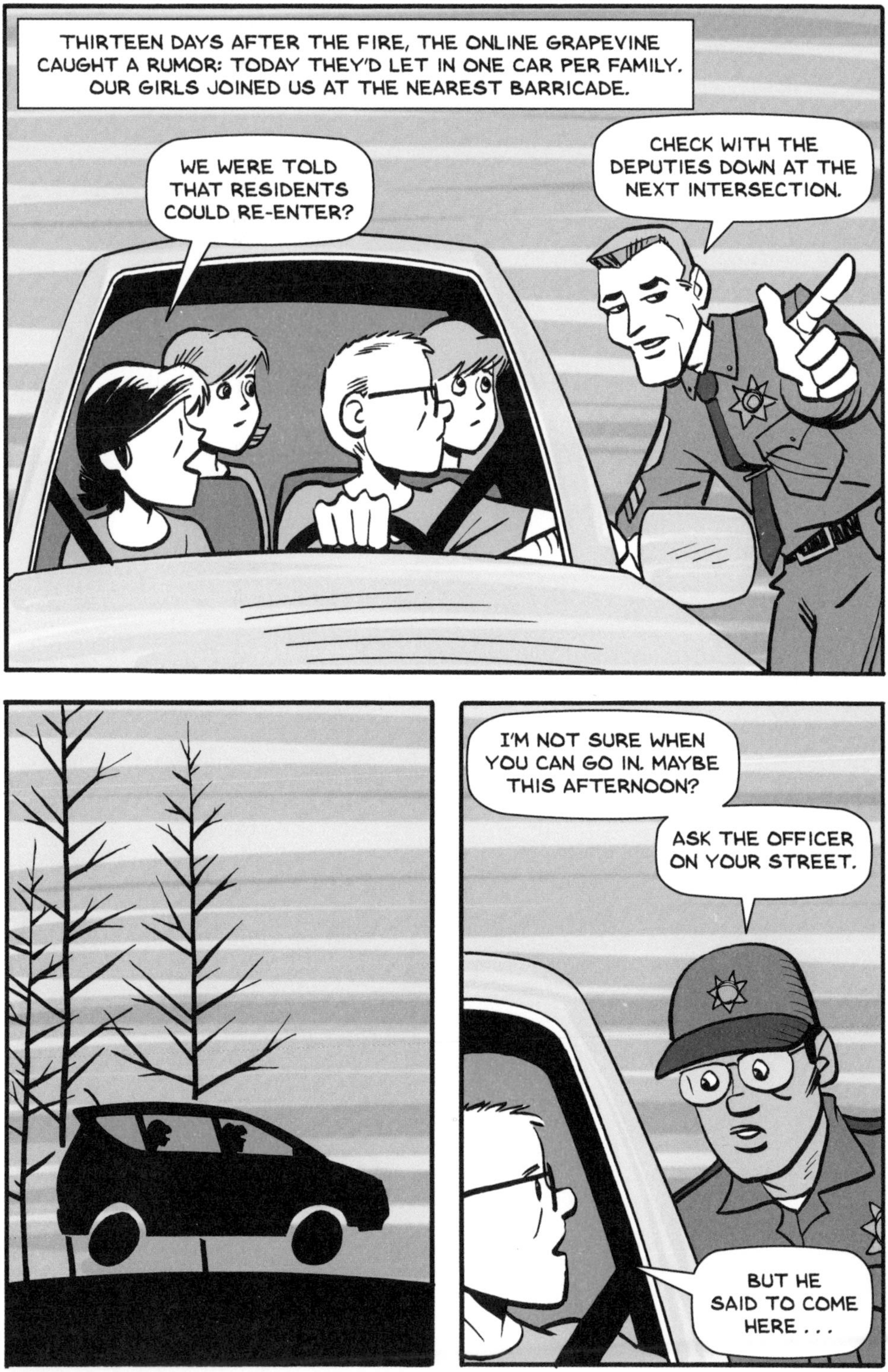
THIRTEEN DAYS AFTER THE FIRE, THE ONLINE GRAPEVINE CAUGHT A RUMOR: TODAY THEY'D LET IN ONE CAR PER FAMILY. OUR GIRLS JOINED US AT THE NEAREST BARRICADE.
WE WERE TOLD THAT RESIDENTS COULD RE-ENTER?
CHECK WITH THE DEPUTIES DOWN AT THE NEXT INTERSECTION.
I'M NOT SURE WHEN YOU CAN GO IN. MAYBE THIS AFTERNOON?
ASK THE OFFICER ON YOUR STREET.
BUT HE SAID TO COME HERE . . .

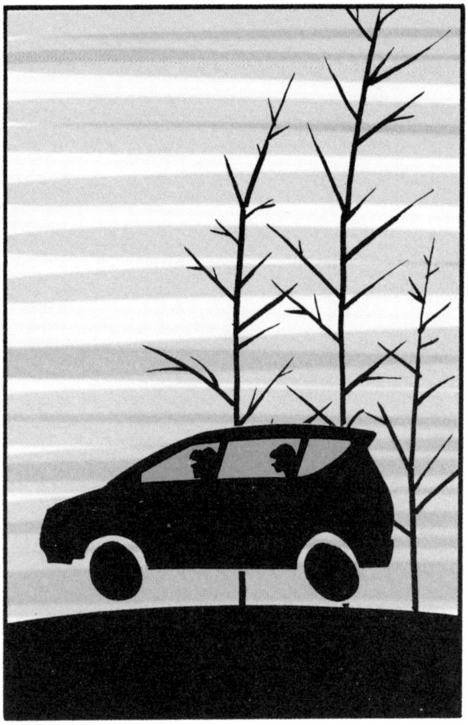

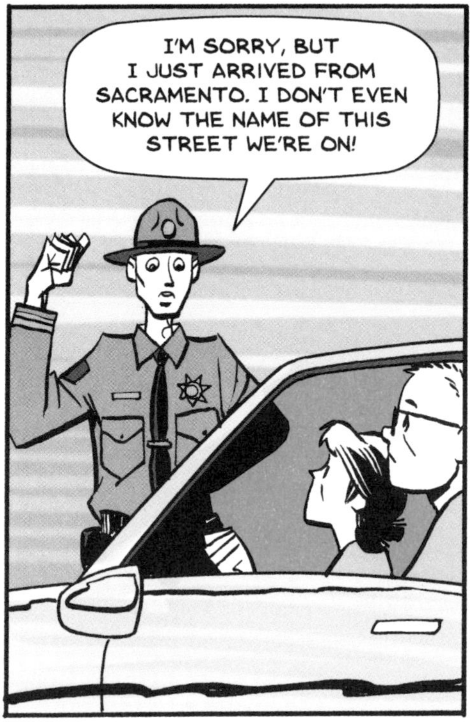
I'M SORRY, BUT I JUST ARRIVED FROM SACRAMENTO. I DON'T EVEN KNOW THE NAME OF THIS STREET WE'RE ON!

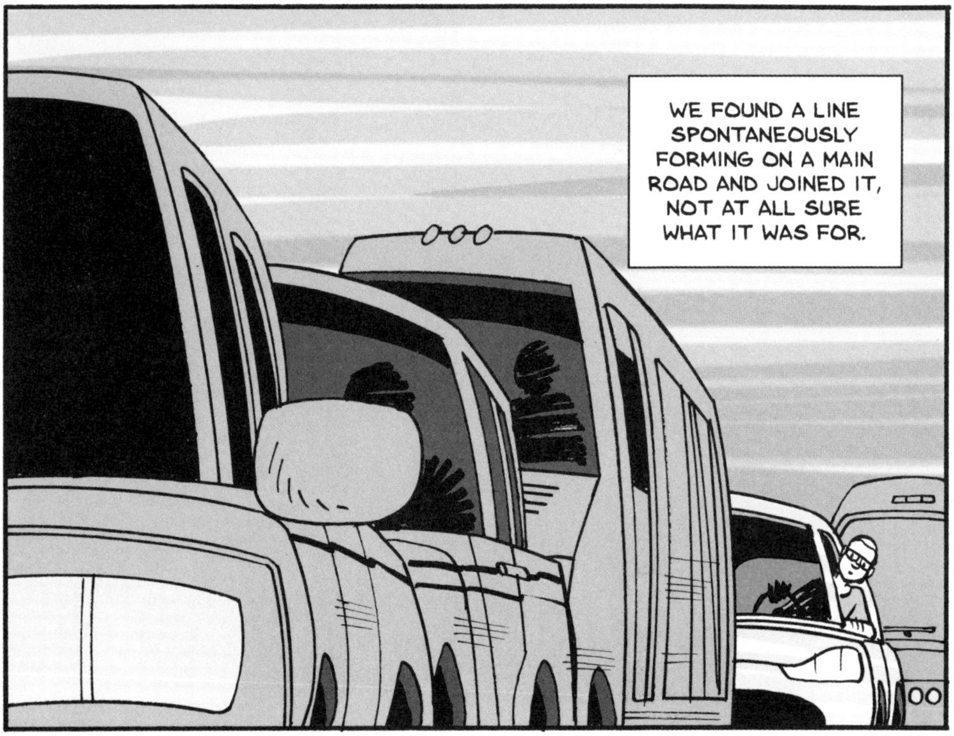
WE FOUND A LINE SPONTANEOUSLY FORMING ON A MAIN ROAD AND JOINED IT, NOT AT ALL SURE WHAT IT WAS FOR.

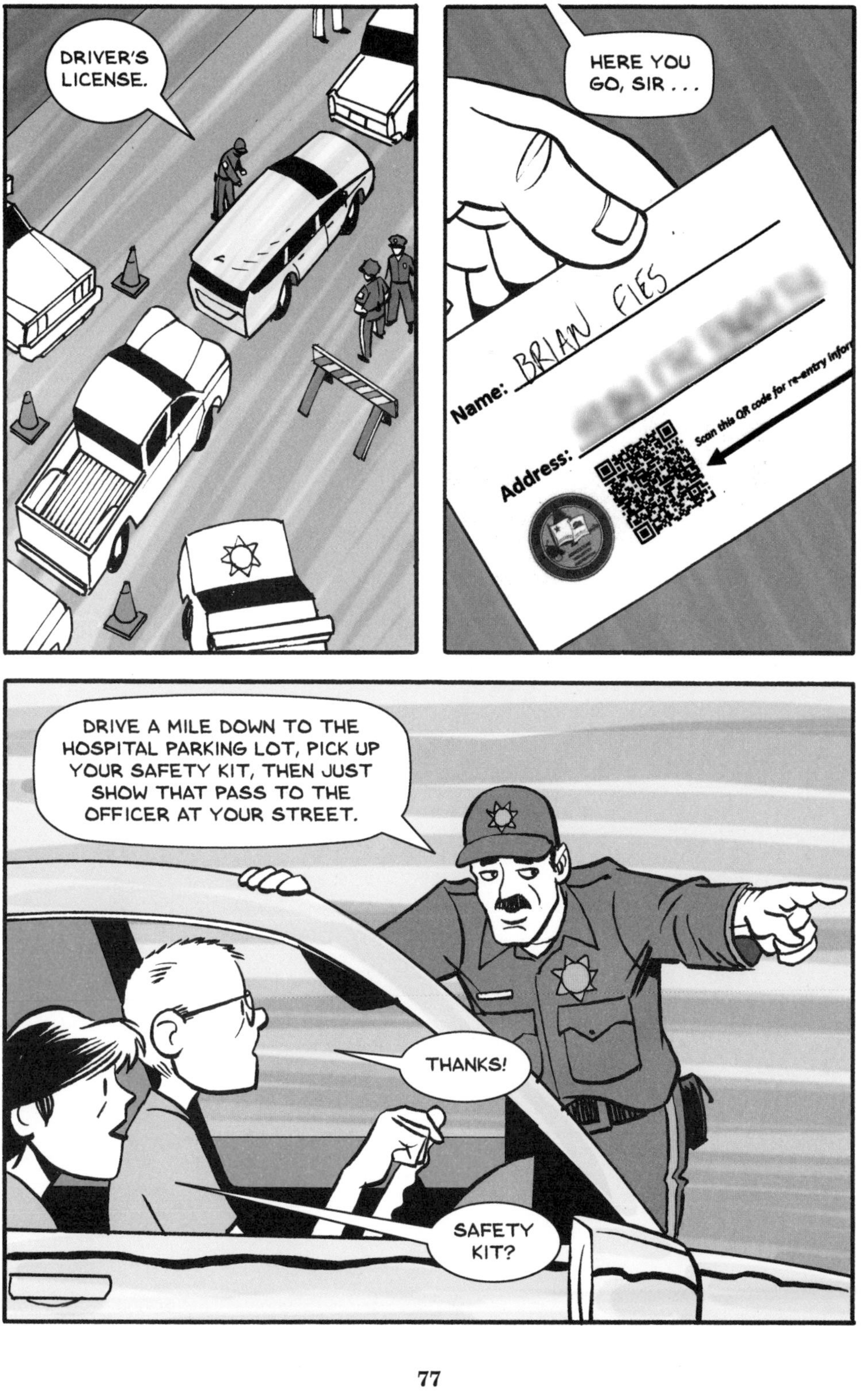
DRIVER'S LICENSE.
HERE YOU GO, SIR . . .
Name: BRIAN FIES
Address:
Scan this QR code for re-entry
DRIVE A MILE DOWN TO THE HOSPITAL PARKING LOT, PICK UP YOUR SAFETY KIT, THEN JUST SHOW THAT PASS TO THE OFFICER AT YOUR STREET.
THANKS!
SAFETY KIT?

THE KIT WAS A LARGE PLASTIC TRASH BAG THAT HELD:

ONE PAIR OF TYVEK COVERALLS AND SHOE COVERS PER PERSON

ONE DUST MASK PER PERSON

ONE PAIR OF LATEX GLOVES PER PERSON

ONE BOTTLE OF WATER PER PERSON

ONE BOOK ON DISASTER RECOVERY WE'D ALREADY BEEN GIVEN SEVERAL COPIES OF

THREE PAGES OF INSTRUCTIONS ON HANDLING HAZARDOUS WASTE

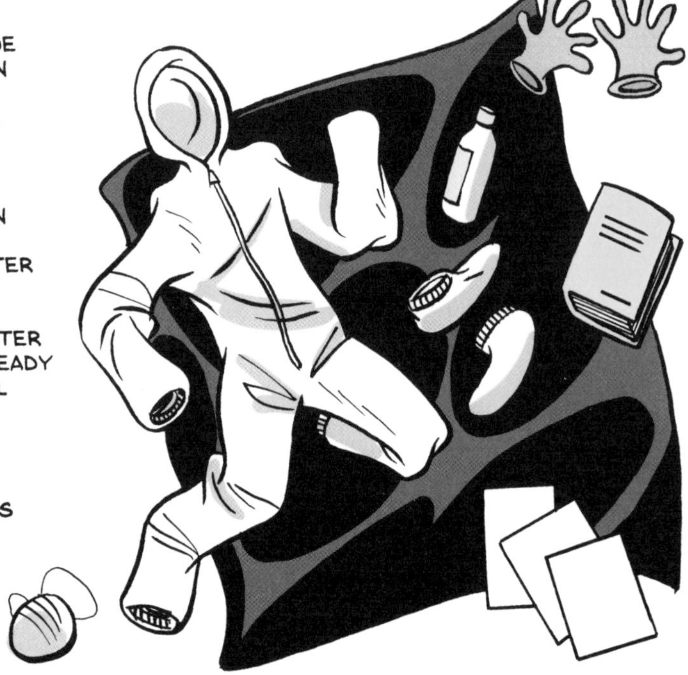

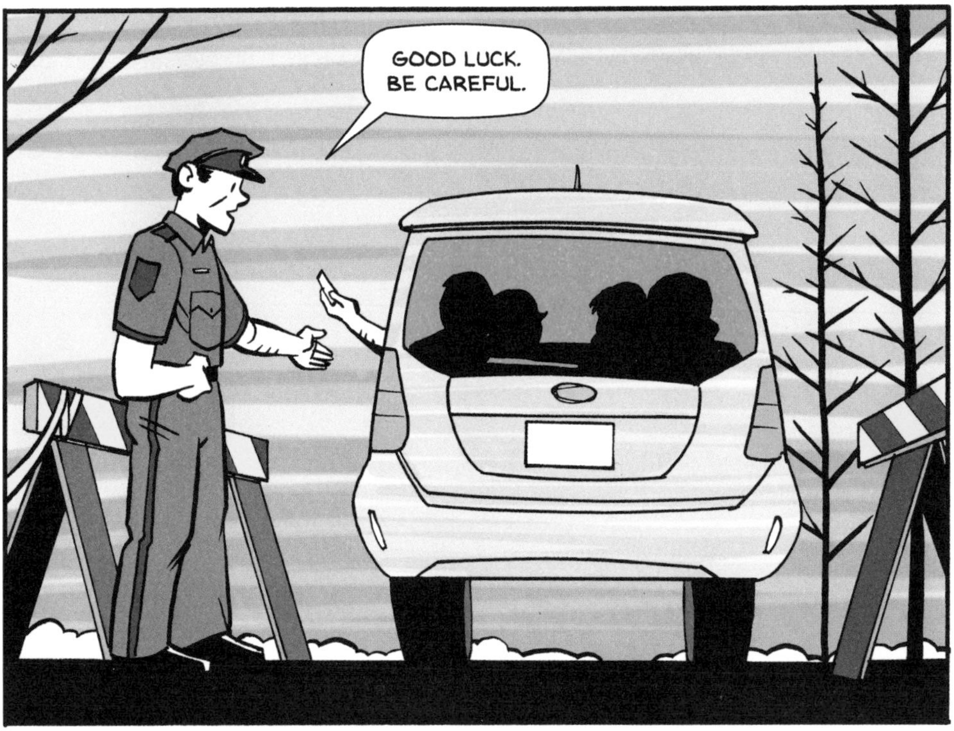
GOOD LUCK. BE CAREFUL.

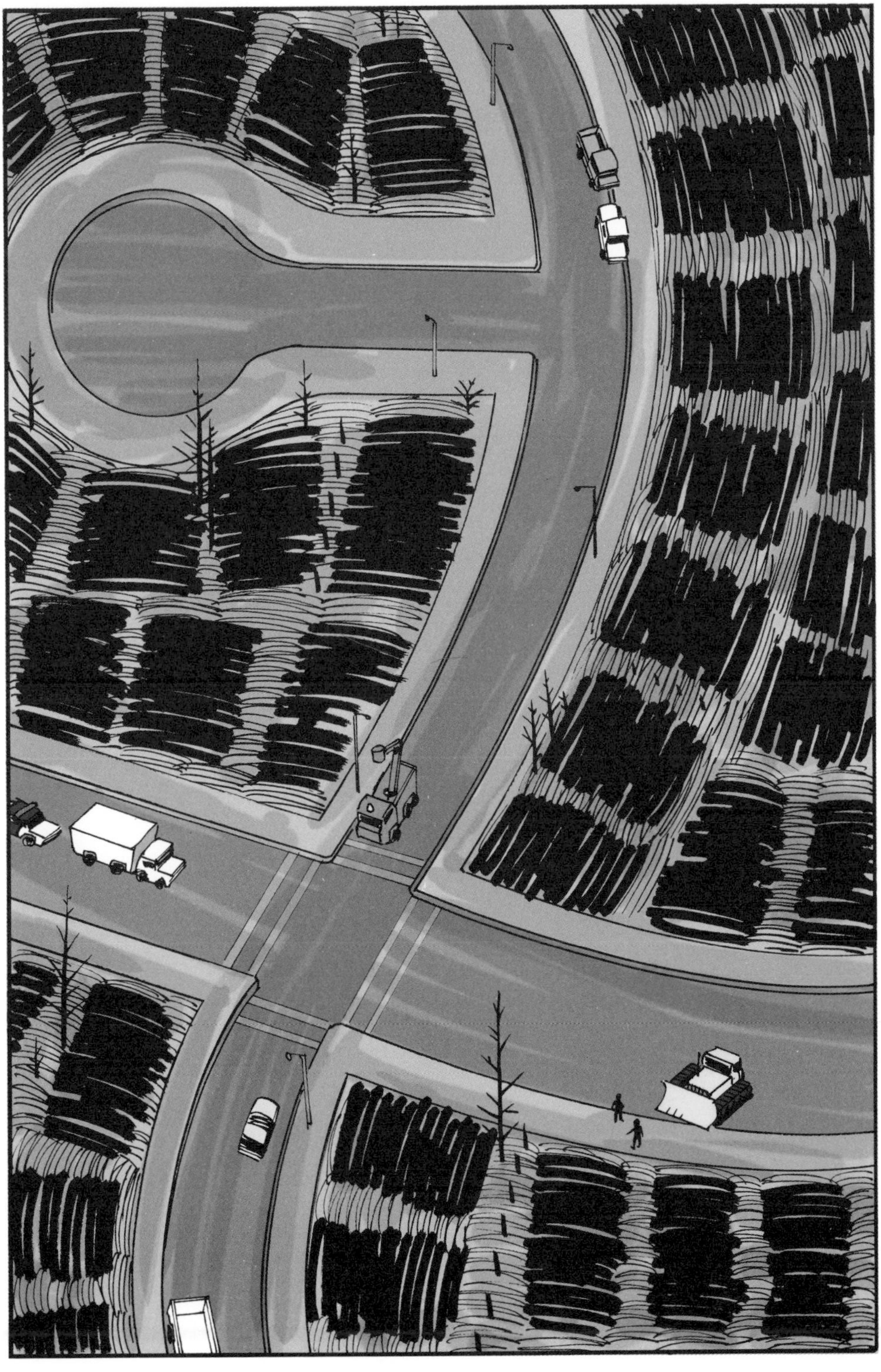

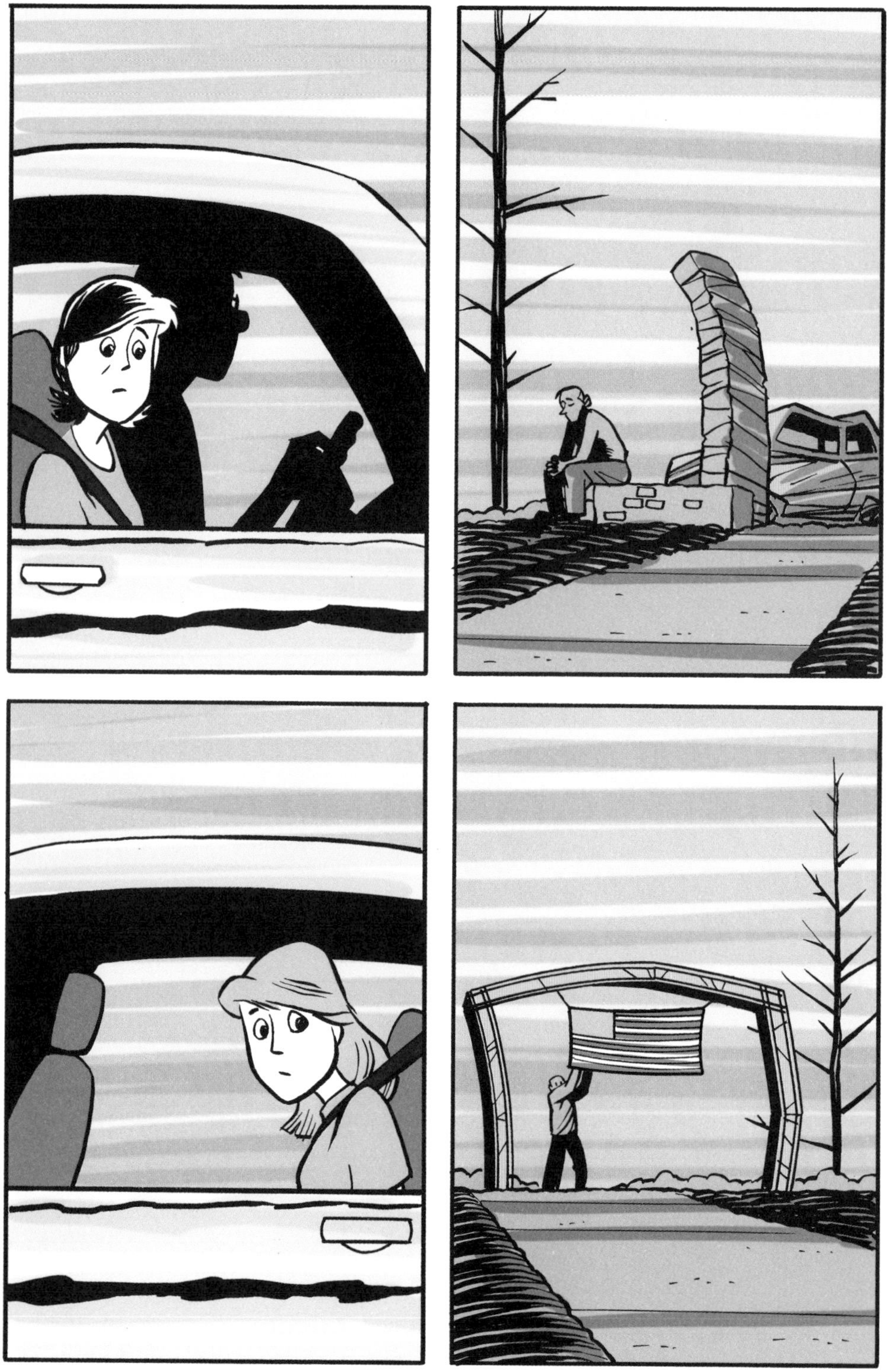

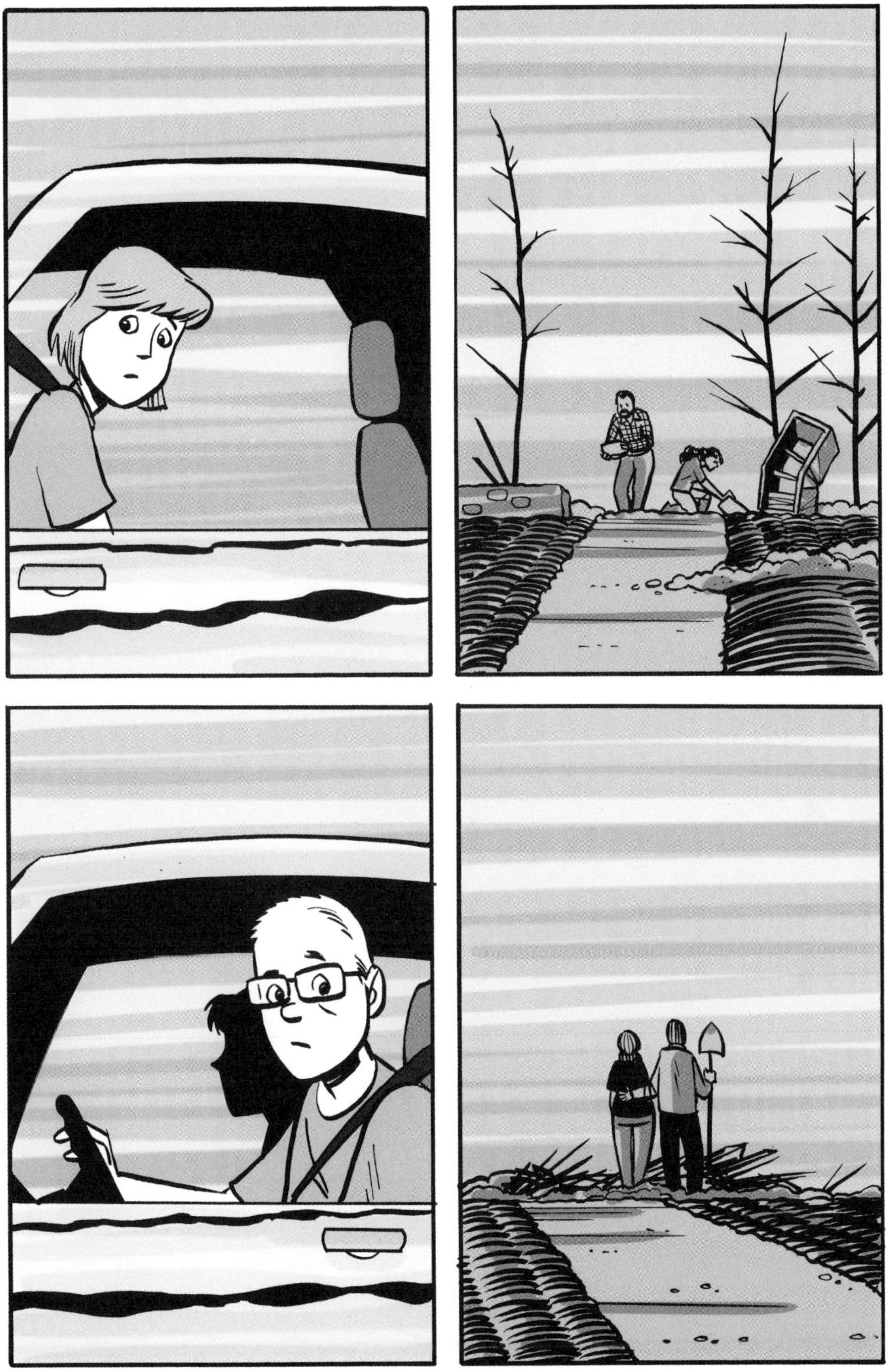

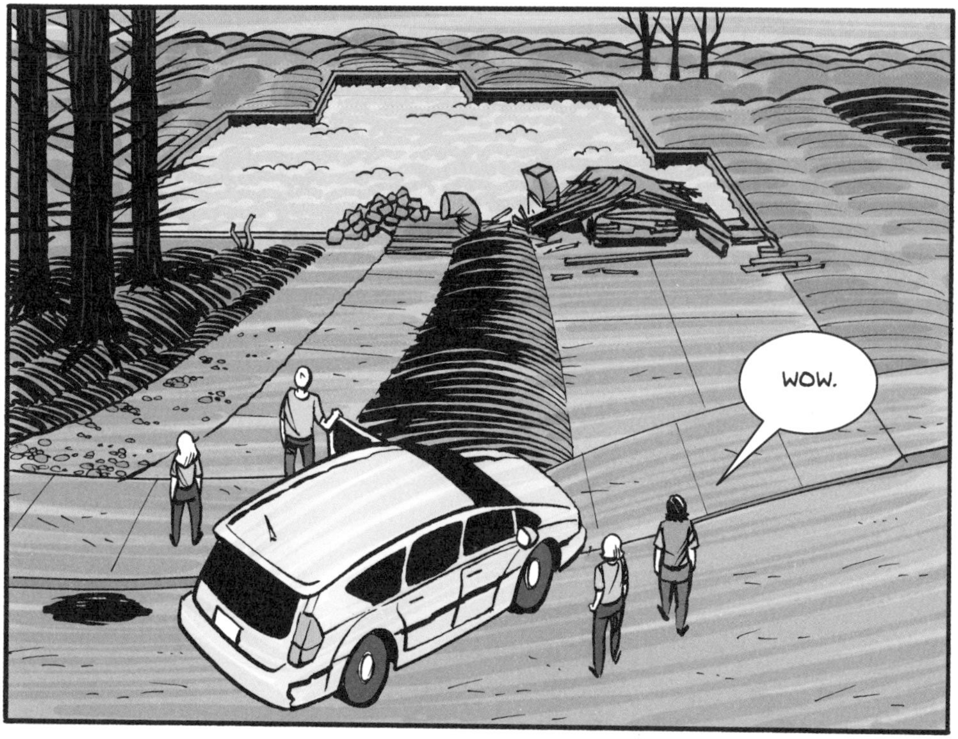
WOW.

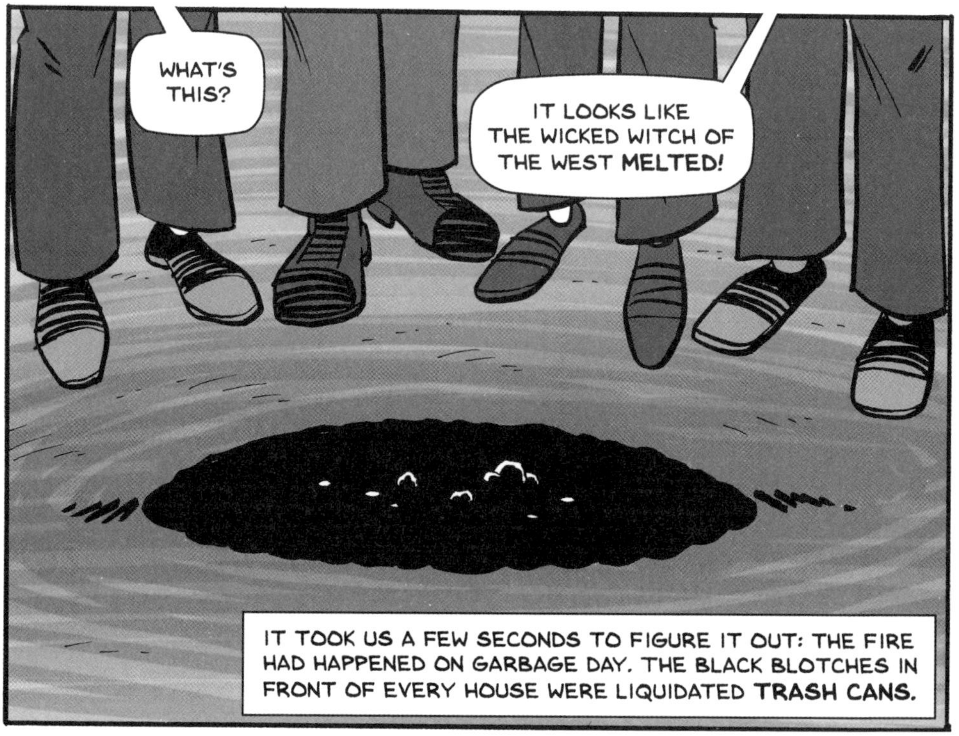
WHAT'S THIS?
IT LOOKS LIKE THE WICKED WITCH OF THE WEST MELTED!
IT TOOK US A FEW SECONDS TO FIGURE IT OUT: THE FIRE HAD HAPPENED ON GARBAGE DAY. THE BLACK BLOTCHES IN FRONT OF EVERY HOUSE WERE LIQUIDATED TRASH CANS.

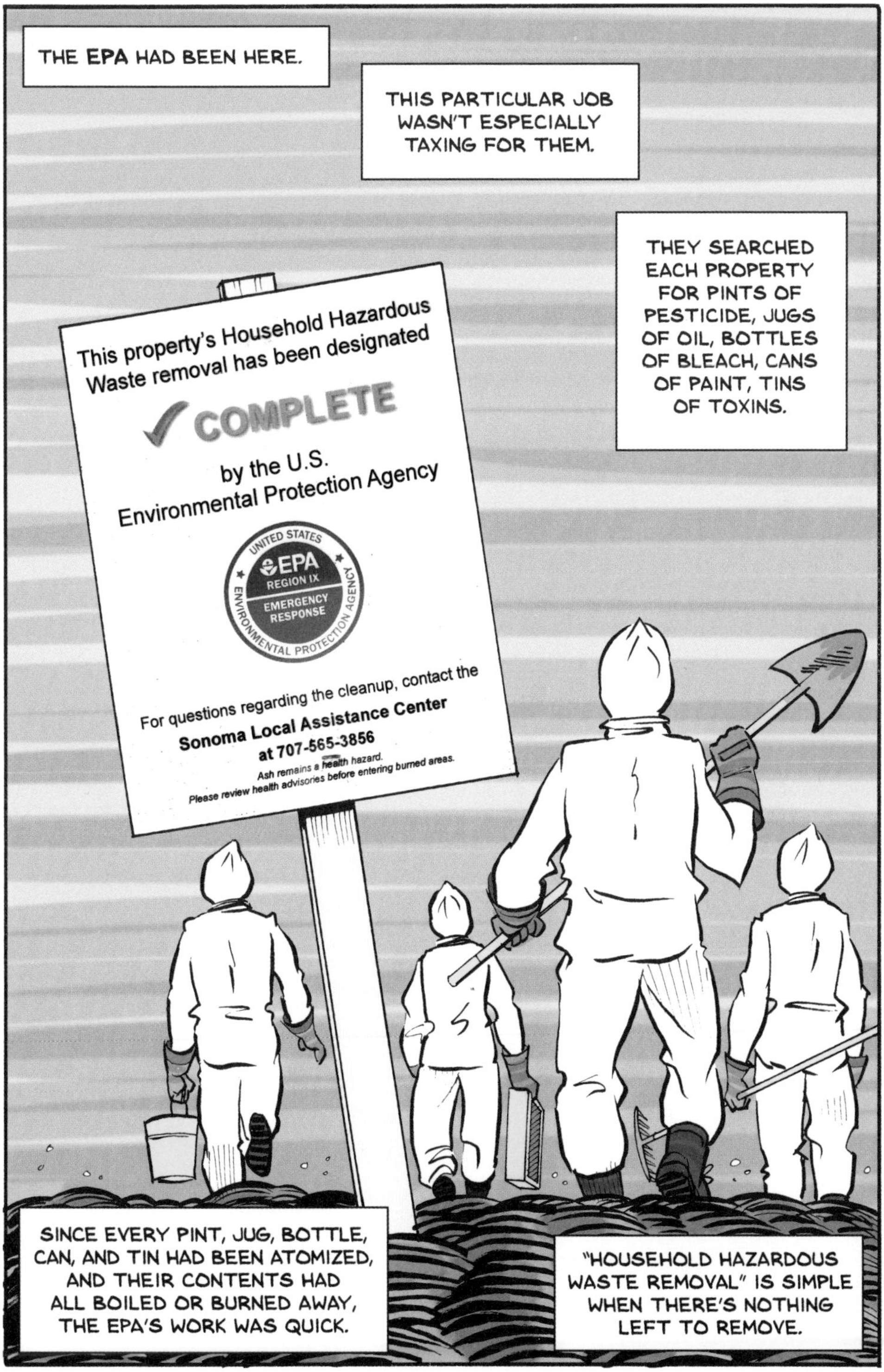
THE EPA HAD BEEN HERE.
THIS PARTICULAR JOB WASN'T ESPECIALLY TAXING FOR THEM.
THEY SEARCHED EACH PROPERTY FOR PINTS OF PESTICIDE, JUGS OF OIL, BOTTLES OF BLEACH, CANS OF PAINT, TINS OF TOXINS.
This property's Household Hazardous Waste removal has been designated
COMPLETE
by the U.S. Environmental Protection Agency
UNITED STATES EPA REGION IX EMERGENCY RESPONSE ENVIRONMENTAL PROTECTION AGENCY
For questions regarding the cleanup, contact the Sonoma Local Assistance Center at 707-565-3856
Ash remains a health hazard. Please review health advisories before entering burned areas.
SINCE EVERY PINT, JUG, BOTTLE, CAN, AND TIN HAD BEEN ATOMIZED, AND THEIR CONTENTS HAD ALL BOILED OR BURNED AWAY, THE EPA'S WORK WAS QUICK.
"HOUSEHOLD HAZARDOUS WASTE REMOVAL" IS SIMPLE WHEN THERE'S NOTHING LEFT TO REMOVE.

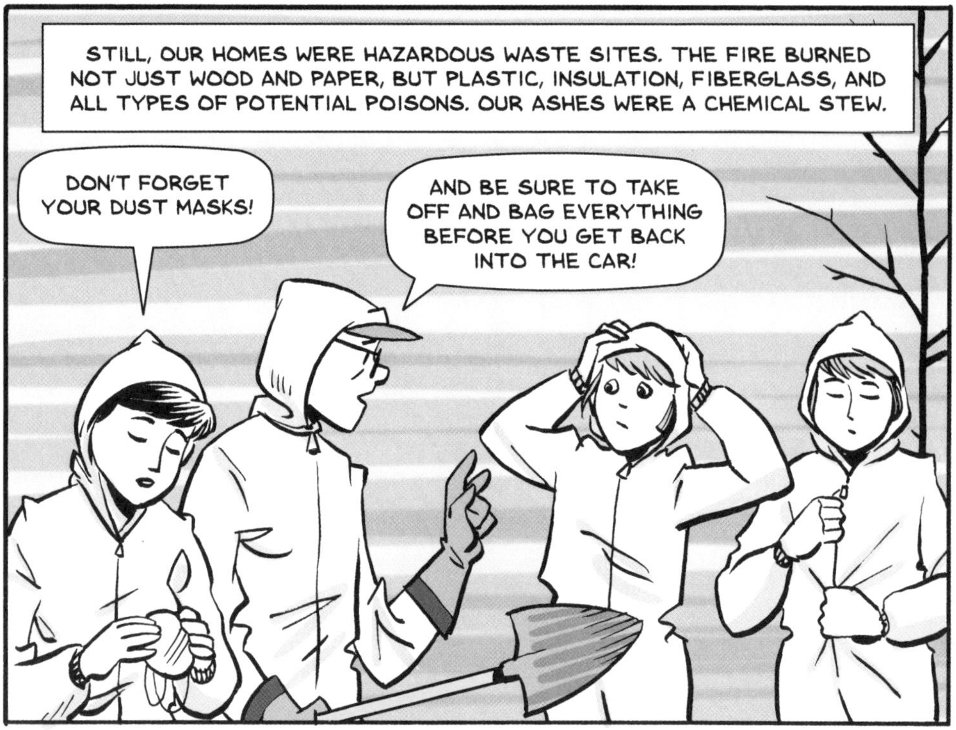
STILL, OUR HOMES WERE HAZARDOUS WASTE SITES. THE FIRE BURNED NOT JUST WOOD AND PAPER, BUT PLASTIC, INSULATION, FIBERGLASS, AND ALL TYPES OF POTENTIAL POISONS. OUR ASHES WERE A CHEMICAL STEW.
DON'T FORGET YOUR DUST MASKS!
AND BE SURE TO TAKE OFF AND BAG EVERYTHING BEFORE YOU GET BACK INTO THE CAR!

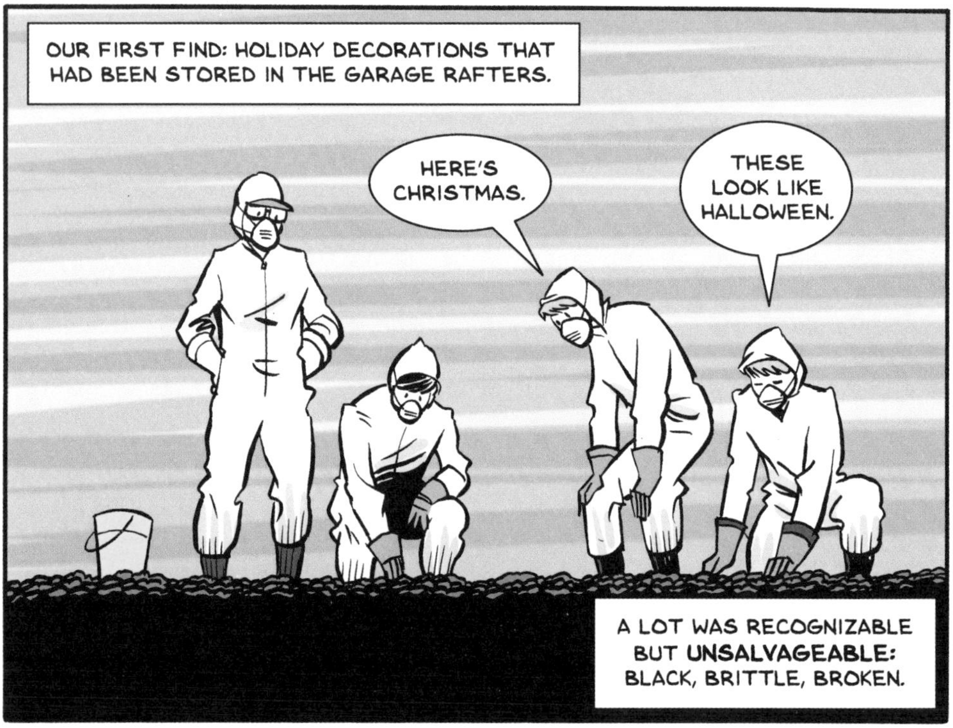
OUR FIRST FIND: HOLIDAY DECORATIONS THAT HAD BEEN STORED IN THE GARAGE RAFTERS.
HERE'S CHRISTMAS.
THESE LOOK LIKE HALLOWEEN.
A LOT WAS RECOGNIZABLE BUT **UNSALVAGEABLE:** BLACK, BRITTLE, BROKEN.

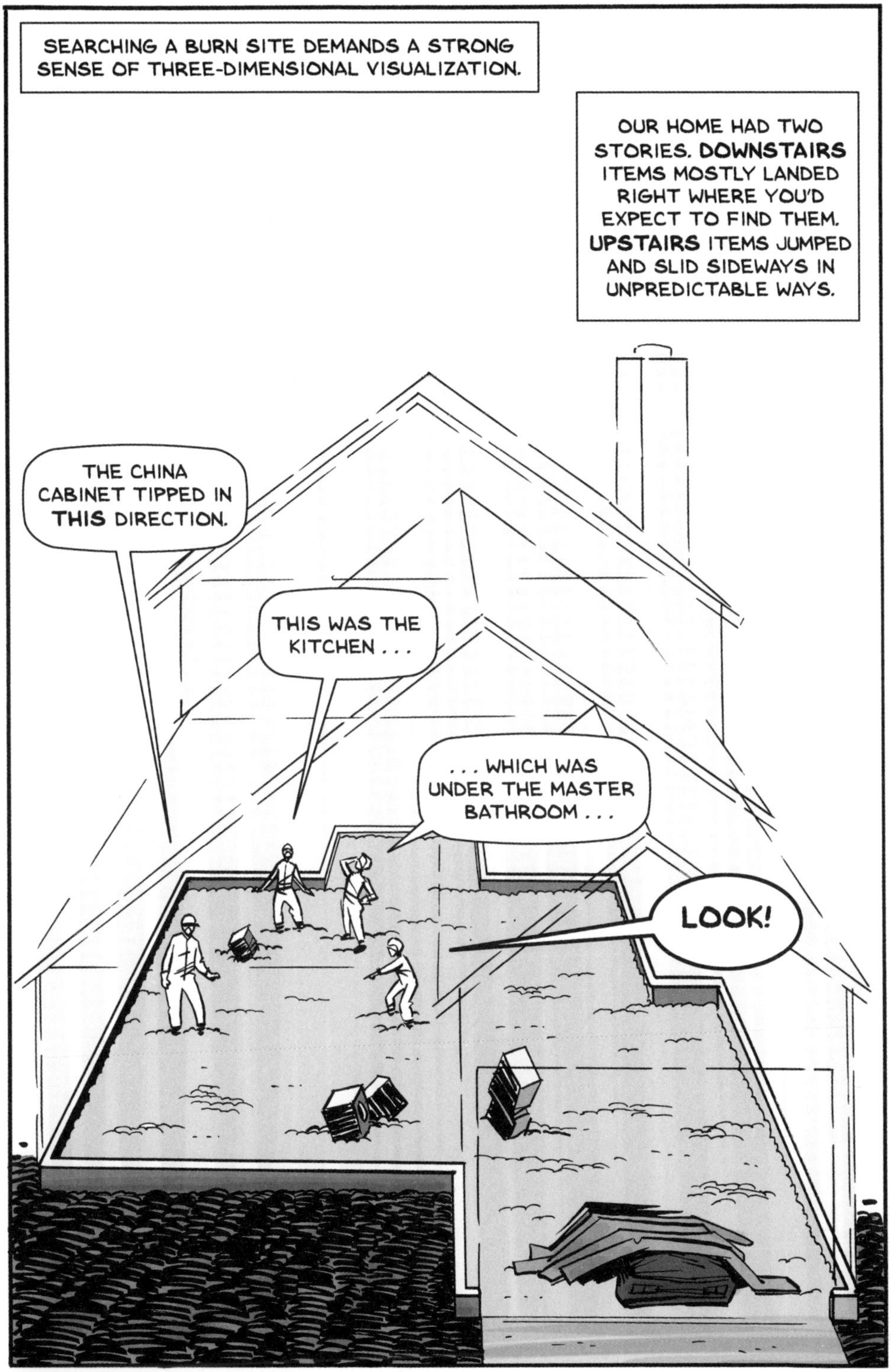
SEARCHING A BURN SITE DEMANDS A STRONG SENSE OF THREE-DIMENSIONAL VISUALIZATION.
OUR HOME HAD TWO STORIES. **DOWNSTAIRS** ITEMS MOSTLY LANDED RIGHT WHERE YOU'D EXPECT TO FIND THEM. **UPSTAIRS** ITEMS JUMPED AND SLID SIDEWAYS IN UNPREDICTABLE WAYS.
THE CHINA CABINET TIPPED IN **THIS** DIRECTION.
THIS WAS THE KITCHEN . . .
. . . WHICH WAS UNDER THE MASTER BATHROOM . . .
LOOK!

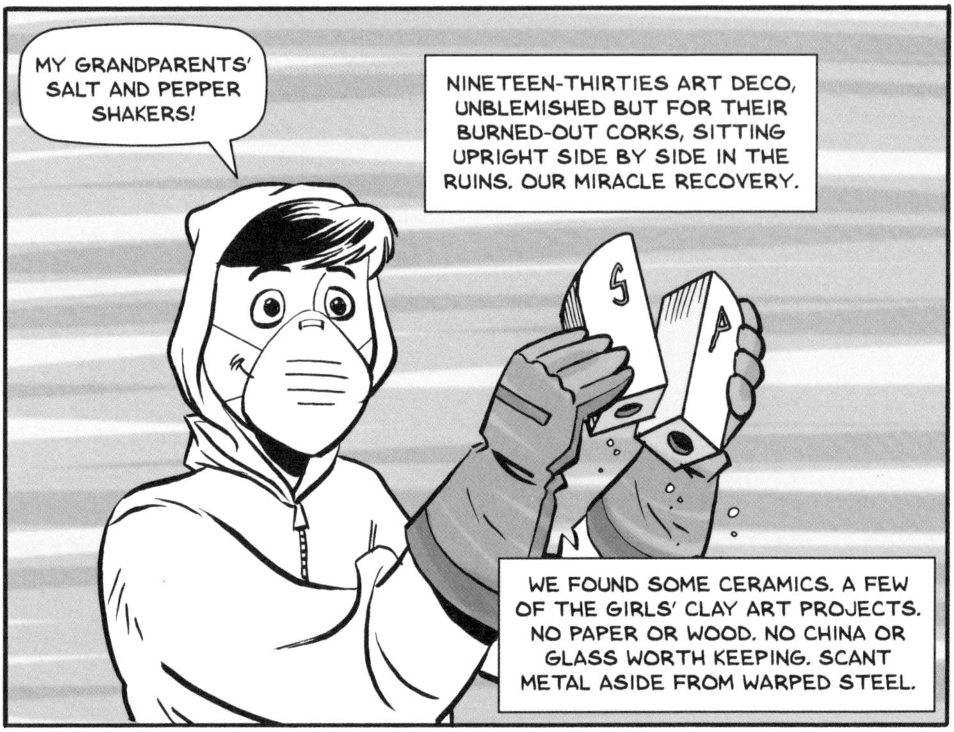
MY GRANDPARENTS' SALT AND PEPPER SHAKERS!
NINETEEN-THIRTIES ART DECO, UNBLEMISHED BUT FOR THEIR BURNED-OUT CORKS, SITTING UPRIGHT SIDE BY SIDE IN THE RUINS. OUR MIRACLE RECOVERY.
S
P
WE FOUND SOME CERAMICS. A FEW OF THE GIRLS' CLAY ART PROJECTS. NO PAPER OR WOOD. NO CHINA OR GLASS WORTH KEEPING. SCANT METAL ASIDE FROM WARPED STEEL.

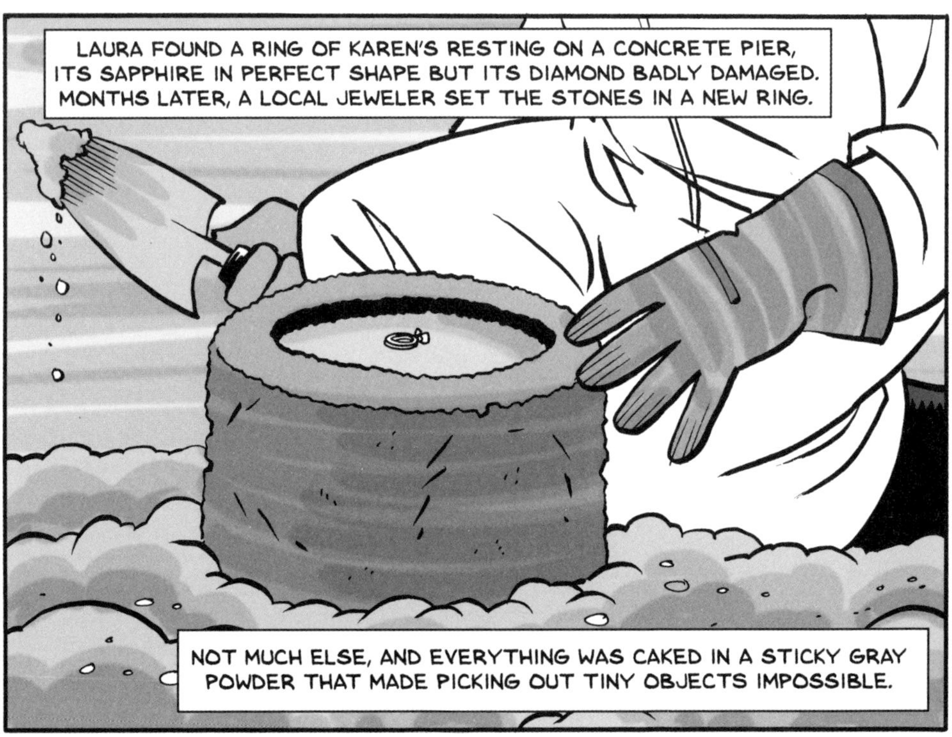
LAURA FOUND A RING OF KAREN'S RESTING ON A CONCRETE PIER, ITS SAPPHIRE IN PERFECT SHAPE BUT ITS DIAMOND BADLY DAMAGED. MONTHS LATER, A LOCAL JEWELER SET THE STONES IN A NEW RING.
NOT MUCH ELSE, AND EVERYTHING WAS CAKED IN A STICKY GRAY POWDER THAT MADE PICKING OUT TINY OBJECTS IMPOSSIBLE.

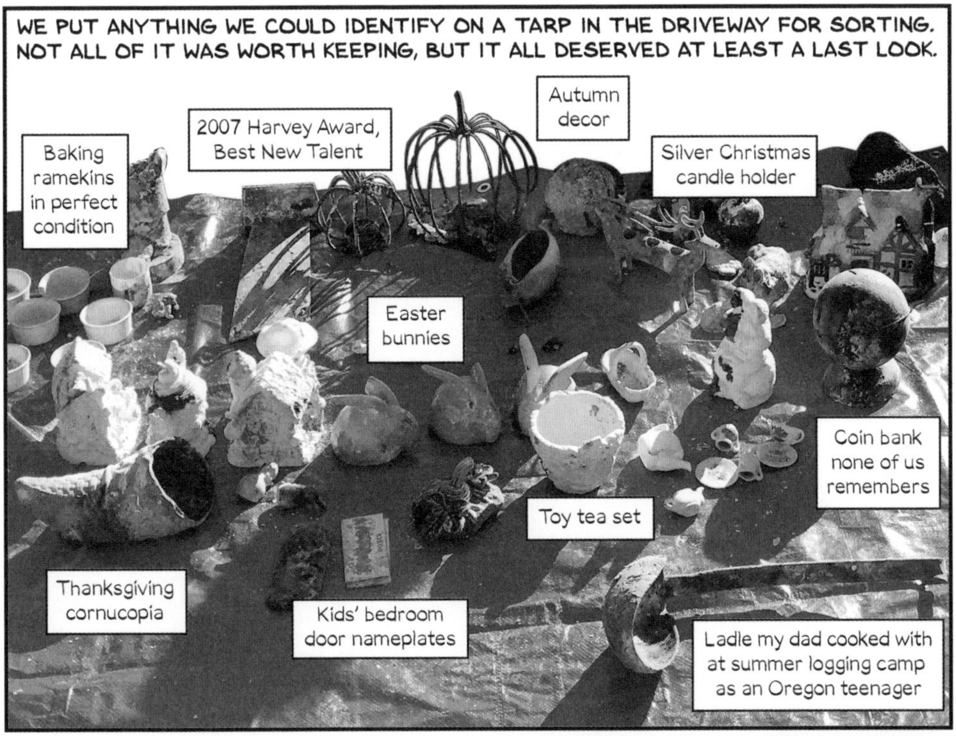
WE PUT ANYTHING WE COULD IDENTIFY ON A TARP IN THE DRIVEWAY FOR SORTING. NOT ALL OF IT WAS WORTH KEEPING, BUT IT ALL DESERVED AT LEAST A LAST LOOK.
Baking ramekins in perfect condition
2007 Harvey Award, Best New Talent
Autumn decor
Silver Christmas candle holder
Easter bunnies
Coin bank none of us remembers
Toy tea set
Thanksgiving cornucopia
Kids' bedroom door nameplates
Ladle my dad cooked with at summer logging camp as an Oregon teenager

MY SECOND GRAPHIC NOVEL WAS TITLED *WHATEVER HAPPENED TO THE WORLD OF TOMORROW?* WE WENT TO QUITE A BIT OF EFFORT TO PRINT IT ON **TWO** TYPES OF PAPER:

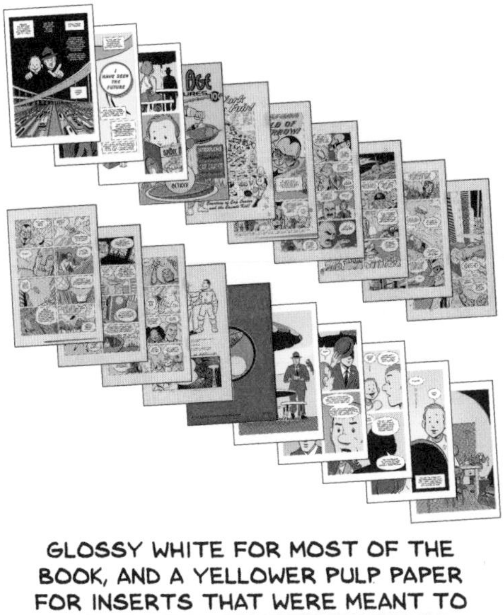

GLOSSY WHITE FOR MOST OF THE BOOK, AND A YELLOWER PULP PAPER FOR INSERTS THAT WERE MEANT TO LOOK LIKE OLD COMIC-BOOK PAGES.

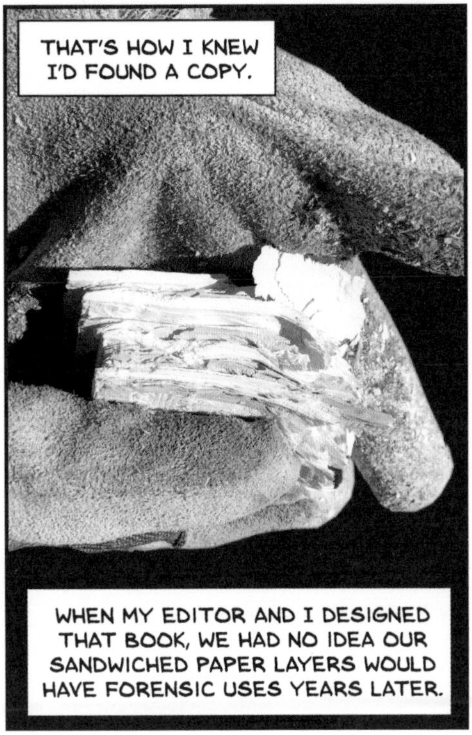
THAT'S HOW I KNEW I'D FOUND A COPY.
WHEN MY EDITOR AND I DESIGNED THAT BOOK, WE HAD NO IDEA OUR SANDWICHED PAPER LAYERS WOULD HAVE FORENSIC USES YEARS LATER.

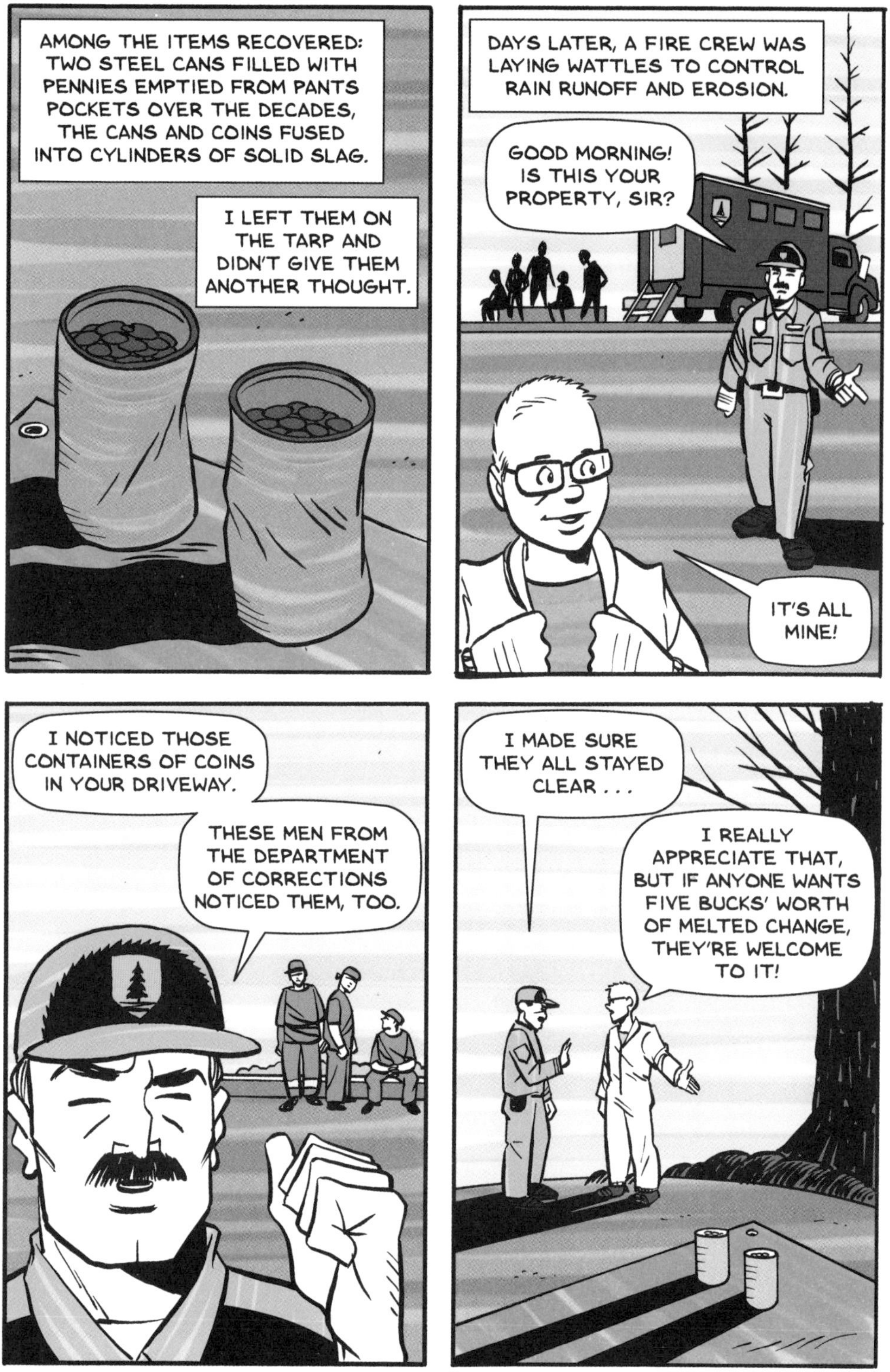
AMONG THE ITEMS RECOVERED: TWO STEEL CANS FILLED WITH PENNIES EMPTIED FROM PANTS POCKETS OVER THE DECADES, THE CANS AND COINS FUSED INTO CYLINDERS OF SOLID SLAG.
I LEFT THEM ON THE TARP AND DIDN'T GIVE THEM ANOTHER THOUGHT.
DAYS LATER, A FIRE CREW WAS LAYING WATTLES TO CONTROL RAIN RUNOFF AND EROSION.
GOOD MORNING! IS THIS YOUR PROPERTY, SIR?
IT'S ALL MINE!
I NOTICED THOSE CONTAINERS OF COINS IN YOUR DRIVEWAY.
THESE MEN FROM THE DEPARTMENT OF CORRECTIONS NOTICED THEM, TOO.
I MADE SURE THEY ALL STAYED CLEAR . . .
I REALLY APPRECIATE THAT, BUT IF ANYONE WANTS FIVE BUCKS' WORTH OF MELTED CHANGE, THEY'RE WELCOME TO IT!

A DAY IN THE NEW LIFE

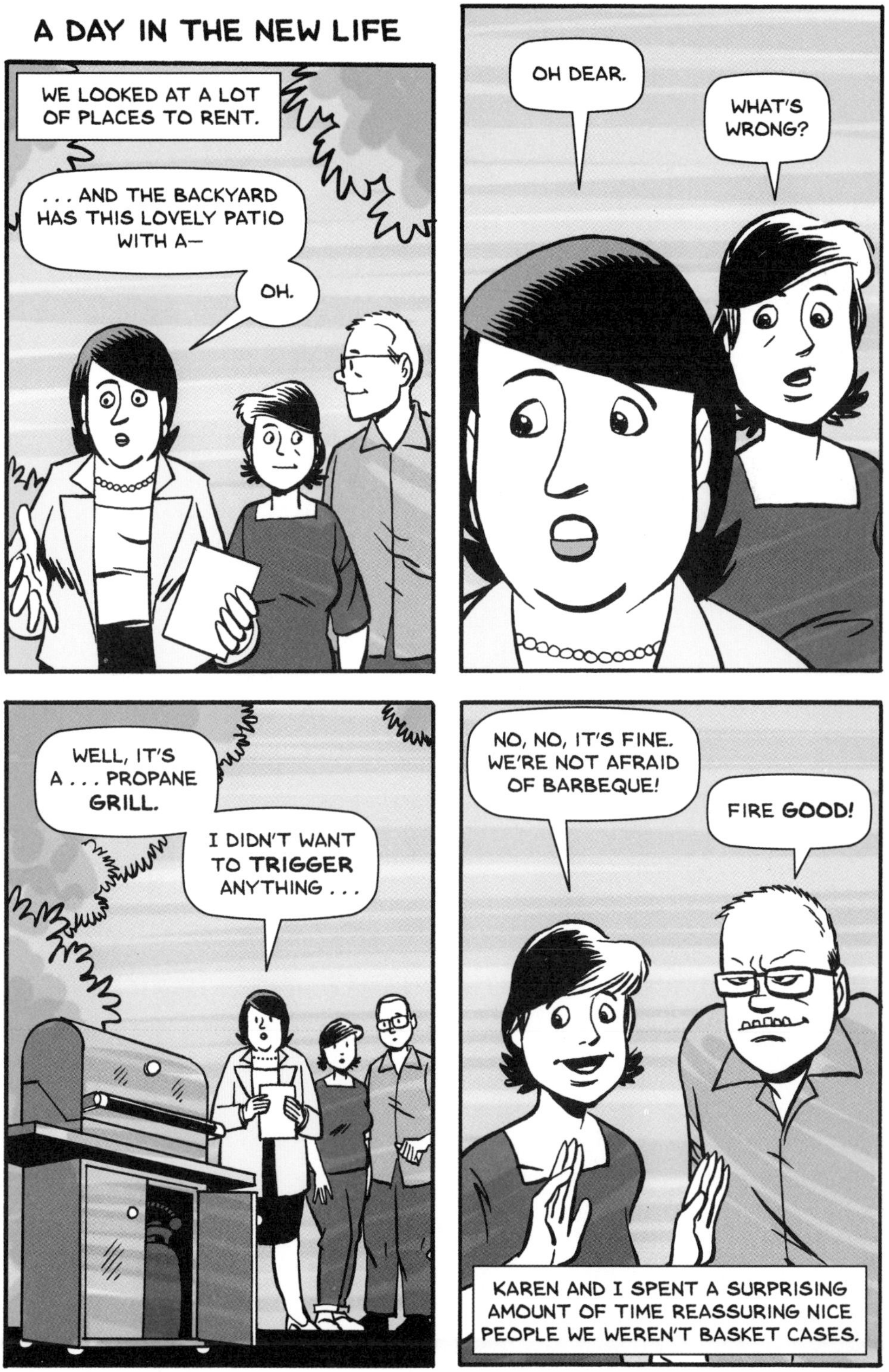

WE LOOKED AT A LOT OF PLACES TO RENT.
. . . AND THE BACKYARD HAS THIS LOVELY PATIO WITH A—
OH.
OH DEAR.
WHAT'S WRONG?
WELL, IT'S A . . . PROPANE GRILL.
I DIDN'T WANT TO TRIGGER ANYTHING . . .
NO, NO, IT'S FINE. WE'RE NOT AFRAID OF BARBEQUE!
FIRE GOOD!
KAREN AND I SPENT A SURPRISING AMOUNT OF TIME REASSURING NICE PEOPLE WE WEREN'T BASKET CASES.

JERRY'S FIRE STORY

JERRY DUNN RECENTLY RETIRED FROM A FORTY-THREE-YEAR CAREER IN SOCIAL SERVICES. HE CARED FOR HIS PARTNER, BILL, WHO AT THE TIME OF THE FIRE WAS SEVENTY AND HAD ALZHEIMER'S DISEASE. THEIR HOUSEMATE, REYNOLDS, WAS NINETY-ONE. THEY LIVED IN SANTA ROSA'S FOUNTAINGROVE NEIGHBORHOOD.

What woke me up was the power outage. I sleep with—or *used to* sleep with, I haven't since the fire—a CPAP mask because I have sleep apnea. So when the power went out the CPAP stopped, and that woke me up.

It was 12:30 in the morning, I remember that vividly. The wind was howling, and the branches of the trees were pounding on our house. I could see out our bedroom window to the east, and all I saw was black. The key thing is, I didn't see any fire.

But I was creeped out. I did training one time about personal safety awareness, and one of the things they said was, if your instincts tell you something's wrong, trust your instincts. I wish I had taken that advice that night, because I felt like something was wrong and I talked myself out of it. I told myself, "Why are you spooked by the wind?"

It was about 2:15 when I heard a lot of cars going down our street. So I got up and walked into the living room, where my windows had a 180-degree view. There I saw the fire coming from a direction I couldn't see before. It looked close.

I yelled at the guys to get up. I had to help Bill get dressed. I put a T-shirt on him but didn't put his arms into it, so it was just hanging around his neck. We fixed that later in the car.

All of a sudden there was a pounding on our door. It was the Santa Rosa police, and they said, "You need to get out now. When you pull out of your driveway, turn left—that's the only way you can go."

We didn't have time to think about what to take. We got in the garage and Reynolds said to me, "How are you going to open the door without power?" I said, "Oh, just watch me!" I released the latch, and although it was a heavy sucker and I've struggled lifting it before, with adrenaline, it was no problem.

No matter how much reality is staring you in the face, denial is so powerful. We pulled out into the driveway, live red embers falling everywhere like rain, and I was starting to worry the car might catch on fire. But I stopped and got out. Reynolds said, "What the hell are you doing?" I said, "I'm gonna pull down the garage door! I don't want people to steal our stuff!" Because it never occurred to me I wouldn't be coming back, even in that extreme situation.

The thing I remember so vividly, I'll never forget this: We got on the freeway going south and I looked in my rearview mirror, and it looked like all of Santa Rosa was on fire.

JERRY LEARNED TWO DAYS LATER THAT HIS HOME WAS GONE WHEN A FRIEND OF HIS SON'S SHOT VIDEO OF THE SCENE.

It didn't feel real at first. Our family was intact, and that's what mattered. We were in a hotel. I knew I had to find more permanent shelter, and I knew that was going to be hard to do. We needed a staging area: someplace we wouldn't have to move out of every night, preferably something that wasn't a hotel where we'd have to go out to eat every meal. That was difficult on Bill.

I started to house-hunt. That was my project. That and getting a car for Reynolds, so if I was gone they weren't stranded. Like Maslow's hierarchy of needs, right? You need this first, then you need that next.

The most difficult thing about all this was turning old stuff off and getting new stuff on—the utility company, the phone company. I made thirty calls to AT&T, and each one lasted at least half an hour.

JERRY IS ALSO A SONGWRITER.

I lost more than a hundred pieces of songs I wrote but never finished. I had a cassette tape of about thirty songs I wrote and recorded on a cheap keyboard in the eighties, and I always wanted to go back and redo them. Now they're gone.

THE SAME DAY THEY MOVED INTO A LONG-TERM RENTAL, REYNOLDS FELL AND BROKE HIS HIP.

That was the icing on the cake. Poor Reynolds. He's a great patient, but he had a week when the doctors insisted his hip wasn't broken and he was miserable, in great pain. He could hardly walk at all. Reynolds really helps immensely with Bill. I was trying to do all this stuff, then trying to take care of both of them.

I'm a lousy nurse anyway. I remember I just sat down and thought, "I'm not going to be able to get through this." But Reynolds recovered and so did I.

BEFORE ALZHEIMER'S, BILL HAD BEEN A SUCCESSFUL INTERIOR DESIGNER.

Bill designed some of our furniture and set up a lot of our house. If he had his full faculties, he'd probably almost enjoy this. What fun to design the house all over again! He doesn't get to do that. The flip side is he doesn't seem to be overly concerned about it.

There are times, with all the work I'm doing to rebuild this house, that I ask, "Who am I doing it for?"

A couple of times Bill has said, "Well, we're going home today!" I tell him, "No, we're not, honey. We're not going home for a long time."

BILL'S ALZHEIMER'S DISEASE PROGRESSED QUICKLY FOLLOWING THE FIRE. THREE MONTHS AFTER THIS INTERVIEW WAS CONDUCTED, HE DIED. THREE WEEKS AFTER THAT, REYNOLDS DIED AFTER A BRIEF ILLNESS. THEY NEVER RETURNED HOME. ∎

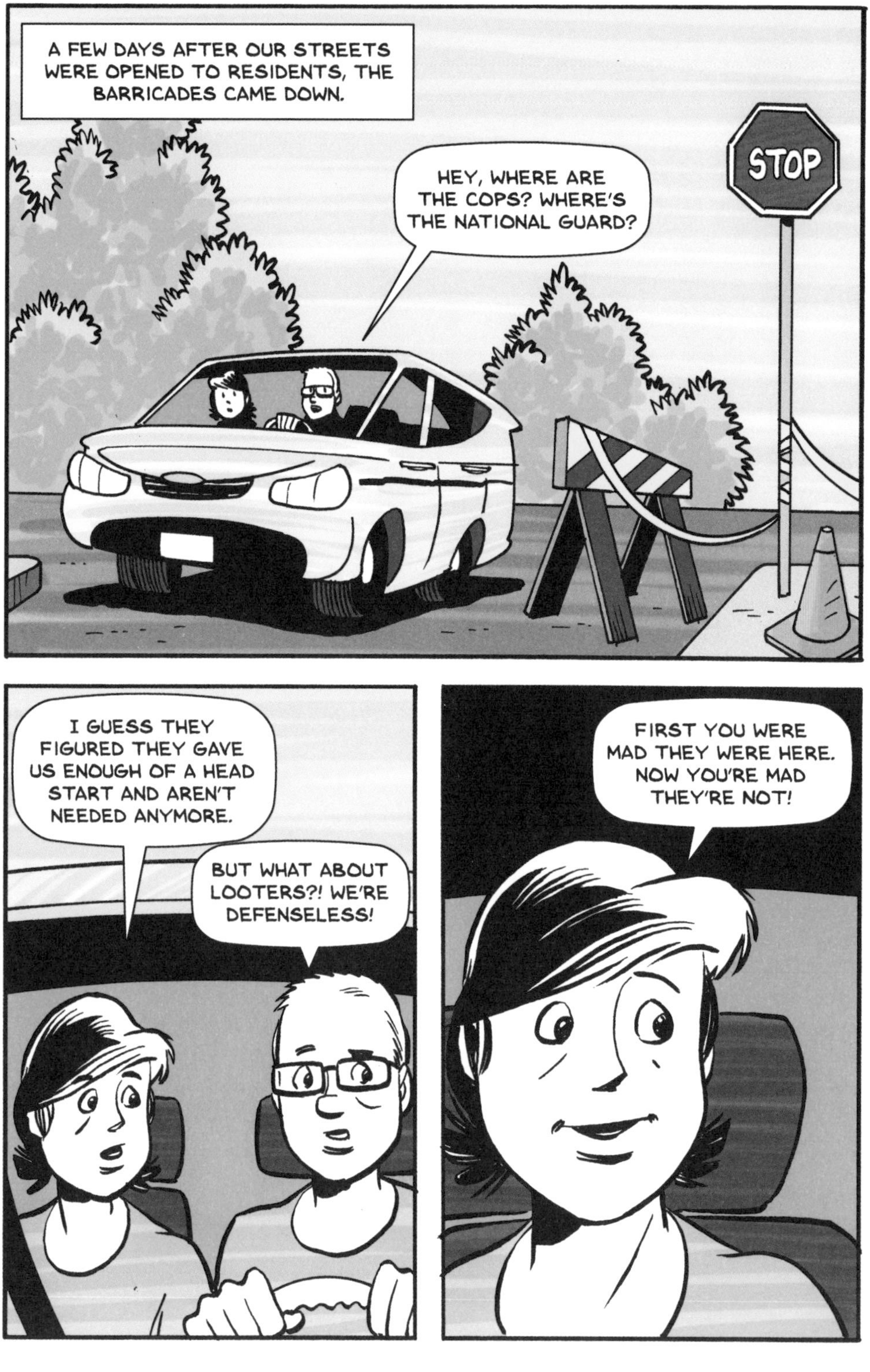

A FEW DAYS AFTER OUR STREETS WERE OPENED TO RESIDENTS, THE BARRICADES CAME DOWN.
HEY, WHERE ARE THE COPS? WHERE'S THE NATIONAL GUARD?
STOP
I GUESS THEY FIGURED THEY GAVE US ENOUGH OF A HEAD START AND AREN'T NEEDED ANYMORE.
BUT WHAT ABOUT LOOTERS?! WE'RE DEFENSELESS!
FIRST YOU WERE MAD THEY WERE HERE. NOW YOU'RE MAD THEY'RE NOT!

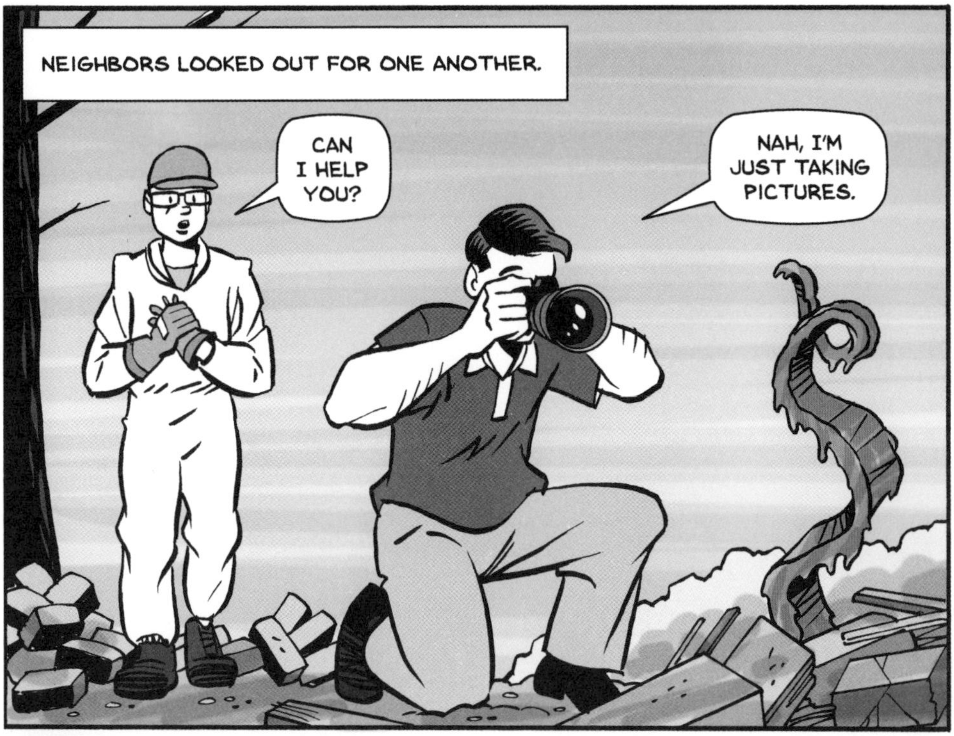
NEIGHBORS LOOKED OUT FOR ONE ANOTHER.
CAN I HELP YOU?
NAH, I'M JUST TAKING PICTURES.

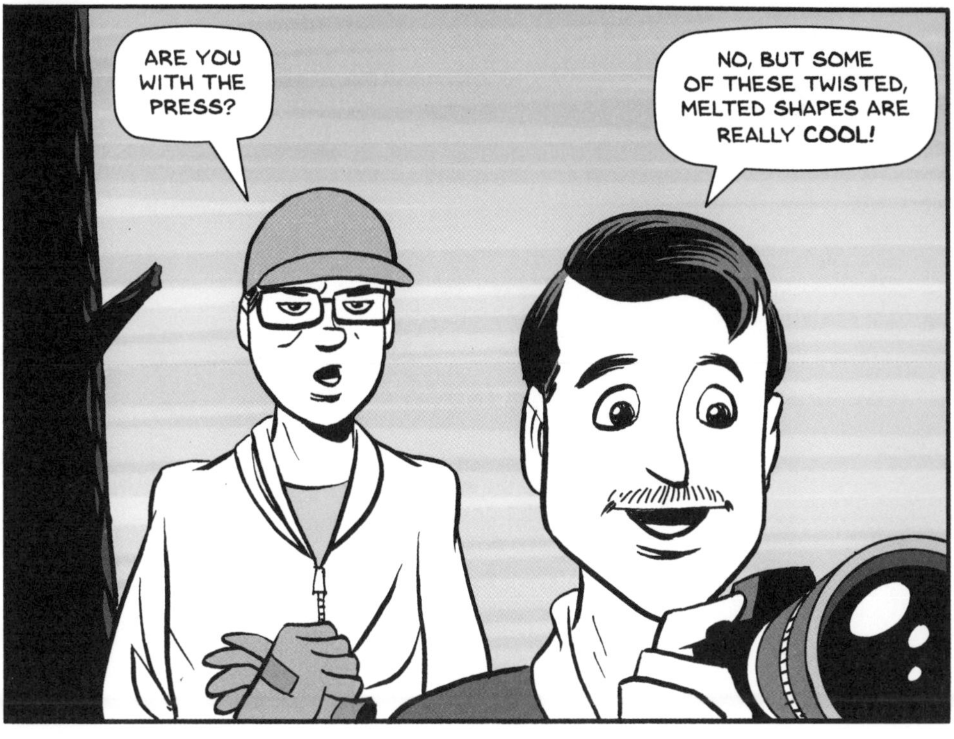
ARE YOU WITH THE PRESS?
NO, BUT SOME OF THESE TWISTED, MELTED SHAPES ARE REALLY **COOL!**

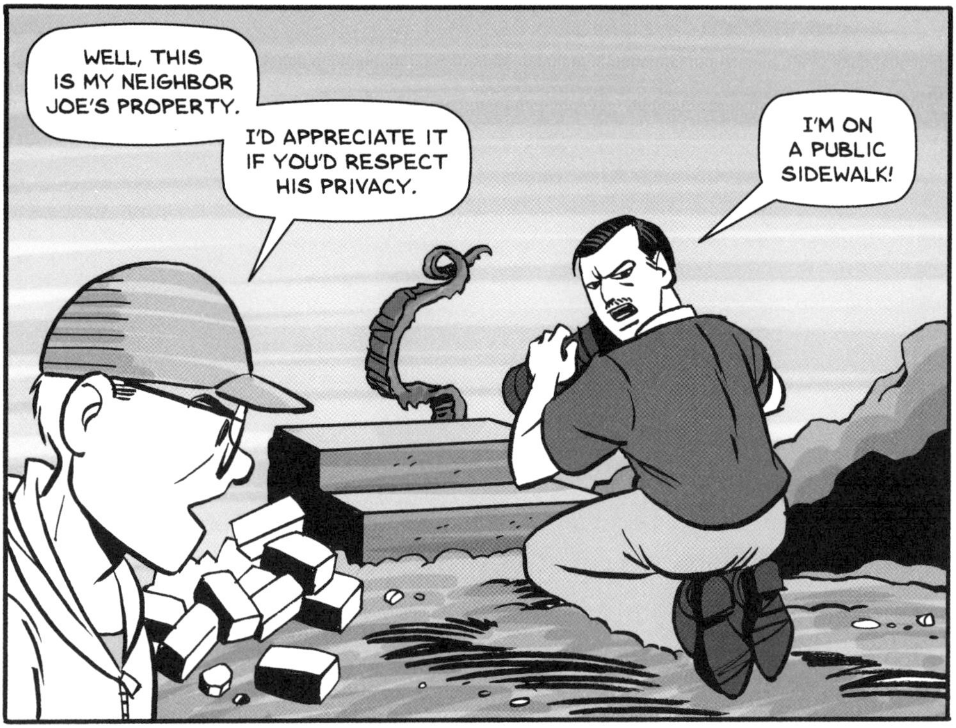
WELL, THIS IS MY NEIGHBOR JOE'S PROPERTY.
I'D APPRECIATE IT IF YOU'D RESPECT HIS PRIVACY.
I'M ON A PUBLIC SIDEWALK!

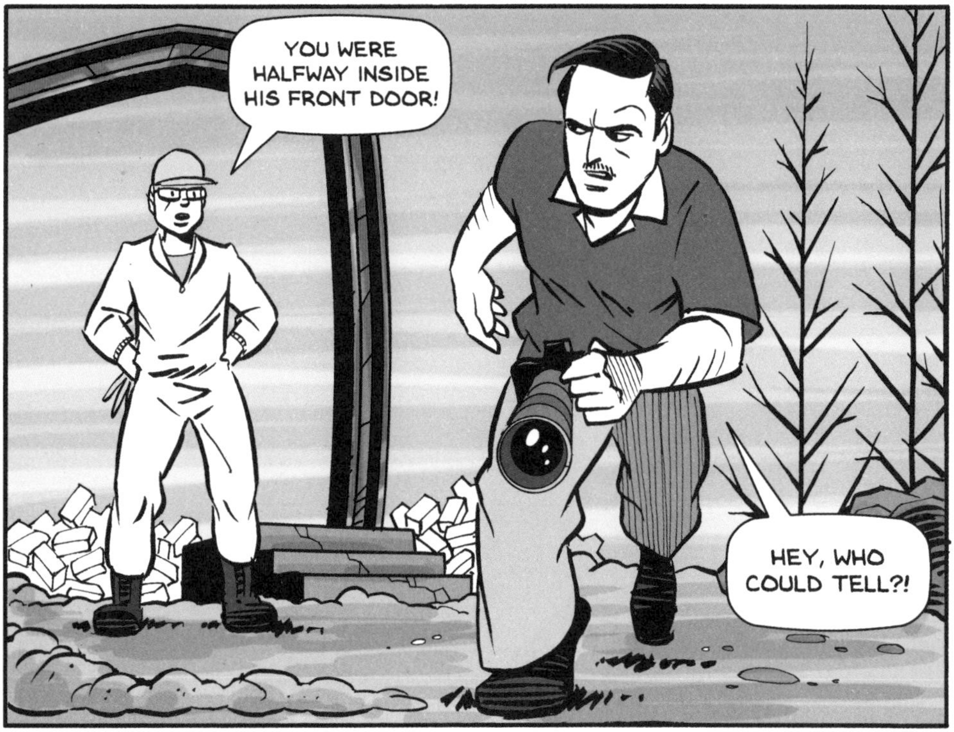
YOU WERE HALFWAY INSIDE HIS FRONT DOOR!
HEY, WHO COULD TELL?!

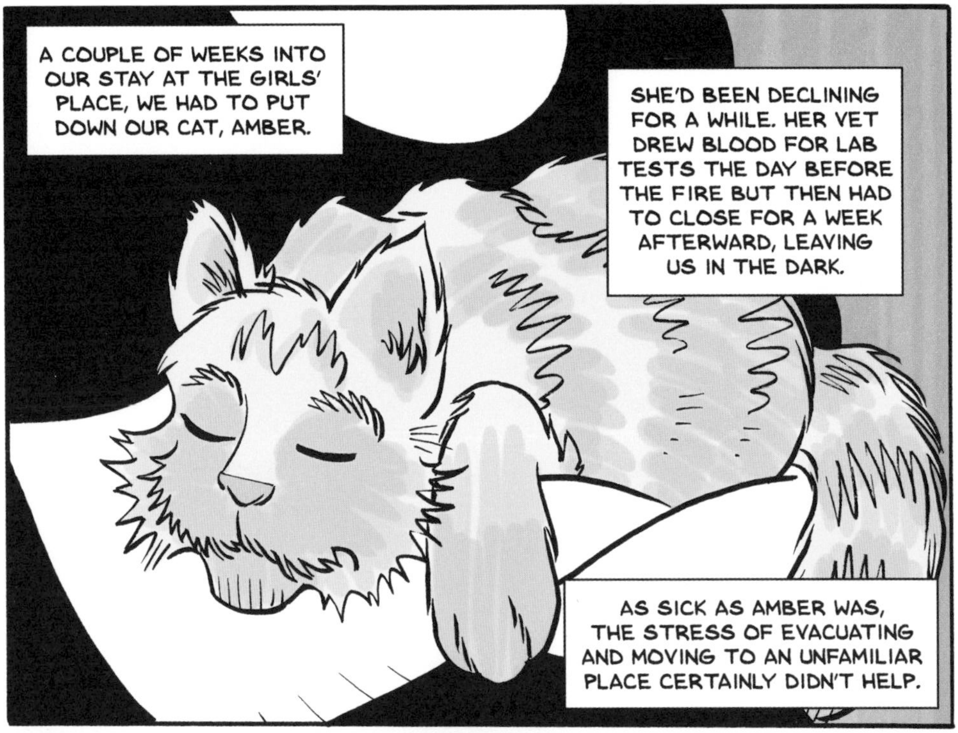
A COUPLE OF WEEKS INTO OUR STAY AT THE GIRLS' PLACE, WE HAD TO PUT DOWN OUR CAT, AMBER.
SHE'D BEEN DECLINING FOR A WHILE. HER VET DREW BLOOD FOR LAB TESTS THE DAY BEFORE THE FIRE BUT THEN HAD TO CLOSE FOR A WEEK AFTERWARD, LEAVING US IN THE DARK.
AS SICK AS AMBER WAS, THE STRESS OF EVACUATING AND MOVING TO AN UNFAMILIAR PLACE CERTAINLY DIDN'T HELP.

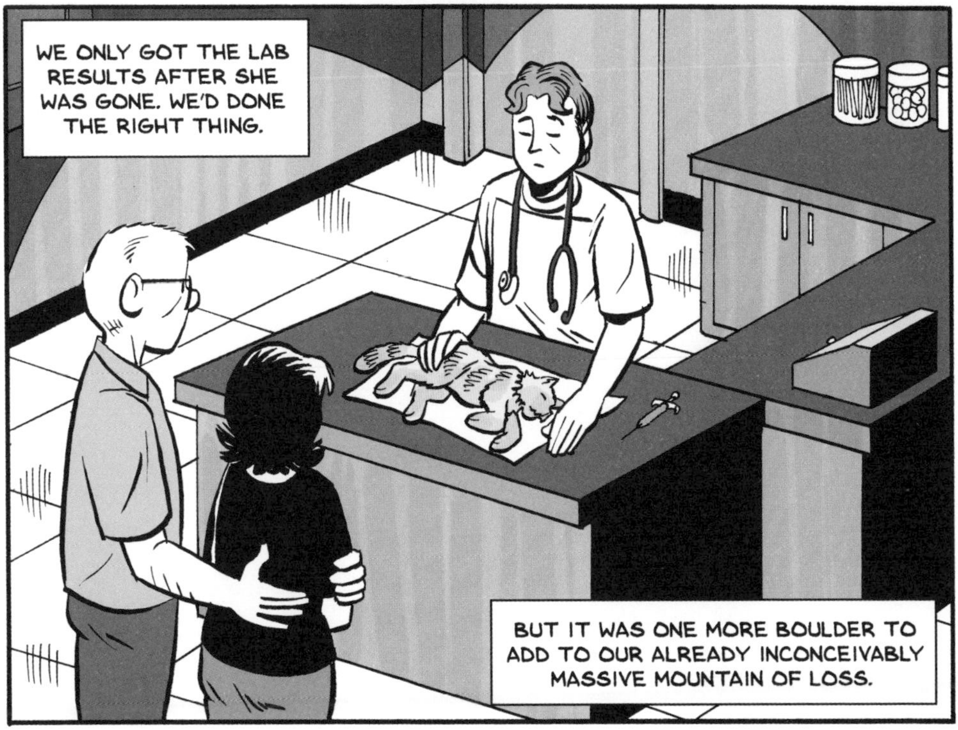
WE ONLY GOT THE LAB RESULTS AFTER SHE WAS GONE. WE'D DONE THE RIGHT THING.
BUT IT WAS ONE MORE BOULDER TO ADD TO OUR ALREADY INCONCEIVABLY MASSIVE MOUNTAIN OF LOSS.

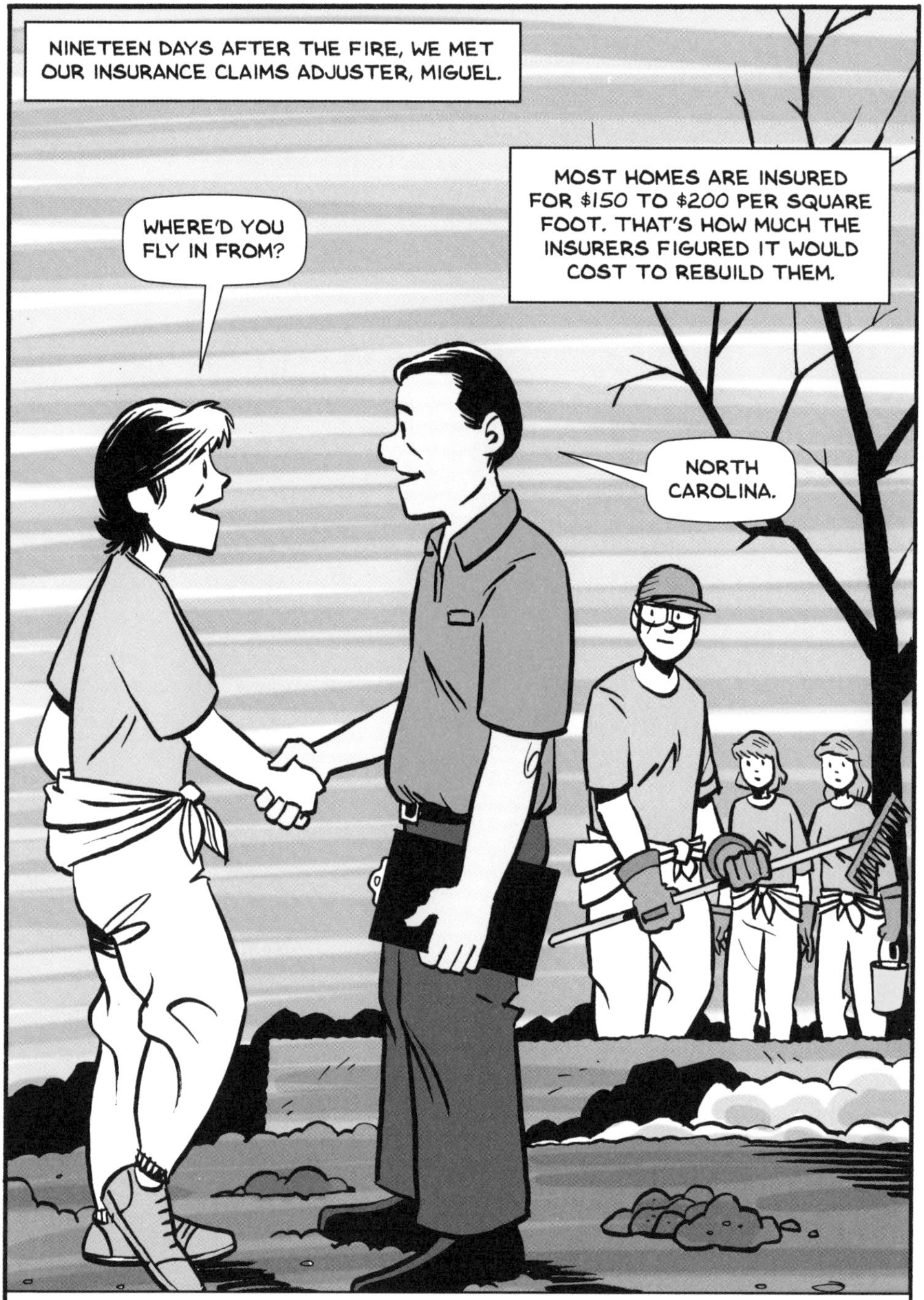
NINETEEN DAYS AFTER THE FIRE, WE MET OUR INSURANCE CLAIMS ADJUSTER, MIGUEL.
WHERE'D YOU FLY IN FROM?
MOST HOMES ARE INSURED FOR $150 TO $200 PER SQUARE FOOT. THAT'S HOW MUCH THE INSURERS FIGURED IT WOULD COST TO REBUILD THEM.
NORTH CAROLINA.
IF ONLY ONE OR TWO HOUSES HAD BURNED, THAT MIGHT HAVE BEEN ALL RIGHT. BUT THERE WON'T BE ENOUGH CONCRETE, LUMBER, OR LABOR IN NORTHERN CALIFORNIA TO REBUILD 6,200 HOMES. **SUPPLY AND DEMAND:** THE BEST COST ESTIMATES NOW ARE $300 TO $500 PER SQUARE FOOT OR MORE.

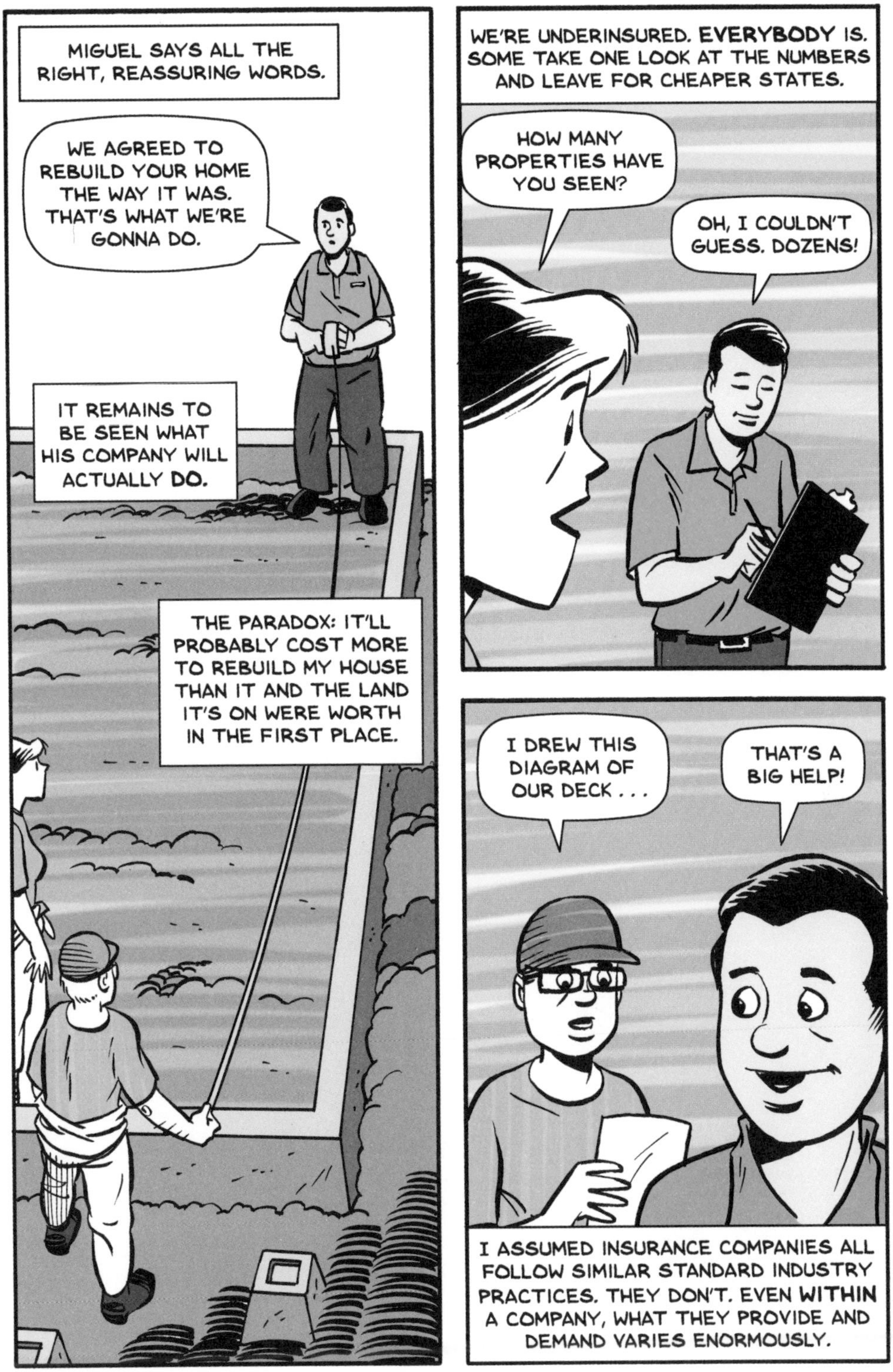
MIGUEL SAYS ALL THE RIGHT, REASSURING WORDS.
WE AGREED TO REBUILD YOUR HOME THE WAY IT WAS. THAT'S WHAT WE'RE GONNA DO.
IT REMAINS TO BE SEEN WHAT HIS COMPANY WILL ACTUALLY **DO.**
THE PARADOX: IT'LL PROBABLY COST MORE TO REBUILD MY HOUSE THAN IT AND THE LAND IT'S ON WERE WORTH IN THE FIRST PLACE.
WE'RE UNDERINSURED. **EVERYBODY** IS. SOME TAKE ONE LOOK AT THE NUMBERS AND LEAVE FOR CHEAPER STATES.
HOW MANY PROPERTIES HAVE YOU SEEN?
OH, I COULDN'T GUESS. DOZENS!
I DREW THIS DIAGRAM OF OUR DECK . . .
THAT'S A BIG HELP!
I ASSUMED INSURANCE COMPANIES ALL FOLLOW SIMILAR STANDARD INDUSTRY PRACTICES. THEY DON'T. EVEN **WITHIN** A COMPANY, WHAT THEY PROVIDE AND DEMAND VARIES ENORMOUSLY.

LUCKILY, OUR INSURER DID **NOT** REQUIRE WHAT MANY OTHERS DID: A VALUATION OF EVERYTHING THEIR CLIENTS OWNED.

EVERY PLATE, CUP, FORK, POT, PAN, MICROWAVE, WAFFLE IRON, COOKBOOK, BOWL, COFFEE MAKER, MIXER, BLENDER, TOASTER, TUMBLER, DISH TOWEL, TEA CUP, TONG, AND TRIVET.

EVERY COUCH, CHAIR, FOOTSTOOL, END TABLE, COFFEE TABLE, BOOKCASE, BOOK, MIRROR, RUG, CARPET, CABINET, LAMP, CURTAIN, PILLOW, CLOCK, TOWEL, BLANKET, BEDSHEET, TV, CD, AND DVD.

EVERY SHIRT, SKIRT, SWEATER, SUIT, DRESS, PANTS, SHORTS, SOCKS, SHOES, BOOTS, COAT, AND TIE; EVERY BICYCLE, LADDER, RAKE, SHOVEL, SCREWDRIVER, SPRINKLER, AND HOSE.

EVERY LAPTOP, TABLET, MONITOR, TELEPHONE, SCANNER, DESK, FILING CABINET, STORAGE CHEST, PAPER CLIP, STAPLER, NOTEPAD, CALENDAR, SCISSORS, THINGAMAJIG, KNICKKNACK, AND DOODAD.

EVERY THING.

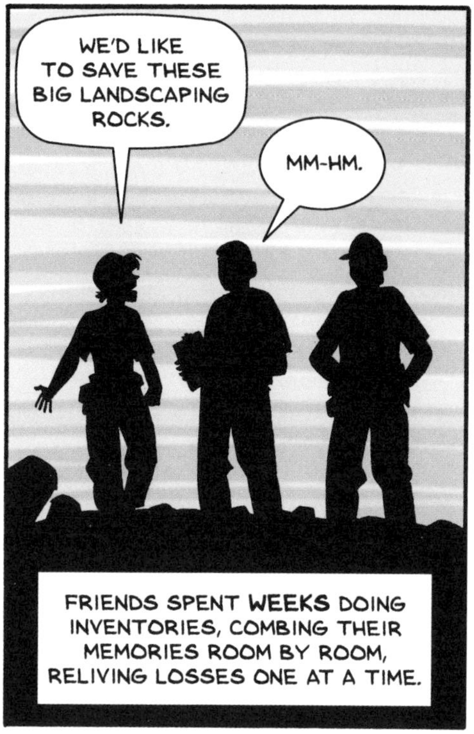
WE'D LIKE TO SAVE THESE BIG LANDSCAPING ROCKS.
MM-HM.
FRIENDS SPENT **WEEKS** DOING INVENTORIES, COMBING THEIR MEMORIES ROOM BY ROOM, RELIVING LOSSES ONE AT A TIME.

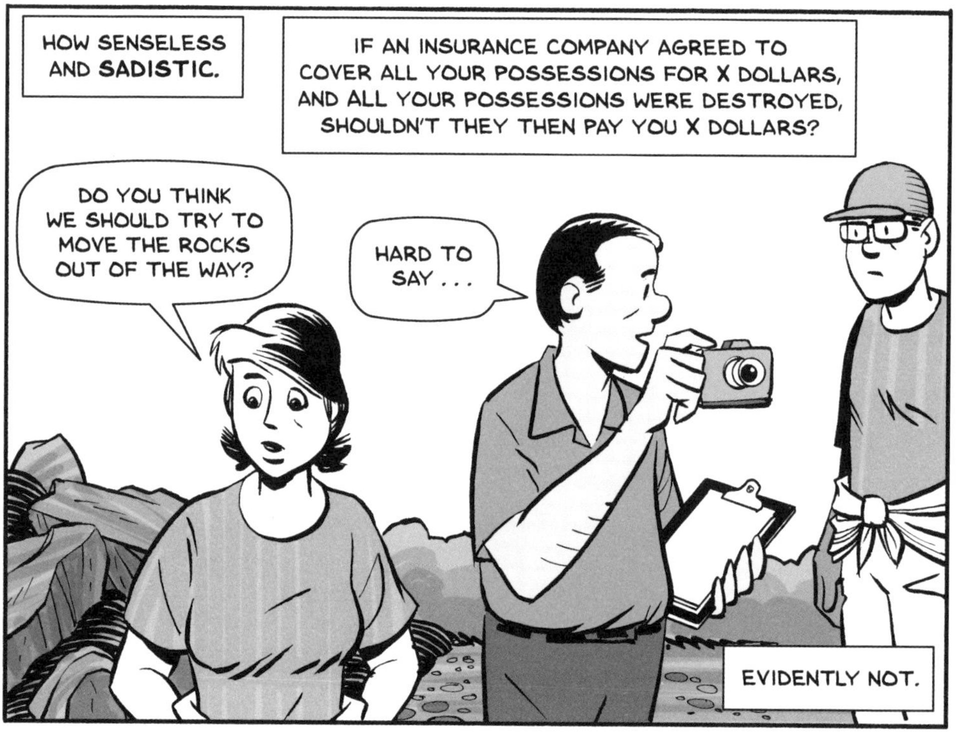
HOW SENSELESS AND **SADISTIC.**
IF AN INSURANCE COMPANY AGREED TO COVER ALL YOUR POSSESSIONS FOR X DOLLARS, AND ALL YOUR POSSESSIONS WERE DESTROYED, SHOULDN'T THEY THEN PAY YOU X DOLLARS?
DO YOU THINK WE SHOULD TRY TO MOVE THE ROCKS OUT OF THE WAY?
HARD TO SAY . . .
EVIDENTLY NOT.

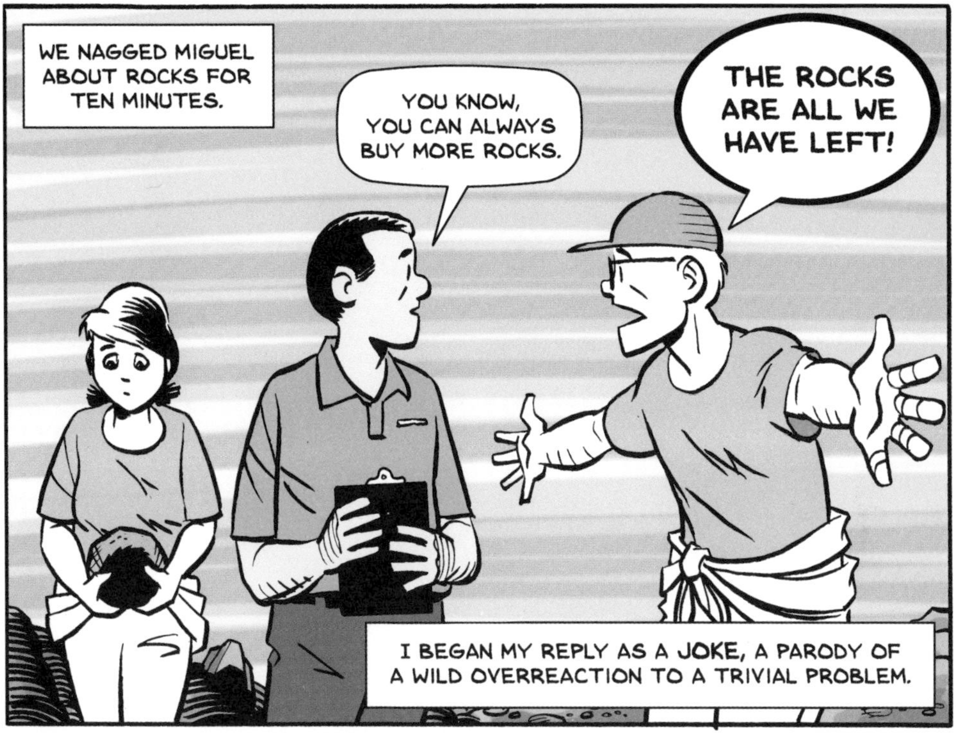
WE NAGGED MIGUEL ABOUT ROCKS FOR TEN MINUTES.
YOU KNOW, YOU CAN ALWAYS BUY MORE ROCKS.
THE ROCKS ARE ALL WE HAVE LEFT!
I BEGAN MY REPLY AS A JOKE, A PARODY OF A WILD OVERREACTION TO A TRIVIAL PROBLEM.

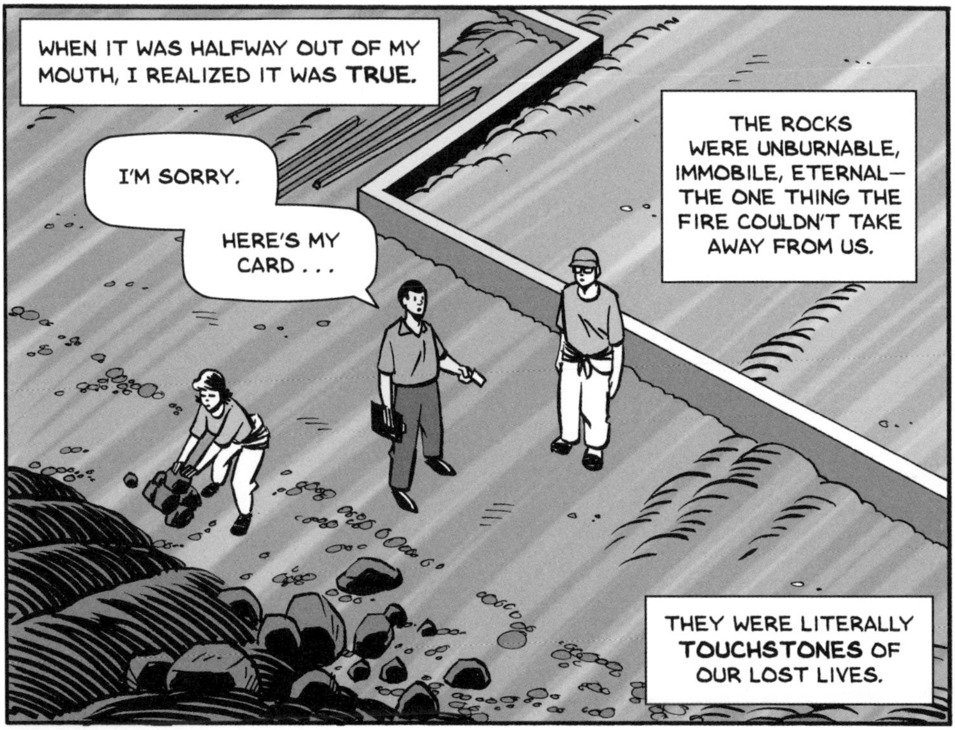
WHEN IT WAS HALFWAY OUT OF MY MOUTH, I REALIZED IT WAS TRUE.
I'M SORRY.
HERE'S MY CARD . . .
THE ROCKS WERE UNBURNABLE, IMMOBILE, ETERNAL— THE ONE THING THE FIRE COULDN'T TAKE AWAY FROM US.
THEY WERE LITERALLY TOUCHSTONES OF OUR LOST LIVES.

A DAY IN THE NEW LIFE

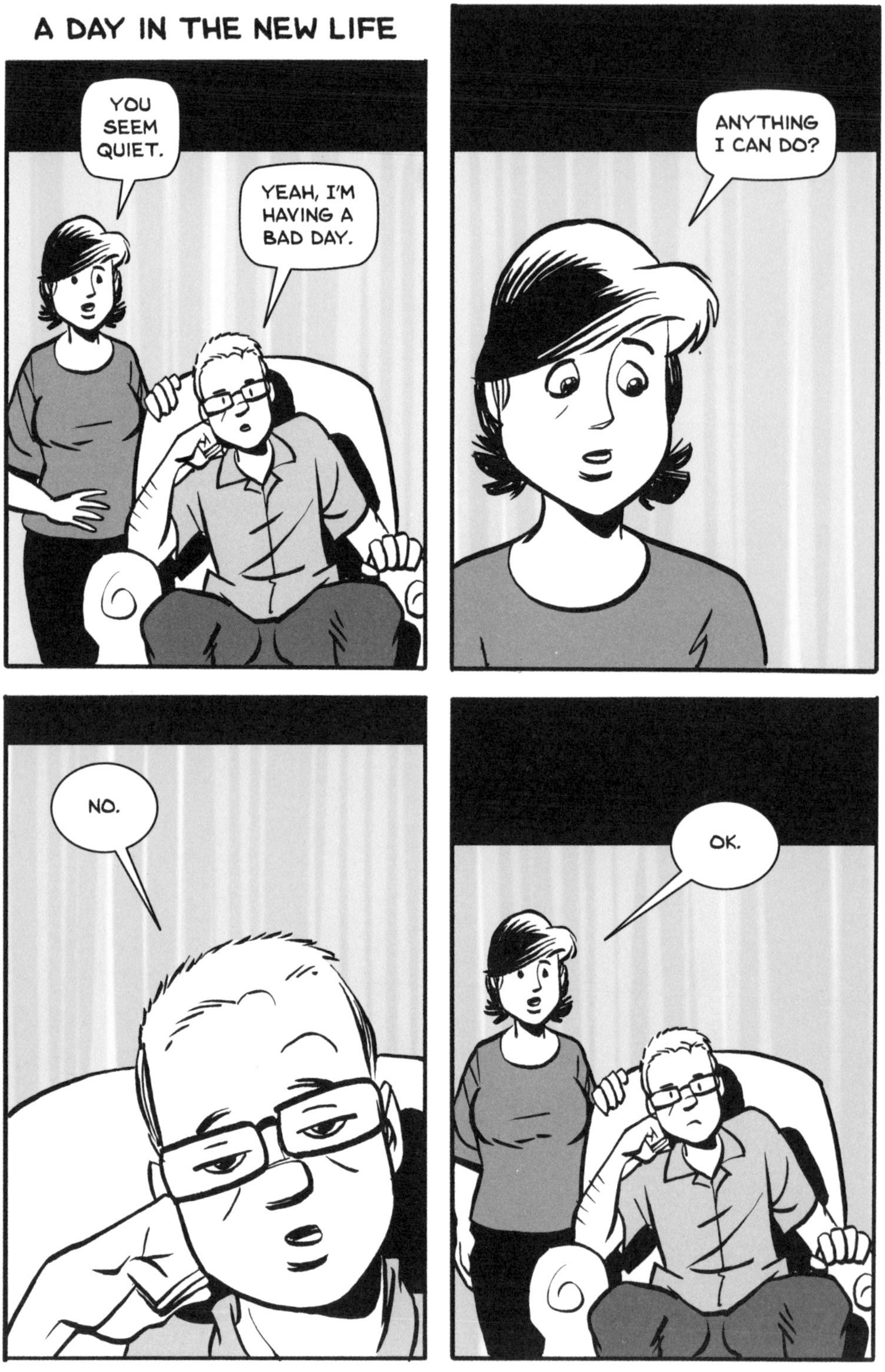
YOU SEEM QUIET.
YEAH, I'M HAVING A BAD DAY.
ANYTHING I CAN DO?
NO.
OK.

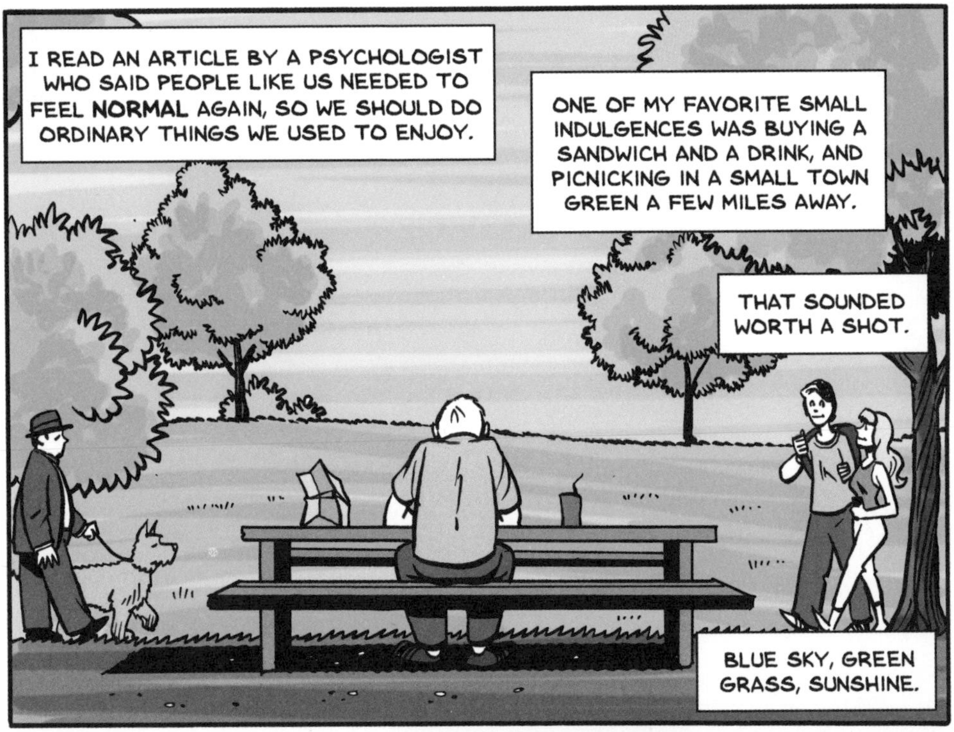
I READ AN ARTICLE BY A PSYCHOLOGIST WHO SAID PEOPLE LIKE US NEEDED TO FEEL **NORMAL** AGAIN, SO WE SHOULD DO ORDINARY THINGS WE USED TO ENJOY.
ONE OF MY FAVORITE SMALL INDULGENCES WAS BUYING A SANDWICH AND A DRINK, AND PICNICKING IN A SMALL TOWN GREEN A FEW MILES AWAY.
THAT SOUNDED WORTH A SHOT.
BLUE SKY, GREEN GRASS, SUNSHINE.

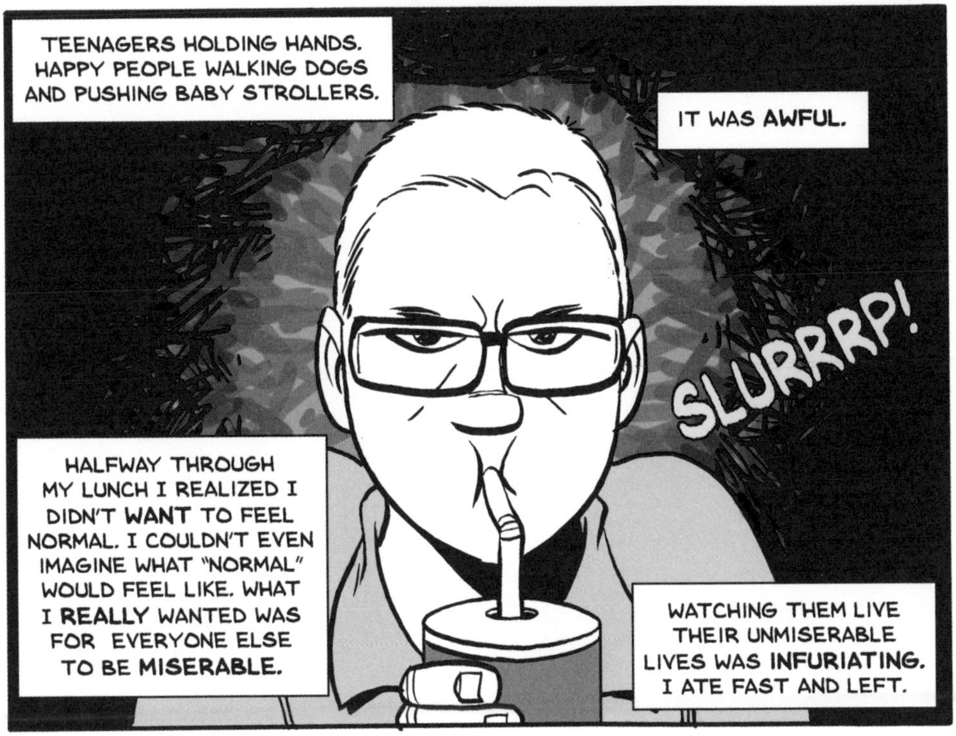
TEENAGERS HOLDING HANDS. HAPPY PEOPLE WALKING DOGS AND PUSHING BABY STROLLERS.
IT WAS **AWFUL.**
SLURRRP!
HALFWAY THROUGH MY LUNCH I REALIZED I DIDN'T **WANT** TO FEEL NORMAL. I COULDN'T EVEN IMAGINE WHAT "NORMAL" WOULD FEEL LIKE. WHAT I **REALLY** WANTED WAS FOR EVERYONE ELSE TO BE **MISERABLE.**
WATCHING THEM LIVE THEIR UNMISERABLE LIVES WAS **INFURIATING.** I ATE FAST AND LEFT.

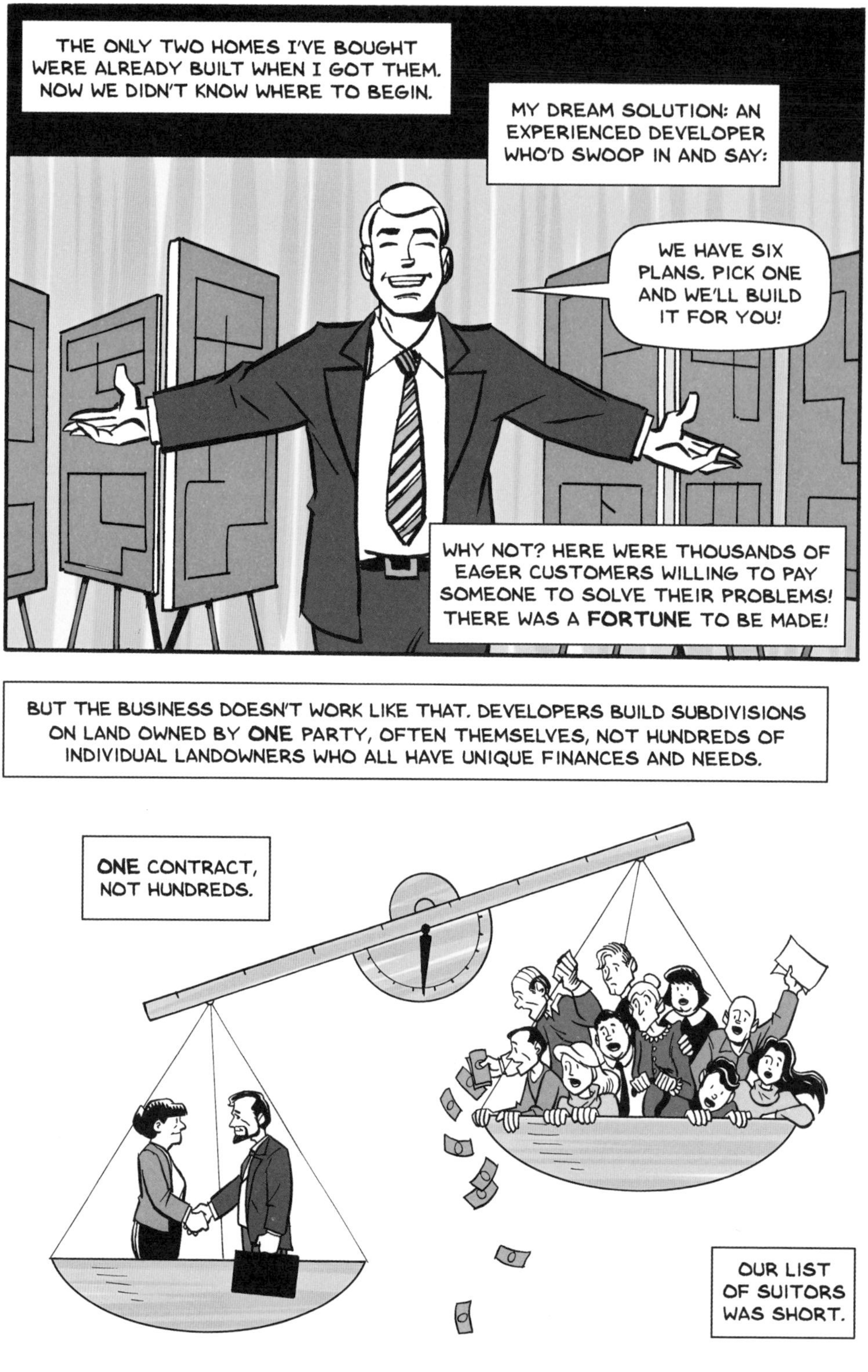
THE ONLY TWO HOMES I'VE BOUGHT WERE ALREADY BUILT WHEN I GOT THEM. NOW WE DIDN'T KNOW WHERE TO BEGIN.
MY DREAM SOLUTION: AN EXPERIENCED DEVELOPER WHO'D SWOOP IN AND SAY:
WE HAVE SIX PLANS. PICK ONE AND WE'LL BUILD IT FOR YOU!
WHY NOT? HERE WERE THOUSANDS OF EAGER CUSTOMERS WILLING TO PAY SOMEONE TO SOLVE THEIR PROBLEMS! THERE WAS A **FORTUNE** TO BE MADE!
BUT THE BUSINESS DOESN'T WORK LIKE THAT. DEVELOPERS BUILD SUBDIVISIONS ON LAND OWNED BY **ONE** PARTY, OFTEN THEMSELVES, NOT HUNDREDS OF INDIVIDUAL LANDOWNERS WHO ALL HAVE UNIQUE FINANCES AND NEEDS.
ONE CONTRACT, NOT HUNDREDS.
OUR LIST OF SUITORS WAS SHORT.

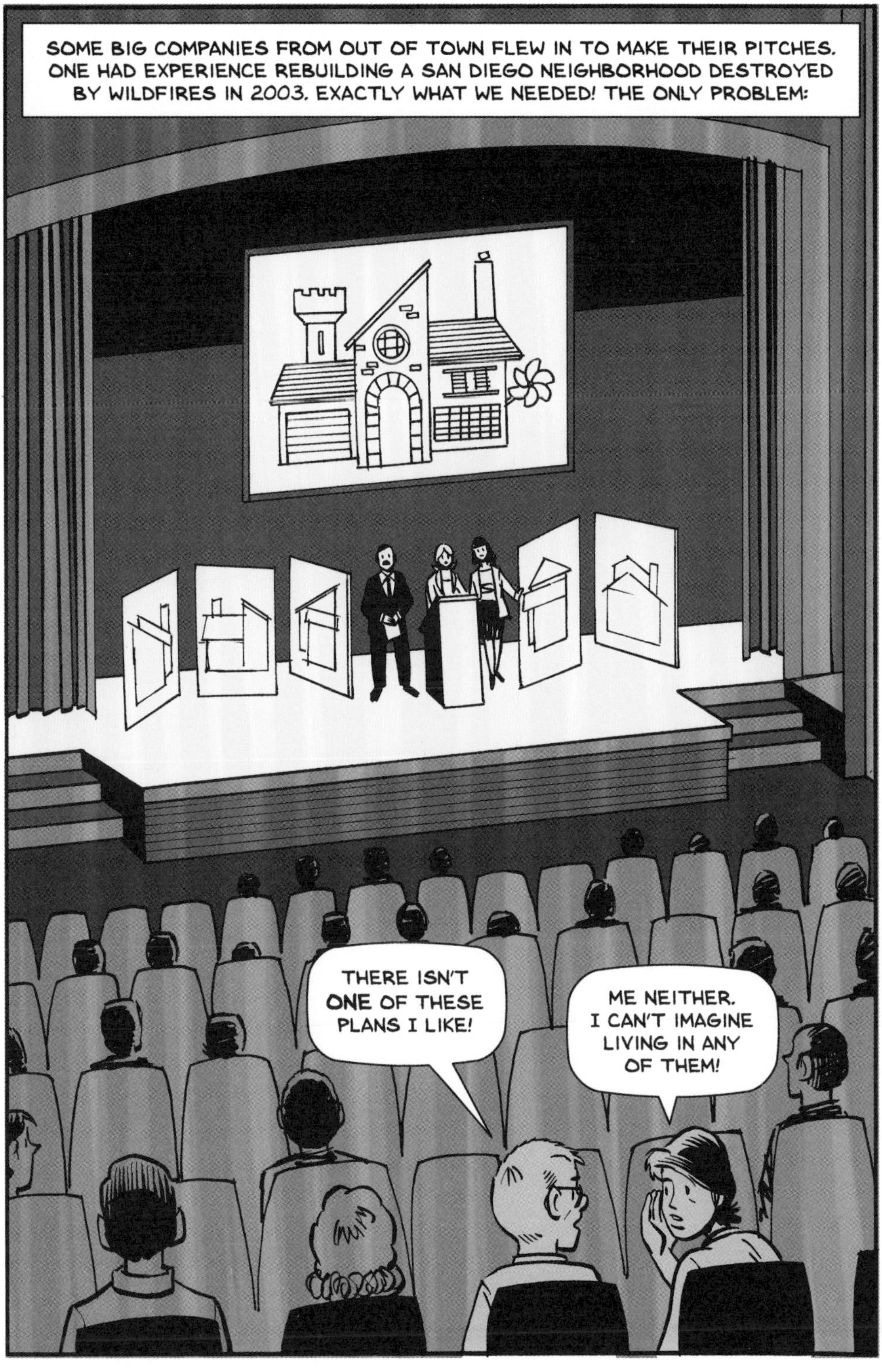
SOME BIG COMPANIES FROM OUT OF TOWN FLEW IN TO MAKE THEIR PITCHES. ONE HAD EXPERIENCE REBUILDING A SAN DIEGO NEIGHBORHOOD DESTROYED BY WILDFIRES IN 2003. EXACTLY WHAT WE NEEDED! THE ONLY PROBLEM:
THERE ISN'T **ONE** OF THESE PLANS I LIKE!
ME NEITHER. I CAN'T IMAGINE LIVING IN ANY OF THEM!

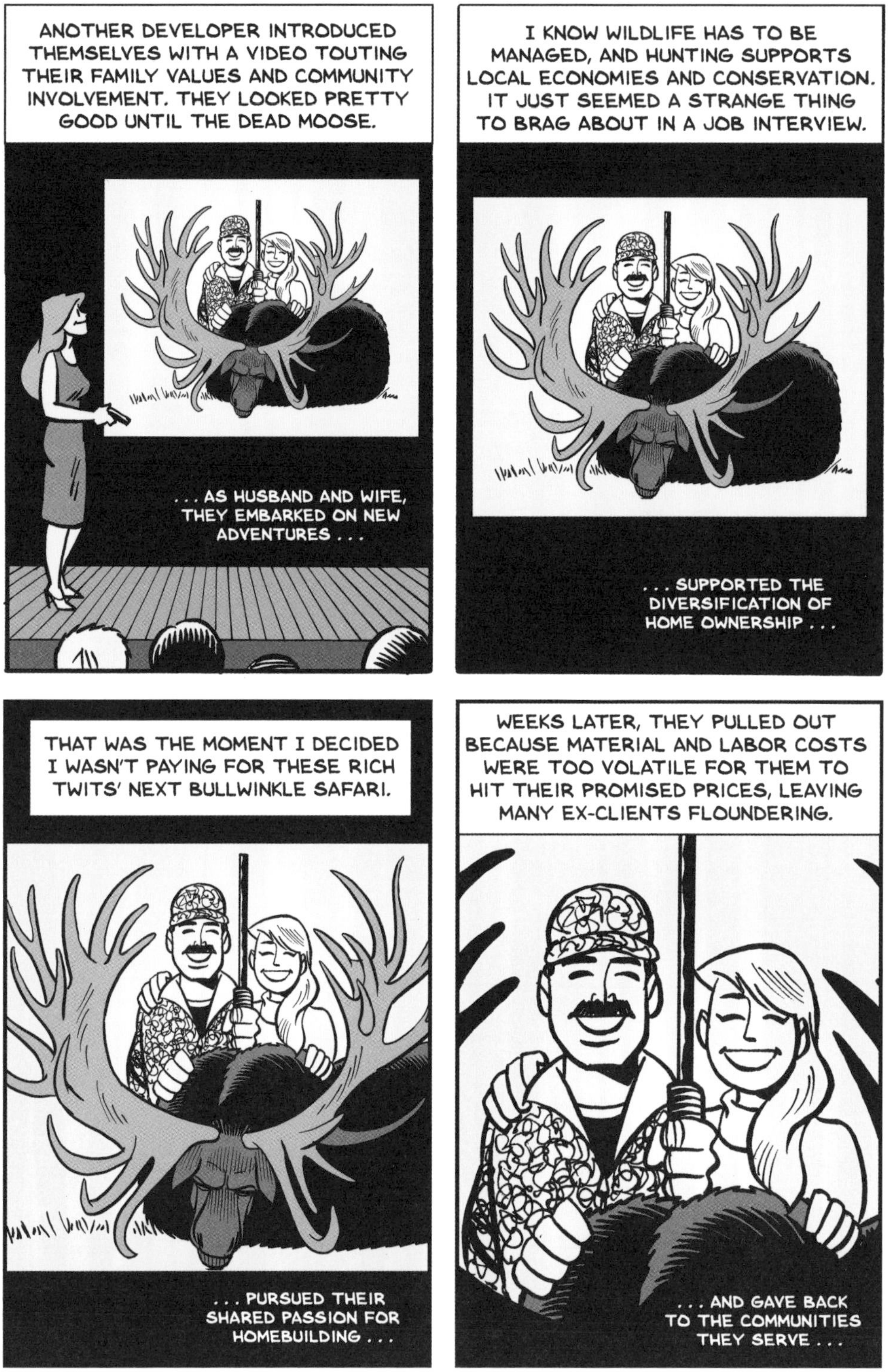
ANOTHER DEVELOPER INTRODUCED THEMSELVES WITH A VIDEO TOUTING THEIR FAMILY VALUES AND COMMUNITY INVOLVEMENT. THEY LOOKED PRETTY GOOD UNTIL THE DEAD MOOSE.
. . . AS HUSBAND AND WIFE, THEY EMBARKED ON NEW ADVENTURES . . .
I KNOW WILDLIFE HAS TO BE MANAGED, AND HUNTING SUPPORTS LOCAL ECONOMIES AND CONSERVATION. IT JUST SEEMED A STRANGE THING TO BRAG ABOUT IN A JOB INTERVIEW.
. . . SUPPORTED THE DIVERSIFICATION OF HOME OWNERSHIP . . .
THAT WAS THE MOMENT I DECIDED I WASN'T PAYING FOR THESE RICH TWITS' NEXT BULLWINKLE SAFARI.
. . . PURSUED THEIR SHARED PASSION FOR HOMEBUILDING . . .
WEEKS LATER, THEY PULLED OUT BECAUSE MATERIAL AND LABOR COSTS WERE TOO VOLATILE FOR THEM TO HIT THEIR PROMISED PRICES, LEAVING MANY EX-CLIENTS FLOUNDERING.
. . . AND GAVE BACK TO THE COMMUNITIES THEY SERVE . . .

AFTER LIVING WITH OUR GIRLS A MONTH, WE FOUND A RENTAL THROUGH AN IN-LAW OF A WOMAN KAREN WORKS WITH. EVERY GOOD BREAK COMES VIA FRIENDS AND LUCK.

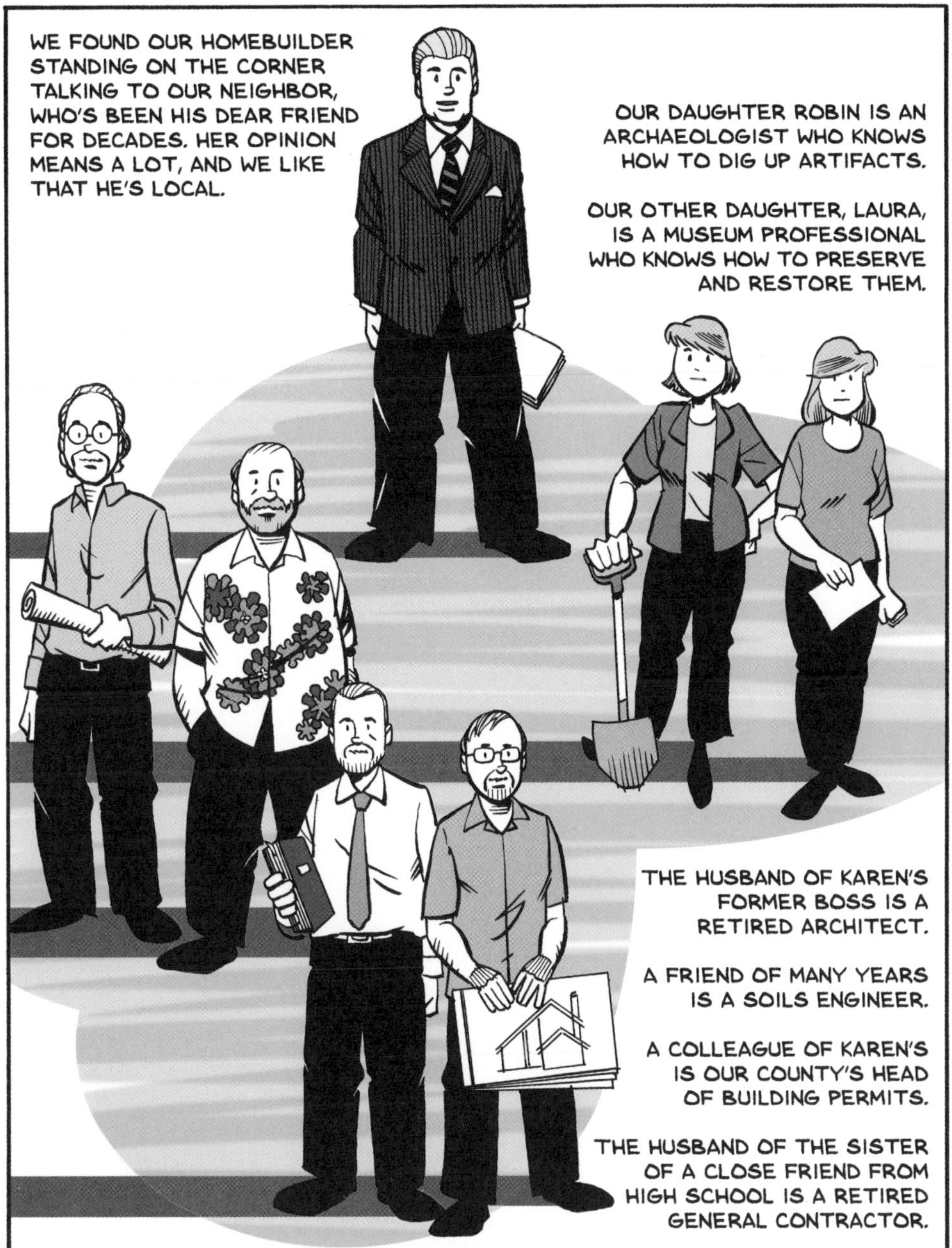
WE FOUND OUR HOMEBUILDER STANDING ON THE CORNER TALKING TO OUR NEIGHBOR, WHO'S BEEN HIS DEAR FRIEND FOR DECADES. HER OPINION MEANS A LOT, AND WE LIKE THAT HE'S LOCAL.
OUR DAUGHTER ROBIN IS AN ARCHAEOLOGIST WHO KNOWS HOW TO DIG UP ARTIFACTS.
OUR OTHER DAUGHTER, LAURA, IS A MUSEUM PROFESSIONAL WHO KNOWS HOW TO PRESERVE AND RESTORE THEM.
THE HUSBAND OF KAREN'S FORMER BOSS IS A RETIRED ARCHITECT.
A FRIEND OF MANY YEARS IS A SOILS ENGINEER.
A COLLEAGUE OF KAREN'S IS OUR COUNTY'S HEAD OF BUILDING PERMITS.
THE HUSBAND OF THE SISTER OF A CLOSE FRIEND FROM HIGH SCHOOL IS A RETIRED GENERAL CONTRACTOR.

NOT **ONCE** IN MY LIFE HAD I NEEDED TO BUILD A HOME, DIG UP ARTIFACTS, PRESERVE AND RESTORE THEM, DRAFT A BLUEPRINT, ENGINEER SOILS, PULL A BUILDING PERMIT, OR EVEN HIRE A GENERAL CONTRACTOR. NOW I HAD TO DO THEM **ALL**. THE LEARNING CURVE WAS A CLIFF. EVERYONE WAS GENEROUS WITH THEIR ADVICE. TO WEATHER THIS DISASTER, WE'D HAVE TO WORK EVERY ANGLE AND CALL IN EVERY FAVOR WE COULD.

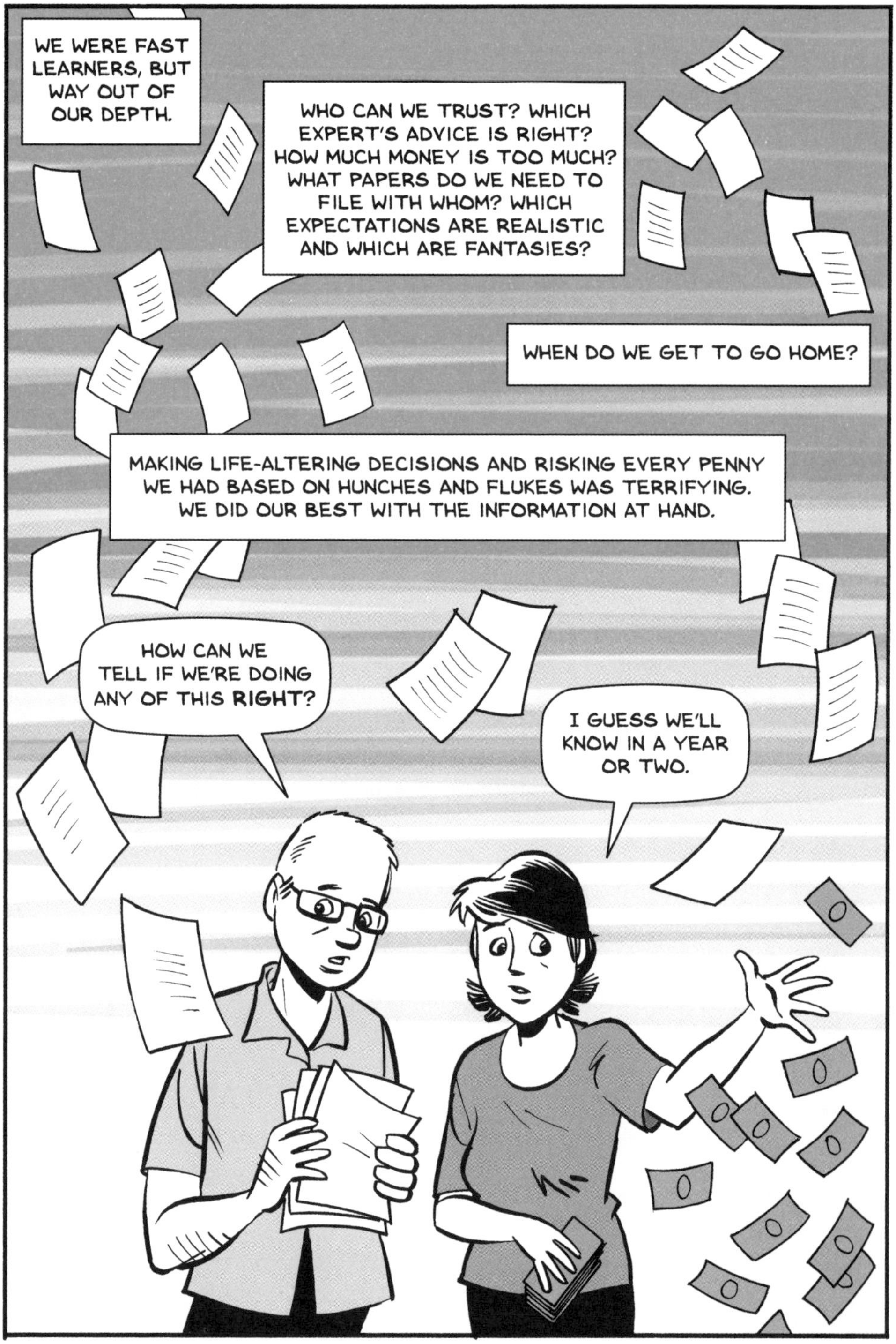
WE WERE FAST LEARNERS, BUT WAY OUT OF OUR DEPTH.
WHO CAN WE TRUST? WHICH EXPERT'S ADVICE IS RIGHT? HOW MUCH MONEY IS TOO MUCH? WHAT PAPERS DO WE NEED TO FILE WITH WHOM? WHICH EXPECTATIONS ARE REALISTIC AND WHICH ARE FANTASIES?
WHEN DO WE GET TO GO HOME?
MAKING LIFE-ALTERING DECISIONS AND RISKING EVERY PENNY WE HAD BASED ON HUNCHES AND FLUKES WAS TERRIFYING. WE DID OUR BEST WITH THE INFORMATION AT HAND.
HOW CAN WE TELL IF WE'RE DOING ANY OF THIS **RIGHT**?
I GUESS WE'LL KNOW IN A YEAR OR TWO.

MORE THAN I'D LIKE, OUR FATE DEPENDED ON THE KINDNESS OF STRANGERS.

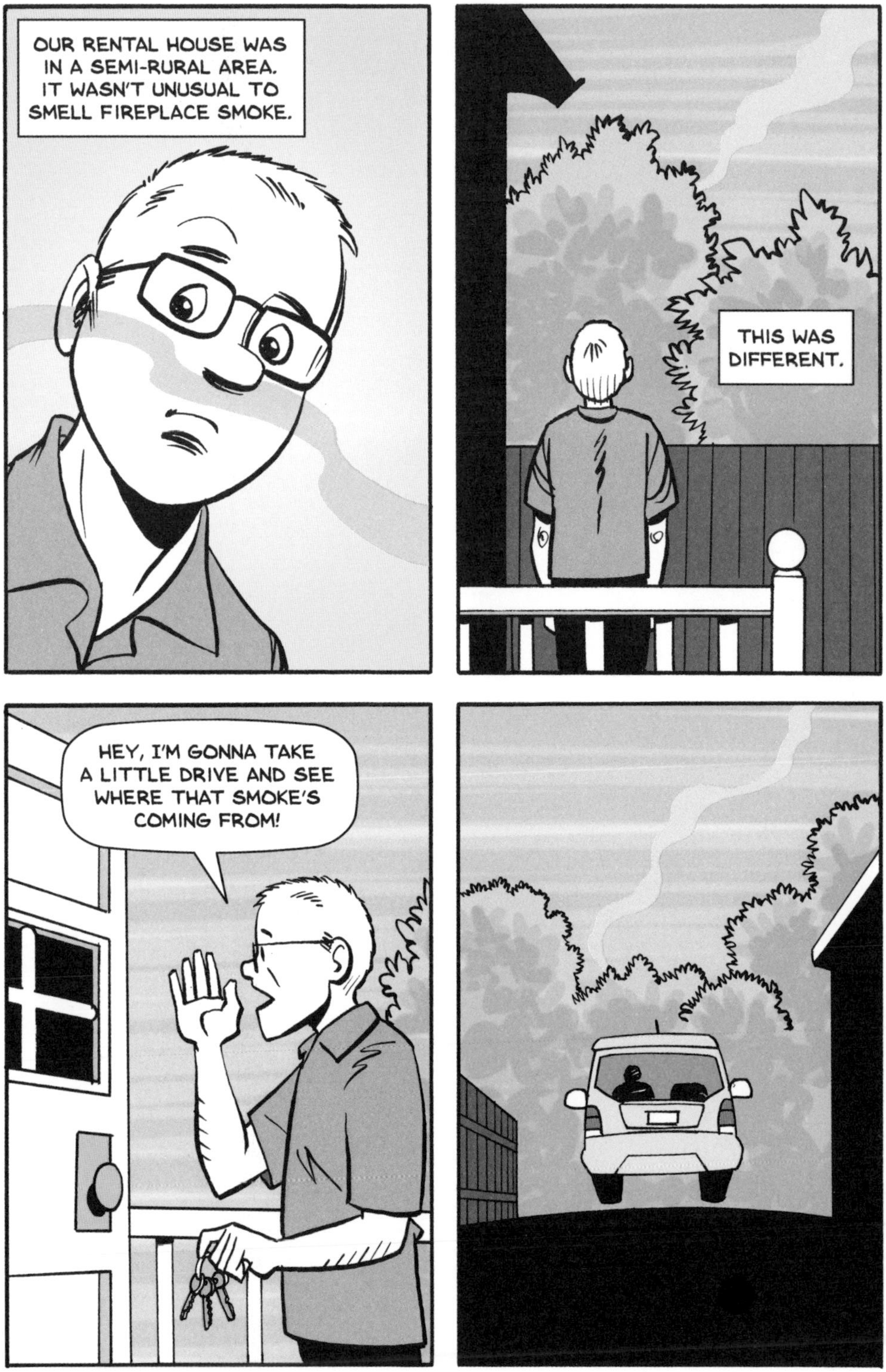

OUR RENTAL HOUSE WAS IN A SEMI-RURAL AREA. IT WASN'T UNUSUAL TO SMELL FIREPLACE SMOKE.
THIS WAS DIFFERENT.
HEY, I'M GONNA TAKE A LITTLE DRIVE AND SEE WHERE THAT SMOKE'S COMING FROM!

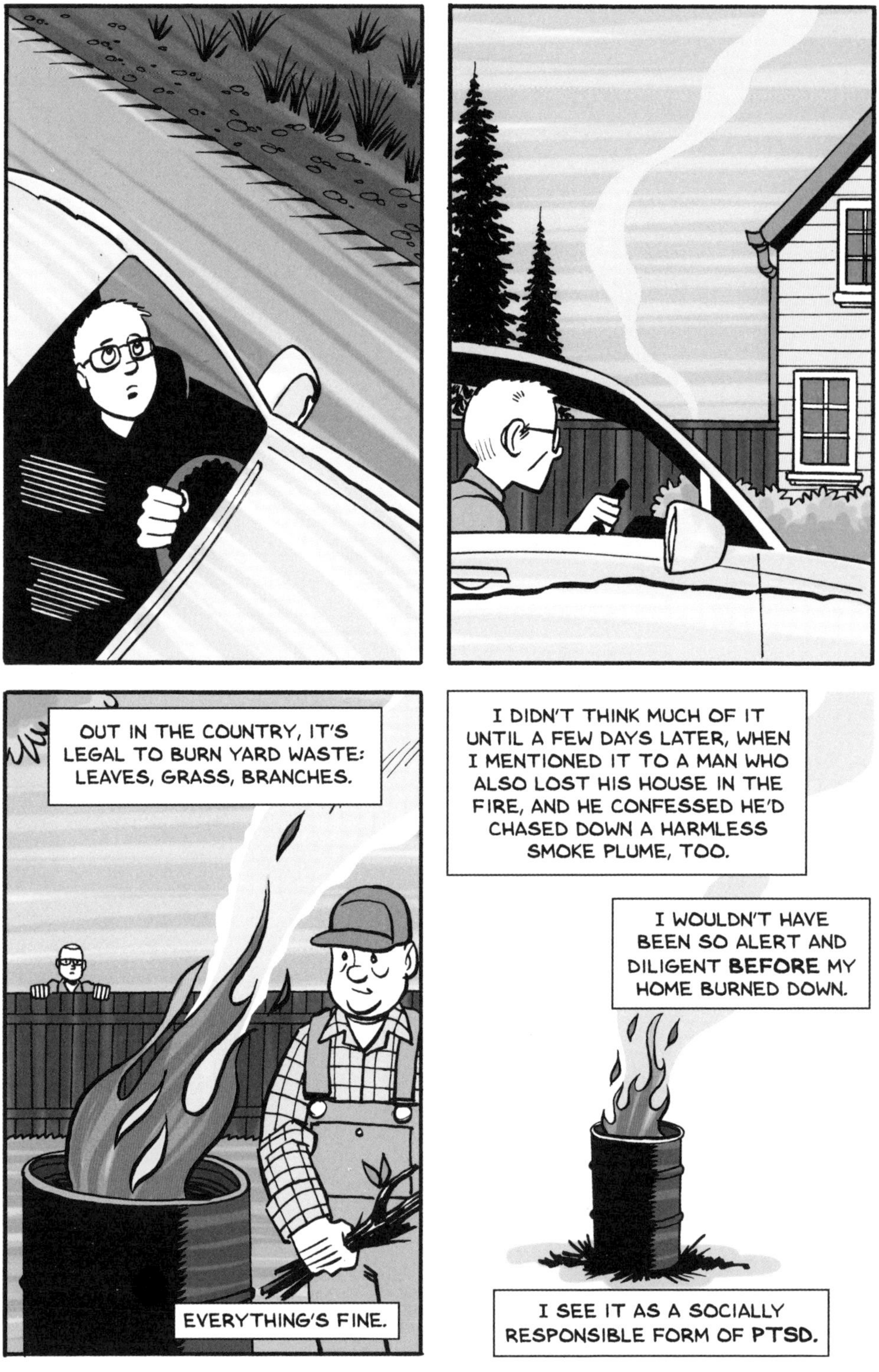
OUT IN THE COUNTRY, IT'S LEGAL TO BURN YARD WASTE: LEAVES, GRASS, BRANCHES.
EVERYTHING'S FINE.
I DIDN'T THINK MUCH OF IT UNTIL A FEW DAYS LATER, WHEN I MENTIONED IT TO A MAN WHO ALSO LOST HIS HOUSE IN THE FIRE, AND HE CONFESSED HE'D CHASED DOWN A HARMLESS SMOKE PLUME, TOO.
I WOULDN'T HAVE BEEN SO ALERT AND DILIGENT **BEFORE** MY HOME BURNED DOWN.
I SEE IT AS A SOCIALLY RESPONSIBLE FORM OF **PTSD.**

A DAY IN THE NEW LIFE

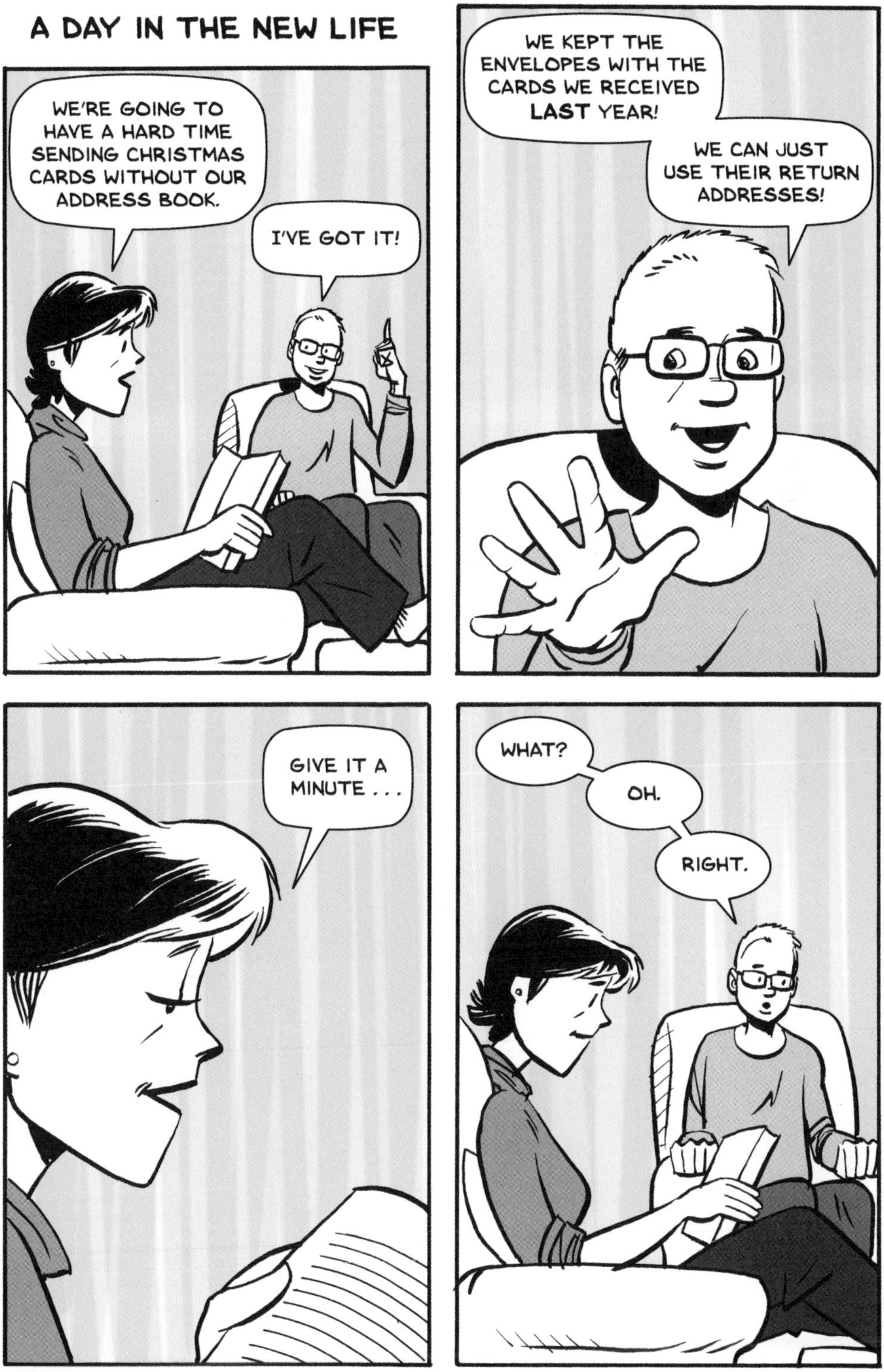
WE'RE GOING TO HAVE A HARD TIME SENDING CHRISTMAS CARDS WITHOUT OUR ADDRESS BOOK.
I'VE GOT IT!
WE KEPT THE ENVELOPES WITH THE CARDS WE RECEIVED **LAST** YEAR!
WE CAN JUST USE THEIR RETURN ADDRESSES!
GIVE IT A MINUTE . . .
WHAT?
OH.
RIGHT.

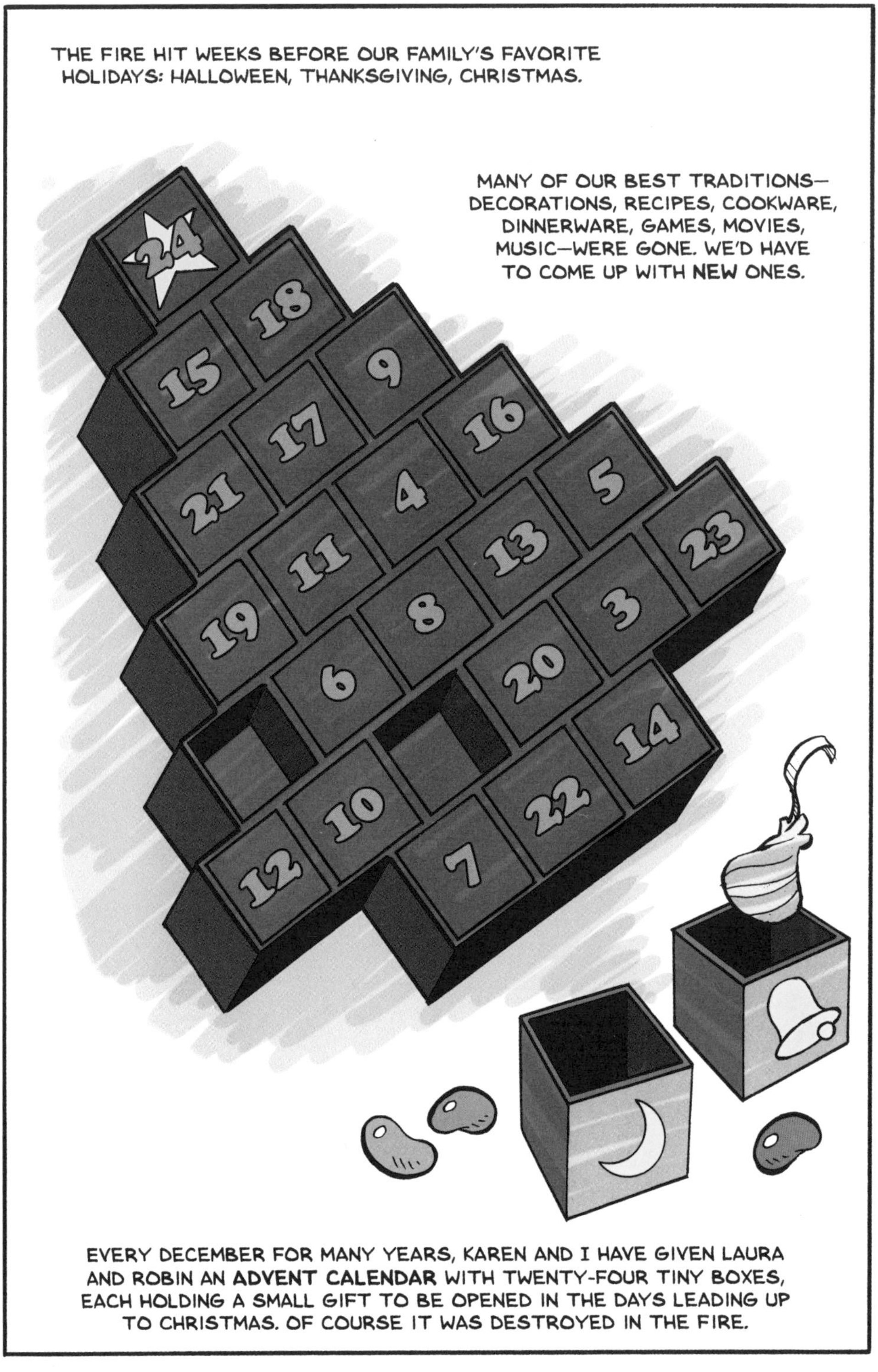
THE FIRE HIT WEEKS BEFORE OUR FAMILY'S FAVORITE HOLIDAYS: HALLOWEEN, THANKSGIVING, CHRISTMAS.
MANY OF OUR BEST TRADITIONS—DECORATIONS, RECIPES, COOKWARE, DINNERWARE, GAMES, MOVIES, MUSIC—WERE GONE. WE'D HAVE TO COME UP WITH NEW ONES.
EVERY DECEMBER FOR MANY YEARS, KAREN AND I HAVE GIVEN LAURA AND ROBIN AN **ADVENT CALENDAR** WITH TWENTY-FOUR TINY BOXES, EACH HOLDING A SMALL GIFT TO BE OPENED IN THE DAYS LEADING UP TO CHRISTMAS. OF COURSE IT WAS DESTROYED IN THE FIRE.

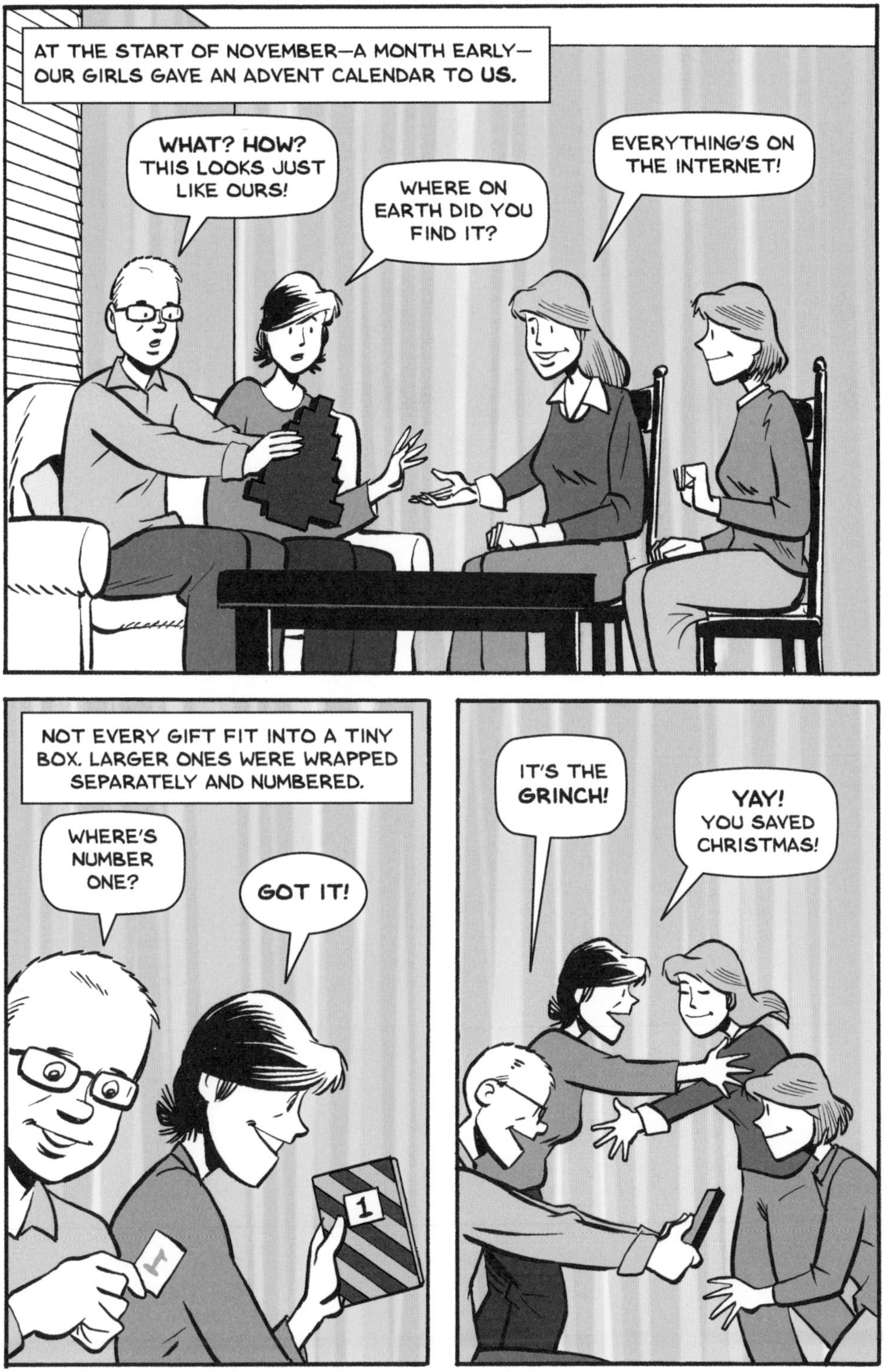
AT THE START OF NOVEMBER—A MONTH EARLY—OUR GIRLS GAVE AN ADVENT CALENDAR TO US.
WHAT? HOW? THIS LOOKS JUST LIKE OURS!
WHERE ON EARTH DID YOU FIND IT?
EVERYTHING'S ON THE INTERNET!
NOT EVERY GIFT FIT INTO A TINY BOX. LARGER ONES WERE WRAPPED SEPARATELY AND NUMBERED.
WHERE'S NUMBER ONE?
GOT IT!
1
IT'S THE GRINCH!
YAY! YOU SAVED CHRISTMAS!

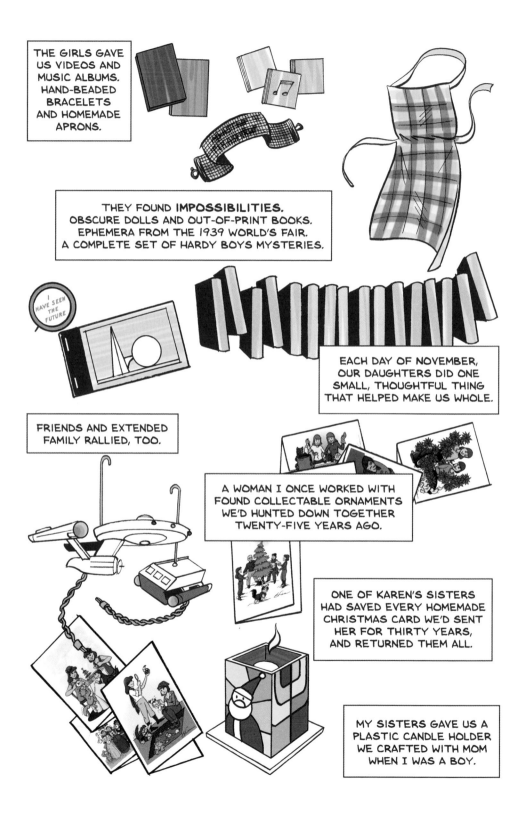

THE GIRLS GAVE US VIDEOS AND MUSIC ALBUMS. HAND-BEADED BRACELETS AND HOMEMADE APRONS.

THEY FOUND **IMPOSSIBILITIES**. OBSCURE DOLLS AND OUT-OF-PRINT BOOKS. EPHEMERA FROM THE 1939 WORLD'S FAIR. A COMPLETE SET OF HARDY BOYS MYSTERIES.

I HAVE SEEN THE FUTURE

EACH DAY OF NOVEMBER, OUR DAUGHTERS DID ONE SMALL, THOUGHTFUL THING THAT HELPED MAKE US WHOLE.

FRIENDS AND EXTENDED FAMILY RALLIED, TOO.

A WOMAN I ONCE WORKED WITH FOUND COLLECTABLE ORNAMENTS WE'D HUNTED DOWN TOGETHER TWENTY-FIVE YEARS AGO.

ONE OF KAREN'S SISTERS HAD SAVED EVERY HOMEMADE CHRISTMAS CARD WE'D SENT HER FOR THIRTY YEARS, AND RETURNED THEM ALL.

MY SISTERS GAVE US A PLASTIC CANDLE HOLDER WE CRAFTED WITH MOM WHEN I WAS A BOY.

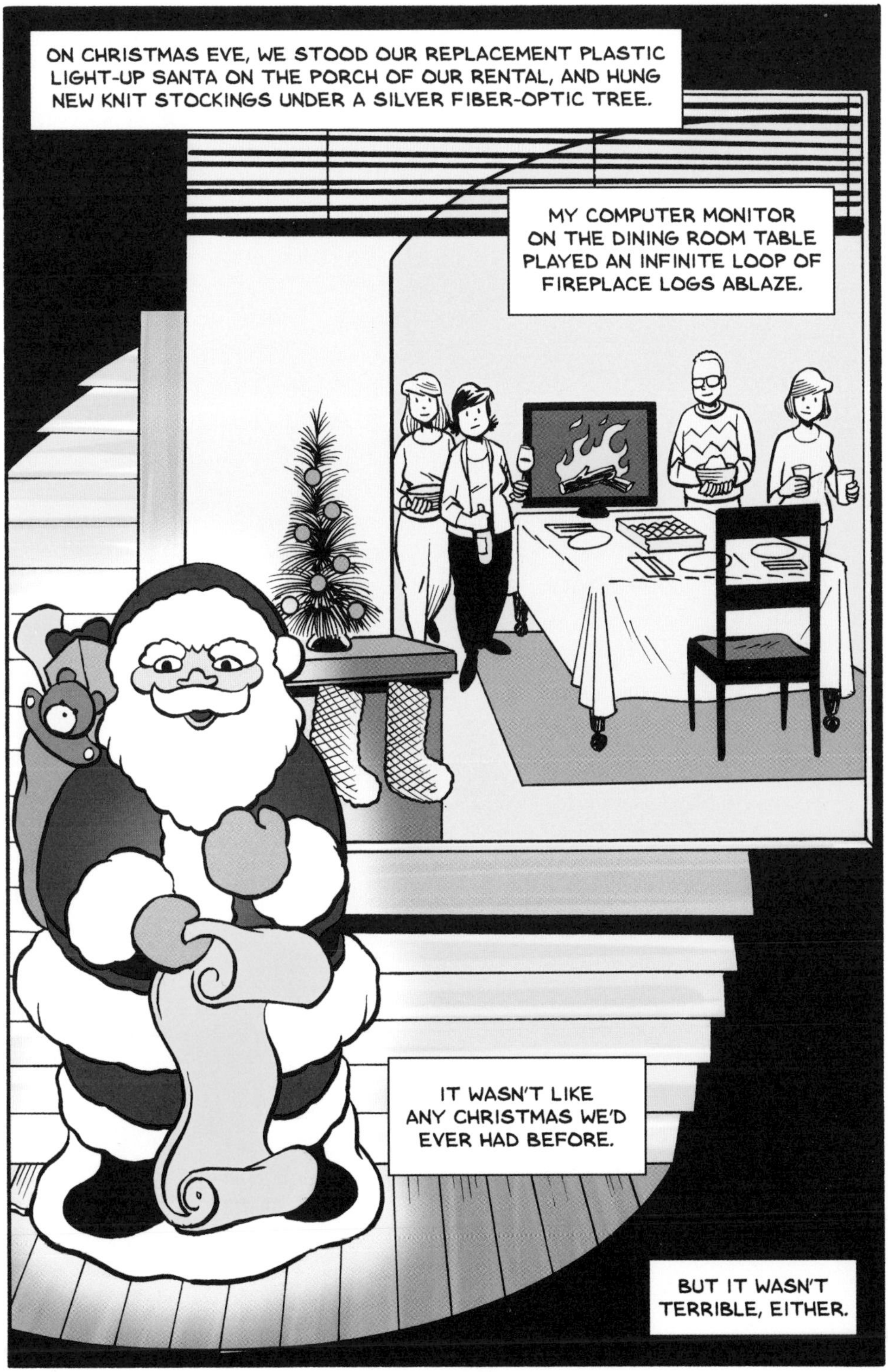
ON CHRISTMAS EVE, WE STOOD OUR REPLACEMENT PLASTIC LIGHT-UP SANTA ON THE PORCH OF OUR RENTAL, AND HUNG NEW KNIT STOCKINGS UNDER A SILVER FIBER-OPTIC TREE.
MY COMPUTER MONITOR ON THE DINING ROOM TABLE PLAYED AN INFINITE LOOP OF FIREPLACE LOGS ABLAZE.
IT WASN'T LIKE ANY CHRISTMAS WE'D EVER HAD BEFORE.
BUT IT WASN'T TERRIBLE, EITHER.

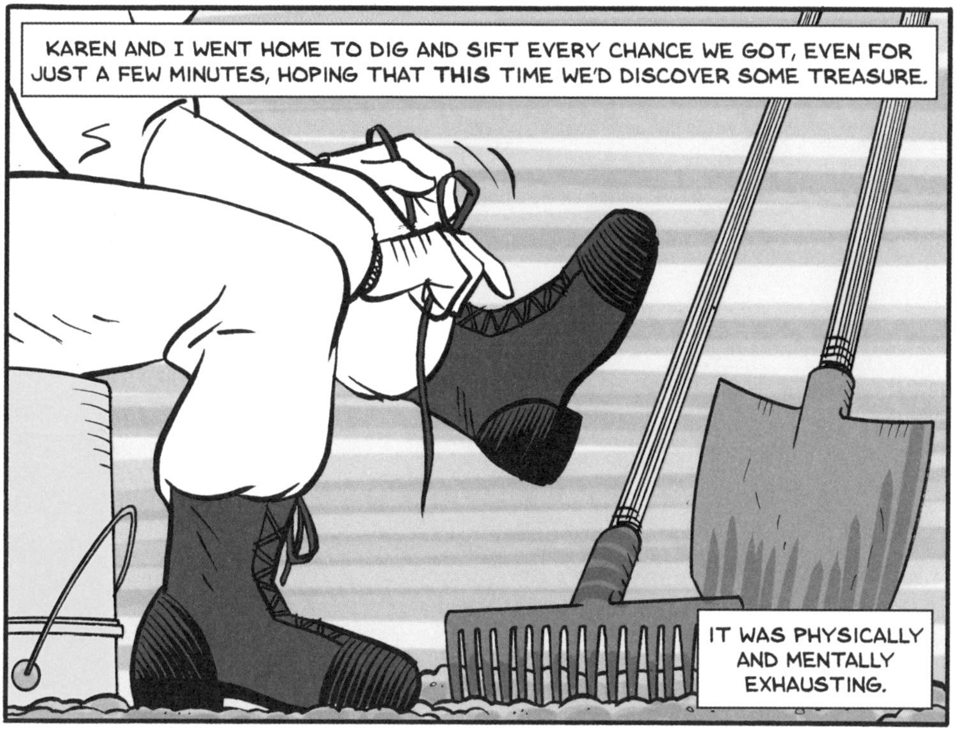
KAREN AND I WENT HOME TO DIG AND SIFT EVERY CHANCE WE GOT, EVEN FOR JUST A FEW MINUTES, HOPING THAT THIS TIME WE'D DISCOVER SOME TREASURE.
IT WAS PHYSICALLY AND MENTALLY EXHAUSTING.

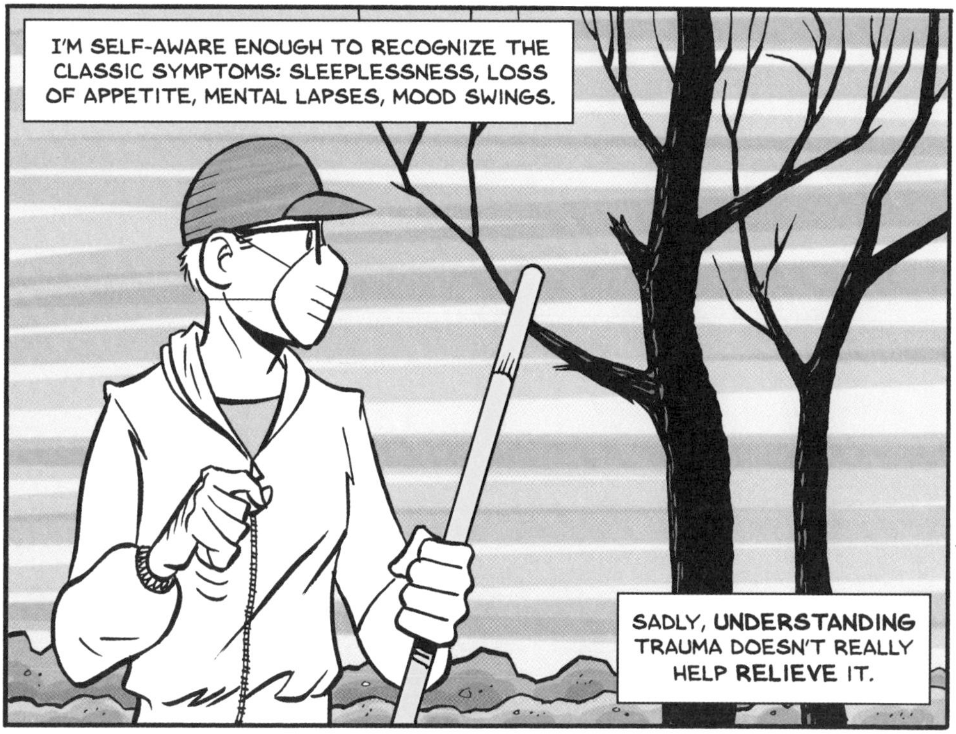
I'M SELF-AWARE ENOUGH TO RECOGNIZE THE CLASSIC SYMPTOMS: SLEEPLESSNESS, LOSS OF APPETITE, MENTAL LAPSES, MOOD SWINGS.
SADLY, UNDERSTANDING TRAUMA DOESN'T REALLY HELP RELIEVE IT.

SOME NEIGHBORS WERE SO WOUNDED THEY NEVER HAD THE HEART TO RETURN AT ALL.

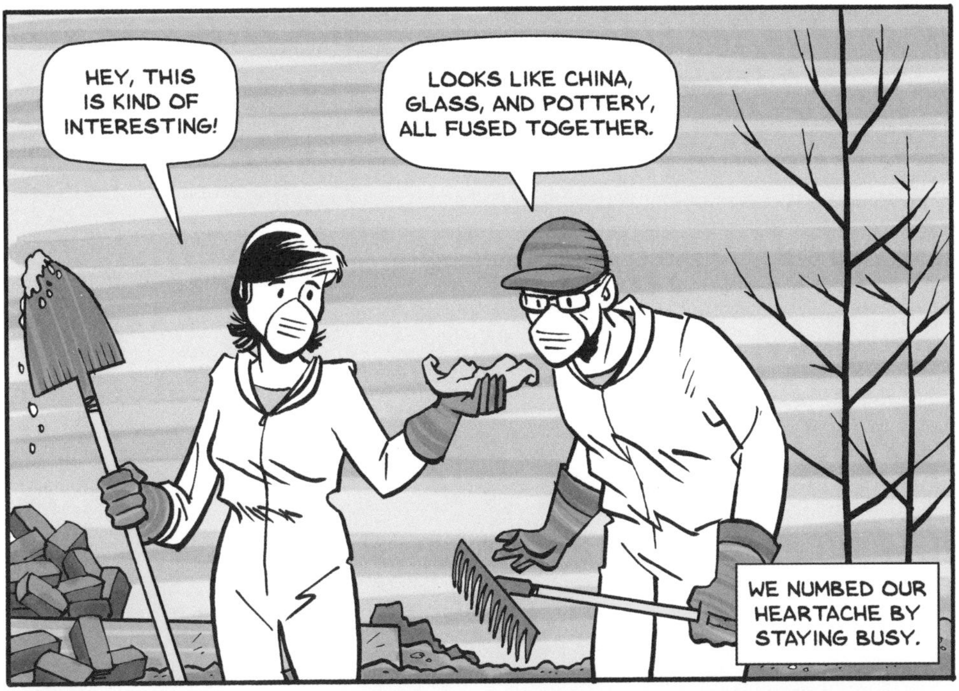
HEY, THIS IS KIND OF INTERESTING!
LOOKS LIKE CHINA, GLASS, AND POTTERY, ALL FUSED TOGETHER.
WE NUMBED OUR HEARTACHE BY STAYING BUSY.

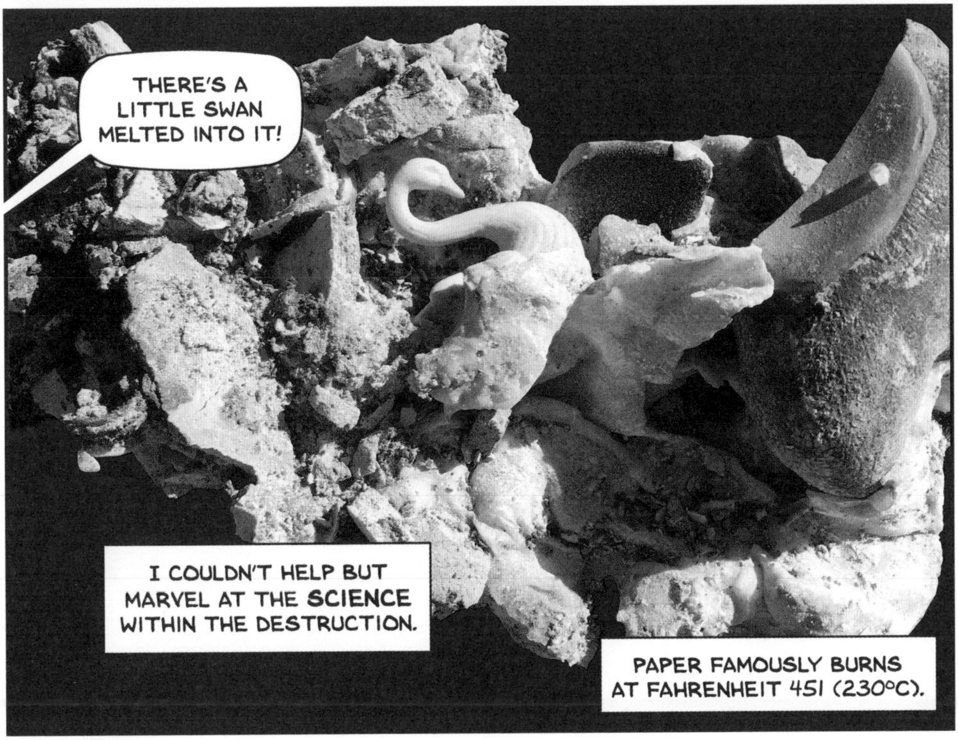
THERE'S A LITTLE SWAN MELTED INTO IT!
I COULDN'T HELP BUT MARVEL AT THE SCIENCE WITHIN THE DESTRUCTION.
PAPER FAMOUSLY BURNS AT FAHRENHEIT 451 (230°C).

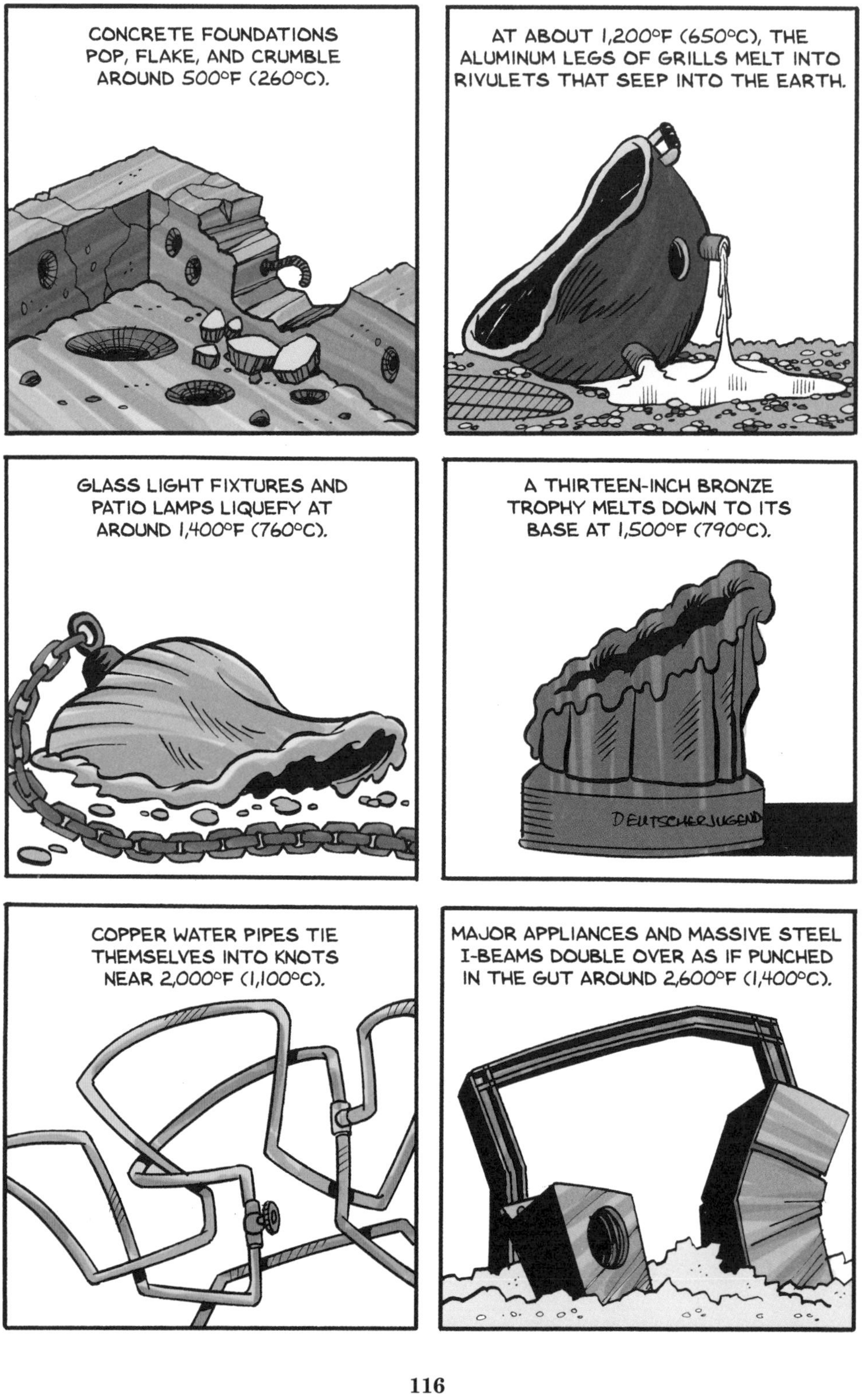
CONCRETE FOUNDATIONS POP, FLAKE, AND CRUMBLE AROUND 500°F (260°C).
AT ABOUT 1,200°F (650°C), THE ALUMINUM LEGS OF GRILLS MELT INTO RIVULETS THAT SEEP INTO THE EARTH.
GLASS LIGHT FIXTURES AND PATIO LAMPS LIQUEFY AT AROUND 1,400°F (760°C).
A THIRTEEN-INCH BRONZE TROPHY MELTS DOWN TO ITS BASE AT 1,500°F (790°C).
DEUTSCHERJUGEND
COPPER WATER PIPES TIE THEMSELVES INTO KNOTS NEAR 2,000°F (1,100°C).
MAJOR APPLIANCES AND MASSIVE STEEL I-BEAMS DOUBLE OVER AS IF PUNCHED IN THE GUT AROUND 2,600°F (1,400°C).

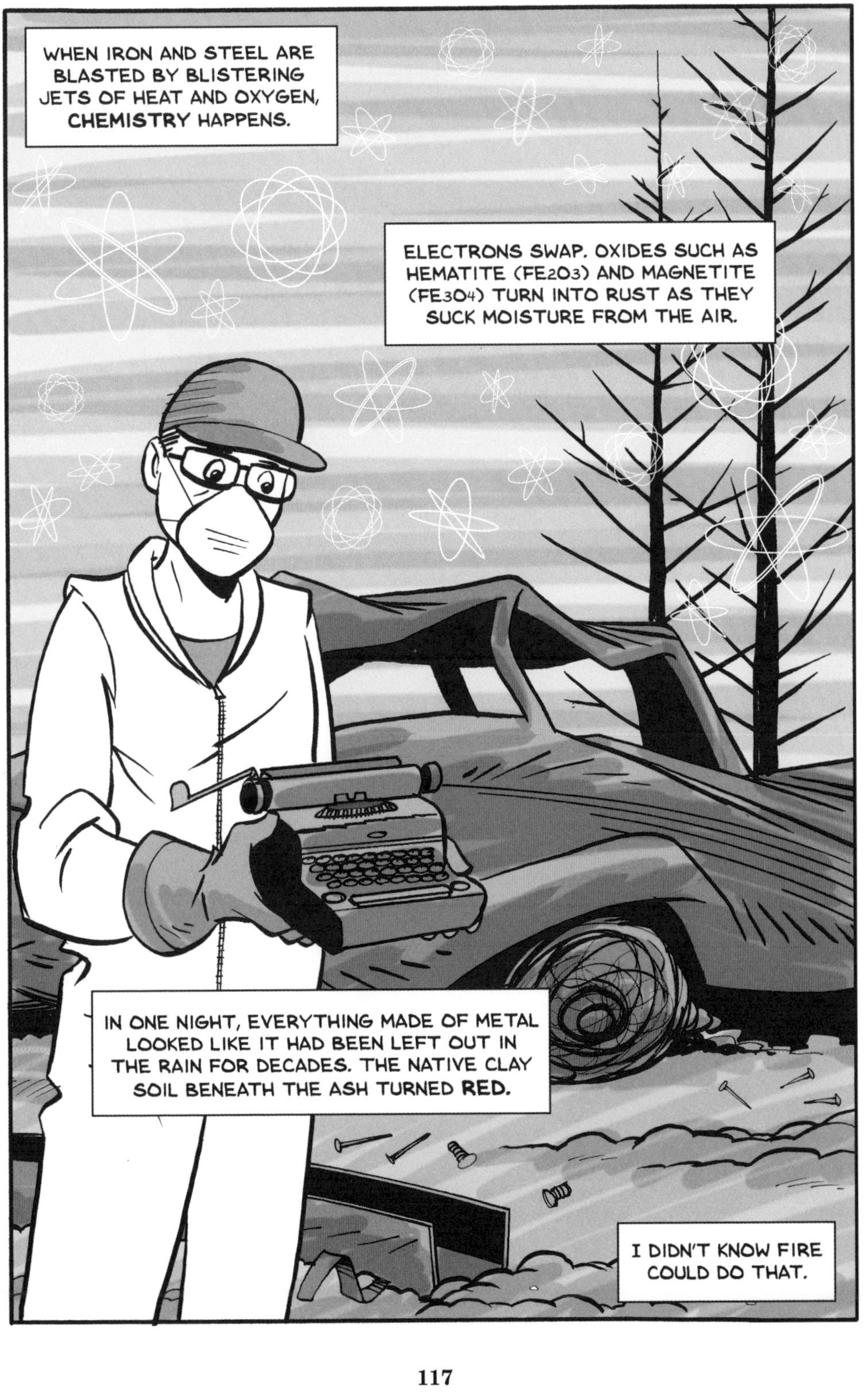
WHEN IRON AND STEEL ARE BLASTED BY BLISTERING JETS OF HEAT AND OXYGEN, **CHEMISTRY** HAPPENS.
ELECTRONS SWAP. OXIDES SUCH AS HEMATITE (FE2O3) AND MAGNETITE (FE3O4) TURN INTO RUST AS THEY SUCK MOISTURE FROM THE AIR.
IN ONE NIGHT, EVERYTHING MADE OF METAL LOOKED LIKE IT HAD BEEN LEFT OUT IN THE RAIN FOR DECADES. THE NATIVE CLAY SOIL BENEATH THE ASH TURNED **RED.**
I DIDN'T KNOW FIRE COULD DO THAT.

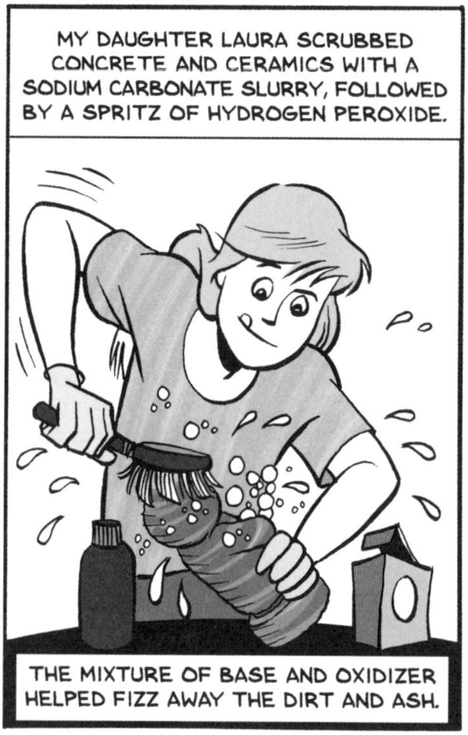
MY DAUGHTER LAURA SCRUBBED CONCRETE AND CERAMICS WITH A SODIUM CARBONATE SLURRY, FOLLOWED BY A SPRITZ OF HYDROGEN PEROXIDE.
THE MIXTURE OF BASE AND OXIDIZER HELPED FIZZ AWAY THE DIRT AND ASH.

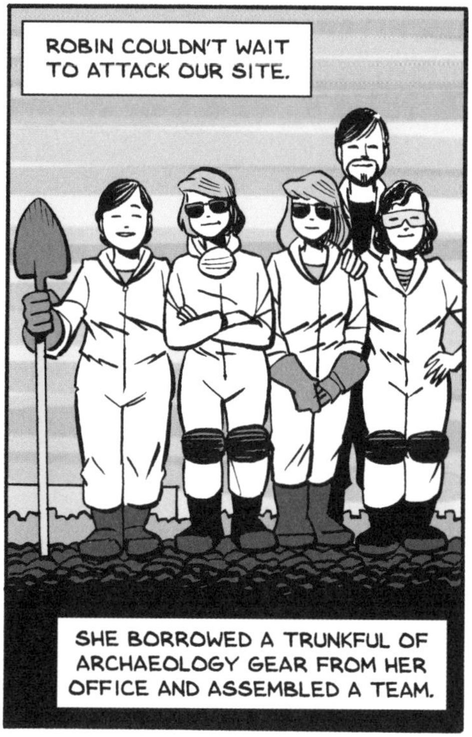
ROBIN COULDN'T WAIT TO ATTACK OUR SITE.
SHE BORROWED A TRUNKFUL OF ARCHAEOLOGY GEAR FROM HER OFFICE AND ASSEMBLED A TEAM.

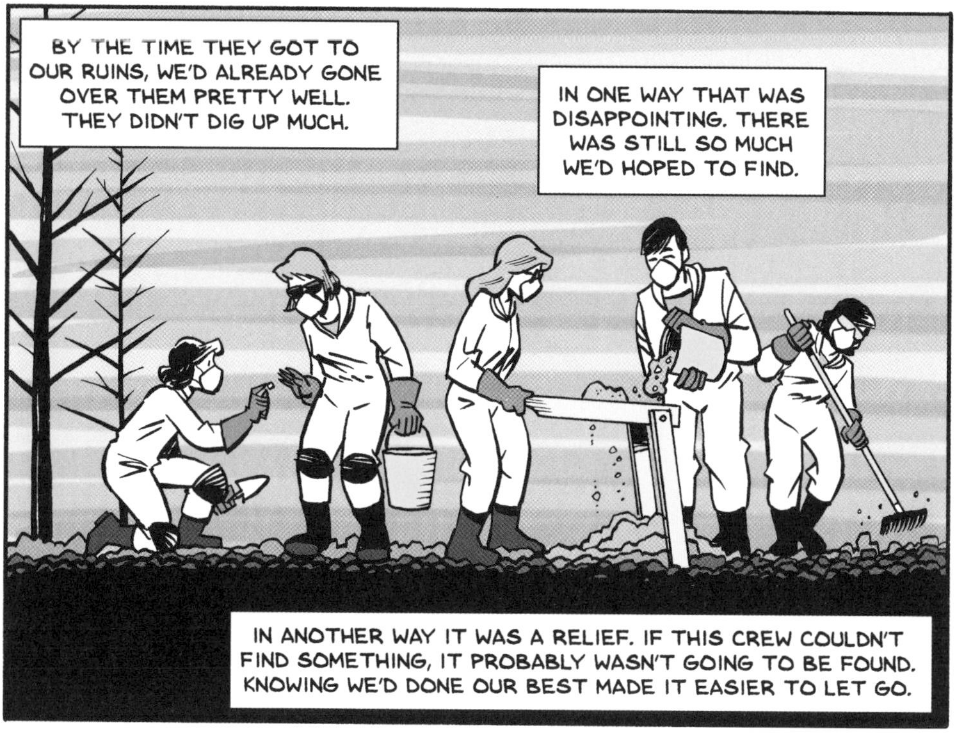
BY THE TIME THEY GOT TO OUR RUINS, WE'D ALREADY GONE OVER THEM PRETTY WELL. THEY DIDN'T DIG UP MUCH.
IN ONE WAY THAT WAS DISAPPOINTING. THERE WAS STILL SO MUCH WE'D HOPED TO FIND.
IN ANOTHER WAY IT WAS A RELIEF. IF THIS CREW COULDN'T FIND SOMETHING, IT PROBABLY WASN'T GOING TO BE FOUND. KNOWING WE'D DONE OUR BEST MADE IT EASIER TO LET GO.

Archaeology 101

A standard archaeological tool is the rocking screen, a wooden frame about two feet square with metal mesh and two hinged legs.

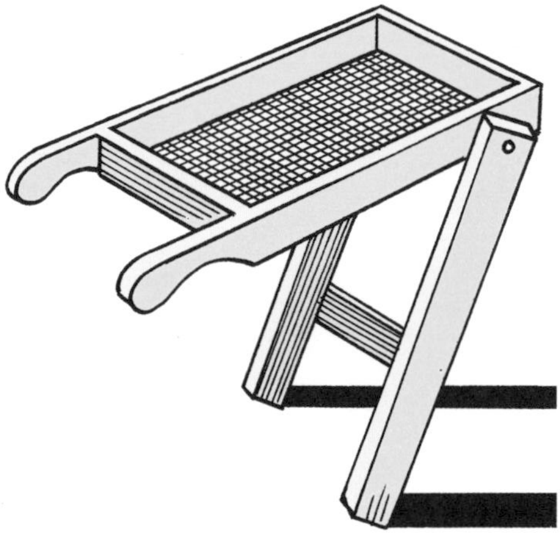

1.

With the screen lying on the ground, fill it with one bucket of debris to be examined.

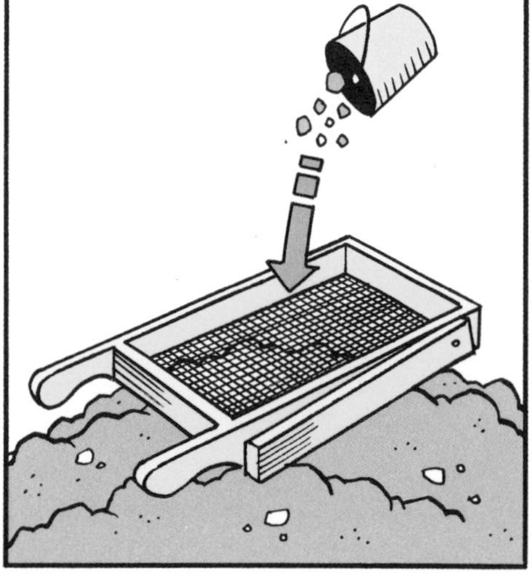

2.

Grasp the screen and pull it up in one confident fluid motion.

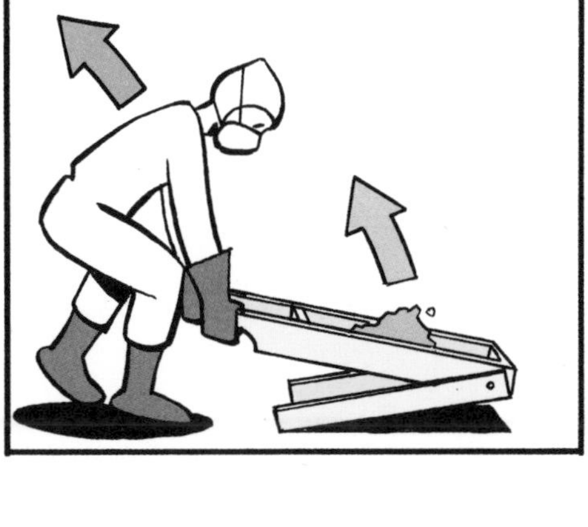

3.

Skitter the screen's legs over the ground until the frame whacks your shins.

Curse.

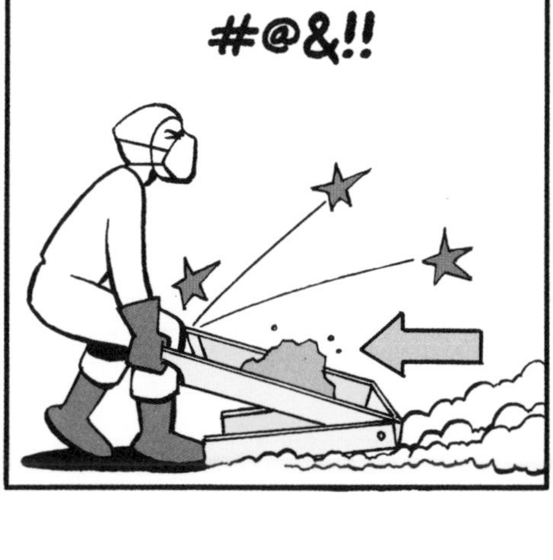
#@&!!

4.

Bracing a hinged leg with your foot, grasp the screen and pull it up in one confident fluid motion.

5.

Shake the screen vigorously to sift small particles and dust. Apologize to anyone downwind.

HEY!

6.

While supporting the screen with one hand, use a trowel to examine debris. Imagine you saw something shiny; fail to find it. Lose your place and start over.

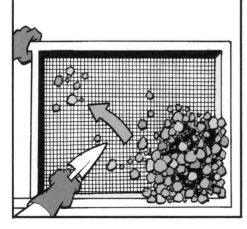

7.

When done, tip debris onto waste pile. Apologize to anyone downwind.

Repeat.

HEY!

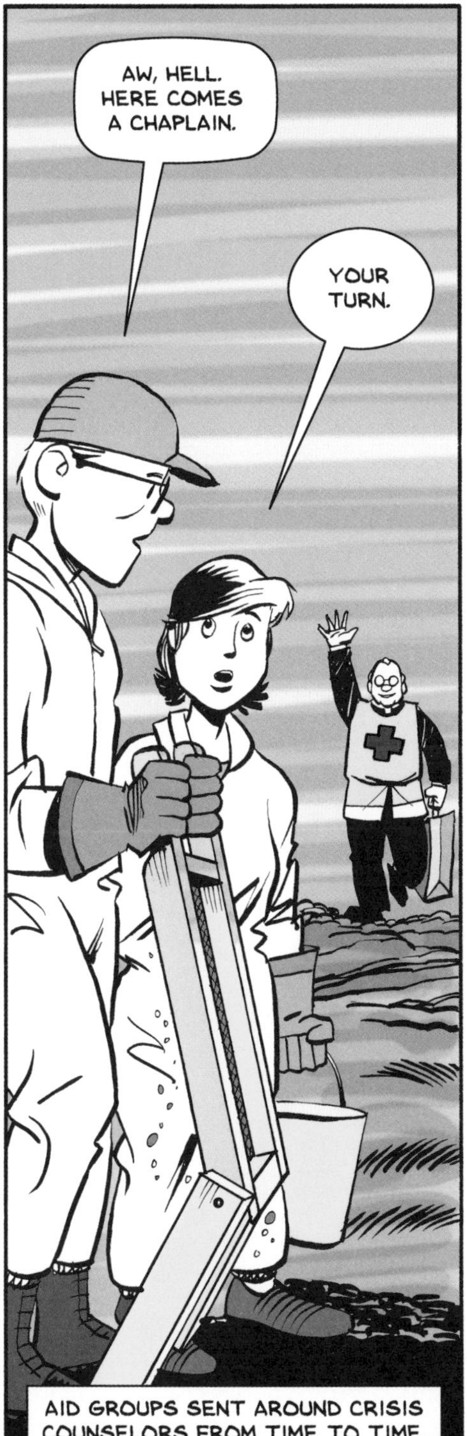
AW, HELL. HERE COMES A CHAPLAIN.
YOUR TURN.
AID GROUPS SENT AROUND CRISIS COUNSELORS FROM TIME TO TIME.

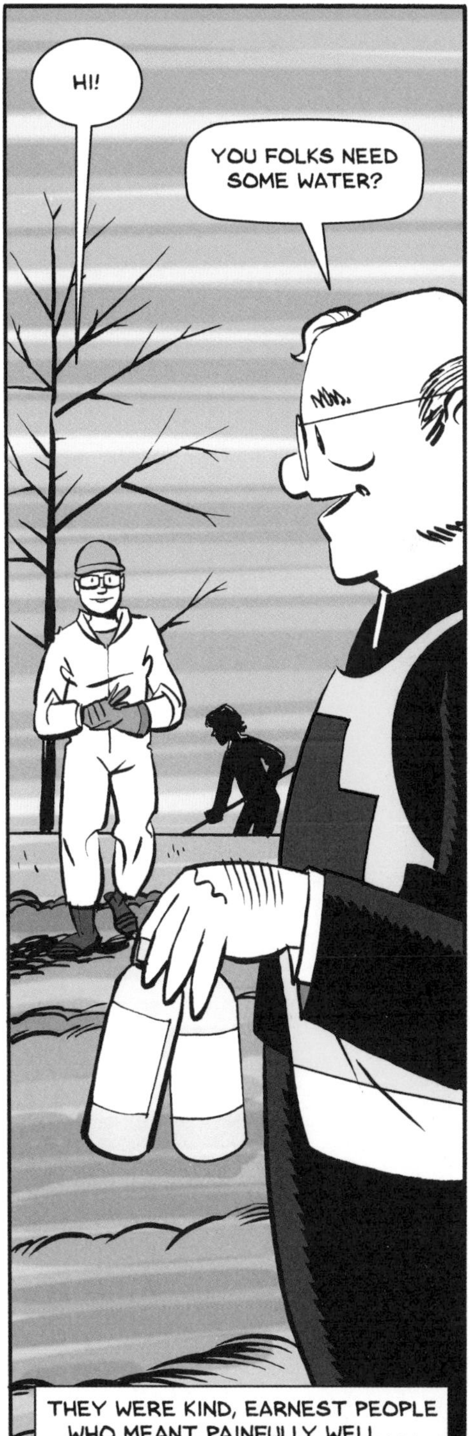
HI!
YOU FOLKS NEED SOME WATER?
THEY WERE KIND, EARNEST PEOPLE WHO MEANT PAINFULLY WELL . . .

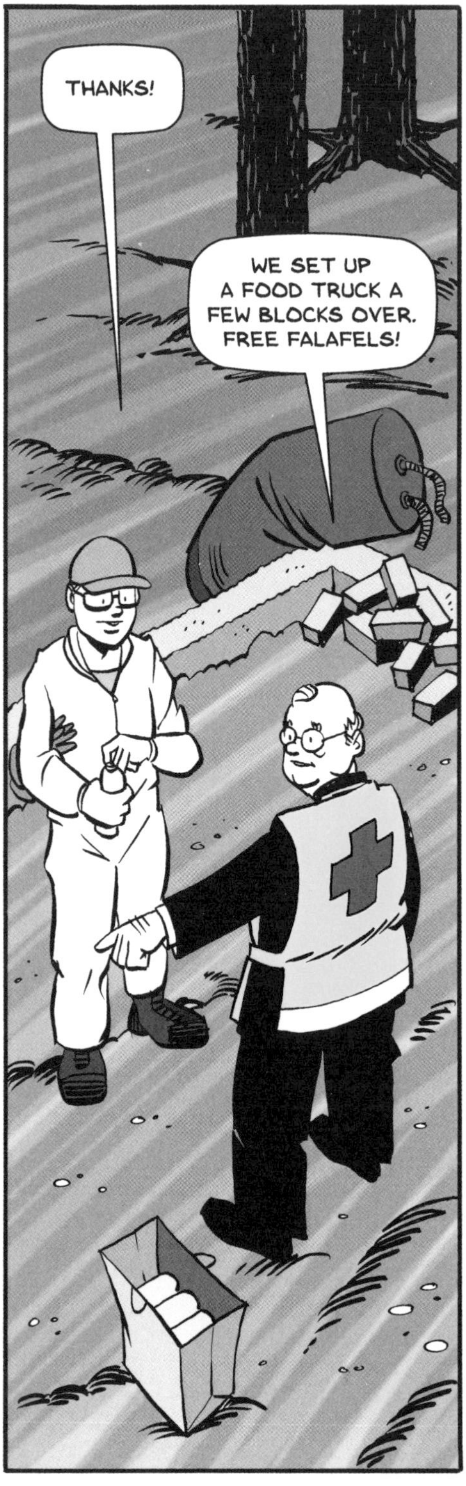
THANKS!
WE SET UP A FOOD TRUCK A FEW BLOCKS OVER. FREE FALAFELS!

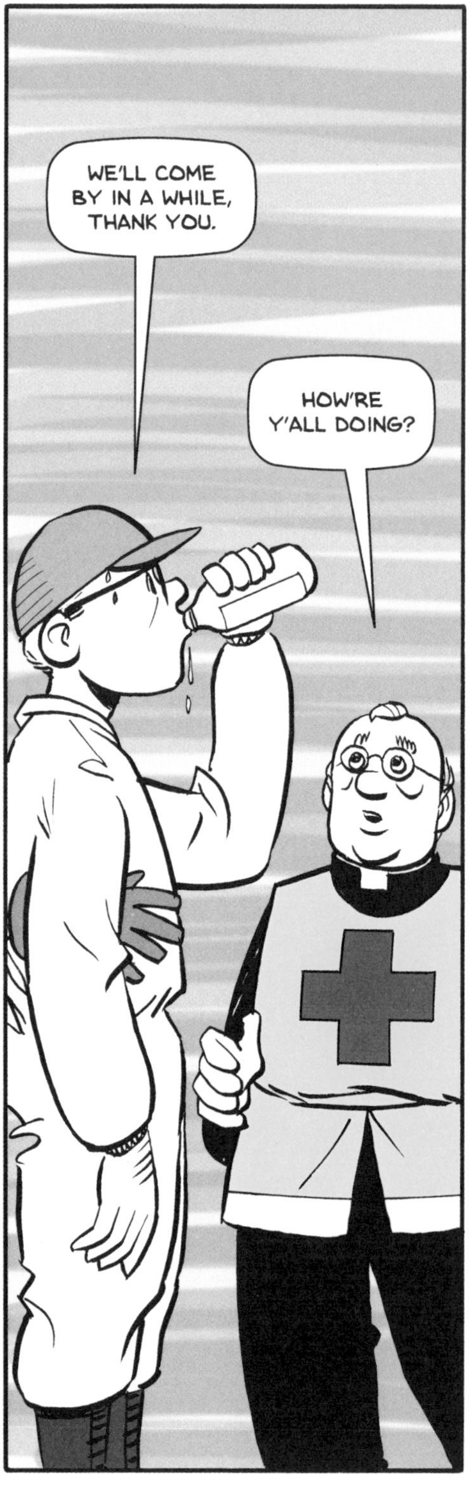
WE'LL COME BY IN A WHILE, THANK YOU.
HOW'RE Y'ALL DOING?

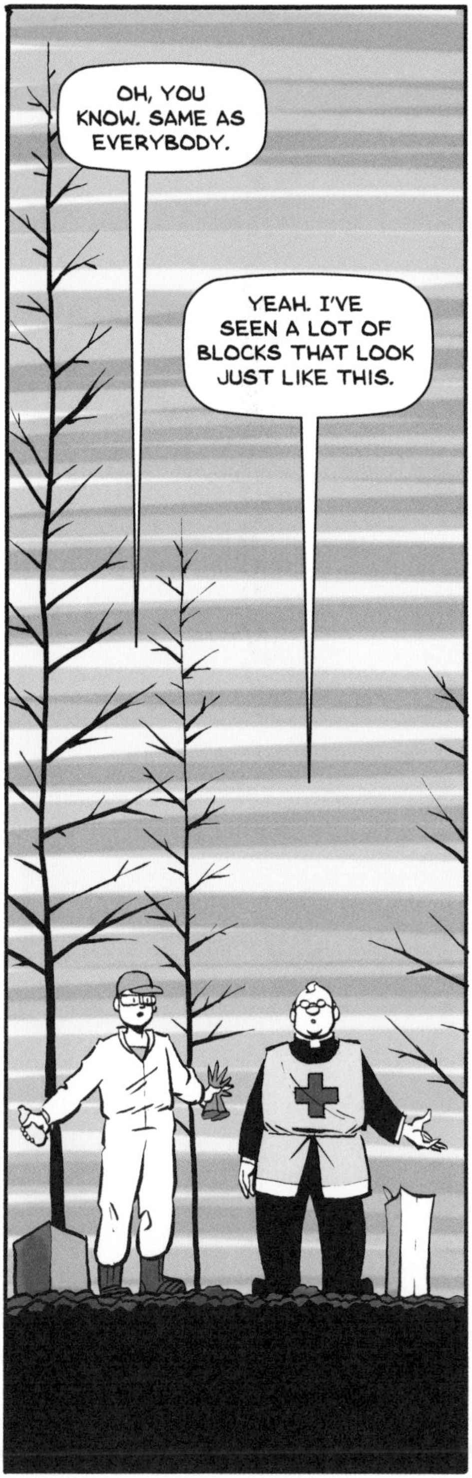
OH, YOU KNOW. SAME AS EVERYBODY.
YEAH. I'VE SEEN A LOT OF BLOCKS THAT LOOK JUST LIKE THIS.

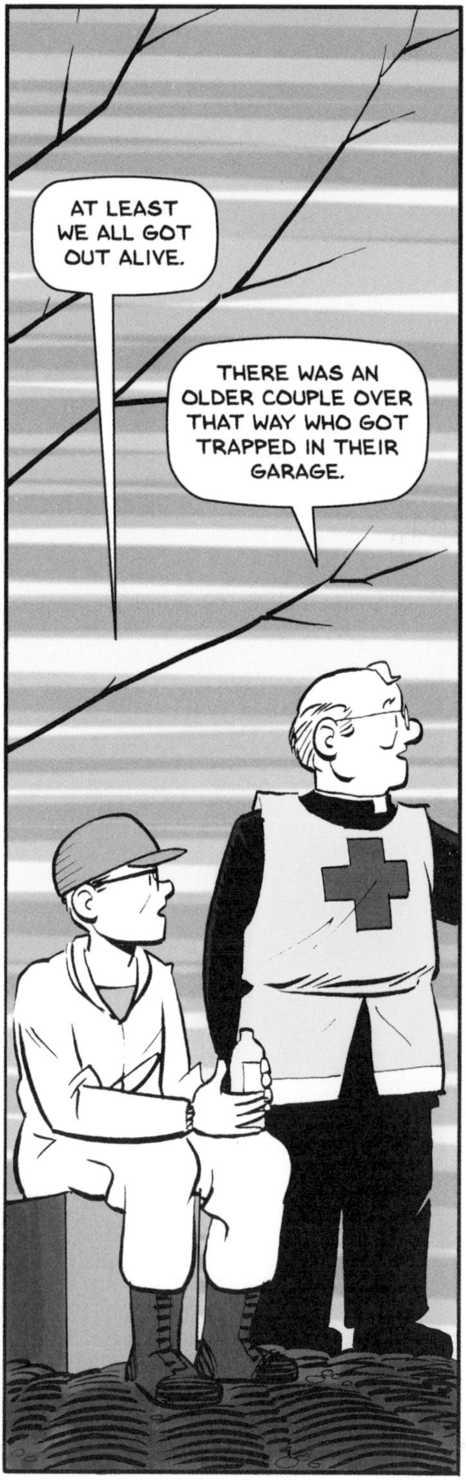
AT LEAST WE ALL GOT OUT ALIVE.
THERE WAS AN OLDER COUPLE OVER THAT WAY WHO GOT TRAPPED IN THEIR GARAGE.

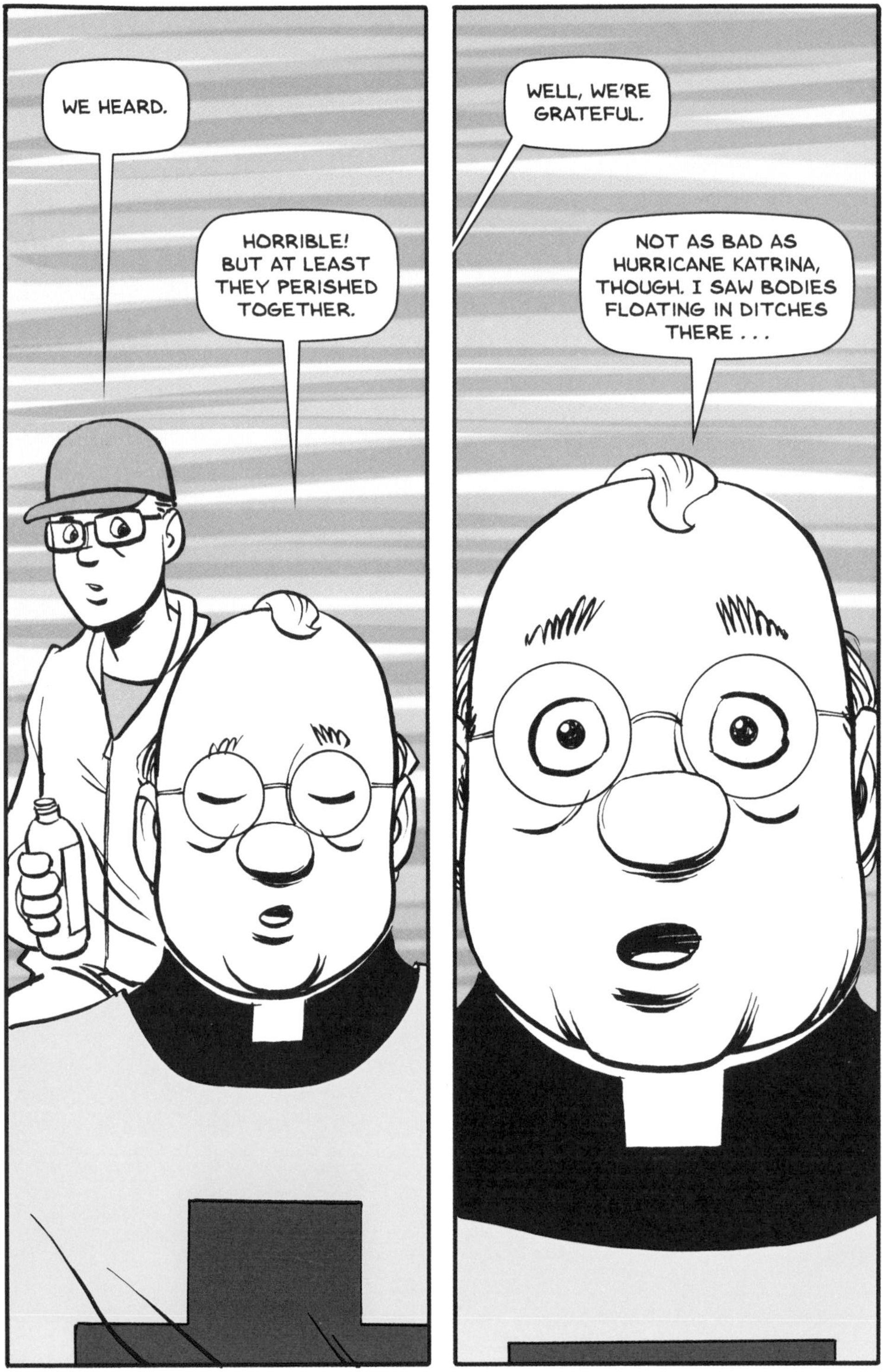
WE HEARD.
HORRIBLE! BUT AT LEAST THEY PERISHED TOGETHER.
WELL, WE'RE GRATEFUL.
NOT AS BAD AS HURRICANE KATRINA, THOUGH. I SAW BODIES FLOATING IN DITCHES THERE . . .

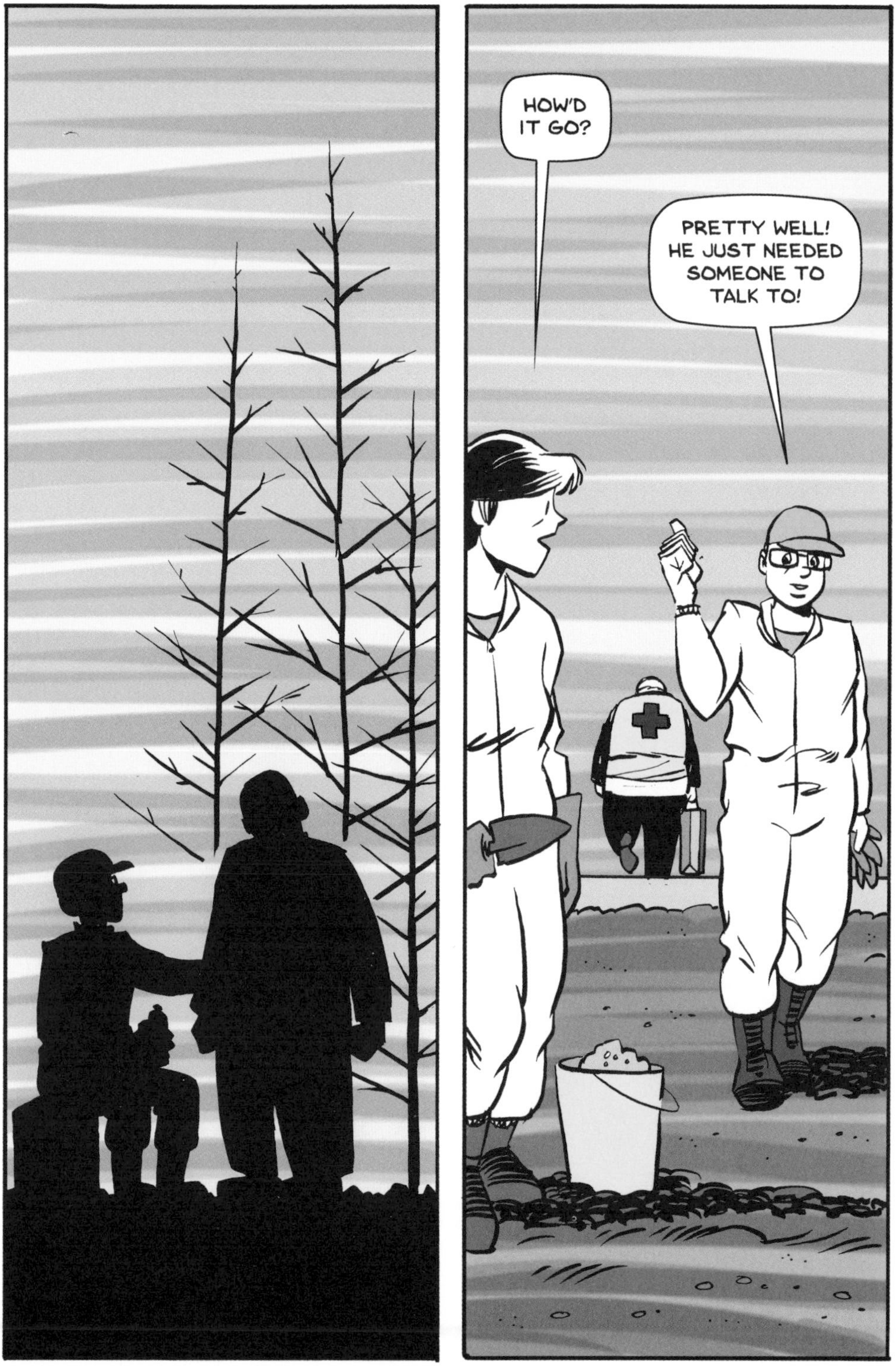
HOW'D IT GO?
PRETTY WELL! HE JUST NEEDED SOMEONE TO TALK TO!

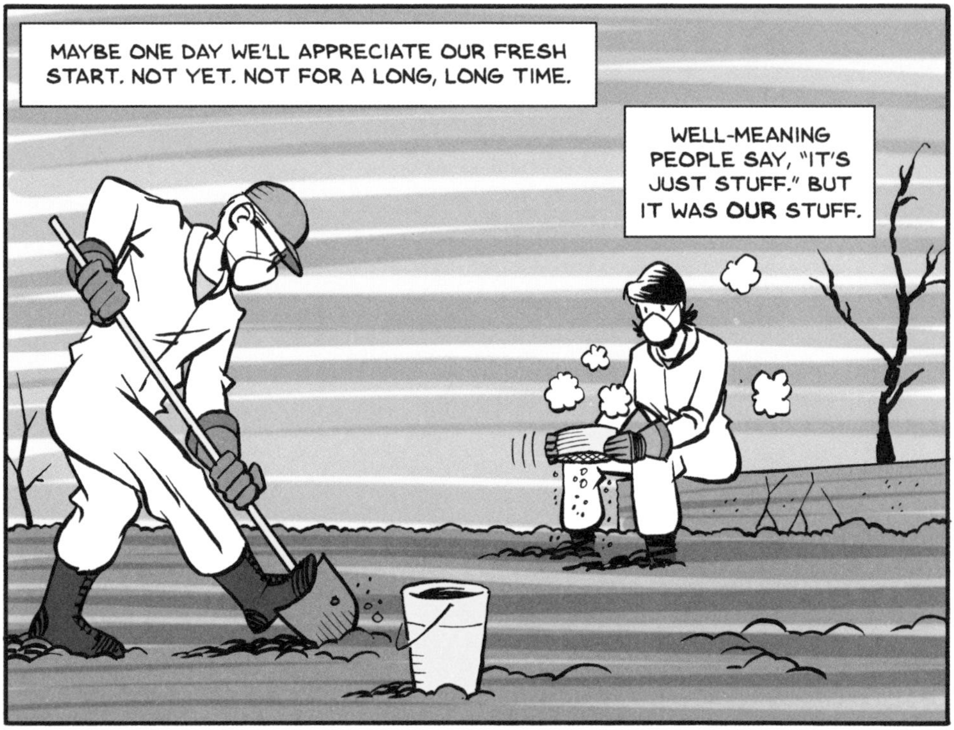
MAYBE ONE DAY WE'LL APPRECIATE OUR FRESH START. NOT YET. NOT FOR A LONG, LONG TIME.
WELL-MEANING PEOPLE SAY, "IT'S JUST STUFF." BUT IT WAS **OUR** STUFF.

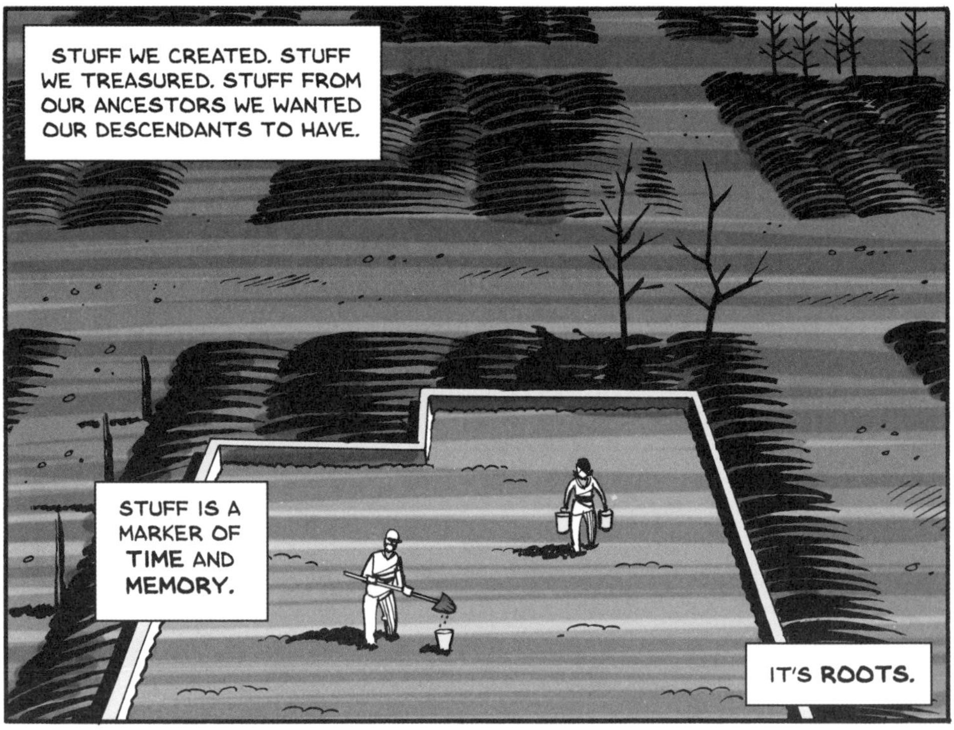
STUFF WE CREATED. STUFF WE TREASURED. STUFF FROM OUR ANCESTORS WE WANTED OUR DESCENDANTS TO HAVE.
STUFF IS A MARKER OF **TIME** AND **MEMORY**.
IT'S **ROOTS**.

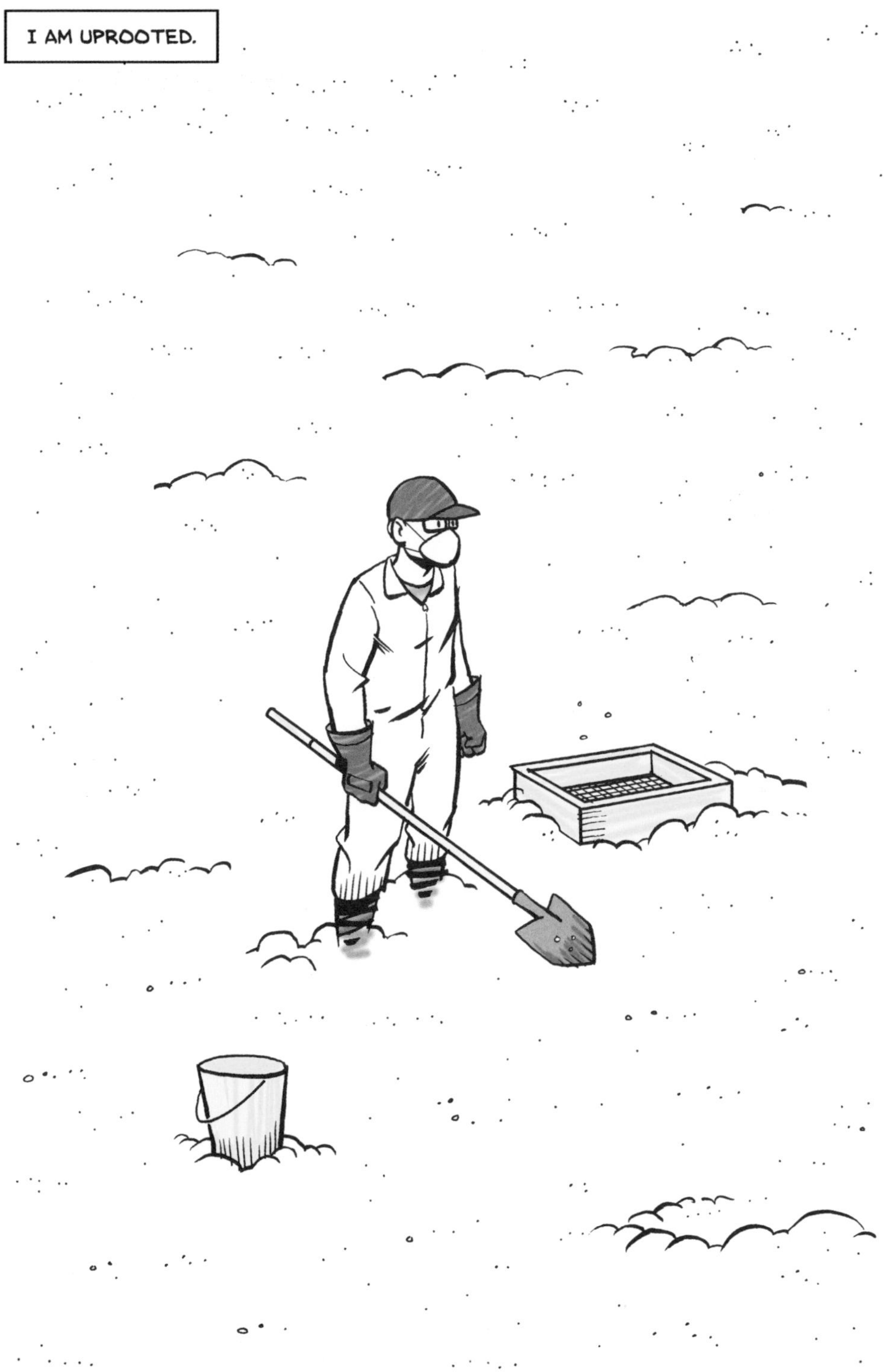
I AM UPROOTED.

SUNNY'S FIRE STORY

BRADLEY SUNSHINE HACKWELL AND HIS GIRLFRIEND, KATELYN, LIVED IN THE HILLS BETWEEN CALISTOGA AND SANTA ROSA, IN THE PATH OF THE TUBBS FIRE. SUNNY, TWENTY-SIX, IS A CONSTRUCTION WORKER WHO SERVED WITH THE U.S. ARMY IN AFGHANISTAN.

I was working security for an Indian casino at the time. I worked really early in the morning, so I was already in bed by 9 P.M. Around 11:30 my girlfriend and our roommate woke me up saying, "Get up, we've gotta get out of the house!" I was pissed because I had to wake up early and thought my friend was playing a joke on me. When I saw Katelyn's face, I knew something was wrong.

I went outside immediately and could see a glow above the tree line. I thought, "Holy crap, this is real!" My roommate's already gone, he's down the road. As I ran back inside to grab Katelyn, the power turned off, so I knew the fire was close.

We hopped into her Tahoe and as soon as we turned onto the main road, everything was engulfed in flames. Left side and right side. With the wind, it looked like waves of flame rolling across the road. Our windows were up but you could feel the heat inside the vehicle, like a sunburn on your face.

Katelyn's freaking out. I've been in worse situations, so I'm quiet. I'm just trying to get through it and calm her down. It's a bad situation, you've got to keep your cool, but if you stop moving, your tires melt and you die.

What I took out of the Army and used in the fire is this: you can't freak out. You've got to stay stress-free and focus on what you're doing. Take emotion out of it. If you freeze, if you take a breath, you could lose your chance at either breathing again or saving a friend.

In Afghanistan, there were a lot of situations where I didn't know what to do. I just knew what was in front of me and what I *could* do at that moment.

A couple of cars slowed down because there were flames in front of us, so I swerved in front of them and gunned it. They fell in right behind me, and before I know it there's two, three, four cars behind us and I'm leading the way through a firestorm.

I did two tours, four years—10th Mountain Division, 1st Battalion, 32nd Infantry Regiment. South Kandahar Province. We basically patrolled, and for six months we built COPs (command operating posts) for the Afghan National Army. It's called "peacekeeping"—kind of like being a police officer, you just walk around and have a presence to deter stupid things from happening. Which, really honestly, just set us up for getting shot at.

How you respond in a situation has more to do with experience than training. Just because someone teaches you something doesn't mean you're going to do it right.

I was building a tower during my first deployment in Afghanistan. We had to stack sandbags. And we hear two pops and two snaps. A pop shot is when you hear gunfire. The snap? That's a bullet breaking the sound barrier, which means it's next to you. So if you hear a pop shot, you just keep walking normal. But if you hear a snap, you get down. Real quick. Or you return fire.

I'd probably been shot at seven or eight times in the first month I was there, so I was used to it, but not like I was at the end of my deployment, when I was keen to every sound and sight. So we're getting the sandbags stacked all nice, and we hear two snaps go by. And then two more snaps. Then the wood cracks right next to us on the top of the tower.

One guy jumps off the tower, another rolls into the tower, and I'm standing there with a sandbag in my hands. Just standing there, not moving. My buddy says, "Get down, you idiot!" and grabs my boot and pulls me inside the tower.

I didn't have experience then. I got a lot more practice after that.

We made it through the firestorm to a bunch of sheriff's cars. The fire's maybe twenty or thirty feet behind us. They rushed us through and we all met at a parking lot to make sure everybody got out and was fine.

After that, Katelyn and I went to the casino hotel and watched the news to see if our house burned down. Sure enough, it did. Me being a casino employee, I had a hook on a room, so we stayed there for three months and a week.

FEMA was no help. We'd been renting the bottom floor of a big three-story house. Other people lived on the other floors. So when I applied for FEMA, they had about nine or ten people applying from the same address. One person got approved and everybody else got denied. They couldn't understand how more than one household could live at one address. They thought it was a scam.

I burned through savings. I burned through everything just trying to survive. We didn't even know if we were going to be able to eat. Thank God I had family here or we would've been on the streets.

SUNNY'S LANDLORD, MIKE, WHOSE HOUSE ALSO BURNED DOWN, OFFERED HIM A CONSTRUCTION JOB.

Katelyn and I were going to move to Tennessee. California is just too expensive. But Mike gave me a job and kept me working. Now I'm making really good money.

It means a lot to help people rebuild their homes. I'm all about the community. I feel like I have to give more because I see everybody else giving more. There's always someone in worse shape than me. I'm blessed. ∎

A DAY IN THE NEW LIFE

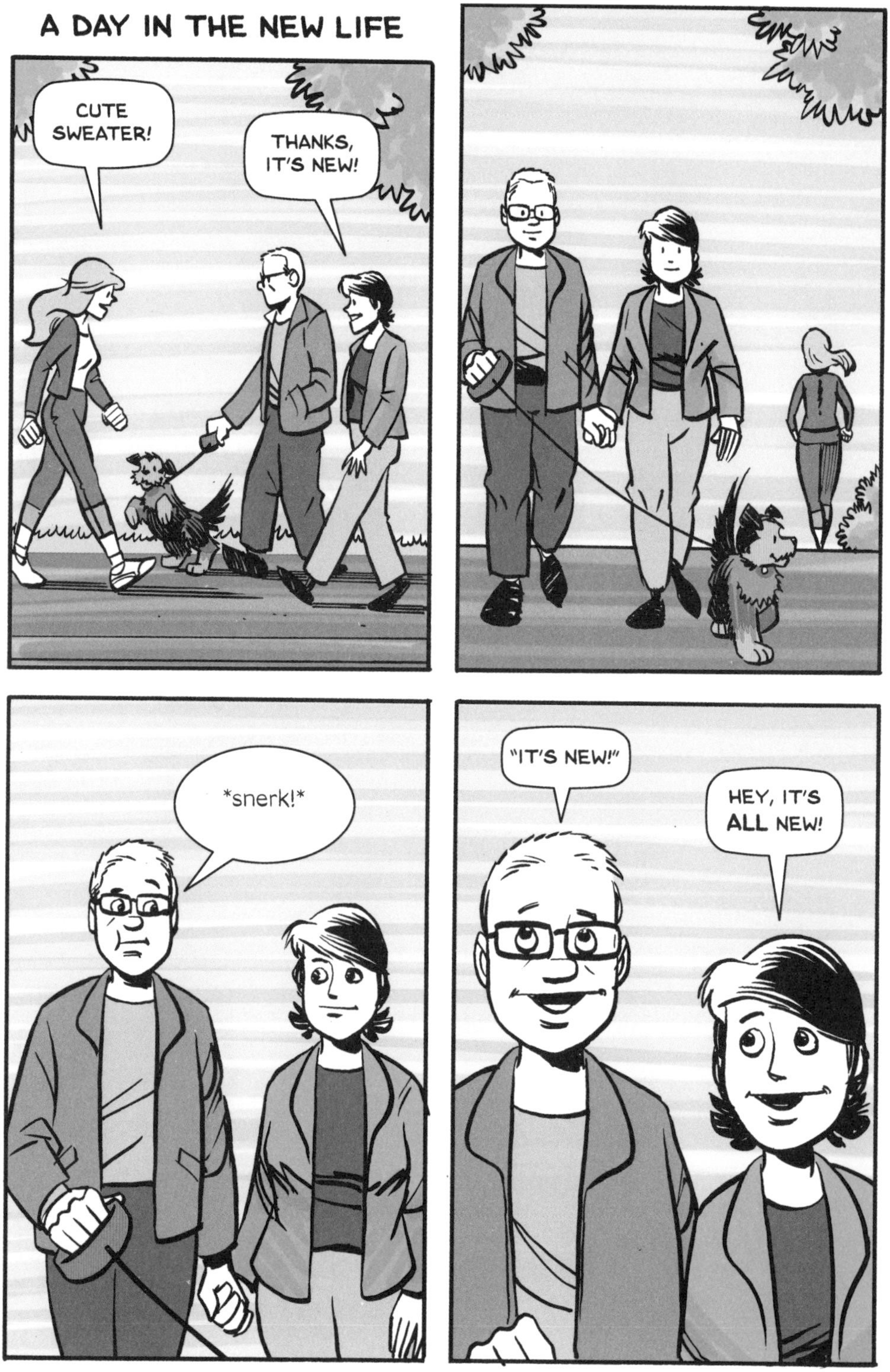
CUTE SWEATER!
THANKS, IT'S NEW!
snerk!
"IT'S NEW!"
HEY, IT'S ALL NEW!

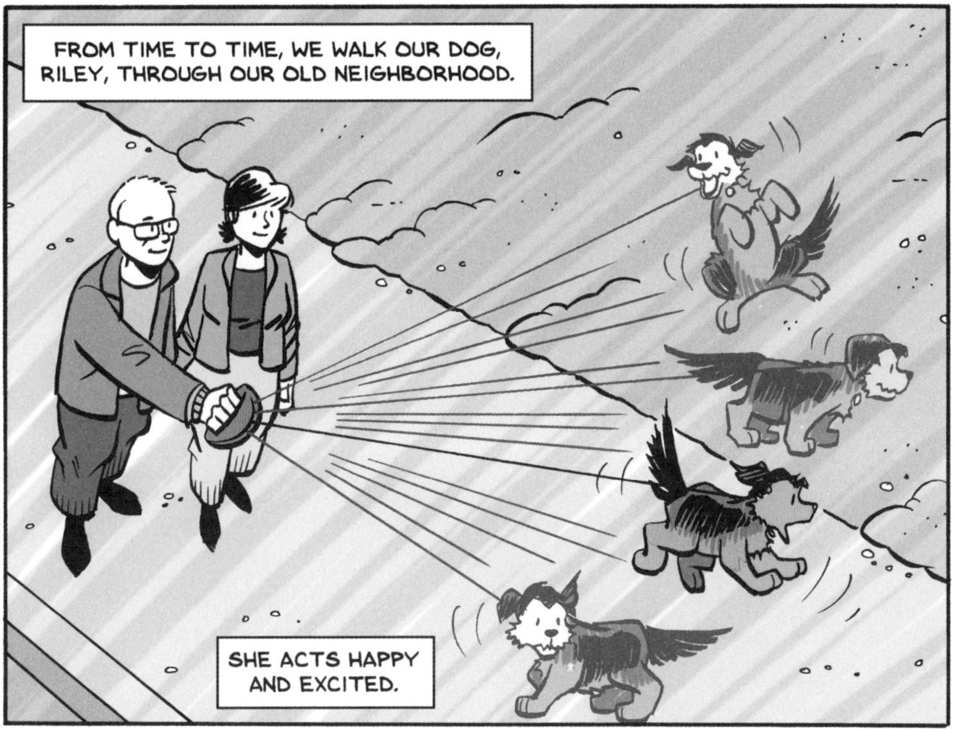
FROM TIME TO TIME, WE WALK OUR DOG, RILEY, THROUGH OUR OLD NEIGHBORHOOD.
SHE ACTS HAPPY AND EXCITED.

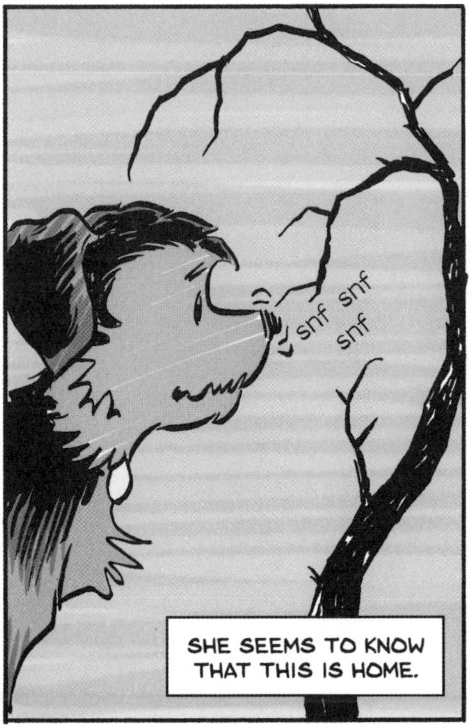
snf snf snf
SHE SEEMS TO KNOW THAT THIS IS HOME.

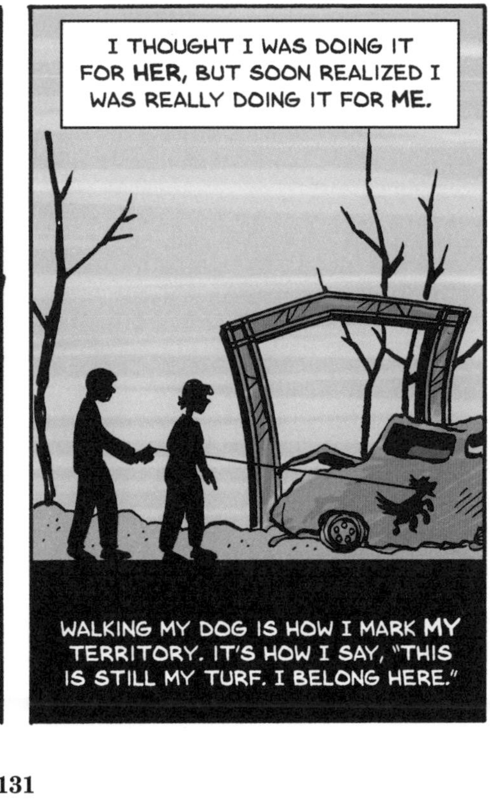
I THOUGHT I WAS DOING IT FOR HER, BUT SOON REALIZED I WAS REALLY DOING IT FOR ME.
WALKING MY DOG IS HOW I MARK MY TERRITORY. IT'S HOW I SAY, "THIS IS STILL MY TURF. I BELONG HERE."

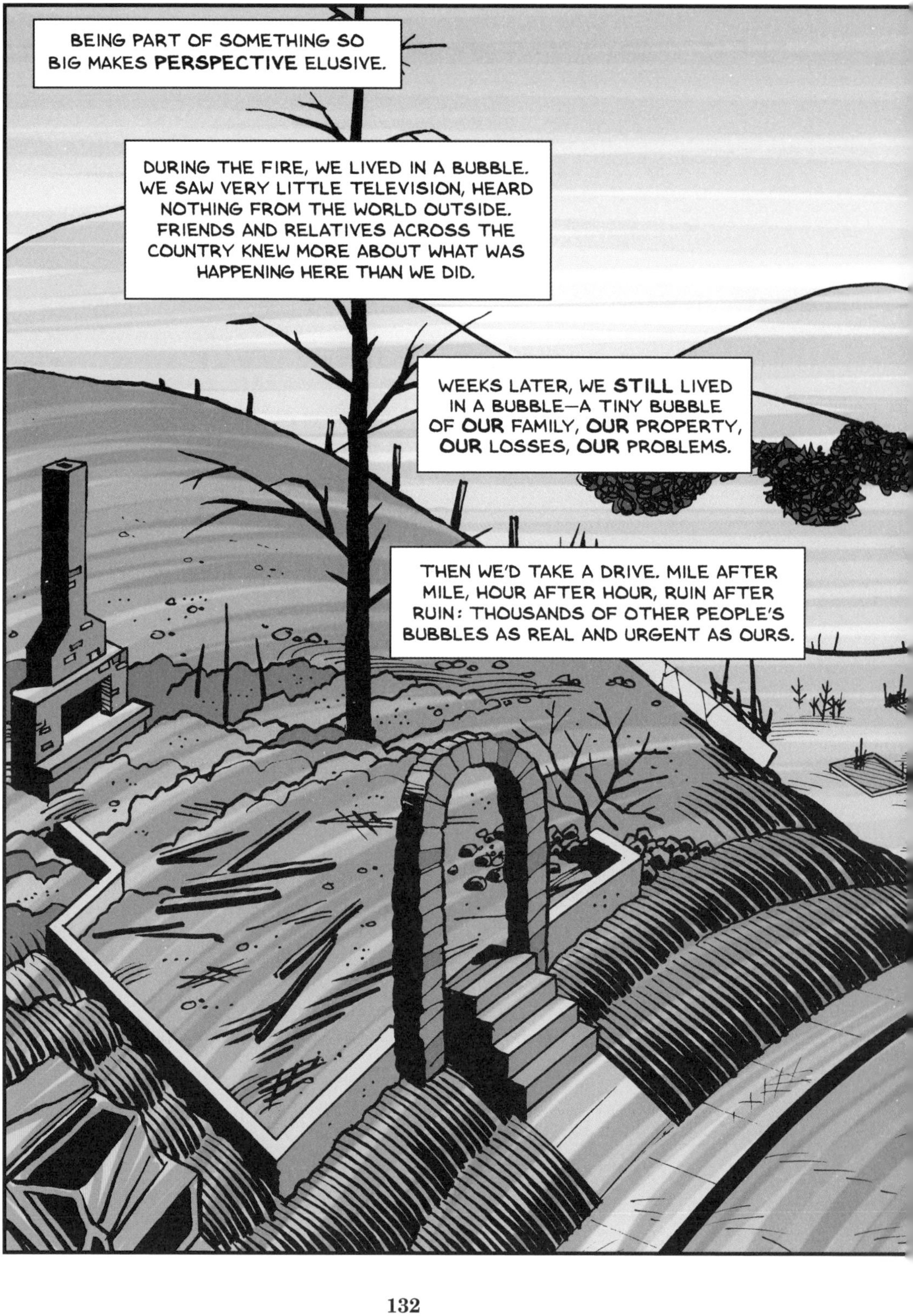
BEING PART OF SOMETHING SO BIG MAKES **PERSPECTIVE** ELUSIVE.
DURING THE FIRE, WE LIVED IN A BUBBLE. WE SAW VERY LITTLE TELEVISION, HEARD NOTHING FROM THE WORLD OUTSIDE. FRIENDS AND RELATIVES ACROSS THE COUNTRY KNEW MORE ABOUT WHAT WAS HAPPENING HERE THAN WE DID.
WEEKS LATER, WE **STILL** LIVED IN A BUBBLE—A TINY BUBBLE OF **OUR** FAMILY, **OUR** PROPERTY, **OUR** LOSSES, **OUR** PROBLEMS.
THEN WE'D TAKE A DRIVE. MILE AFTER MILE, HOUR AFTER HOUR, RUIN AFTER RUIN: THOUSANDS OF OTHER PEOPLE'S BUBBLES AS REAL AND URGENT AS OURS.

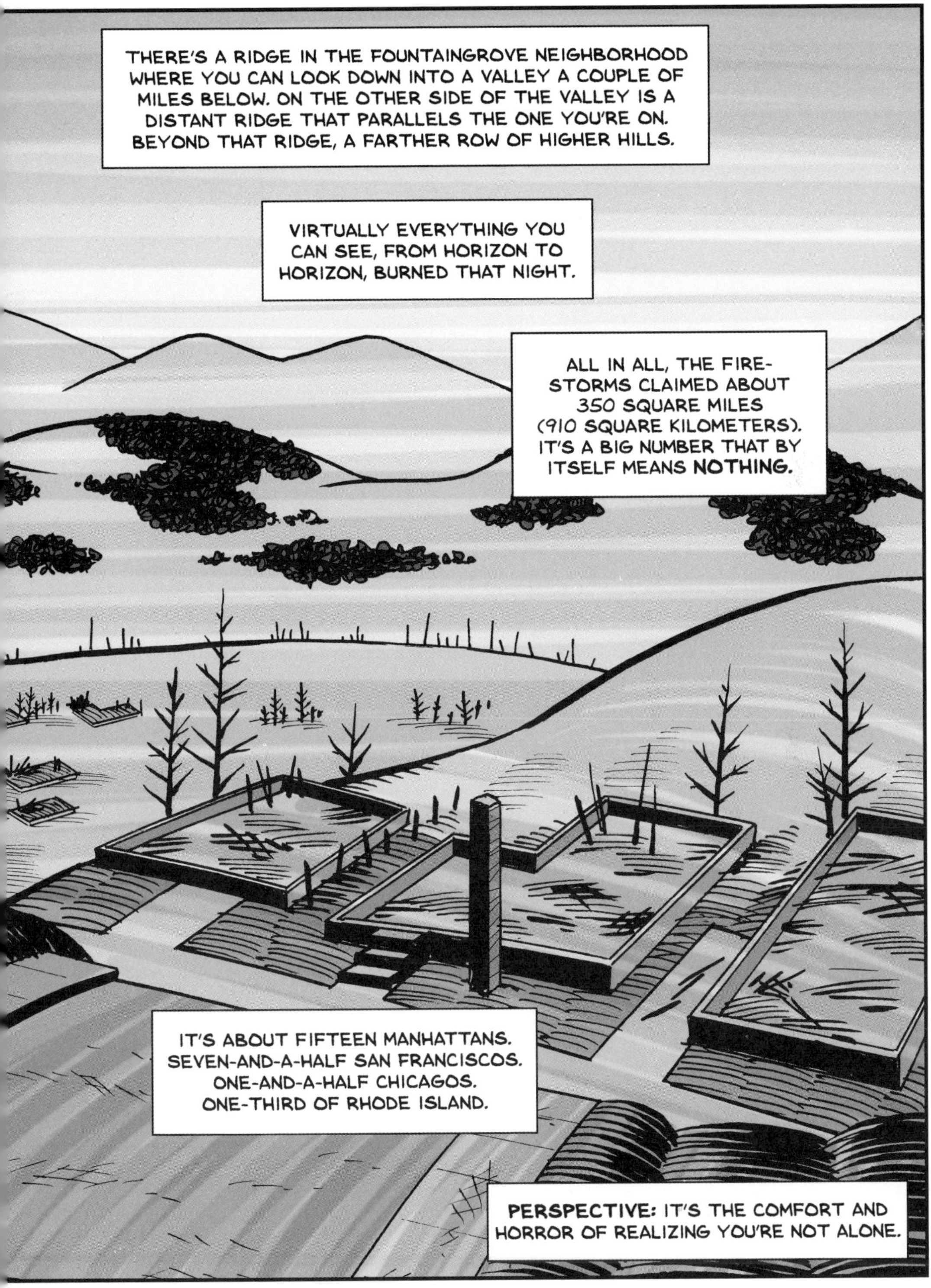
THERE'S A RIDGE IN THE FOUNTAINGROVE NEIGHBORHOOD WHERE YOU CAN LOOK DOWN INTO A VALLEY A COUPLE OF MILES BELOW. ON THE OTHER SIDE OF THE VALLEY IS A DISTANT RIDGE THAT PARALLELS THE ONE YOU'RE ON. BEYOND THAT RIDGE, A FARTHER ROW OF HIGHER HILLS.
VIRTUALLY EVERYTHING YOU CAN SEE, FROM HORIZON TO HORIZON, BURNED THAT NIGHT.
ALL IN ALL, THE FIRE-STORMS CLAIMED ABOUT 350 SQUARE MILES (910 SQUARE KILOMETERS). IT'S A BIG NUMBER THAT BY ITSELF MEANS **NOTHING.**
IT'S ABOUT FIFTEEN MANHATTANS. SEVEN-AND-A-HALF SAN FRANCISCOS. ONE-AND-A-HALF CHICAGOS. ONE-THIRD OF RHODE ISLAND.
PERSPECTIVE: IT'S THE COMFORT AND HORROR OF REALIZING YOU'RE NOT ALONE.

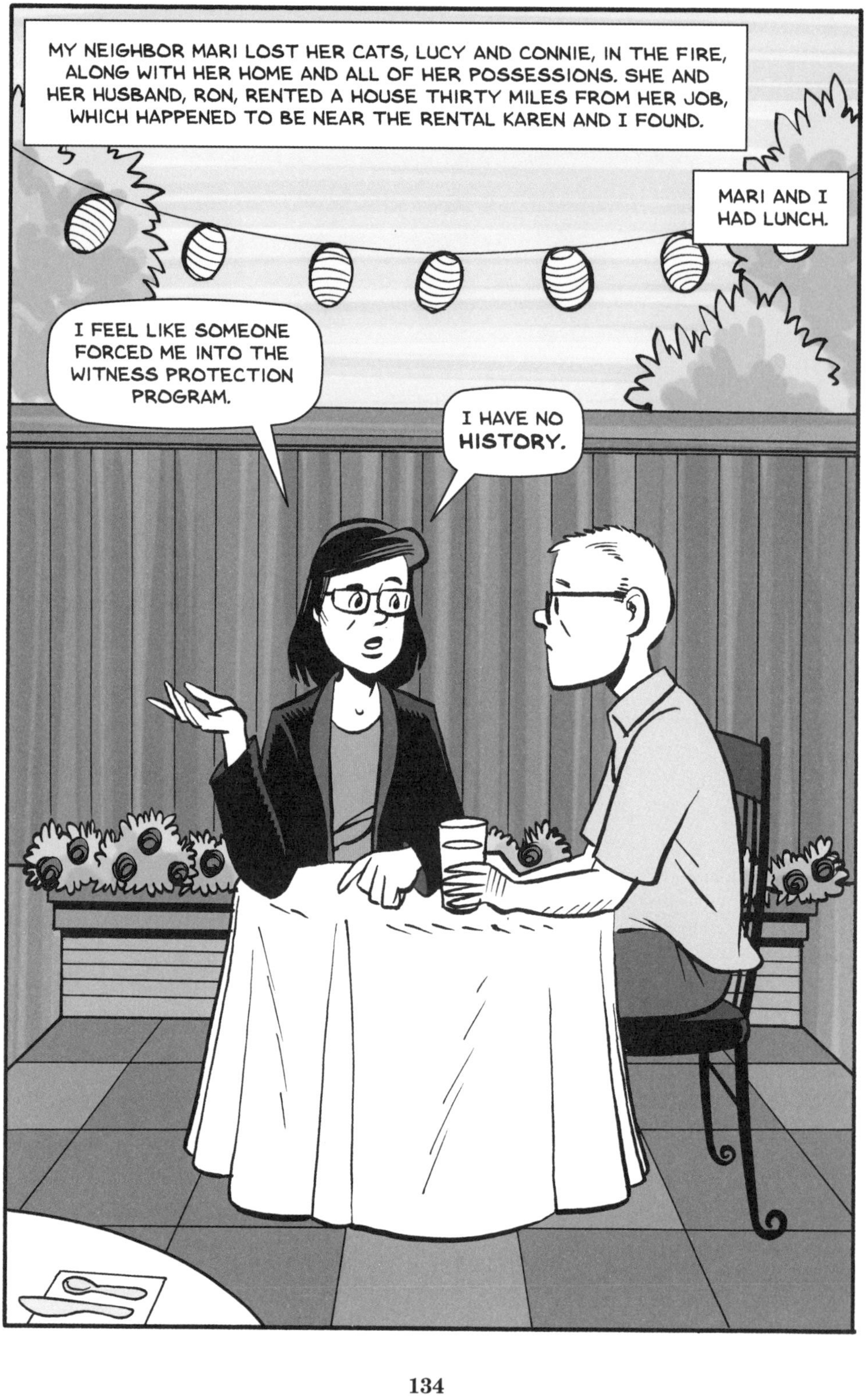
MY NEIGHBOR MARI LOST HER CATS, LUCY AND CONNIE, IN THE FIRE, ALONG WITH HER HOME AND ALL OF HER POSSESSIONS. SHE AND HER HUSBAND, RON, RENTED A HOUSE THIRTY MILES FROM HER JOB, WHICH HAPPENED TO BE NEAR THE RENTAL KAREN AND I FOUND.
MARI AND I HAD LUNCH.
I FEEL LIKE SOMEONE FORCED ME INTO THE WITNESS PROTECTION PROGRAM.
I HAVE NO **HISTORY.**

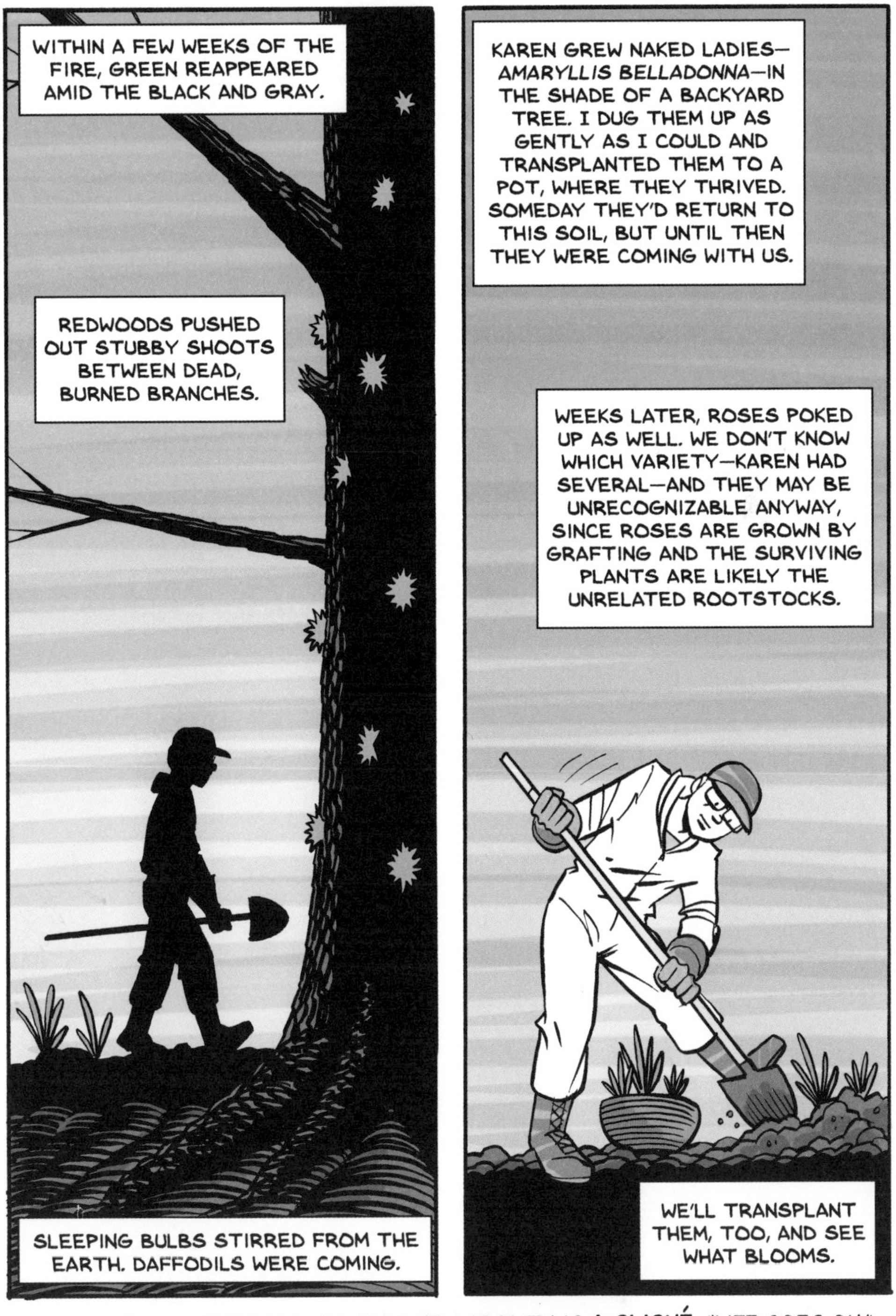
WITHIN A FEW WEEKS OF THE FIRE, GREEN REAPPEARED AMID THE BLACK AND GRAY.
REDWOODS PUSHED OUT STUBBY SHOOTS BETWEEN DEAD, BURNED BRANCHES.
SLEEPING BULBS STIRRED FROM THE EARTH. DAFFODILS WERE COMING.
KAREN GREW NAKED LADIES—*AMARYLLIS BELLADONNA*—IN THE SHADE OF A BACKYARD TREE. I DUG THEM UP AS GENTLY AS I COULD AND TRANSPLANTED THEM TO A POT, WHERE THEY THRIVED. SOMEDAY THEY'D RETURN TO THIS SOIL, BUT UNTIL THEN THEY WERE COMING WITH US.
WEEKS LATER, ROSES POKED UP AS WELL. WE DON'T KNOW WHICH VARIETY—KAREN HAD SEVERAL—AND THEY MAY BE UNRECOGNIZABLE ANYWAY, SINCE ROSES ARE GROWN BY GRAFTING AND THE SURVIVING PLANTS ARE LIKELY THE UNRELATED ROOTSTOCKS.
WE'LL TRANSPLANT THEM, TOO, AND SEE WHAT BLOOMS.

AS A LITERARY METAPHOR, ALL THIS NEW GROWTH IS A **CLICHÉ**: "LIFE GOES ON." STILL, THAT DOESN'T MAKE IT UNTRUE, AND IT'S MARVELOUS TO SEE. FLOWERS AND TREES CAN COME BACK, CHANGED AND SCARRED BUT STILL BEAUTIFUL. SO CAN WE.

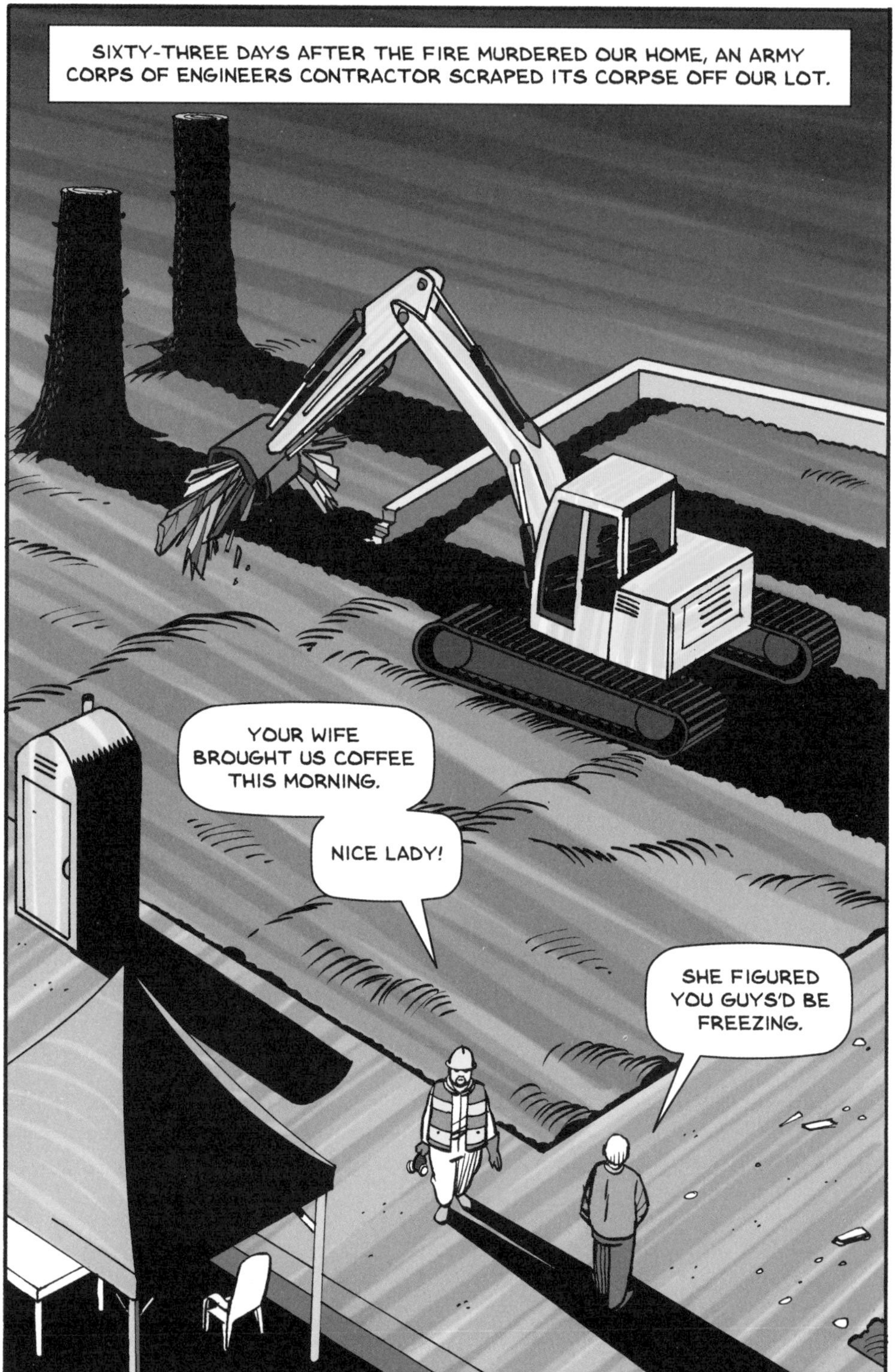
SIXTY-THREE DAYS AFTER THE FIRE MURDERED OUR HOME, AN ARMY CORPS OF ENGINEERS CONTRACTOR SCRAPED ITS CORPSE OFF OUR LOT.
YOUR WIFE BROUGHT US COFFEE THIS MORNING.
NICE LADY!
SHE FIGURED YOU GUYS'D BE FREEZING.

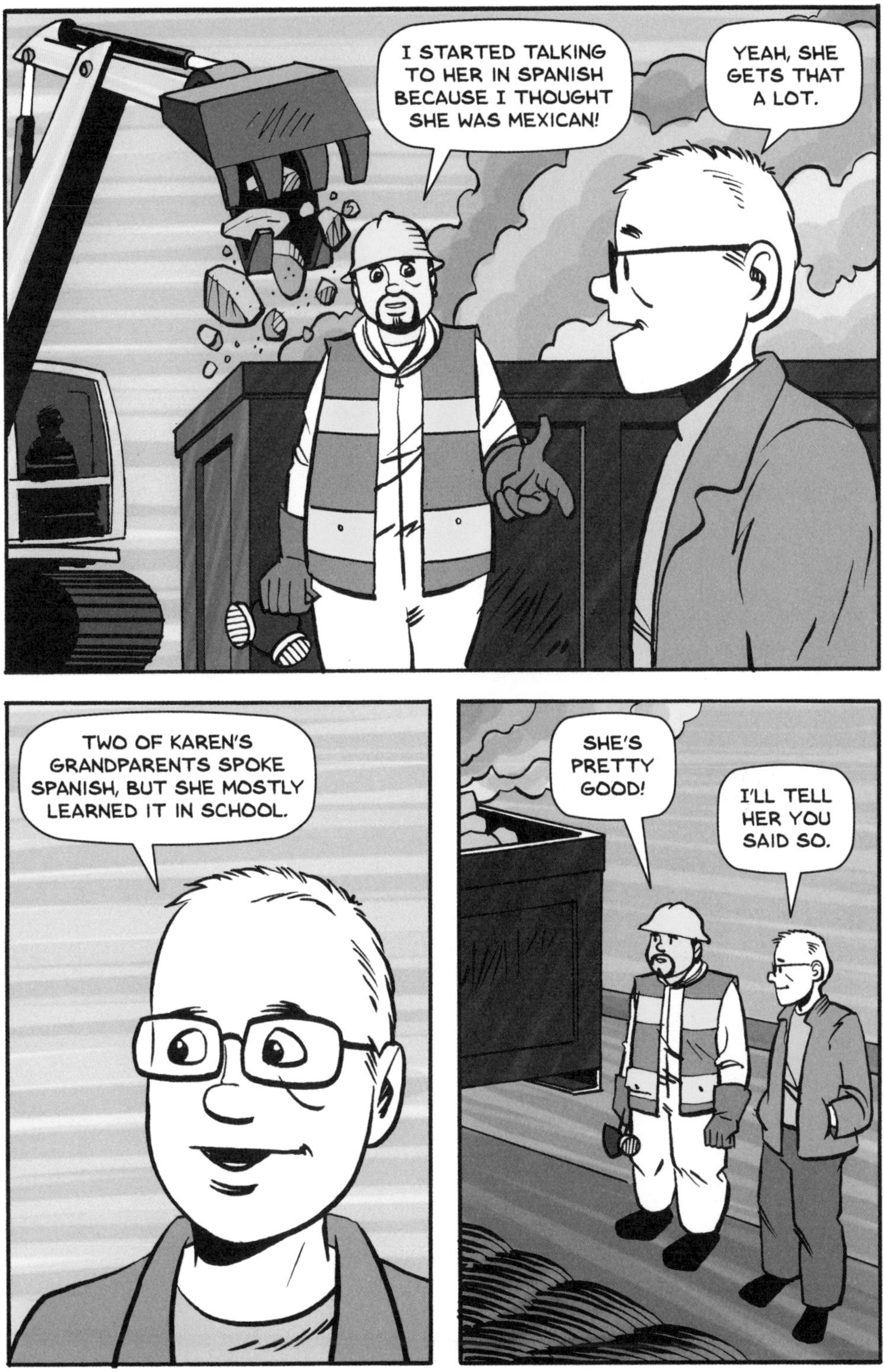
I STARTED TALKING TO HER IN SPANISH BECAUSE I THOUGHT SHE WAS MEXICAN!
YEAH, SHE GETS THAT A LOT.
TWO OF KAREN'S GRANDPARENTS SPOKE SPANISH, BUT SHE MOSTLY LEARNED IT IN SCHOOL.
SHE'S PRETTY GOOD!
I'LL TELL HER YOU SAID SO.

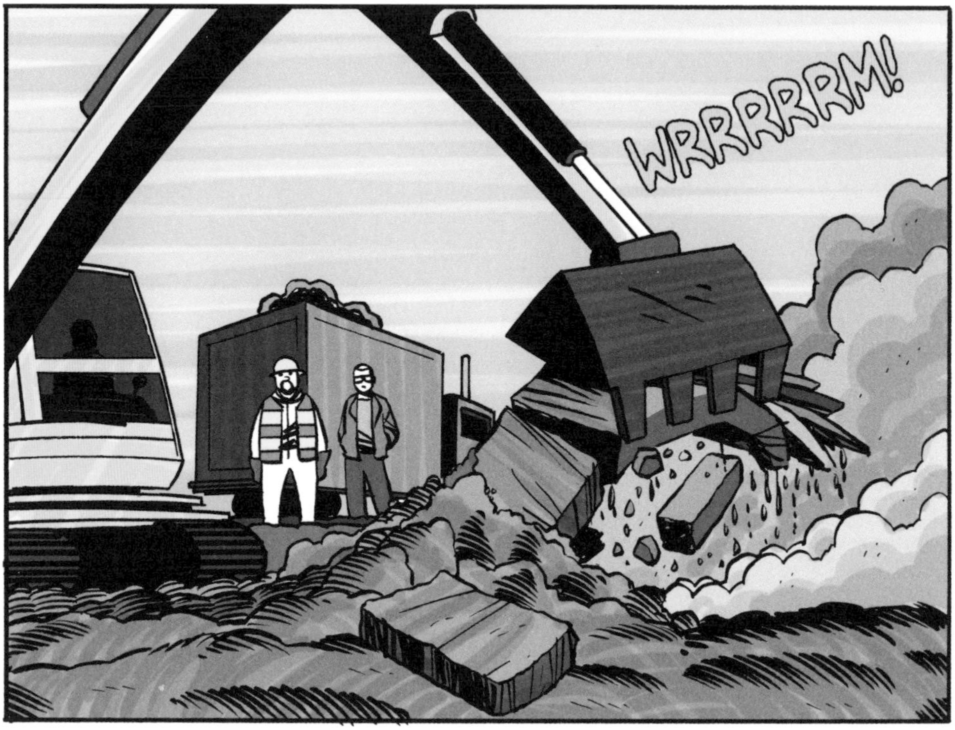
WRRRRRM!

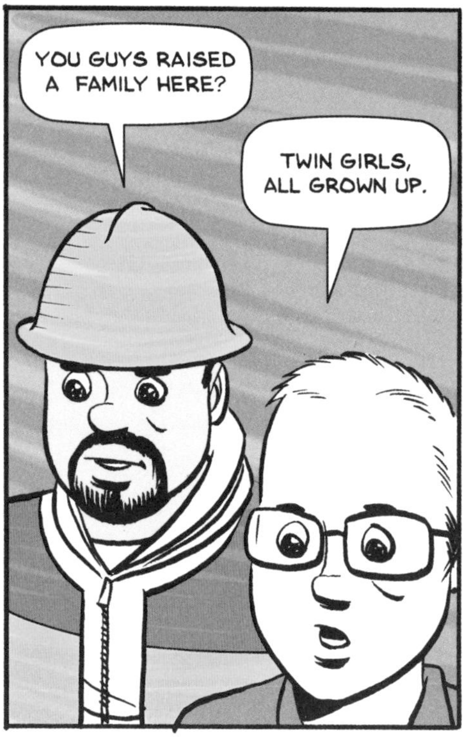
YOU GUYS RAISED A FAMILY HERE?
TWIN GIRLS, ALL GROWN UP.

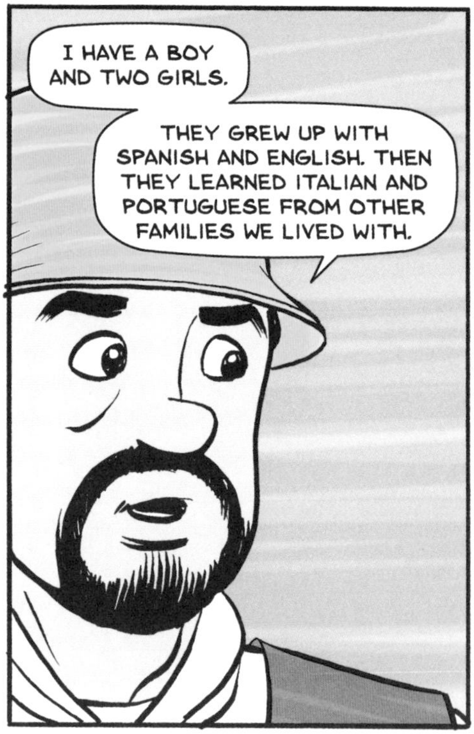
I HAVE A BOY AND TWO GIRLS.
THEY GREW UP WITH SPANISH AND ENGLISH. THEN THEY LEARNED ITALIAN AND PORTUGUESE FROM OTHER FAMILIES WE LIVED WITH.

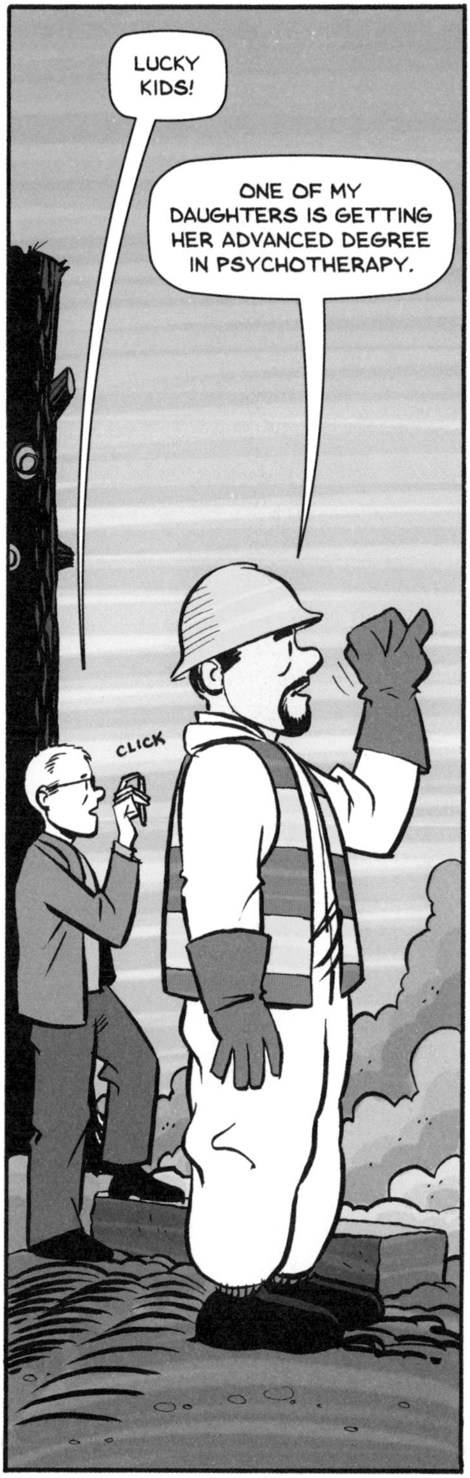
LUCKY KIDS!
ONE OF MY DAUGHTERS IS GETTING HER ADVANCED DEGREE IN PSYCHOTHERAPY.
CLICK

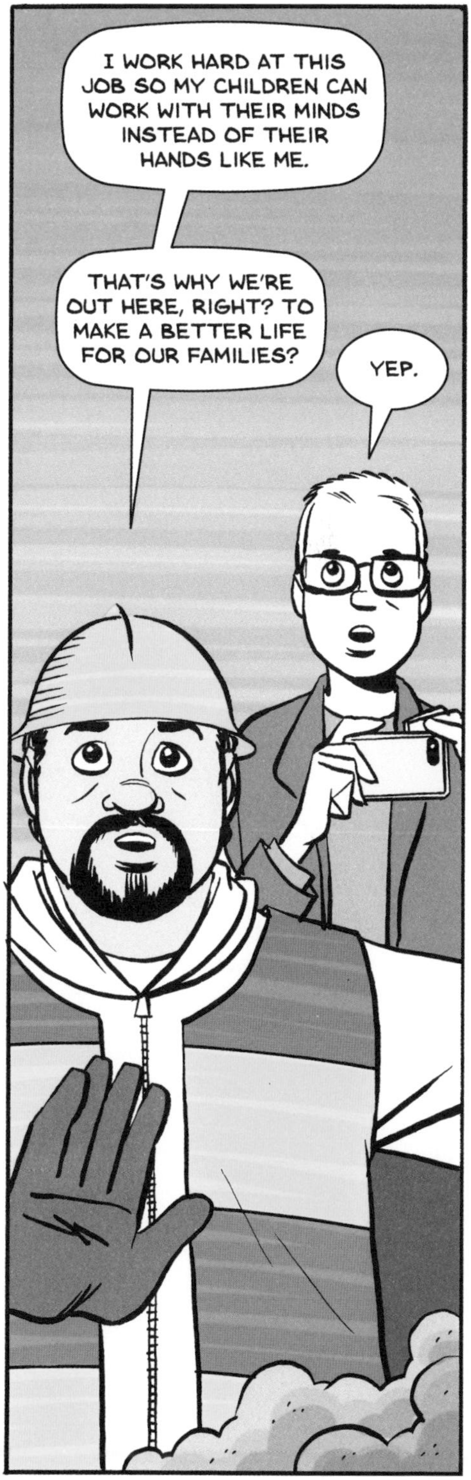
I WORK HARD AT THIS JOB SO MY CHILDREN CAN WORK WITH THEIR MINDS INSTEAD OF THEIR HANDS LIKE ME.
THAT'S WHY WE'RE OUT HERE, RIGHT? TO MAKE A BETTER LIFE FOR OUR FAMILIES?
YEP.

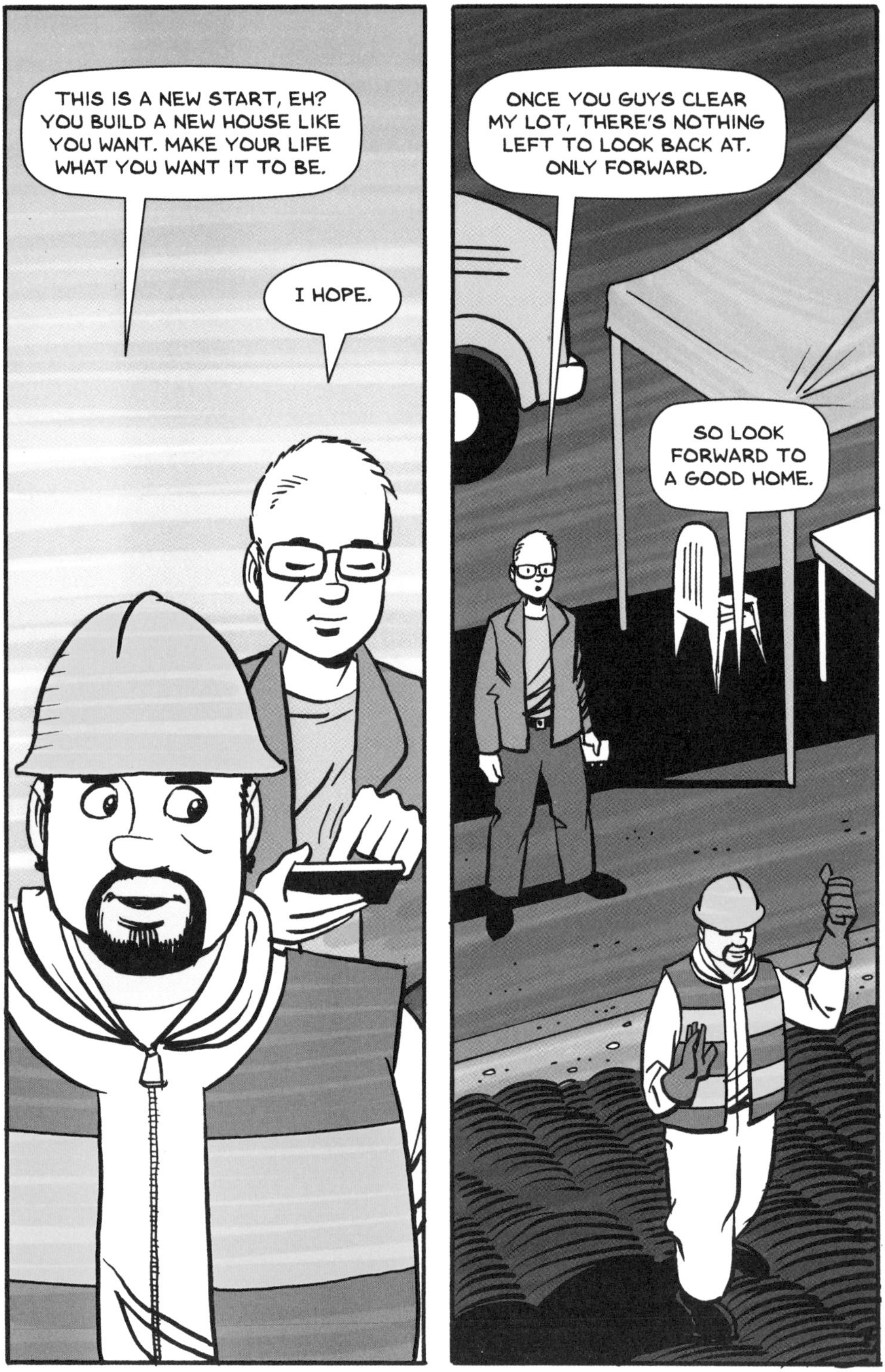
THIS IS A NEW START, EH? YOU BUILD A NEW HOUSE LIKE YOU WANT. MAKE YOUR LIFE WHAT YOU WANT IT TO BE.
I HOPE.
ONCE YOU GUYS CLEAR MY LOT, THERE'S NOTHING LEFT TO LOOK BACK AT. ONLY FORWARD.
SO LOOK FORWARD TO A GOOD HOME.

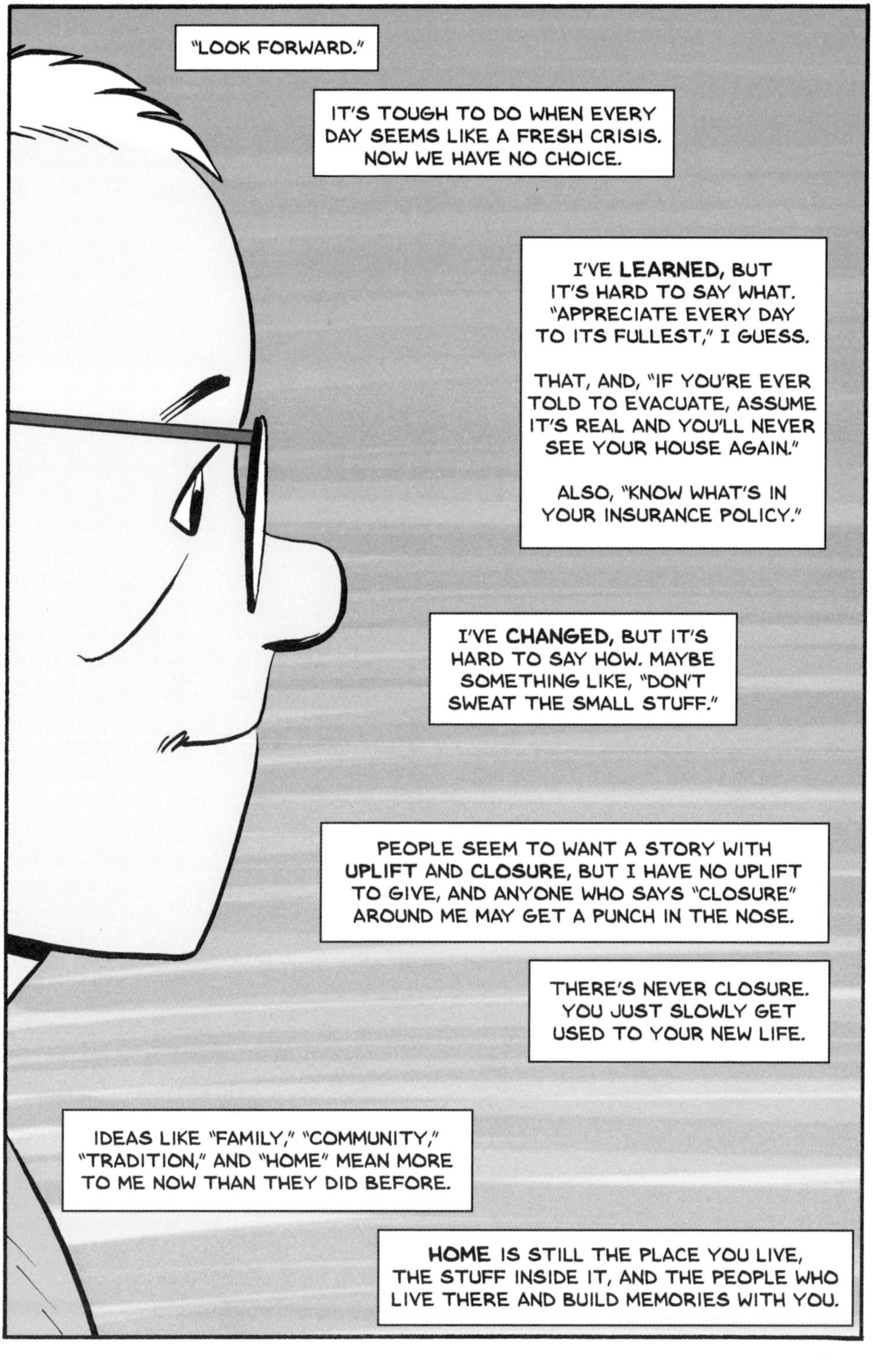
"LOOK FORWARD."
IT'S TOUGH TO DO WHEN EVERY DAY SEEMS LIKE A FRESH CRISIS. NOW WE HAVE NO CHOICE.
I'VE **LEARNED,** BUT IT'S HARD TO SAY WHAT. "APPRECIATE EVERY DAY TO ITS FULLEST," I GUESS.
THAT, AND, "IF YOU'RE EVER TOLD TO EVACUATE, ASSUME IT'S REAL AND YOU'LL NEVER SEE YOUR HOUSE AGAIN."
ALSO, "KNOW WHAT'S IN YOUR INSURANCE POLICY."
I'VE **CHANGED,** BUT IT'S HARD TO SAY HOW. MAYBE SOMETHING LIKE, "DON'T SWEAT THE SMALL STUFF."
PEOPLE SEEM TO WANT A STORY WITH **UPLIFT** AND **CLOSURE,** BUT I HAVE NO UPLIFT TO GIVE, AND ANYONE WHO SAYS "CLOSURE" AROUND ME MAY GET A PUNCH IN THE NOSE.
THERE'S NEVER CLOSURE. YOU JUST SLOWLY GET USED TO YOUR NEW LIFE.
IDEAS LIKE "FAMILY," "COMMUNITY," "TRADITION," AND "HOME" MEAN MORE TO ME NOW THAN THEY DID BEFORE.
HOME IS STILL THE PLACE YOU LIVE, THE STUFF INSIDE IT, AND THE PEOPLE WHO LIVE THERE AND BUILD MEMORIES WITH YOU.

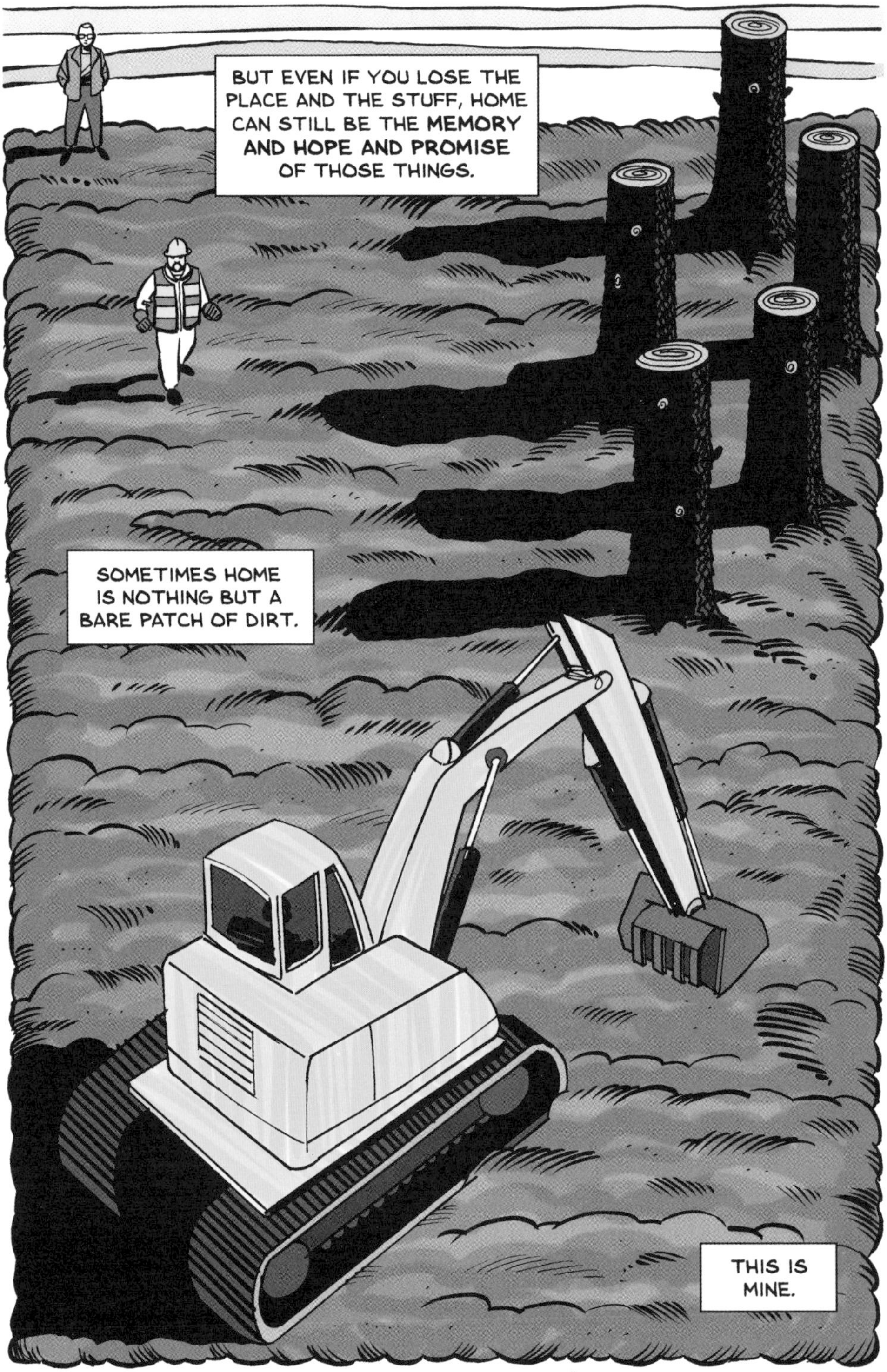
BUT EVEN IF YOU LOSE THE PLACE AND THE STUFF, HOME CAN STILL BE THE **MEMORY AND HOPE AND PROMISE** OF THOSE THINGS.
SOMETIMES HOME IS NOTHING BUT A BARE PATCH OF DIRT.
THIS IS MINE.

AFTERWORD

Karen and I evacuated our home north of Santa Rosa, California, at around 1:30 A.M. on Monday, October 9, 2017. Based on when our neighbors began getting text messages from their home security systems, we think our neighborhood burned around 2:30 A.M.

The first photo I shot as I walked back to the area later that morning is time-stamped 8:04 A.M. It took the firestorm less than six hours to scour a good-sized subdivision from the planet.

The next day, in addition to buying shoes and other necessities, I also bought the only art supplies I could find: a pad of low-quality pulp paper, one permanent marker, a fine-point felt-tip pen, and four colored highlighters. That afternoon, I began writing and drawing *A Fire Story*.

I've done journalism before, and *A Fire Story* felt like journalism to me. Someone called it my way of "bearing witness," and I couldn't put it better than that. I was there. I saw these extraordinary events. I had to tell what it was like the best way I knew how: in the form of a comic.

I drew the original eighteen pages of *A Fire Story* over parts of four days, and posted them online on October 13 and 15, 2017. They immediately went viral. News outlets picked up the story, and soon it had been featured on CNN, the *Washington Post, Entertainment Weekly, Mother Jones*, San Francisco newspapers and TV stations, and more.

To say my feelings about all that were conflicted is an understatement. Karen and I were dealing with a mind-numbing disaster while I was also hosting reporters

and TV crews in our daughters' little apartment. There was no joy in the experience, but there was satisfaction in people reading our story and saying it helped them understand what it was like to be there. People who'd been through the fire with us said I got it right.

Around 700,000 people read the original comic on my blog, and another three million or so saw an animated version produced by San Francisco PBS station KQED that was picked up by National Public Radio (NPR). KQED producer Kelly Whalen came to my girls' place to record Karen and me reciting scripted lines from our own lives, which Farrin Abbott expertly animated and edited. KQED couldn't have been more sensitive and respectful, and I loved the short film they produced, which won a regional Emmy Award for Best Public/Current/ Community Affairs—Feature/Segment on June 2, 2018.

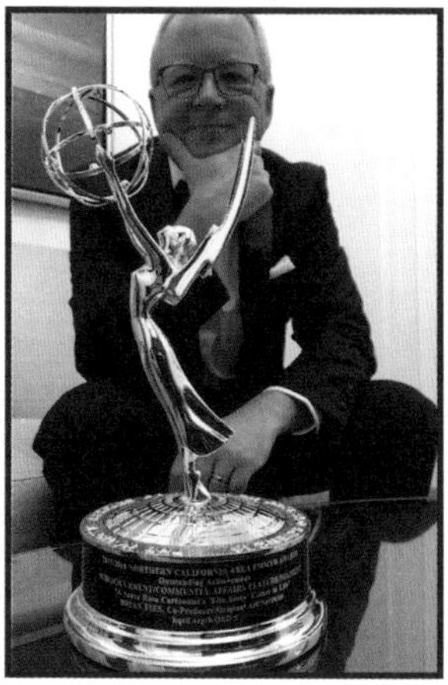

I didn't write about my work on the original *Fire Story* webcomic, or the attention and commotion that went with it, in this book. Although this *Fire Story* is a graphic memoir, it isn't just *my* story; it's the story of thousands of people who lost everything, and hundreds of thousands who were affected less directly but still traumatically. Compared to the enormity of that universal experience, my particular unique situation was irrelevant.

The following pages are the original webcomic written and drawn in the few days immediately after the fire. My editor and I debated how to incorporate them into this book. They have a storytelling energy and urgency that comes from being created on the ground in the moment. But they're also a crude, slapdash record of me drawing as fast as I could with crummy materials on the worst days of my life.

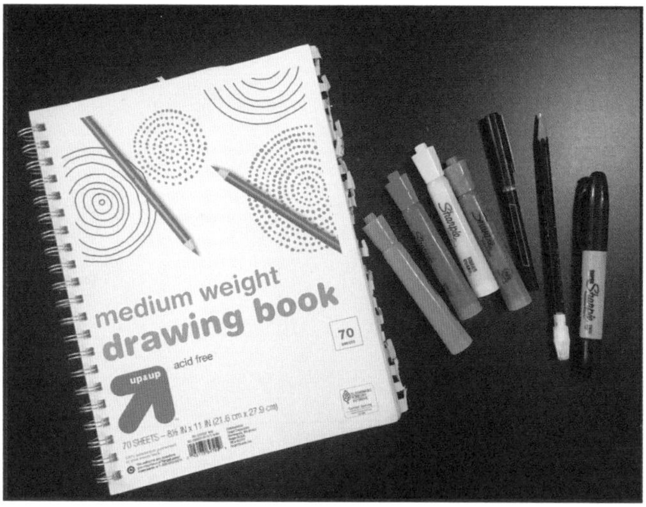
medium weight
drawing book
70
acid free
up&up

While I completely understand that the original story's spontaneity is part of what makes it worthwhile, I always considered it a rough first draft—part of the bigger story told in this book. I'm proud to include it here and happy I could take another crack at it.

I wish the fire hadn't happened. Since it did, I'm glad I was able to wring this small, good thing out of such a terrible disaster. I eventually laid to rest my ambivalence about telling *A Fire Story*. The way I see it, the fire owes me one.

My family is doing fine. We are rebuilding.

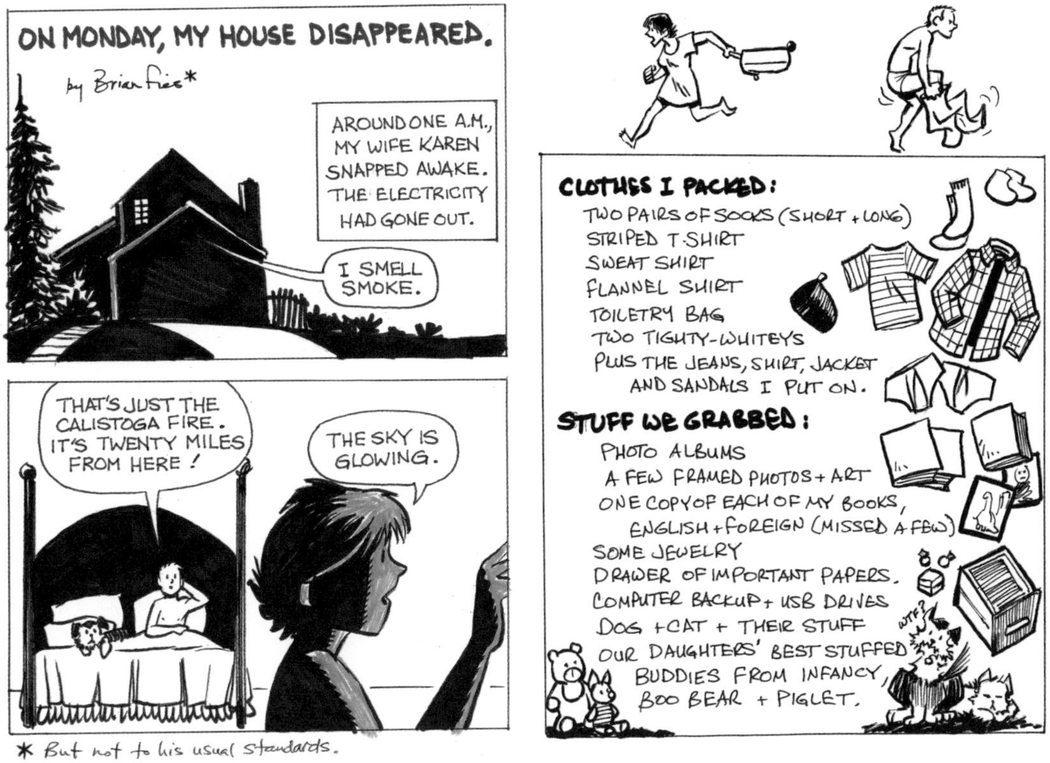
ON MONDAY, MY HOUSE DISAPPEARED.
by Brian Fies*
AROUND ONE A.M., MY WIFE KAREN SNAPPED AWAKE. THE ELECTRICITY HAD GONE OUT.
I SMELL SMOKE.
THAT'S JUST THE CALISTOGA FIRE. IT'S TWENTY MILES FROM HERE!
THE SKY IS GLOWING.
* But not to his usual standards.
CLOTHES I PACKED:
TWO PAIRS OF SOCKS (SHORT + LONG)
STRIPED T-SHIRT
SWEAT SHIRT
FLANNEL SHIRT
TOILETRY BAG
TWO TIGHTY-WHITEYS
PLUS THE JEANS, SHIRT, JACKET AND SANDALS I PUT ON.
STUFF WE GRABBED:
PHOTO ALBUMS
A FEW FRAMED PHOTOS + ART
ONE COPY OF EACH OF MY BOOKS, ENGLISH + FOREIGN (MISSED A FEW)
SOME JEWELRY
DRAWER OF IMPORTANT PAPERS.
COMPUTER BACKUP + USB DRIVES
DOG + CAT + THEIR STUFF
OUR DAUGHTERS' BEST STUFFED BUDDIES FROM INFANCY, BOO BEAR + PIGLET.
WTF?

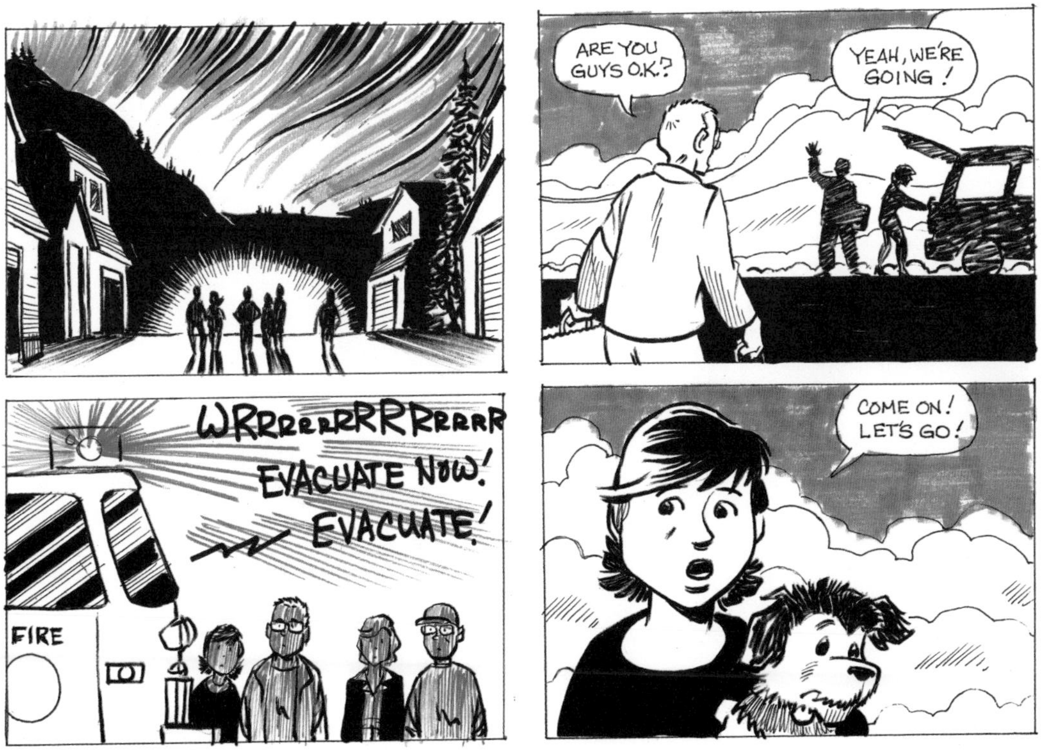
ARE YOU GUYS O.K.?
YEAH, WE'RE GOING!
WRRRRRRRRRRRRRR
EVACUATE NOW!
EVACUATE!
FIRE
COME ON! LET'S GO!

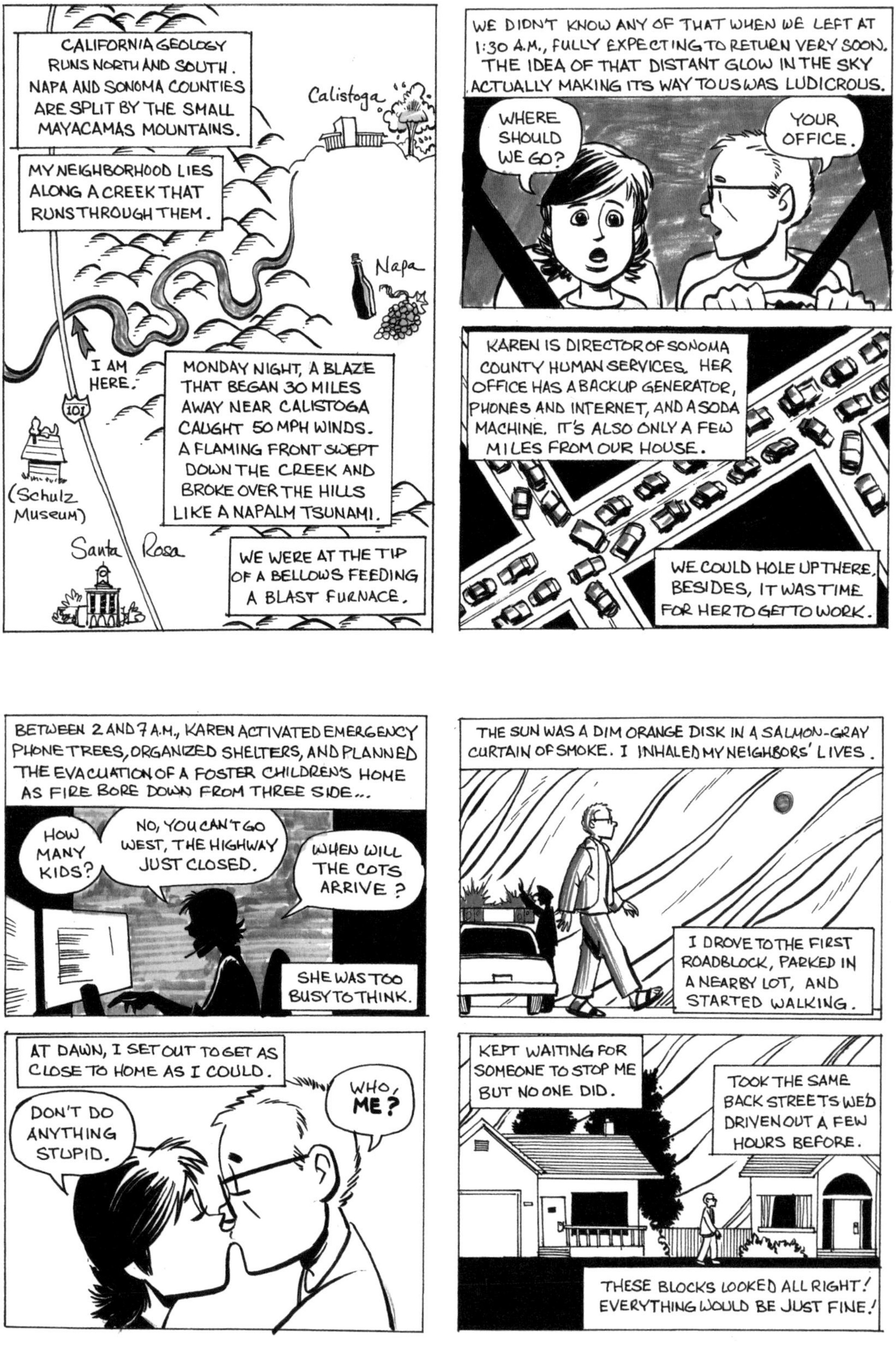
CALIFORNIA GEOLOGY RUNS NORTH AND SOUTH. NAPA AND SONOMA COUNTIES ARE SPLIT BY THE SMALL MAYACAMAS MOUNTAINS.
MY NEIGHBORHOOD LIES ALONG A CREEK THAT RUNS THROUGH THEM.
Calistoga
Napa
I AM HERE.
101
(Schulz Museum)
Santa Rosa
MONDAY NIGHT, A BLAZE THAT BEGAN 30 MILES AWAY NEAR CALISTOGA CAUGHT 50 MPH WINDS. A FLAMING FRONT SWEPT DOWN THE CREEK AND BROKE OVER THE HILLS LIKE A NAPALM TSUNAMI.
WE WERE AT THE TIP OF A BELLOWS FEEDING A BLAST FURNACE.
WE DIDN'T KNOW ANY OF THAT WHEN WE LEFT AT 1:30 A.M., FULLY EXPECTING TO RETURN VERY SOON. THE IDEA OF THAT DISTANT GLOW IN THE SKY ACTUALLY MAKING ITS WAY TO US WAS LUDICROUS.
WHERE SHOULD WE GO?
YOUR OFFICE.
KAREN IS DIRECTOR OF SONOMA COUNTY HUMAN SERVICES. HER OFFICE HAS A BACKUP GENERATOR, PHONES AND INTERNET, AND A SODA MACHINE. IT'S ALSO ONLY A FEW MILES FROM OUR HOUSE.
WE COULD HOLE UP THERE. BESIDES, IT WAS TIME FOR HER TO GET TO WORK.
BETWEEN 2 AND 7 A.M., KAREN ACTIVATED EMERGENCY PHONE TREES, ORGANIZED SHELTERS, AND PLANNED THE EVACUATION OF A FOSTER CHILDREN'S HOME AS FIRE BORE DOWN FROM THREE SIDE...
HOW MANY KIDS?
NO, YOU CAN'T GO WEST, THE HIGHWAY JUST CLOSED.
WHEN WILL THE COTS ARRIVE?
SHE WAS TOO BUSY TO THINK.
THE SUN WAS A DIM ORANGE DISK IN A SALMON-GRAY CURTAIN OF SMOKE. I INHALED MY NEIGHBORS' LIVES.
I DROVE TO THE FIRST ROADBLOCK, PARKED IN A NEARBY LOT, AND STARTED WALKING.
AT DAWN, I SET OUT TO GET AS CLOSE TO HOME AS I COULD.
DON'T DO ANYTHING STUPID.
WHO, ME?
KEPT WAITING FOR SOMEONE TO STOP ME BUT NO ONE DID.
TOOK THE SAME BACK STREETS WE'D DRIVEN OUT A FEW HOURS BEFORE.
THESE BLOCKS LOOKED ALL RIGHT! EVERYTHING WOULD BE JUST FINE!

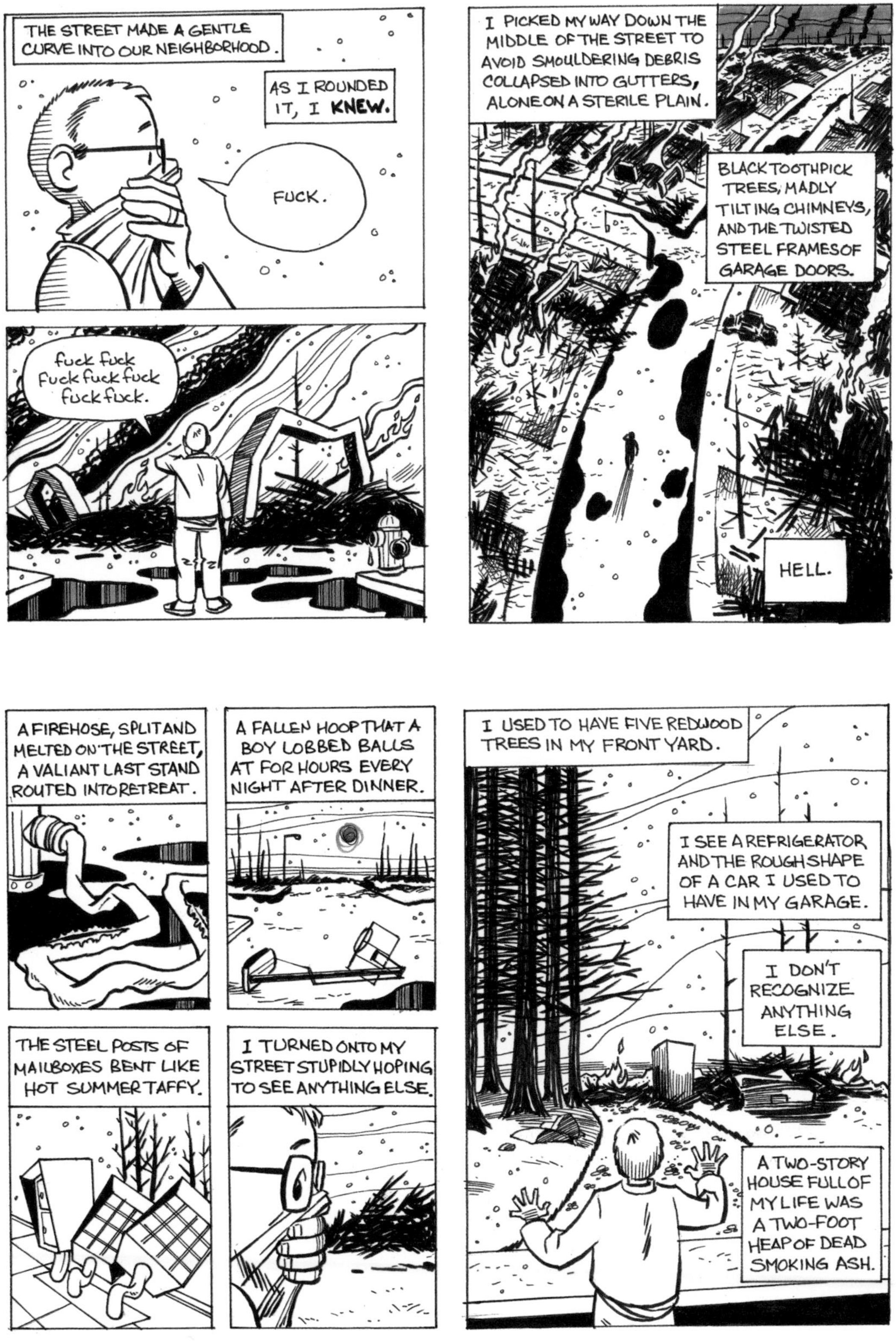
THE STREET MADE A GENTLE CURVE INTO OUR NEIGHBORHOOD.
AS I ROUNDED IT, I KNEW.
FUCK.
fuck fuck fuck fuck fuck fuck fuck.
I PICKED MY WAY DOWN THE MIDDLE OF THE STREET TO AVOID SMOULDERING DEBRIS COLLAPSED INTO GUTTERS, ALONE ON A STERILE PLAIN.
BLACK TOOTHPICK TREES, MADLY TILTING CHIMNEYS, AND THE TWISTED STEEL FRAMES OF GARAGE DOORS.
HELL.
A FIREHOSE, SPLIT AND MELTED ON THE STREET, A VALIANT LAST STAND ROUTED INTO RETREAT.
A FALLEN HOOP THAT A BOY LOBBED BALLS AT FOR HOURS EVERY NIGHT AFTER DINNER.
THE STEEL POSTS OF MAILBOXES BENT LIKE HOT SUMMER TAFFY.
I TURNED ONTO MY STREET STUPIDLY HOPING TO SEE ANYTHING ELSE.
I USED TO HAVE FIVE REDWOOD TREES IN MY FRONT YARD.
I SEE A REFRIGERATOR AND THE ROUGH SHAPE OF A CAR I USED TO HAVE IN MY GARAGE.
I DON'T RECOGNIZE ANYTHING ELSE.
A TWO-STORY HOUSE FULL OF MY LIFE WAS A TWO-FOOT HEAP OF DEAD SMOKING ASH.

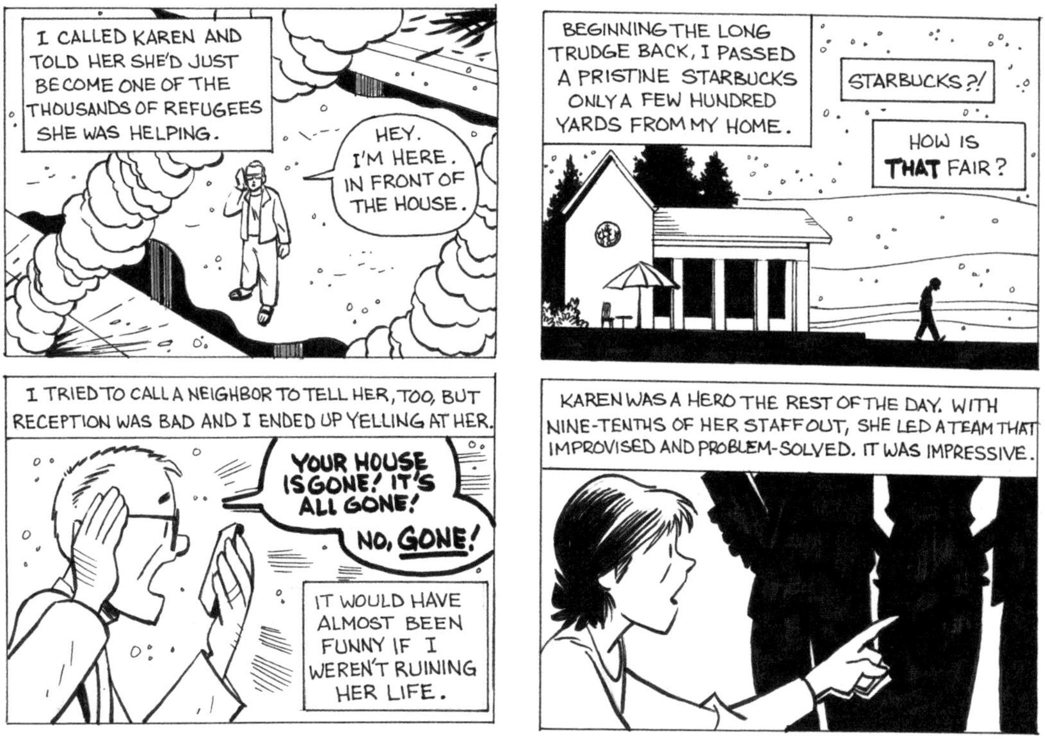
I CALLED KAREN AND TOLD HER SHE'D JUST BECOME ONE OF THE THOUSANDS OF REFUGEES SHE WAS HELPING.
HEY. I'M HERE. IN FRONT OF THE HOUSE.
BEGINNING THE LONG TRUDGE BACK, I PASSED A PRISTINE STARBUCKS ONLY A FEW HUNDRED YARDS FROM MY HOME.
STARBUCKS?!
HOW IS **THAT** FAIR?
I TRIED TO CALL A NEIGHBOR TO TELL HER, TOO, BUT RECEPTION WAS BAD AND I ENDED UP YELLING AT HER.
YOUR HOUSE IS GONE! IT'S ALL GONE!
NO, GONE!
IT WOULD HAVE ALMOST BEEN FUNNY IF I WEREN'T RUINING HER LIFE.
KAREN WAS A HERO THE REST OF THE DAY. WITH NINE-TENTHS OF HER STAFF OUT, SHE LED A TEAM THAT IMPROVISED AND PROBLEM-SOLVED. IT WAS IMPRESSIVE.

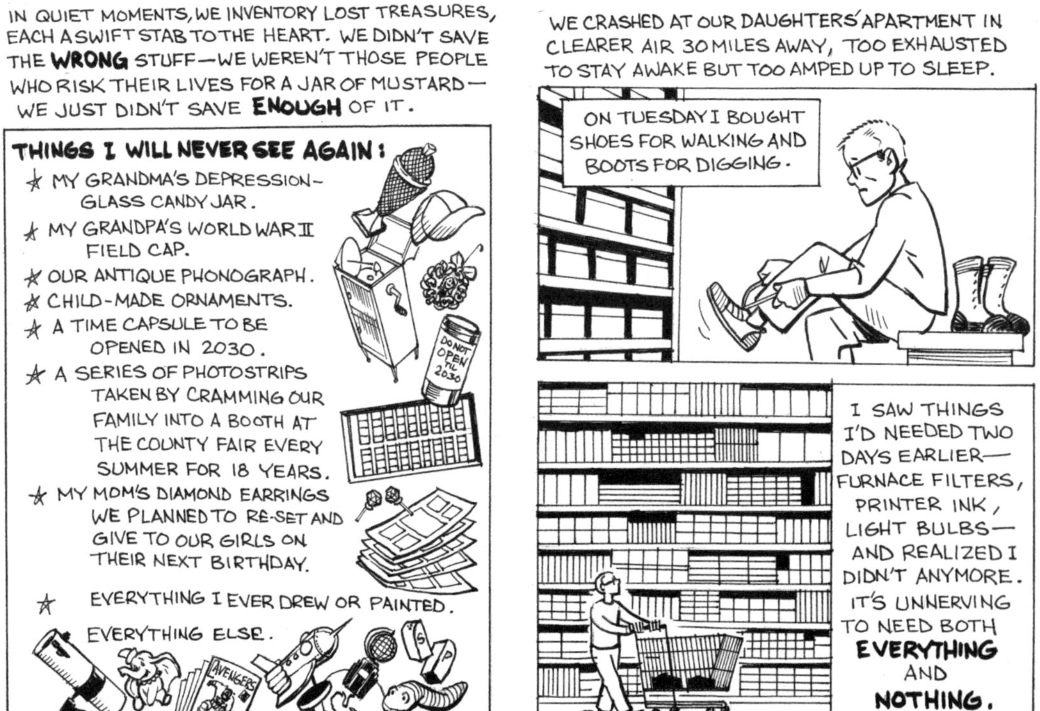
IN QUIET MOMENTS, WE INVENTORY LOST TREASURES, EACH A SWIFT STAB TO THE HEART. WE DIDN'T SAVE THE **WRONG** STUFF—WE WEREN'T THOSE PEOPLE WHO RISK THEIR LIVES FOR A JAR OF MUSTARD—WE JUST DIDN'T SAVE **ENOUGH** OF IT.
THINGS I WILL NEVER SEE AGAIN:
MY GRANDMA'S DEPRESSION-GLASS CANDY JAR.
MY GRANDPA'S WORLD WAR II FIELD CAP.
OUR ANTIQUE PHONOGRAPH.
CHILD-MADE ORNAMENTS.
A TIME CAPSULE TO BE OPENED IN 2030.
A SERIES OF PHOTOSTRIPS TAKEN BY CRAMMING OUR FAMILY INTO A BOOTH AT THE COUNTY FAIR EVERY SUMMER FOR 18 YEARS.
MY MOM'S DIAMOND EARRINGS WE PLANNED TO RE-SET AND GIVE TO OUR GIRLS ON THEIR NEXT BIRTHDAY.
EVERYTHING I EVER DREW OR PAINTED.
EVERYTHING ELSE.
DO NOT OPEN TIL 2030
AVENGERS
WE CRASHED AT OUR DAUGHTERS' APARTMENT IN CLEARER AIR 30 MILES AWAY, TOO EXHAUSTED TO STAY AWAKE BUT TOO AMPED UP TO SLEEP.
ON TUESDAY I BOUGHT SHOES FOR WALKING AND BOOTS FOR DIGGING.
I SAW THINGS I'D NEEDED TWO DAYS EARLIER—FURNACE FILTERS, PRINTER INK, LIGHT BULBS—AND REALIZED I DIDN'T ANYMORE. IT'S UNNERVING TO NEED BOTH **EVERYTHING** AND **NOTHING**.

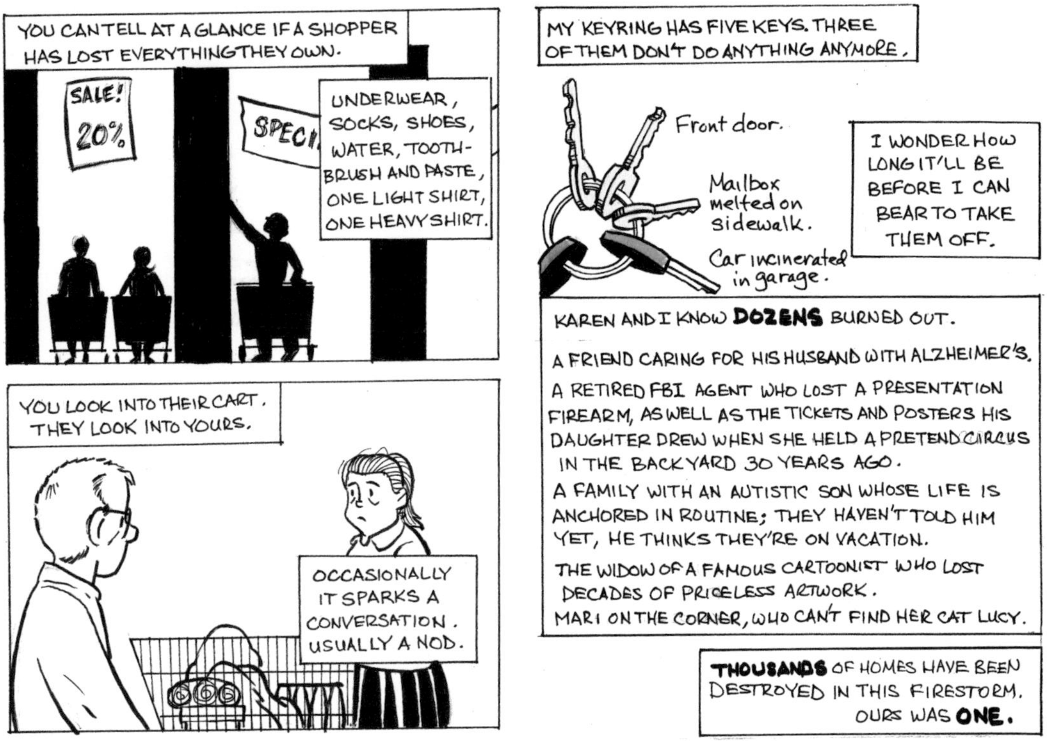
YOU CAN TELL AT A GLANCE IF A SHOPPER HAS LOST EVERYTHING THEY OWN.
SALE! 20%
SPECI
UNDERWEAR, SOCKS, SHOES, WATER, TOOTH-BRUSH AND PASTE, ONE LIGHT SHIRT, ONE HEAVY SHIRT.
YOU LOOK INTO THEIR CART. THEY LOOK INTO YOURS.
OCCASIONALLY IT SPARKS A CONVERSATION. USUALLY A NOD.
MY KEYRING HAS FIVE KEYS. THREE OF THEM DON'T DO ANYTHING ANYMORE.
Front door.
Mailbox melted on sidewalk.
Car incinerated in garage.
I WONDER HOW LONG IT'LL BE BEFORE I CAN BEAR TO TAKE THEM OFF.
KAREN AND I KNOW DOZENS BURNED OUT.
A FRIEND CARING FOR HIS HUSBAND WITH ALZHEIMER'S.
A RETIRED FBI AGENT WHO LOST A PRESENTATION FIREARM, AS WELL AS THE TICKETS AND POSTERS HIS DAUGHTER DREW WHEN SHE HELD A PRETEND CIRCUS IN THE BACKYARD 30 YEARS AGO.
A FAMILY WITH AN AUTISTIC SON WHOSE LIFE IS ANCHORED IN ROUTINE; THEY HAVEN'T TOLD HIM YET, HE THINKS THEY'RE ON VACATION.
THE WIDOW OF A FAMOUS CARTOONIST WHO LOST DECADES OF PRICELESS ARTWORK.
MARI ON THE CORNER, WHO CAN'T FIND HER CAT LUCY.
THOUSANDS OF HOMES HAVE BEEN DESTROYED IN THIS FIRESTORM. OURS WAS ONE.

The pages below were posted on October 31, 2017, after readers asked how we were doing.

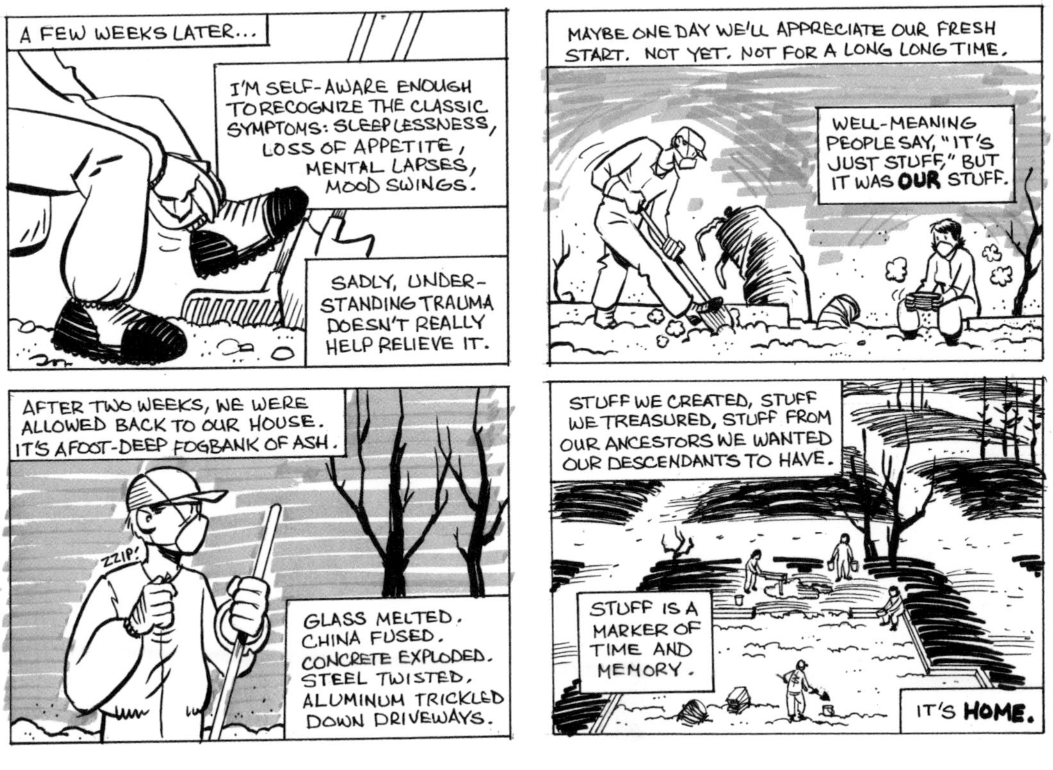
A FEW WEEKS LATER...
I'M SELF-AWARE ENOUGH TO RECOGNIZE THE CLASSIC SYMPTOMS: SLEEPLESSNESS, LOSS OF APPETITE, MENTAL LAPSES, MOOD SWINGS.
SADLY, UNDER-STANDING TRAUMA DOESN'T REALLY HELP RELIEVE IT.
AFTER TWO WEEKS, WE WERE ALLOWED BACK TO OUR HOUSE. IT'S A FOOT-DEEP FOGBANK OF ASH.
ZZIP!
GLASS MELTED. CHINA FUSED. CONCRETE EXPLODED. STEEL TWISTED. ALUMINUM TRICKLED DOWN DRIVEWAYS.
MAYBE ONE DAY WE'LL APPRECIATE OUR FRESH START. NOT YET. NOT FOR A LONG LONG TIME.
WELL-MEANING PEOPLE SAY, "IT'S JUST STUFF," BUT IT WAS OUR STUFF.
STUFF WE CREATED, STUFF WE TREASURED, STUFF FROM OUR ANCESTORS WE WANTED OUR DESCENDANTS TO HAVE.
STUFF IS A MARKER OF TIME AND MEMORY.
IT'S HOME.

NOTES

Unless otherwise credited, all photos and artwork in *A Fire Story* are by the author, who mostly still draws with ink on paper.

Page 37: Photo copyright © 2017 Michael W. Harkins, used with permission and thanks.

Page 40: Satellite photo: NASA Earth Observatory image by Joshua Stevens, using MODIS data from LANCE/EOSDIS Rapid Response.

Large and small fires broke out all over the state during the night of October 8–9, 2017, due to a combination of sustained dry weather and unusually hot, strong winds blowing from the east. I consulted final incident reports produced by the California Department of Forestry and Fire Prevention (Cal Fire) to compile the following list of major fires (in order of area burned):

- Nuns Fire, Napa and Sonoma counties: 56,556 acres, 1,355 structures, 3 deaths
- Atlas Fire, Napa and Solano counties: 51,624 acres, 783 structures, 6 deaths
- Tubbs Fire, Napa and Sonoma counties: 36,807 acres, 5,636 structures (including my home), 22 deaths
- Redwood Valley Fire, Mendocino County: 36,523 acres, 546 structures, 9 deaths
- Pocket Fire, Sonoma County: 17,357 acres, 6 structures
- Cascade Fire, Yuba County: 9,989 acres, 264 structures, 4 deaths
- Cherokee Fire, Butte County: 8,417 acres, 6 structures
- LaPorte Fire, Butte County: 6,151 acres, 74 structures
- Sulphur Fire, Lake County: 2,207 acres, 150 structures
- Highway 37 Fire, Sonoma County: 1,660 acres, 30 structures
- Lobo Fire, Nevada County: 821 acres, 47 structures

Those fires account for the 8 counties, 8,900 structures, and 44 deaths mentioned in the text. In addition, the Bear Fire, which began in Santa Cruz County on October 16, 2017, burned 391 acres and destroyed 6 structures. An unrelated series of wildfires, the largest of them the Thomas Fire, struck southern California in early December 2017. In July and August 2018, the Mendocino Complex Fire, about forty miles north of Santa Rosa, burned more than 300,000 acres to become the largest wildfire in California history.

Page 48: Information regarding the number and cost of U.S. disasters in 2017 is from the National Oceanic and Atmospheric Administration's (NOAA) National Centers for Environmental Information (ncdc.noaa.gov). In this context, a "major disaster" is one that was declared under the Stafford Disaster Relief and Emergency Assistance Act, which was invoked fifty-seven times in 2017, mostly due to fires and hurricanes.

In addition to assistance provided by the County of Sonoma, FEMA, and other government agencies, several organizations came forward to gather and distribute contributions:

- The Redwood Credit Union's North Bay Fire Relief Fund (redwoodcu.org/fire-relief) collected more than $32 million. Some of those dollars were used to meet fire victims' immediate food and housing needs, others were given as cash. My family received $2,000 from this fund. Redwood Credit Union stopped accepting donations for its Fire Relief Fund in February 2018.

- Tipping Point (tippingpoint.org/relief) raised more than $33 million, much of it through two high-profile "Band Together Bay Area" rock concerts. The group is distributing the proceeds over time for fire relief, recovery, and rebuilding efforts. Much of their support has been given in the form of grants to local nonprofits and other organizations providing direct assistance.

- Community Foundation Sonoma County (sonomacf.org) established the Sonoma County Resilience Fund to address the area's mid- to long-term recovery. The Community Foundation is focusing its efforts on what it identifies as three key areas of greatest need:

  - helping individuals impacted by the fires
  - healing the long-term effects of trauma
  - finding housing solutions for the community

If you're moved to help, I would recommend a contribution to the Sonoma County Resilience Fund.

Also, as mentioned on **page 51**, Creative Sonoma (creativesonoma.org), a program of the Sonoma County Economic Development Board, provided cash grants to artists—including me—to replace destroyed art equipment and supplies.

The Red Cross deployed quickly and provided funding for both short- and long-term needs. Many other public and private groups, too numerous to name, provided invaluable aid and support to fire victims in the days and months following the disaster. My thanks and appreciation to them all.

Page 146: Emmy photo by Karen Fies (June 2, 2018). XO.